Pop Goes the Decade

Pop Goes the Decade

The Eighties

THOMAS HARRISON

GREENWOOD™

An Imprint of ABC-CLIO, LLC
Santa Barbara, California • Denver, Colorado

Library of Congress Cataloging-in-Publication Data

Names: Harrison, Thomas, author.
Title: Pop goes the decade: The eighties / Thomas Harrison.
Description: Santa Barbara, California : Greenwood, an imprint of ABC-CLIO, LLC, 2017. |
    Series: Pop goes the decade | Includes bibliographical references and index.
Identifiers: LCCN 2016057518 (print) | LCCN 2017034330 (ebook) | ISBN 9781440836671 (e-book) |
    ISBN 9781440836664 (hard copy : acid-free paper)
Subjects: LCSH: Popular culture—United States—History—20th century. |
    United States—Civilization—1970– | United States—Social life and customs—1971–
Classification: LCC E169.12 (ebook) | LCC E169.12 .H3774 2017 (print) | DDC 306.0973—dc23
LC record available at https://lccn.loc.gov/2016057518

ISBN: 978-1-4408-3666-4
EISBN: 978-1-4408-3667-1

21 20 19 18 17   1 2 3 4 5

This book is also available as an eBook.

Greenwood
An Imprint of ABC-CLIO, LLC

ABC-CLIO, LLC
130 Cremona Drive, P.O. Box 1911
Santa Barbara, California 93116-1911
www.abc-clio.com

This book is printed on acid-free paper ∞

Manufactured in the United States of America

Contents

Timeline

1980   President Jimmy Carter withdraws the United States from the SALT II treaty with the Soviet Union in response to their invasion of Afghanistan. The president would also prevent the U.S. Olympic team from competing in the Summer Olympics held in Moscow that year.

Ronald Reagan is elected president of the United States.

Broadway receipts top $200 million.

Heaven's Gate, by Michael Cimino, opens and generates $40 million, far less than its breakeven point (its budget was a staggering $44 million). The sheer immensity of this flop made the film industry much more cautious of large-budget films by directors with total control.

The Broadway production of *Grease* closes, becoming the longest-running show in Broadway history at that time.

Important American albums released: Bruce Springsteen's *The River,* Prince's *Dirty Mind,* Pat Benatar's *Crimes of Passion,* Billy Joel's *Glass Houses,* and Barbra Streisand's *Guilty.*

Important films released: *Airplane! American Gigolo, Blues Brothers, The Empire Strikes Back, Ordinary People,* and *The Shining.*

1981   Ronald Reagan is inaugurated as president. On the same day, 52 American hostages that had been taken in Iran in 1979 are freed.

Important American albums released: Van Halen's *Fair Warning,* Journey's *Escape,* Stevie Nicks's *Bella Donna,* Styx's *Paradise Theater,* and Kim Carnes's *Mistaken Identity.*

Important films released: *Chariots of Fire, Body Heat, Raiders of the Lost Ark,* and *On Golden Pond.*

1982   The United States and the Soviet Union begin the START discussions to negotiate a reduction in nuclear weapons by each country.

U.S. Marines arrive in Lebanon as part of a multinational force following an Israeli invasion.

Unemployment reaches 10.7 percent, the highest level since before World War II.

Important American albums released: Michael Jackson's *Thriller*, Bruce Springsteen's *Nebraska*, Prince's *1999*, John Cougar's *American Fool*, and Toto's *Toto IV*.

Important films released: *Gandhi, Blade Runner, E.T.: The Extra Terrestrial*, and *Tootsie*.

1983   The American public learns that the Central Intelligence Agency (CIA) has been assisting the contras (rebels in Nicaragua) secretly.

A suicide bomber at the U.S. Marines compound in Beirut kills 241 marines and sailors.

Important American albums released: Lionel Richie's *Can't Slow Down*, Billy Joel's *An Innocent Man*, Metallica's *Kill 'Em All*, Madonna's *Madonna*, Cyndi Lauper's *She's So Unusual*, and Huey Lewis and the News's *Sports*.

Important films released: *Terms of Endearment, The Right Stuff, The Big Chill, Scarface*, and *The Killing Fields*.

1984   The new U.S. embassy in Beirut is destroyed by a terrorist bombing.

The International Court of Justice issues a decree for the United States to pay reparations to Nicaragua and to refrain from assisting rebels in the future. The U.S. government responds by noting that the Court has no jurisdiction over the matter.

President Reagan is reelected for another four-year term.

Important American albums released: Prince's *Purple Rain*, Bruce Springsteen's *Born in the U.S.A.*, Talking Heads' *Stop Making Sense*, Van Halen's *1984*, Tina Turner's *Private Dancer*, and Madonna's *Like a Virgin*.

Important films released: *Out of Africa, Ghostbusters, The Karate Kid, Gremlins*, and *Brazil*.

1985   President Reagan ships antitank weapons to Iran with the hopes that Western hostages would be released (only one eventually was).

President Reagan meets with Soviet premier Mikhail Gorbachev, but the so-called Star Wars space defense system plans prevent them from making an agreement on missile reduction.

Congress repeals the Clark Amendment, which had prevented the United States from assisting either side in the Angola war. With its repeal, assistance is provided alongside a coalition of other countries, including Saudi Arabia and France.

Important American albums released: Prince's *Around the World in a Day*, John Cougar Mellencamp's *Scarecrow*, Whitney Houston's *Whitney Houston*, Sonic Youth's *Bad Moon Rising*.

Important films released: *Back to the Future, Rambo, Hannah and Her Sisters, The Color Purple, The Breakfast Club*, and *Out of Africa*.

1986   United States declares a state of emergency with Libya. The year is marked with some limited naval conflicts, and eventually an attack by U.S. warplanes. A bomb explodes at a West German nightclub frequented by American military personnel, killing one army sergeant, injuring 50 others and injuring 250 civilians.

The Lebanese press reveals that contrary to official policies, the United States has been trading missiles with Iran in exchange for hostages. The situation becomes known as "the Iran-contra missile crisis."

President Reagan and Soviet premier Mikhail Gorbachev meet in Iceland to reactivate discussions for an arms-control treaty and plan a 1987 meeting in Washington, D.C.

Important American albums released: Paul Simon's *Graceland*, Beastie Boys' *Licensed to Ill*, Bon Jovi's *Slippery When Wet*, Run-D.M.C.'s *Raising Hell*, Madonna's *True Blue*, and Janet Jackson's *Control*.

Important films released: *The Last Emperor, Full Metal Jacket, Top Gun, Crocodile Dundee, Ferris Bueller's Day Off*, and *Platoon*.

1987   The Tower Commission report blames the Iran-contra affair on National Security Council director Robert McFarlane, Lieutenant Colonel Oliver North, Admiral John Poindexter, and former CIA director William Casey, while also criticizing President Reagan for letting it go on, apparently by benign neglect. Reagan publicly accepts "full responsibility," but he also claims that he did not know that Iranian arms sales were distributed to the contra rebels.

An Iraqi jet erroneously fires a missile at the *USS Starke* as it escorts Iraqi oil tankers in the Persian Gulf through mines placed by Iranians, killing 37 American sailors.

President Reagan and Premier Gorbachev sign the Intermediate Nuclear Forces (INF) Treaty, eliminating medium-range nuclear missiles.

Important American albums released: Guns 'N' Roses' *Appetite for Destruction*, Whitney Houston's *Whitney*, Dolly Parton, Linda Ronstadt, and Emmylou Harris's *Trio*, Prince's *Sign 'o' the Times*, Michael Jackson's *Bad*, and Eric B. & Rakim's *Paid in Full*.

1988   A federal grand jury freezes all Iranian assets in the United States. A separate grand jury in Florida indicts Panamanian dictator Manuel Noriega on drug-trafficking charges. The United States invades Panama later that year to capture Noriega.

Poindexter, North, and two others are indicted on charges relating to the Iran-contra affair, while Robert McFarlane pleads guilty to four counts of illegally withholding information from Congress during the investigation.

George H. W. Bush is elected president of the United States.

Important American albums released: Public Enemy's *It Takes a Nation of Millions to Hold Us Back*, N.W.A.'s *Straight Outta Compton*, Metallica's *. . . And Justice for All*, Tracy Chapman's *Tracy Chapman*, and R.E.M.'s *Green*.

Important films released: *Rain Man, Dangerous Liaisons, Coming to America, Die Hard, Beetlejuice,* and *Who Framed Roger Rabbit?*

1989   George H. W. Bush is inaugurated as president.

Oliver North is found guilty on three felony charges, receiving a sentence including a $20,000 fine, a three-year suspended prison sentence, two years of probation, and 1,200 hours of community service.

President Bush vetoes a bill raising the minimum wage to $4.55 an hour.

Important American albums released: Don Henley's *End of the Innocence,* Beastie Boys' *Paul's Boutique,* De La Soul's *3 Feet and Rising,* Tom Petty's *Full Moon Fever,* Madonna's *Like a Prayer,* and Janet Jackson's *Rhythm Nation 1814.*

Important films released: *Driving Miss Daisy, Field of Dreams, Batman, Dead Poets Society,* and *Do the Right Thing.*

Background and Introduction

When the 1980s started, many parts of American society were in turmoil. The American people had endured the long and controversial Vietnam War, which had just ended. Political strife exasperated by the Watergate scandal that embroiled President Richard Nixon and his administration had led to Nixon's resignation (the first time in history for a U.S. president). The U.S. economy had fallen significantly, especially due to the rising price of oil, as the United States relied on sources in the Middle East, who had raised prices to their highest ever. The Middle East was undergoing a good deal of upheaval, which also affected oil prices. In short, the general feeling among Americans was not positive as the decade began. This introduction will discuss some of the issues that led to this general sense of apathy (if not negativity) that permeated American society.

AFRICAN AMERICANS IN POPULAR CULTURE BEFORE THE 1980s

The rights of African Americans have been violated since the United States became a country in the 18th century (and even earlier). Until the end of the Civil War, the horrors of slavery were the most obvious example of how poorly humans could treat others, particularly in the Southern part of the United States. Though slavery ended officially with the passage of the Thirteenth Amendment in 1864, Jim Crow laws passed subsequently had made discrimination legal in the majority of Southern states, and depending on the locations, the laws sanctioned varying degrees of prejudice.

In the 1960s, African Americans found a leader in Dr. Martin Luther King, Jr., to help in the struggle for equal rights through peaceful protest and civil disobedience. However, that decade was also a time for the rise of more militant groups, such as the Black Panthers, who took more aggressive and violent means to agitate for civil rights. Dr. King was assassinated in 1968, but the wave of African American activism continued, bringing forth policies that worked to the benefit of a variety of ethnicities and genders. Jesse Jackson founded Operation PUSH—whose acronym stands for "People United to Save [later Serve] Humanity"—in 1971. Equal rights among all ethnicities have been a strong aspect of the civil rights movement. Following his failed presidential bid in 1984, Jackson founded the Rainbow Coalition, with a similar goal. The groups (which merged in the 1990s) advocated equal access to all aspects of American society, but unfortunately, the United States has decades of discussion and growth ahead of it in order to fully realize true equality.

Yet the 1970s was a fruitful period for the inclusion of African Americans in popular culture. Charles Gordone was the first African American playwright to win the Pulitzer Prize, for his play *No Place to Be Somebody*. The 1970s was also a time that saw a growing number of movies cast predominantly African American actors—a significant breakthrough even though those films were made for a predominantly African American audience. There was even a specific name for the genre—blaxploitation—and these were primarily action flicks that revolved around crime, horror, or police and detective plots. Early films in this category included *Sweet Sweetback's Baadasssss Song* (1971), about one African American man's fight against white authority; and the Hollywood feature *Shaft* (1971), about John Shaft (Richard Roundtree), a private detective trying to find a kidnapped little girl. *Shaft* is significant because it was the first in the genre to receive attention from an audience outside the African American community, and it became a model for blaxploitation genre: plenty of action, and a soundtrack based on funk and soul music from the 1970s. For his theme song for *Shaft*, Issac Hayes won an Oscar for Best Original Song, and the movie soundtrack won a few Grammys as well.

A notable crime movie in this genre was *Foxy Brown* (1974), starring Pam Grier as a woman fighting a drug gang that had murdered her government agent boyfriend. Grier's sexuallity was a central element in this movie, enabling the viewers to see how an attractive woman could also be strong (and black). *Blacula* (1972) was a surprise hit, starring William Marshall as Mamuwalde, an African prince who becomes a vampire in the 18th century by getting locked in a coffin while visiting Dracula in Transylvania. Two hundred years later, two unsuspecting interior designers purchase the coffin and bring it to Los Angeles, unknowingly releasing the vampire. Mamuwalde shows his gratitude for his freedom by beginning a killing spree. *Three the Hard Way* (1974) was an action film starring former professional football star Jim Brown alongside Fred Williamson and Jim Kelley. The trio fought Monroe Feather (Jay Robinson), an evil white supremacist plotting to release a serum into municipal water systems that will only harm African Americans. *Super Fly* (1972) focused on Youngblood Priest (Ron O'Neil), a drug dealer struggling to leave the profession after two drug addicts rob and beat him. Curtis Mayfield wrote the music for the film, featuring funk and soul, which epitomized the genres at their height in the 1970s.

Critics of blaxploitation films claimed that their African American writers and directors were essentially being race traitors, playing into and indeed reinforcing stereotypes of them from the Caucasian community. Though they may have had a point, it is undeniable that African Americans were becoming more prevalent in the movie industry one way or another, and at least it was a start for them. By the end of the 1970s and the start of the 1980s, African American actors were being seen in prominent roles alongside Caucasian actors, including Billy Dee Williams in *The Empire Strikes Back* (1980) and Carl Weathers in *Rocky* (1976) and *Rocky II* (1979).

The funk music that developed out of the counterculture movement in the late 1960s was gaining strength as its own genre during the 1970s. Bands that played that funky music included Sly and the Family Stone, Mother's Finest, the Isley Brothers, the O'Jays, and most predominantly, two groups led by George Clinton, Parliament and Funkadelic (with shared members, and often referred to as P-Funk, collectively). Other artists from the 1960s, such as James Brown and Stevie Wonder, began to incorporate elements of funk into their music as well, with effective results.

Eventually, the mainstream record industry became more interested in funk and began to adapt its elements into a more commercialized version known as *disco*. Disco was the most popular genre in the late 1970s, and it was frequently at odds with the rock fan base. Disco utilized the rhythms and harmonies of funk but infused a dance beat that repeated hypnotically for the duration of each song, primarily so large groups of people could dance together at discotheques (whose name was shortened to *discos* or *disco clubs*) in a repetitious way, with few surprises about how the music would develop.

African American themes in television were beginning to emerge on mainstream networks in the 1970s for the first time. *Good Times, Sanford and Son, The Jeffersons*, and *What's Happening?* featured overwhelmingly African American casts, with few Caucasian actors (even in supporting roles). *The Jeffersons* was particularly groundbreaking, as a mixed-race couple, Tom and Helen Willis (Franklin Cover and Roxie Roker), were major characters, and their relationship was quite a source of aggravation and chagrin for the main character, George Jefferson (Sherman Helmsley). *Sanford and Son* starred a junkyard dealer, Fred Sanford (Redd Foxx), and his son Lamont (Desmond Wilson). When the elder Sanford experienced stress—of any kind, and no matter what amount—he would clutch his heart and act as though he was going to have a heart attack, proclaiming, "I'm comin' to join you, honey" (his late wife, Elizabeth). His interactions with his sister-in-law, the abrasive Aunt Esther (LaWanda Page), were a reliable source of stress, and the two would verbally prod each other mercilessly in some of the most eagerly anticipated portions of every episode.

As a result of the struggle for equal rights, African Americans were receiving more opportunities in popular culture. For example, Cheryl Browne, representing Iowa, became the first African American contestant in the Miss America pageant in 1971. (But there wouldn't be an African American Miss America until Vanessa Williams won the pageant in 1983.)

WOMEN'S RIGHTS

In the 1960s and 1970s, women's rights made significant progress in the United States. The National Organization of Women (NOW) marched on Washington in 1970, demanding passage of the Equal Rights Amendment, a controversial proposal that was debated throughout the decade and never passed (though it did get to the stage where states had to ratify it—but not enough did). Other court cases helped clarify how the U.S. Constitution should be interpreted to protect the rights of women. In *Reed vs. Reed* (1971), Cecil and Sally Reed, a married couple who were separated, were each trying to gain custody of the remains of their deceased, adopted son. In the state law of Idaho, where the Reeds lived, "males must be preferred to females" in custody matters, but Mrs. Reed's attorney argued that the law violated the Equal Protection clause of the Constitution, which states that equal protection under the law cannot be denied "to any person within its jurisdiction." The Supreme Court ultimately found that the Idaho law was unconstitutional, resulting in a decision for Mrs. Reed. *Eisenstadt v. Baird* (1972) considered a similar argument. William Baird was distributing conceptive devices after a lecture at Boston University. Baird handed one to an unmarried 19-year-old woman, and the local sheriff arrested him for breaking a Massachusetts law stating that no one who was not a doctor or pharmacist could give an unmarried woman a contraceptive. In the Baird case, the court ruled that the marital status of a woman did not matter when it came to receiving contraceptives. *Schultz v. Wheaton Glass Co.* (1970) helped make strides for equal pay for both men and women doing the same position. It also prohibited giving a woman a lesser title in order to pay her less.

Not all these cases were ruled in favor of the woman, though. In 1978, a decision was made in *Oregon v. Rideout*, a case that would make rape of a spouse (or domestic partner) illegal; it was not passed. The reasoning for the law not passing was because a jury could not determine when sex was nonconsensual. *Geduldig v. Aiello* (1974) was a California case that questioned if a woman should be allowed to keep health insurance simply because she becomes pregnant. It was decided in the judgment that the "list of conditions covered by the disability insurance system is not exclusive. Furthermore, there are conditions not covered by the system that affect both men and women. The excluded conditions do not affect women alone."

New pieces of legislation were passed to help the cause of equal rights for women. The Equal Credit Discrimination Act (1974) prevented people from being discriminated against based on their race, color, religion, national origin, sex, marital status, or age. The Pregnancy Discrimination Act (1978) protected women if they became (or were planning on becoming) pregnant in the workplace. Pregnant women were also not required to take time off if they wanted to continue to work.

The 1970s was a time when female leaders published writings arguing for equal treatment. Kate Millett wrote *Sexual Politics* (1971), arguing that sex has had a male-dominated power, while *Our Bodies, Ourselves* (1976), helped women learn more about their own bodies from a feminist point of view, including pregnancy, abortion, and postpartum depression. Susan Brownmiller, in *Against Our Will* (1975), led an important discussion on how women are viewed and treated with regard to rape, particularly the idea that rape represents a man exerting power over a woman. The founder of the National Women's Political Caucus, Gloria Steinem, gave an infamous speech, "Address to the Women of America," in 1971, which discussed the need for a revolution in how gender and race is viewed in the United States. Even First Lady Betty Ford, married to Republican president Gerald Ford, openly supported the Equal Rights Amendment and was pro-choice in wake of the 1971 *Roe v. Wade* decision legalizing abortion. In the 1970s, women were allowed into the various service academies of the U.S. armed forces, including ones who graduated in 1976 as female pilots.

Thanks to the strides made in the 1970s, a higher percentage of the workforce was made up of women than at any time in history. The power of women was celebrated, and women in the workplace gained more prominent positions; by the 1980s, fashion styles were reflected in the "power suit" design, featuring shoulder pads. By the 1980s, the focus of women's rights changed from equal rights to establishing new interpretations of sexuality and pornography. Discussions in the 1980s were beginning to debate how the media portrays women, particularly in magazines that sexualized them, such as *Playboy, Penthouse,* and *Hustler.* While some argued that celebrating a woman's sexuality was part of the sexual revolution, largely furthered by the development of the birth control pill and the passing of *Roe v. Wade*, others contended that selling magazines with nude women in provocative poses objectified them. The development of music videos in the 1980s made this discussion more vibrant throughout the decade.

THE PRESIDENCY

In this period of history, the United States had been in considerable disarray since the assassination of President John F. Kennedy in 1963, and the controversies over both the civil rights and women's rights movements discussed earlier in this chapter caused a great deal of unrest from coast to coast. The most problematic issue that emerged at the end of the late 1960s and into the 1970s was the Vietnam War. Though the Democratic president Lyndon B. Johnson accelerated the efforts to have the United States enter the war in the 1960s, by the 1970s it was expected that the new Republican president Richard Nixon, elected in 1968, would withdraw American soldiers from the battlefield quickly. Although Nixon began to replace American troops with Vietnamese troops in 1969 and tried to negotiate with the North Vietnamese, his efforts to end the war were not successful in a timely enough manner for the American people. Instead, the bombings increased, and Nixon did not complete the withdrawal until the beginning of his second term in office. The conscription draft of young American men ended in 1973, which had been a strong point of contention by critics of the war since its beginning.

Nixon was in favor of a "New Federalism" program that would advocate stronger state rights in lieu of federal oversight. Nixon also helped alleviate the tensions of the Cold War with his diplomatic trip to China (the first for an American president). Unfortunately, Nixon is best remembered for the Watergate scandal, where he tried to cover up a 1972 break-in at the Democratic National Committee headquarters in the Watergate Hotel. The investigation into this incident also exposed that Nixon's administration had participated in the surveillance of political enemies, and that the break-in at the Watergate Hotel was just one of the spying activities that Nixon's administration did against American citizens. Additional controversy came with an investigation into Vice President Spiro Agnew's tax documents, which led to his resignation; he was replaced by Representative Gerald R. Ford. Impeachment proceedings in response to these revelations had begun, and when it became clear that Nixon had lost support among his own political party, he decided to resign before he could be impeached. He became the only president to resign from the office in U.S. history. Ford became elevated to the presidency, making a little bit more history (Ford is the only person ever to hold the offices of vice president and president without being elected to either one).

President Ford did his best to keep the country together, even saying that the "long national nightmare was finally over." Ford also worked for the release of prisoners of war from the Vietnam conflict. However, the Republican Party was less than enthusiastic about Ford; they were critical of his plan to cede the Panama Canal back to the host country, though the United States had paid for its construction years before. Moreover, Ford was saddled with an economy in which inflation and unemployment were both rising at an alarming rate. He championed the "Whip Inflation Now" (WIN) campaign, appealing to the American public for their help in controlling spending in order to reduce unemployment. His most controversial action, though, was his full pardon of Nixon; many in Washington (not to mention the country) wanted Nixon prosecuted and convicted for his crimes, and the pardon caused some speculation that there could have been a deal between the two men so that Ford could become president. Ultimately, Ford's pardon was a contributing factor toward his loss of the 1976 presidential election to his Democratic opponent, Jimmy Carter.

Carter was seen as an outsider; his status of being outside the Washington circle, often seen as a place of madness by voters disgusted by Johnson's Vietnam, Nixon's Watergate scandal, and Ford's pardon. Carter represented a fresh, new start for the country. His presidency was highlighted by a foreign policy in the Middle East that brought Israel and Egypt together for a peace deal for the first time in history. Carter also helped develop SALT II, a new antiballistic missile treaty with the Soviet Union, as well as a new energy policy.

But Carter's presidency was hampered by high unemployment and high inflation, partly because of the 1979 energy crisis, which resulted in long lines at gas stations, and even gas shortages. A period of stagflation occurred, in which inflation increases while incomes and the market value of the country's products remain the same.

Then, in November 1979, a group of Iranian students took hostages at the U.S. Embassy in Tehran. This crisis (and the failed attempt to save the hostages) was a particularly low mark on Carter's presidency. Although a few of the hostages were released early, most of them were held for 444 days. The Iranian crisis was not exclusively Carter's doing—it was at least in part a reaction to long-standing U.S. policy supporting the Shah of Iran, who had just been overthrown—but it contributed to his public image as a weak leader, especially after the failed rescue attempt. This may have helped Ronald

Reagan defeat Carter in the 1980 presidential election. The general feeling among Americans was that change was needed to help rejuvenate the economy—in particular, that growth had to occur at nearly any cost, even if the national debt skyrocketed.

The Iran hostage crisis was certainly one of the first troubling events from the Middle East, to be followed by many others. The tensions in the region have had reverberations that have affected the United States (not to mention the rest of the world) well into the 21st century.

MOVEMENTS IN POP AND DISCO MUSIC

When a country is in poor economic standing, its popular music tends to reflect the change in one of two ways: a return to older styles, reflecting a sense of longing for times past; or a more elaborate style, to help people forget their troubles. Americans were trying to find things to celebrate during a period riddled with feelings of apathy about the politicians in Washington, as discussed previously. The bicentennial year of 1976 was a time for Americans to acknowledge the entire 200-year history of the United States, rather than just the difficulties of the previous 10 years.

Musically, disco was a combination of funk as it had developed in the early 1970s, traditional pop, soul, and salsa. The funk aspect was the strongest element, as it represented a segment of African American music and culture in the 1960s' civil rights and psychedelic era, which continued into the early 1970s. The string and horn sections found in the bigger, Motown-influenced music of the late 1960s had a strong influence on the Philadelphia sound in the early 1970s. Both styles of music influenced American pop, replacing the strings and horn sections with the use of synthesizers by the end of the 1970s. The soul part of disco manifested itself in the vocal delivery, especially by female singers. The salsa facet of disco comes from the rhythmic drive of the music of Mexican records released by Salsoul Records in New York City.

Initially, disco was the music of underground dance clubs for gay and Latino audiences, particularly in New York and Philadelphia. Music producer Tom Moulton created an important element, the extended remix, which featured long "break-down" sections for the audience to dance to, allowing them to continue doing so for a longer period of time.

The dancing itself had its roots in the psychedelic period, in which concerts by groups such as the Grateful Dead, Jefferson Airplane, and later, Pink Floyd would feature long songs that patrons, many under the influence of a hallucinogenic drug or two, would be able to sway along to. These groups had an impact on one of the top funk groups of the late 1960s and early 1970s, Sly and the Family Stone, which became a favorite in the African American underground. In time, private dance parties were formed in New York that expanded into clubs frequented by African Americans and Latinos.

In 1974, the songwriting team of Kenneth Gamble and Leon A. Huff released a disco single, "TSOP (The Sound of Philadelphia)" as the theme song for *Soul Train*, a nationally syndicated television show geared toward African Americans. Because it was so easy to dance to, the song was a hit, introducing a new set of fans to disco. Other songs appeared that had disco-remix elements to them, such as "I Will Survive" from Gloria Gaynor. Miami-based KC and the Sunshine Band became national recording sensations because of a string of number one hits that incorporated the disco style. Donna Summer, a soul singer/song-writer, incorporated disco elements into her song "Love to Love You Baby," which went to No. 2 on the charts.

By 1977, disco music had moved into mainstream dance clubs in the inner cities, especially New York. An established English trio, the Bee Gees, changed from their "British Invasion" pop style of the 1960s and early 1970s to one with disco elements, featured most prominently in their songs for the soundtrack to the movie *Saturday Night Fever* (1977). Chic, featuring funk guitarist and pro-ducer Niles Rogers, released a string of hits that were national successes (their best known was probably 1978's "Le Freak"). The Jackson 5 began to incorpo-rate the sound into their music as well, and groups as wide-ranging as Kiss, Queen, the Beach Boys, and the Rolling Stones all jumped upon the craze. Disco had hit its commercial peak, and it seemed only natural that parodies, such as the Memphis-based disc jockey Rick Dees's hit "Disco Duck," would emerge.

As expected with any new trend, a movement sprang up against disco. Most of the opposition came from the rock community, eventually joined by the punk rock community. Disco did not feature the guitar in prominent parts—funk guitar was a rhythmic instrument—so it is unsurprising that criticism would be strong from the segments of the music industry that featured power-ful guitar performances. Rock artists openly criticized disco in the press, and Chicago rock disc jockey Steve Dahl even went as far as hosting an event to blow up disco albums at a baseball game on July 12, 1979.

Some supporters of disco countered with the charge that because it started in the gay, African American, and Latino communities, there were racial and even homophobic undertones beneath the criticism. However, it is more likely that this was the inevitable backlash against a trend that had become so popu-lar. The synthesizers that were used for disco were repurposed in the 1980s with the development of the new wave genre, which took the sound in a whole new direction for a new decade.

ROCK AND COUNTRY MUSIC

Following the popularity of psychedelic and blues music, hard rock/heavy metal became one of the most popular musical genres in the early part of the 1970s. (Though there was a clear distinction between hard rock and heavy metal by the middle of the 1980s, the terms were used synonymously throughout the 1970s.) The most prominent groups in the 1970s were British—Led Zeppelin, Queen, Deep Purple, Nazareth, and Black Sabbath. But a few American groups achieved respectable levels of popularity as well, including Aerosmith, Ted Nugent, Kiss, and, toward the end of the decade, Van Halen.

Aerosmith's style was certainly influenced by the blues, not only from the traditional version, but also from the secondary influence of the Rolling Stones.

What separated Aerosmith from the Stones, though, was that the group was also influenced by glam rock of the era. Aerosmith's hits ranged from the blues-based "Train Kept A Rollin' (All Night Long)" (from *Get Your Wings*, 1974) and "Big Ten Inch (Record)" (from *Toys in the Attic*, 1975), to heavier-rocking tunes such as "Draw the Line" (from *Draw the Line*, 1977), "Toys in the Attic" (from *Toys in the Attic*) and "Back in the Saddle" (from *Rocks*, 1976). Aerosmith's biggest hits of this period were "Dream On" (from *Aerosmith*, 1973) and "Walk this Way" and "Sweet Emotion" (both of the latter from *Toys in the Attic*). Though substance abuse plagued many members of the group (including lead singer Steven Tyler and lead guitarist Joe Perry) throughout the 1970s, the group became sober in the 1980s and has gone on to enjoy a substantial career since.

Kiss has been one of the most loved (and most hated) groups to come out of the 1970s. Supporters point to the success of songs such as "Rock and Roll All Night" (from *Alive!*, 1975) and "Detroit Rock City," "Shout It Out Loud," and the romantic ballad "Beth" (all from *Destroyer*, 1976)—however, none of these became top-charting singles, and neither did any of their others. Rather, their audience has always embraced the full albums as art pieces on their own, as well as their legendary live shows. What made Kiss stand out were their onstage and offstage personas, with each band member playing a particular character that gave Kiss an air of mystery. In the 1970s, few had seen the members without their makeup, adding to their mystique. Merchandise sales for the group were significant, and the persona gimmick was a brilliant move spearheaded by the leaders of the group, Paul Stanley and Gene Simmons. Both Aerosmith and Kiss were important influences on the most popular genre of the 1980s: hard rock.

Other versions of American rock that became popular in the 1970s included the less aggressive, "arena rock" groups, such as Journey, Cheap Trick, Boston, Foreigner, Kansas, and Styx. All of these bands gained support in the latter half of the 1970s, and enjoyed varying degrees of success in the 1980s. Progressive rock, delivered by the British groups Yes, Pink Floyd, and Genesis, as well as the Canadian band Rush, incorporated intricate arrangements and sophisticated lyrical content, often influenced by the psychedelic era. These groups experienced varying degrees of change in direction in the 1980s.

Jazz-influenced rock was successful in the 1970s for both Blood, Sweat, and Tears and Chicago, but with the development of synthesizer technology in the 1980s, they had a difficult time staying relevant. The glam rock of T. Rex and Mott the Hoople was also popular in the early 1970s, but it gave way to the new wave music of the 1980s. The blues influence in rock of the late 1960s was still prevalent, but with a definitive twist: Eric Clapton embraced pop and reggae styles, while the Texas-based ZZ Top moved toward a hard rock sound.

Some forms of rock and country music in the 1970s were idiomatic of the decade, such as soft rock, which was popular in the early 1970s. Several groups scored hits in this genre, including the Carpenters, the Osmonds, The Captain and Tennille, Bread, and Fleetwood Mac. Many of the classic soft rock artists of the 1970s were singer-songwriters, such as Jackson Browne, Jim Croce, John Denver, Carole King, Billy Joel, Kris Kristofferson, Don McLean, Joni Mitchell,

Carly Simon, Paul Simon, and James Taylor, and a few of them continued their success into the next decade.

Another important development in the 1970s was country rock, which infused the two popular genres together. The most significant representative of this type of music is the Eagles. Hailing from Southern California, the Eagles are one of the best-selling recording artists of all time. Their eponymous album, released in 1972, included the hit songs "Take It Easy," "Witchy Woman," and "Peaceful Easy Feeling," which featured drums, bass, and acoustic and electric guitars alongside more blues- and country-oriented instruments such as slide guitar and banjo. "Tequila Sunrise" and "Desperado" were released on their 1973 concept album *Desperado* and again featured rock, blues, and country instrumentation, including the Dobro and mandolin. *On the Border* (1974) included the hits "Already Gone," "James Dean," and "Best of My Love," while the follow-up, *One of These Nights* (1975), included "Lyin' Eyes," "Take It to the Limit," and the title track. Their *Greatest Hits (1971–1975)* was the best-selling album of the 1970s and remains the second-highest-selling album of all time (behind Michael Jackson's *Thriller*). It was followed by two more records: *Hotel California* (1976), with the singles "New Kid in Town," "Life in the Fast Lane" and the title track; and *The Long Run* (1979), with the singles "Heartache Tonight" and the title track, before the band experienced an ugly, acrimonious breakup in 1980.

Lynrd Skynrd (pronounced *'lĕh-'nérd 'skin-'nérd*), from Jacksonville, Florida, brought a definitive regional flavor to their Southern-tinged rock and are now considered pioneers of the genre. Their first album featured three major hits: "Gimme Three Steps," "Simple Man," and one of their best-known songs, "Free Bird." Their second album, *Second Helping* (1974), included the hits "Don't Ask Me No Questions" and "Sweet Home Alabama." The group's next albums were *Nuthin' Fancy* (1975) and *Gimme Back My Bullets* (1976). Tragically, an airplane crash killed three members of the group before the release of *Street Survivors* (1977), which featured two more hits, "What's Your Name" and "You Got That Right."

Other country-influenced rock artists were important contributors to the rock landscape in the 1970s. Linda Ronstadt had eight platinum albums and a string of hit singles (most notably "You're No Good," "That'll Be the Day," "It's So Easy," and "Blue Bayou"), and The Marshall Tucker Band and the Allman Brothers were also noteworthy.

In the 1970s, country music featured two styles: the Bakersfield sound, featuring California artists Buck Owens and Merle Haggard, and a highly produced style called Countrypolitan that featured traditional country writing alongside the inclusion of orchestral instruments. Countrypolitan opened the doors to a mainstream country sound that made big stars of its proponents, including Glen Campbell, Charlie Rich, Olivia Newton-John, Anne Murray, Tammy Wynette, and John Denver. Campbell's hit, "Rhinestone Cowboy," helped bring country music to a mainstream market for the first time since country elements were included in early rock and roll. Wynette's "Stand By Your Man" was one of the decade's most successful crossover country songs. Australian Olivia Newton-John had a breakthrough single, "Let Me Be There," as did Canadian Anne Murray, with "Snowbird."

Two important trends emerged in country music in the 1970s. Artists such as Jessi Colter, Tompall Glaser, Waylon Jennings, and Willie Nelson were considered outlaw singers whose music featured traditional country aspects infused with rock and blues influences, particularly on the album the four of them collaborated on, *Wanted! The Outlaws* (1976). The other trend was more accepted by the mainstream: pop country. Stars such as Crystal Gayle, Barbara Mandrell, Dolly Parton, and Kenny Rogers would become known in households that had not embraced country music before. Helped by many Countrypolitan elements, pop country incorporated pop songwriting and producing into its sound. Kenny Rogers had a string of hits, including "Lucille," "The Gambler," "Daytime Friends," and "Coward of the County." Mandrell's hits included "Sleeping Single in a Double Bed" and "(If Loving You Is Wrong) I Don't Want to Be Right," and in the 1980s, she starred with her sisters on a television variety show, *Barbara Mandrell and the Mandrell Sisters*. Parton had significant crossover success with the songs "I Will Always Love You," "Here You Go Again," "Two Doors Down," and "Heartbreaker," and she parlayed that popularity into a movie career, starting with a role in *Nine to Five* (1980). The success of pop country helped popularize country in the 1980s to the extent that it evolved into a new subgenre called *urban country.*

In the late 1970s, punk rock emerged in New York, particularly at the club CBGB, and it was popularized by the glam band the New York Dolls in the early part of the decade. The punk scene in New York included the Ramones, Blondie, and the Talking Heads. The scene was influential enough that when an English clothing designer, Malcolm McLaren, noticed it, he took the recordings and fashion ideas back to London with the intention of starting a new fashion trend. He even went as far as putting together a punk band of local youths, the Sex Pistols, which although they had no major hit singles in the United States, were still very influential.

Punk music certainly had its share of critics, some of whom would even go as far as saying that the music was not difficult to perform (with the implication that therefore, punkers were not "real" musicians). The mainstream success of the genre in the United States was limited; however, in Britain, the punk movement found favor with a disenchanted youth, so the Sex Pistols and other punk groups achieved a greater popularity. The cultural impact of punk in the United States was limited to the underground in both New York and Los Angeles in the late 1970s.

FILMS

The 1970s was a particularly fertile period for films, especially for ones with sequels. One of the most significant movies of all time in terms of cultural impact was the science-fiction epic *Star Wars* (1977), in which Luke Skywalker, a farm boy on a desert planet, joins a rebel alliance to fight the tyrranical Empire, who has been ruling the galaxy. Along the way, he learns from an older mentor that he can access and channel a mystical Force that can give him enhanced abilities. Luke becomes a pilot and flies on a heroic mission to save Princess Leia with the help of a space smuggler and his faithful sidekick.

The movie was so groundbreaking primarily because of its use of special effects. Director George Lucas had the team at his company, Industrial Light and Magic (ILM), create these effects using inventive camera tricks and miniaturized space vehicles in ways that had not been accomplished before. The sequels to this movie, which were released in the 1980s, were among the most popular movies of the decade.

The Godfather (1970) and its sequel, *The Godfather Part II* (1974), told not only about a criminal syndicate in the early 1930s, 1940s, and 1950s, but also about immigrants coming to the United States, and the feeling of dedication within a tight-knit family. *Rocky* (1976) and *Rocky II* (1979) followed the exploits of an unknown, poor boxer from Philadelphia who gets an opportunity to fight for the heavyweight crown twice, illustrating how someone can overcome obstacles to accomplish a lifelong dream. The *James Bond* movie franchise was successful in the 1970s in spite of the fact that the lead character was played by two different men. *Diamonds Are Forever,* starring the original Bond, Sean Connery, was released in 1971. Roger Moore filled the role for the rest of the Bond films released in the 1970s, *Live and Let Die* (1973), *The Man with the Golden Gun* (1974), *The Spy Who Loved Me* (1977), and *Moonraker* (1979). The success of those movies may have convinced the producers that the value of the franchise lay in the elements of Bond himself rather than the actor who played him, and since then, there have been several more changes in the casting of the role.

The 1970s was also known as a fertile time for the movie musical. Many film versions of the Charles Dickens 1843 literary classic *A Christmas Carol* have been released over the years; the 1970 version, *Scrooge,* featured a unique musical treatment. The most popular musical made into a movie in this period was *Grease* (1978), based on the 1971 Broadway musical. Featuring two of the top movie and music stars of the late 1970s, John Travolta and Olivia Newton-John, the film and soundtrack were among the top hits in the late 1970s. Its setting, in a high school in the 1950s, and sense of nostalgia made many baby boomers relate to the movie, while younger fans fell in love with the romantic storyline and catchy songs.

L. Frank Baum's 1900 novel *The Wonderful Wizard of Oz* had already been made into a film classic in 1939, but by 1974, a new African American treatment of the story emerged on Broadway: *The Wiz: The Super Soul Musical of the Wizard of Oz.* The musical's film version, *The Wiz* (1977), was developed by Motown Records, which had purchased the rights to it. The label cast two of their top artists into prominent roles: Diana Ross as Dorothy and Michael Jackson as the Scarecrow. As Dorothy and her fellow travelers move along the yellow brick road to Oz, they sing soul and funk songs instead of the original classics, which was intended to make the film more appealing to an African American audience. And it was, but a mainstream fan base also responded warmly to the film.

The *Rocky Horror Picture Show* (1975) was a comedic, satirical view of horror B-movies. A newlywed couple is stranded when their car breaks down. Seeking help, they enter the home of a scientist and his bizarre world of characters. When released, the movie was not a commercial success, but it went on to have a strong cult following in the decades since, fueled by midnight showings where the audience would come dressed as the movie's colorful characters and act out the scenes and musical numbers. *Willy Wonka and the Chocolate Factory* (1971) features elements of a musical with memorable songs such as "The Candy Man" and "Pure Imagination," and it has become a children's classic.

As noted previously, Vietnam was still on the minds of many Americans in the 1970s. By the latter part of the decade, films were beginning to be made about the war. *Apocalypse Now* (1979) chronicles the story of a highly decorated colonel who has gone rogue and taken his battalion into Cambodia. A lieutenant colonel in the special forces has been tasked with hunting down the colonel and kill him before he can attack again. *The Deer Hunter* (1978) tells the story of three Russian Americans living in western Pennsylvania who go to war in Vietnam. One of the soldiers is wounded and returns to a military hospital, another is mentally harmed from the conflict, and one returns to Pennsylvania, coming to terms to what has happened to his friends. There were also movies that, while they were not directly about the war, had connections to it; for instance, the main character of *Taxi Driver* (1976) is an unstable Vietnam veteran; and the musical *Hair* (1979) focuses on a young draftee and his friends on their way to the induction center.

The 1970s featured a significant number of classic, blockbuster movies. *Superman* (1978) was a new twist on the classic comic character and introduced Christopher Reeve to the world. *Star Trek: The Movie* (1979) was similar, in that it was a new retelling of the hit television show from the 1960s, with the same characters, but enhanced by the more modern filmmaking technology of the period. *Close Encounters of the Third Kind* (1977), directed by Steven Spielberg, focuses on a group of people and their encounters with aliens, a theme that fit well with a growing interest in alien visitations to Earth in the 1970s. *Saturday Night Fever* (1977) tells the story of a young man struggling in life but finding success as a disco dancer in New York City. *Jaws* (1975) focuses on a series of attacks on swimmers by a massive great white shark off the coastline of Martha's Vineyard, Massachusetts, presenting the story as a kind of horror film. The action comedy *Smokey and the Bandit* (1977) takes advantage of a new interest in country music, as discussed earlier in the chapter.

A number of blockbuster movies from this period were set in earlier decades. *The Sting* (1973), set in the Depression-era 1930s, features two swindlers trying to cheat a top mobster out of money through a "big con." *Summer of '42* (1971), a coming-of-age, comedy-drama set during World War II, tells the tale of three teenage boys, one of whom is infatuated with a new bride whose husband has gone to war. *American Graffiti* (1973) is a teen movie set in California in 1962 that focuses on growing up in an environment of cars, drive-ins, and girls.

As innocent as the previous teen-oriented movies were, the comedy *National Lampoon's Animal House* (1979) was raunchy. Set on the campus of the fictional Faber College, the movie's action centers around the exploits of an out-of-control fraternity in 1962. Well received by both critics and audiences, *Animal House* paved the way for later hit entries from National Lampoon, such as *National Lampoon's Vacation* (1983) and *National Lampoon's Christmas Vacation* (1989), and teen-oriented sex comedies like the *American Pie* series in the late 1990s and *The Hangover* series in the 21st century.

Other notable releases include the science fiction thriller *Alien* (1979); *One Flew Over the Cuckoo's Nest* (1975), a drama set in a mental health facility; and the comic western *Blazing Saddles* (1974), cowritten and directed by Mel Brooks.

The 1970s also saw shifts in the horror film, wherein the genre became more elaborate and violent than in previous years. *The Exorcist* (1973) shows a graphic transformation of a possessed little girl and the valiant efforts by a priest to save her. *The Omen* (1976) features a U.S. government official and his wife who adopt a little boy who turns out to be the son of Satan. The boy, Damien, becomes increasingly violent toward animals and eventually even attacks his own family. The diplomat eventually realizes his son's evil lineage and tries to kill Damien, but in the end both he and his wife are killed, and Damien survives. Its sequel, *Damien: Omen II*, advances the story of Damien's life as a preteen. He is beginning to understand his power and begins to use it in a more calculated way. Three more sequels have followed since.

Carrie (1977), Stephen King's first breakthrough in the horror film genre, features a shy teenage girl, Carrie White, who lives with a Christian fundamentalist mother. Carrie is bullied at school, but she finds out that she has telekinetic powers. She is tricked into going to her high school's senior prom and is cruelly harassed by her schoolmates; she strikes back at them with her powers, killing almost everyone. *The Texas Chainsaw Massacre* (1974) was one of the decade's most controversial films, simply because it was so violent. A group of teenagers are terrorized by a madman, known as Leatherface, who not only uses a chainsaw but also a meat hook and hammer to kill his victims. One of the first so-called slasher movies, it was banned in many theaters, which ironically made people curious about it and want to see it (so it probably was more successful than it would have been otherwise). *Halloween* (1978), another slasher movie, was shot so effectively by its director, John Carpenter, that it revolutionized the entire genre and helped define what the horror movie in the 1980s would be like. The film tells the story of a six-year-old boy who murders his older sister and is committed to a psychiatric asylum, but years later, he escapes and starts hunting down people (mostly teenagers) and killing them on Halloween night. The great acclaim and box-office success of *Halloween* spawned several sequels, as well as imitators in the 1980s and beyond.

In short, the important advances in film during the 1970s set up the subsequent decade to be a fruitful period in cinema as well.

TELEVISION IN THE 1970s

With advances in the civil and women's rights movements, it was no surprise that television programs embraced these changes in social attitudes. *All in the Family* (1971–1979) featured Archie Bunker, a conservative bigot who openly spoke disparagingly about practically all minorities, often using terms like "spic" and "nigger" that were extremely offensive, especially for television at the time. He would routinely spar with his liberal son-in-law, Mike, and the audience also grew to love Archie's ditzy wife, Edith. A couple of well-received episodes also involved him sparring with Maude, Edith's (very) liberal cousin, who stood for everything progressive. The popularity of the Maude character led to the launch, in 1972, of a series about her called *Maude* (a development that became known as a *spinoff*). That series became a hit too, running until 1978, and that led to yet another spinoff, *Good Times* (1974–1979), focusing on Maude's African American housekeeper, Esther.

As *Good Times* and other African American–oriented programs set in urban areas (like the aforementioned series *The Jeffersons*, yet another spinoff of *All in the Family*) became more popular, rural shows such as *Hee Haw, Green Acres,* and *The Beverly Hillbillies* lost viewers, and networks started to distance themselves from a "country" type of programming. Similarly, westerns such as *Bonanza, Little House on the Prairie, The Waltons,* and *Gunsmoke* were big hits in the early part of the decade but lost much of their viewership by the end of the decade.

The United States reached the moon in 1969, and the so-called space race with the Soviet Union was beginning to diminish. But the American public retained an interest in space and astronauts; they were used to seeing them on television in real life, so it was natural that they might be interested in watching fictional shows about them. *The Six Million Dollar Man* (1973–1978) focuses on an astronaut who is restored to life with bionic limbs after barely surviving a tragic aircraft accident. With his new strength and speed, he becomes quite an asset to the Office of Scientific Intelligence, a fictional U.S. government agency. *The Bionic Woman* (1976–1978), a spin-off of that show with a similar theme, soon followed. *Battlestar Galatica* (1978–1979), a science fiction show similar to *Star Trek,* was broadcast for only one season, but it still became one of the iconic television shows of the 1970s.

The Incredible Hulk (1978–1982) and *Wonder Woman* (1976–1977) both focused on cartoon heroes fighting crime, often with fantastic storylines. Other more realistic crime-fighting shows such as *Kojak, The Rockford Files, Columbo, Starsky & Hutch, Barnaby Jones,* and *Hawaii Five-O* brought the activities of police detectives to the small screen. Those series all featured policemen as their lead characters, but *Charlie's Angels* (1976–1981) took the genre in a whole new direction. The show featured three beautiful female private investigators working for a male boss whom they never saw. It was a huge hit in the ratings, but it also was tarnished with a negative moniker: "jiggle TV." The idea was that the show was only successful because its (mostly male) audience wanted to watch the scantily clad (and often braless, hence the "jiggle") actresses running around.

A similar philosophy lay behind *Three's Company* (1977–1984), which featured a slinky Suzanne Somers, dressed in skimpy clothing, and suggestive banter between the characters. Fantasy storylines were featured in two of the decade's biggest hits, *The Love Boat* (1977–1986) and *Fantasy Island* (1977–1984). Both had aspects that seemed impossible in real life, whether it be traveling on a cruise ship to find romance or living out your dreams on a secluded island, and viewers flocked to them.

The variety show had been a mainstay on American television since the 1950s. The 1970s was the last decade where that type of show was a prominent part of the television landscape, led by *The Carol Burnett Show* (1967–1978). Burnett became one of the most iconic personalities on television because of her easy-to-understand humor and delivery, as well as excellent writing and personable costars, including Tim Conway, Vicki Lawrence, and Harvey Korman. Another variety hit was *The Flip Wilson Show* (1970–1974), which was also well written. Wilson was a veteran African American comedian, and his character on the show, "Geraldine Jones," was considered one of his most memorable creations, particularly when she spoke of her boyfriend, "Killer" and uttered a phrase that entered the American vernacular, "What you see is what you get!" Other variety shows featured duos, including the wholesome *Donny and Marie* (1976–1979), hosted by two siblings from the Osmonds' singing group. Donny and Marie were well known for their bright smiles and positive, family-oriented content that probably reflected their conservative Mormon upbringing. *The Sonny and Cher Comedy Hour* (1971–1974), led by the namesake popular singing duo of the late 1960s and early 1970s, was a major hit, which made them even more popular. Though married at the show's inception, Sonny and Cher split up in 1974, and the show dissolved shortly thereafter (though it was briefly revived a few years later). Other variety shows included *Tony Orlando and Dawn* and *The Hudson Brothers Show*, both featuring musical groups and enjoying only fleeting success. By the start of the 1980s, the variety show format had disappeared from American television.

The biggest development in television during the 1970s was in daytime television in both game shows and soap operas. *The Hollywood Squares* and *The Match Game* both included guest actors, musicians, and other performers who answered questions. *Family Feud* was another popular game show that emerged in the 1970s, featuring families that would try to identify the most popular answers to surveys. *The Price Is Right* played on network television from 1956 to 1965, and it was revamped and reintroduced in 1972. Daytime audiences made it a huge hit, and it has run ever since. Other prominent games included *Let's Make a Deal*, *The $20,000 Pyramid*, and *The Joker's Wild*. Games that were inspirations for reality programming in the decades that followed included *The Newlywed Game* and *The Gong Show*, with the latter becoming a cultural touchstone of the decade.

Soap operas became significantly more popular, primarily because of the success of *All My Children* and *As the World Turns*, and though *General Hospital* was not very successful in the 1970s, it was a significant hit in the next decade. The success of these shows led to a comedic parody, *Soap*, which ran from 1977 to 1981.

Network news has been a prominent part of television since its inception, and network sports broadcasts followed soon afterward. The three major networks at the time were ABC (American Broadcasting Company), CBS (Columbia Broadcasting System), and NBC (National Broadcasting Company), and each one had a nightly news program. *ABC Network News*, anchored by Howard K. Smith, was the least popular of the three. The other two were *NBC Network News*, with John Chancellor as anchorman (with David Brinkley as commentator); and *CBS Network News*, with the widely popular Walter Cronkite; each enjoyed a similar level of success during the 1970s.

Televised sports were also beginning to become part of the American experience. The biggest development in the 1970s was that *Monday Night Football* premiered in 1970. The program was hosted by Howard Cosell, who had already become an iconic figure in sports broadcasting, and for most of the 1970s, Dan Meredith and Frank Gifford sat alongside him. While Cosell was the veteran broadcast journalist, Meredith and Gifford were both former players, and fans appreciated their contributions; Gifford gave play-by-play narration, and Meredith supplied color commentary. In addition, football games were broadcast on Sunday afternoons, often with two games per network. Games that featured the AFC teams were broadcast on NBC, while the NFC games were broadcast on CBS; the home team would determine which network would show interconference games. Major League Baseball (MLB) games were broadcast on NBC in the beginning of the 1970s, and between both NBC and ABC in the late 1970s. Though the National Basketball Association (NBA) and National Hockey League (NHL) had fleeting success on network television in the 1970s, the success of both *Monday Night Football* and MLB broadcasts led to more lucrative television contracts for all sports in the 1980s.

SPORTS

With the expansion of professional baseball and football onto prime-time network television, it is not surprising that the popularity of both sports was at an all-time high as the 1980s began. MLB was the most popular sport in America at the beginning of the 1970s. The Washington Senators in the American League moved to Dallas in 1972 and became the Texas Rangers. The American League expanded to 14 teams in 1977 with the addition of the Seattle Mariners and the Toronto Blue Jays, who became the second team outside of the United States (the Montreal Expos had been founded in 1969). The American League also implemented the designated hitter rule. Whereas the pitcher was required to bat in the lineup, the new rule allowed the team to designate a specific person to bat for him instead. The new rule encouraged more scoring, as usually pitchers were not effective hitters. Both the expansion to more teams and the designated hitter rule were intended to increase attendance in the American League, as the National League was generally more popular.

The teams who won conference championships (pennants) varied little in the 1970s. The Cincinnatti Reds won four, the Baltimore Orioles, Oakland Athletics, Los Angeles Dodgers, and New York Yankees each won three, the Pittsburgh Pirates won two, and the New York Mets won one. The Athletics won three World Series titles, while the Reds, Yankees, and Pirates won two each and the Orioles won one (the Dodgers and Mets were unfortunately shut out). Of the teams that won multiple World Series, the Athletics, Reds, and Yankees won theirs in back-to-back seasons. Outfielder Reggie Jackson was a part of the three Athletics and two Yankee World Series–winning squads. His ability to raise his play to a high standard at playoff time earned Jackson the nickname "Mr. October." The Reds' four National League pennant–winning squads were led by third baseman Pete Rose and catcher Johnny Bench.

The Super Bowl was developed in the late 1960s as the championship game between the winners of the long-established NFL and the American Football League (AFL), created in 1960. After four Super Bowls, the leagues merged.

The two new conferences, the National Football Conference and the American Football Conference, were divided evenly, with some of the NFL teams moving to the AFC.

The 1970s was a decade known for stingy defenses with nicknames: Pittsburgh's "Steel Curtain," Miami's "No-Name Defense," Minnesota's "Purple People Eaters," and Dallas's "Doomsday Defense." In 1973, Buffalo running back O.J. Simpson became the first in league history to run for 2,000 yards. Two new franchises were created during the decade: the Tampa Bay Buccaneers and the Seattle Seahawks; this brought the total number of franchises in the National Football League to 28, where it remained for nearly 20 years. The most important element of professional football in the 1970s was the increase in popularity of the Super Bowl, which got a somewhat lukewarm reception among the mainstream at the beginning of the decade, but grew increasingly popular in the United States by the end.

The top team of the 1960s, the Green Bay Packers, did not see their success translate into the 1970s. The prime teams of the 1970s were the Dallas Cowboys, Miami Dolphins, and the Pittsburgh Steelers. The Cowboys appeared in five Super Bowls in the 1970s, winning two (Super Bowls VI and XII). The Dolphins also won two Super Bowls (VII and VIII), the first being the only undefeated season in the Super Bowl era. Their second appearance, in 1973, marked the first time a team had played in three straight Super Bowls—but that was also their last appearance until 1984. The Steelers won four Super Bowls in the 1970s (IX, X, XIII, and XIV—the latter was for the 1979 season, but it was actually played in January 1980). Two teams won one Super Bowl each: the Baltimore Colts (V) and the Oakland Raiders (XI).

College football was very popular in the 1970s, as it had been since the 1950s. Like baseball, there were only a few college football teams who kept appearing in and winning the national championship year in and year out. The University of Southern California won three titles, while Nebraska, Notre Dame, and Oklahoma won two apiece and the University of Pittsburgh won one. Other programs that excelled without winning the national championship included Ohio State, Michigan, and Penn State. Oklahoma won the highest percentage of games (nearly 88 percent) during the decade, but since not all teams play the same number of games, that did not mean that they won the most games; Alabama won 103 (compared to Oklahoma's 102). Another distinction that occurred during the 1970s was that for the first time in college football history, the same person won the Heisman Trophy, awarded to college football's most valuable player, twice: Ohio State's running back Archie Griffin, after the 1974 and 1975 seasons.

College basketball in the 1970s increased in popularity throughout the decade. During the late 1960s and early 1970s, college basketball was dominated by the University of California at Los Angeles (UCLA), under the legendary coach John Wooden. UCLA, led by Lew Alcindor (who later changed his named to Kareem Abdul-Jabbar) started the decade by beating Jacksonville and their star Artis Gilmore, and went on to win the national championship three more times, a total of nine in a row between the two decades. After North Carolina State won the 1974 tournament, UCLA came back to win again after the 1974–1975 season. Indiana, Marquette, Kentucky, Michigan State, and Louisville won the rest of the tournament titles of the decade.

Professional basketball was not as popular in the 1970s as it was in later decades. The merger of the NBA and the American Basketball Association (ABA) after the 1976 season was the most significant event of the decade, combining one moderately successful league (the NBA) with a fledging league with star potential (the ABA). The Los Angeles Lakers and Boston Celtics both won two championships in the 1970s. The Lakers won their titles at the beginning (1971–1972) and end (1979–1980) of the decade and appeared in an additional final in 1972–1973. Meanwhile, the Celtics won their championships over a three-year period (1973–1976). The Milwaukee Bucks, the New York Knicks, and Seattle Supersonics won one championship each (and appeared in two other finals), while the Washington Bullets won one and lost two other finals. The only other teams to win, in their only championship appearances, were the Golden State Warriors and the Portland Trail Blazers, whereas the Phoenix Suns lost in their only trip to the finals. In short, just a few teams dominated the NBA. Kareem Abdul-Jabbar won 6 of the 10 Most Valuable Player awards in the 1970s (3 each with the Bucks and the Lakers).

The 1972 Summer Olympics were held in Munich, West Germany, with the United States winning 33 gold medals, 31 silver medals, and 30 bronze metals, second to the Soviet Union in both the gold and overall categories. Swimmer Mark Spitz won seven gold medals for the United States, a record that stood until Michael Phelps won eight golds in 2008. But the Games were marred by a tragic event: a Palestinian terrorist group took nine Israeli athletes hostage and then executed them.

The 1976 games were held in Montreal, Canada, with the United States winning 34 gold, 35 silver, and 25 bronze medals. Decathlete Bruce Jenner won the gold in his event, setting a world record. The American highlight of the game, though, was the performance of the boxing team, with five Americans (Howard Davis, Jr., Sugar Ray Leonard, Leo Randolph, Leon Spinks, and Michael Spinks) winning gold medals—the most in history for a team. Each of these boxers went on to lucrative professional careers in the 1980s.

The 1972 Winter Olympics was held in Sapporo, Japan, with the United States winning three gold, two silver, and three bronze medals; the 1976 games were held in Innsbruck, Austria, with the United States winning three gold, three silver, and four gold medals. Both Winter Games lacked popularity in the United States, but since the 1980 games were going to be held in Lake Placid, New York, the nation started to pay more attention to them.

DRUG USE

The 1960s' counterculture, which advocated some of the most liberal behavior in American history, was a reaction to so-called traditional values that had taken hold since the end of World War II. After spending years experiencing the horrors of war, World War II veterans came back to the United States with the desire to live peaceful lives, and the government stepped in to help them do that in a number of ways, including the GI Bill, which paid for their education. They wanted to raise their families, own their own homes (including the iconic image of the white picket fence), and live out the American Dream.

In reality, however, many of the struggles of society were hidden or ignored, including the struggles to establish equal rights for minorities and women. In addition, by the 1960s, a considerable number of young people were rebelling against traditional values, and in so doing, they began to experiment with drug use and freer sexuality. Marijuana use was most common, followed by hallucinogenics. Marijuana was the most accessible drug, and many people in both the mainstream and the counterculture believed that the drug was relatively harmless. Hallucinogenic drugs such as lysergic acid diethylamide (LSD, known as acid), psilocybin mushrooms, and mescaline (peyote) were popular with the counterculture, who used them at rock concerts that featured long, improvised, nearly avant-garde sections of music. Both types of drugs were hailed as ways for users to experience self-discovery. The popularity of these drugs in the mainstream (or more accurately, the white mainstream community) led to the passage of the U.S. Drug Abuse Regulation and Control Act of 1970.

The 1970s also saw the decline of drugs that had been used in decades prior. Phencyclidine (PCP), a type of animal tranquilizer, had been a popular mood-altering drug in the past, but it caused psychotic episodes among its users, so it lost popularity gradually throughout the decade. Amphetamine "uppers," such as Dexyaml, and barbiturate "downers," such as Seconol, were pills that were widely used in the 1950s and 1960s, but their reputation for causing overdoses, leading to the deaths of Jimi Hendrix and Judy Garland, among many others, took them out of favor.

What was more important to drug users during this period were drugs that would allow them to stay awake late into the evening (all the better for having a good time). Quaaludes were popular for use in party atmospheres such as disco clubs in the late 1970s, as they lowered users' self-consciousness. Amyl nitrate was used extensively in the gay community. Known as "poppers" on the street, the drug allowed involuntary muscles, particularly those of the sphincter, to relax, which enhanced sexual pleasure, but it fell out of favor by the time the 1980s started.

Cocaine, which allowed users to party well into the night, became the drug of choice for many in the disco scene, and soon afterward it became an integral part of yuppie society, as explored later in this book. After the coke high subsided, users would get depressed and eagerly seek out another dose of the drug. The 1980s also saw the development and swift popularity of a by-product, crack, created by cooking the original version of cocaine with baking soda. The mixture would eventually take the form of a rock, which could then be smoked in a pipe. Crack cocaine was inexpensive, so it became a favorite with lower-income, inner-city populations.

In short order, children began being born to crack-using mothers, resulting in substantial birth defects and other abnormalities. The concentrated version of cocaine in rock form was very addictive, and just like the powder version, users felt nearly invincible. The high from crack was so intense because the drug was smoked, not just inhaled, and because lower-income users were more prone to addiction for a variety of reasons, it had a more lethal result on the population. The connection between income level and which version of the drug was used was clear. And thus, many in American society viewed crack as dirty and cheap, while the powder form of cocaine was seen as elegant and sophisticated—but the fact remains that no matter what the form, cocaine is very dangerous.

Most of the baby boomers (born between 1945 and 1964) had left any thoughts of the counterculture and the 1970s party scene behind by the early 1980s, as they became parents and professionals themselves. Many of these parents became conservative and were instrumental in electing Ronald Reagan to the White House in 1980. On the other hand, a good number of them were using cocaine in order to stay active in the workplace, and more and more children were being arrested and jailed for drug possession and use. Reagan's wife, Nancy, led a campaign against drug use called "Just Say No," which advocated for children to resist the temptations of drug use. Many people favored the cause (especially if they did not use), but their peers who used were resistant to "just saying no."

FURTHER READING

Abramson, Albert, and Christopher H. Sterling. *The History of Television, 1942–2000.* Jefferson, NC: McFarland and Company, 2003.

Crepeau, Richard C. *NFL Football: A History of America's New National Pastime.* Champaign, IL: University of Illinois Press, 2014.

Friedman, Lester. *American Cinema of the 1970s: Themes and Variations.* New Brunswick, NJ: Rutgers University Press, 2007.

George-Warren, H., P. Romanowski, and J. Pareles. *The Rolling Stone Encyclopedia of Rock & Roll (Revised and Updated for the 21st Century).* New York: Fireside, 2001.

Kingsbury, Paul. *The Encyclopedia of Country Music.* New York: Oxford University Press, 1998.

Larkin, Colin, ed. *The Encyclopedia of Popular Music.* 4th ed. New York: Oxford, 2006.

MacCambridge, Michael, and Dan Jenkins, eds. *ESPN College Football Encyclopedia: The Complete History of the Game.* Bristol, CT: ESPN, 2005.

Vecsey, George. *Baseball: A History of America's Favorite Game.* New York: Modern Library/Random House, 2008.

Wexman, Virginia Wright. *A History of Film.* 7th ed. New York: Pearson, 2009.

Wood, Robin. *Hollywood from Vietnam to Reagan.* New York: Columbia, 1986.

Exploring Popular Culture

CHAPTER 1

Television

Since the midway point of the 20th century, television has been one of the most important aspects of popular culture in the United States. The reasons for this are obvious: First, television is convenient for viewers, as they can view it in the comfort of their own homes; and second, there are choices on what to watch every minute of the day and night. In the 1980s, there were three primary networks that delivered entertainment via comedy, drama, and action shows, as well as news and sports programming. With the advancement of cable television in the 1980s, the amount, frequency, and variety of those offerings increased incredibly and were a significant aspect of how popular culture felt about American society. This chapter details the important shows of the 1980s.

COMEDY

The top programs at the beginning of the 1980s were ones that had started in the 1970s. *M*A*S*H*, featuring a medical unit in the Korean War, was broadcast until 1983. Central characters in the 1980s period included "Hawkeye" Pierce (Alan Alda), Margaret "Hot Lips" Houlihan (Loretta Swit), B. J. Hunnicutt (Mike Farrell), Corporal Maxwell Klinger (Jamie Farr), Father Francis Mulcahy (William Christopher), Colonel Sherman T. Potter (Harry Morgan), and Charles Winchester III (David Ogden Stiers), all of whom had a variety of personal and interpersonal issues that somehow propelled them through the difficult task of tending to injured soldiers during a war.

What was important about the show was that even though it was comedic in nature, there were hidden commentaries on the role of the United States in the Cold War. In the 1980s, these hints were less veiled in the episodes broadcast while the Vietnam War was still active. Topics could be serious at a moment's notice, which was one of the appealing aspects of the show. Another prevalent narrative was the struggle between wanting a civilian life again for some characters (particularly Winchester, who had an upper-crust upbringing in the Boston elite known as Brahmins, and Klinger, who resorted to dressing in women's clothing to facilitate a discharge from the army), while others were career soldiers (such as Potter). The final episode, "Goodbye, Farewell, and Amen," was broadcast on February 23, 1983. The episode was highly publicized, and at the time of its airing, it was the most watched television event in history (surpassing "Who Shot J. R.?" from the *Dallas* series, discussed later in this chapter).

WKRP in Cincinnati was another program that started in the 1970s, but it was seeing its decline in the early 1980s. Centered on a dysfunctional rock radio station in Ohio, program director Andy Travis (Gary Sandy) is brought in to help the struggling station become relevant. Dr. Johnny Fever (Howard Hesseman), who got fired from his prime Los Angeles gig for saying "booger" on the air, is going through the motions as a DJ in the small market of Cincinnati. Arthur Carlson (Gordon Jump) is the careless general manager who is preoccupied with fishing, not on the well-being of a failing radio station (he only got his job because his mother owns the station). American audiences were initially drawn to receptionist Jennifer Marlow (Loni Anderson) because of her beauty; however, she also possessed a wit and intelligence that somehow allowed her to find a way to keep calm among the chaos. Jennifer is often the recipient of advances from married sales manager Herb Tarlek (Frank Bonner), whose loud clothes and offensive behavior prevents him from landing big accounts for the station. Joining the dysfunction is bumbling news director Les Nessman, Herb's best friend. As the 1980s developed, rock radio was moving away from 1970s' groups, and fans equated the show with irrelevant rock music by the time its run ended in 1983.

The Jeffersons was one of the most important shows in the 1970s because it showcased an African American couple, Louise and George Jefferson (played by Isabel Sanford and Sherman Helmsley, respectively), who had worked their way up to wealth and prominence in New York by having a successful dry cleaning business. The show was also significant because it was one of the first to feature a mixed-race couple, Tom (Franklin Cover) and Helen Willis (Roxie Roker). The show was a spinoff from the successful 1970s' sitcom *All in the Family*. *The Jeffersons* was well received when it debuted in the 1970s, hit a slump for a few years, and then rebounded in the 1980s. In an unfortunate end, the cast was not notified that their show was to be canceled, and the series did not receive a traditional finale, even though it was one of the longest-running programs in television history. The network, CBS, never stated a reason for the show's unexpected and discurtious end.

Mork and Mindy features one of America's most beloved stand-up comedians of all time, Robin Williams. Williams plays Mork, an alien who comes to Earth to observe the human population for his home planet, Ork, which has sent him away because he enjoys laughter (which is forbidden on the planet). Mork befriends Mindy (Pam Dawber), who lives in Boulder, Colorado, and moves into her attic. Mindy's father and grandmother, who, unlike Mindy, do not know that Mork is from another planet, are skeptical of the living arrangements. Williams gives reports to his superiors on Ork at the end of each episode.

Like *WKRP in Cincinnati*, *Mork and Mindy* started in 1978 but quickly became less popular in the 1980s, though the decline actually started in the show's second season, as Mindy's father and grandmother were phased out and a romantic relationship between Mork and Mindy began to develop. By 1982, other characters such as Mork and Mindy's son Merth, played by comic legend Jonathan Winters, had been added, but the show was canceled. Along the way, Williams became well known as a comedian, and the Mork character introduced phrases that became part of the popular vernacular, such as "Nanu-na-nu" (greetings), "Shaz-bot" (a vulgarity), and "KO" (okay).

Taxi was another show that started in the 1970s but only lasted for the first few years of the 1980s. The show revolves around a taxi company and its quick-to-insult dispatcher Louie De Palma (Danny DeVito). Louie is a cruel figure in a cage presiding over a garage full of drivers, including pessimist Alex Reiger (Judd Hirsch); struggling actor Bobby Wheeler (Jeff Conaway); single mother Elaine Nardo (Marilu Henner), who works as a taxi driver on the side from her daytime job as a receptionist; emerging boxer and overall nice guy Tony Banta (Tony Danza); and a former burnout from the 1960s, Jim Ignatowski (Christopher Lloyd). Of these, only Alex is a full-time cab driver, while the others are preoccupied with other parts of their lives. One of the hilarious characters featured on the show is Latka Gravas (Andy Kaufman), who is from a fictional island country called Caspiar, located in the Caspian Sea. Latka is the taxi company's mechanic, and he speaks in either heavily accented English or his own, unintelligible language. Eventually, Louie softens up; toward the end of the series, he starts a relationship with Zena (played by Rhea Perlman, DeVito's real-life wife).

Throughout the show's history, there was a delicate balance between comedy and items that were more emotional. The level of writing and acting was quite high, with many of the actors starring in other productions later (Danza in *Who's the Boss?*, Perlman in *Cheers*, and Hirsch and DeVito in films). The show was successful in the 1970s but fell sharply in 1980.

Barney Miller was a top comedic show for much of the 1970s, but that ended in 1982. The show features Barney Miller, a police captain (Hal Linden) who tries to manage a crew of detectives with all types of insecurities. African American Sergeant Ron Harris (Ron Glass) has a desire (eventually realized) to be a published author and is preoccupied with his appearance, especially his extravagant and heightened fashion sense. Asian American Sergeant Nick Yemana (Jack Soo) is often comedic, particularly when he attempts to be philosophical, and he has trouble making coffee for his colleagues and filing paperwork in a timely manner. Puerto Rican American Sergeant Chano Amenguale (Gregory Sierra) is a hard-working and dedicated detective, seemingly one of the more stable ones in the office. The well-read Arthur Dietrich (Steve Landesberg) speaks many languages and seems to be familiar with every subject.

Fantasy Island started in 1978 and ended in 1984. The premise of the show was unique: normal visitors can have their fantasies fulfilled by coming to the island for a price of $50,000. Some visitors want to meet (or become) a mermaid; others want to be transported to a different time era, attain a longtime dream, or meet a historical figure. However, the story usually involves some type of drama that challenges the guest, and many times, the guest comes to appreciate the circumstances of his or her own life upon leaving the island. The host, Mr. Roarke (Ricardo Montalbán), facilitates the fantasies on the island for his guests, but he often warns them that their fantasies might not turn out the way that they hope.

The guests arrive at the island on an airplane, at which time Roarke's assistant, Tattoo (Hervé Villechaize), goes to a bell tower, ringing the bell while shouting what most viewers hear as "Ze plane! Ze plane!" ("The plane!") in Villechaize's French accent. Roarke is a mysterious figure, whose ability to grant each person's wish is an intriguing thread to the whole series. He provides background to the viewer about each visitor when the guests arrive (via speaking to Tattoo) that effectively sets the stage for the impending episode. Visitors could come to Fantasy Island only once, so there were no recurring guest stars on the show. *Fantasy Island*'s popularity declined after Villechaize left the show and was canceled soon after.

In a manner similar to *Fantasy Island*, *The Love Boat* was another show where guests would be part of the show for just one episode, while a core cast would remain as the crew. One of the unique elements of this show was that there were three story lines, all occurring simultaneously. One would focus on guests in the same group; another involved the guests interacting with the crew; and the crew would have a different underlying story line. Most of the guests' story lines revolved around finding or mending a relationship and had a more serious tone, while the ones that included the crew tended to be broadly comedic. The crew included Captain Merrill Stubing (Gavin MacLeod); the ship's doctor, "Doc" Bricker (Bernie Kopell); yeoman purser "Gopher" Smith (Fred Grandy); bartender Isaac Washington (Ted Lange); photographer "Ace" Evans (Ted McGinley); and Julie McCoy (Lauren Tewes) and her sister, Judy (Pat Klous), who both served as cruise directors. Many of the guests were famous performers or celebrities, either from the past or of the era, ranging from Hollywood royalty (Lillian Gish, Ray Bolger, Gene Kelly, Greer Garson, Farley Granger, Anne Baxter) to stars of TV past and present (Sid Caesar, Loni Anderson, Diahann Carroll, Jim Nabors, David Cassidy) to musicians (Carol Channing, Engelbert Humperdinck, Marilyn McCoo), and even curiosities like Charo, Zsa Zsa Gabor, the Village People, and Andy Warhol. The show lasted until 1987, longer than many of the shows that emerged in the 1970s that lasted into the 1980s.

Diff'rent Strokes was one of the shows of the decade that lasted nearly as long as *The Love Boat*. It tells a classic story, in which a wealthy widower adopts a child or children from poor circumstances so they can have a better life. In this rendition of the tale, the widower, a Caucasian New York millionaire named Philip Drummond (Conrad Bain), had a housekeeper, and toward the end of her life, he promised to take care of her two African American boys, 12-year-old Willis (Todd Bridges) and 8-year-old Arnold (Gary Coleman).

Drummond keeps his word, adopting them and bringing them into his home, which he shares with his 13-year-old daughter Kimberly (Dana Plato) and his new housekeeper, Edna Garrett (Charlotte Rae).

Drummond begins to teach the boys not only about a higher standard of life but social values that they had not experienced before in their lives. Arnold had one of the most identifiable phrases on television at the time, used when speaking to his brother: "What'chu talkin' 'bout, Willis?" In 1982, Rae left *Diff'rent Strokes* for her own show, *The Facts of Life*, and was eventually replaced by Mary Jo Catlett as Pearl Gallagher, the new housekeeper. A twist in the family dynamic occurrs when a new child is adopted, Sam McKinney (Danny Cooksey).

Arnold, the cute, loveable, and outspoken child, was clearly the star of the show. Coleman was nearly the age of the character at the beginning of the show, and his body did not age along with him because of health issues. As a result, the audience kept identifying Coleman as eight years old throughout the eight years that the show aired, which frustrated Coleman during the latter half of the show's run.

The Facts of Life, a spin-off from *Diff'rent Strokes*, featured Edna Garrett, Charlotte Rae's character, in a new role: the housemother at Eastlake Academy, an all-girls boarding school. The show had an impressive run (1979–1988), during which its viewers felt that they were growing up alongside the lead characters. *The Facts of Life* was one of the longest-running shows to feature a mostly female cast.

The first season features spoiled and preppy Blair Warner (Lisa Wheschel), friendly and gullible Natalie Green (Mindy Cohn), tomboy Cindy Webster (Julie Anne Haddock) and the youngest, and only African American girl, "Tootie" Ramsey (Kim Fields). In the second season, Webster was written out and replaced with a new tomboy character, Jo Polniaczek (Nancy McKeon). Throughout the series, a balance between humor and the complicated reality of growing up as a teenage girl was struck, including plots about parental relationships, eating disorders, peer pressure, drug use, and by the last season, sex and losing one's virginity. Edna's character expanded her duties at the school to include being a dietician. In the fifth season, Blair and Jo graduate from the school, and the plot shifts to Edna leaving the school to open a new business, Edna's Edibles. The show continued for three more seasons before Rae began to phase her character out of the program in 1985.

Family Ties, which focused on the exploits of the Keating family, was one of the most iconic television programs of the 1980s, starting in 1982. The family members are the main characters: liberal, former hippie parents (Michael Gross and Meredith Baxter-Birney), products of the 1960s' counterculture, who regularly spar with their teenage, conservative son (Michael J. Fox) and their two daughters (Justine Bateman and Tina Yothers). Bateman played Mallory, the prototypical 1980s' materialistic, fashion-driven, lazy teenage girl, who sides with her brother, Alex, in most of his clashes with their liberal parents, Steven and Elyse. The youngest daughter, Jennifer, is generally seen as the most stable, enjoying her childhood and not bothering with the friction between the political views of her siblings and parents. Eventually, a fourth child, Andrew, is introduced as the youngest brother; Alex promptly begins to guide the boy in his own conservative, capitalist ways.

The show was not just about political friction however; the teens were still growing up, and in the case of Jennifer, right before the viewers' eyes during the show's run, which lasted nearly the entire decade (1982–1989). Both of the teenagers go through struggles with relationships and other typical teenage problems, and throughout the course of the run, the story lines addresses teen pregnancy, censorship, minority effects on property values, and drug addiction. Fox went on to become a star in the *Back to the Future* film series—his character in those movies, Marty McFly, was a perfect complement to Alex Keaton.

Roseanne began its long run on American television in 1988; thus, it was on the air for two years in the 1980s. The show was the top-rated one on television during that time. The Conner family, who lives in rural Illinois, includes two blue-collar parents (Roseanne, played by Roseanne Barr and Dan, played by John Goodman) with three children, Darlene (Sara Gilbert), Becky (Lecy Goranson), and D. J. (Michael Fishman). Roseanne's sister, Jackie (Laurie Metcalf), is another central part of the show. Both sisters work for a plastics company, while Dan works as a contractor. Both Dan and Roseanne are overweight—unusual for TV stars of the era, especially since their weight isn't the subject of the jokes—and indeed, their weight makes the pair approachable to the audience, as it makes it easier for the general person to relate to their characters.

The dynamics in the household center around the female characters: Roseanne is the mother and wife, who is clearly in charge; and Dan is the husband who does not want to get in her way (but he is there for Roseanne in the event of a crisis). The show features teenage daughters who are growing up and dealing with menstrual periods, dating, and drinking, while not holding any of their own opinions back in the process, providing parental friction. D. J. is simply trying to just grow up as a normal boy, and his Aunt Jackie is trying to find a companion. Jackie becomes a police officer in the second season, while Roseanne moves on from the plastics company into a string of dead-end jobs. *Roseanne* became an important part of television because it mimicked the lives of many working Americans in the late 1980s.

Full House was another family-oriented show, but with a more serious setup: the family members in this show have lost their mother/wife to a drunk driver. The father is television sports anchor Danny Tanner (Bob Saget), who is raising his three daughters: Donna Jo, aka D. J. (Candace Cameron), Stephanie (Jodie Sweetin), and Michelle Tanner (played by identical twins Ashley and Mary-Kate Olsen). In order for the family to continue smoothly, Danny decides to ask his brother-in-law, exterminator and struggling rock musician, Jesse Katsopolis (John Stamos), to move in. He also asks his best friend, struggling comedian Joey Gladstone (Dave Coulier), to move in as well. In the second season, Danny becomes a cohost of a local television show, *Wake Up San Francisco*. Danny's new cohost, Rebecca Donaldson (Lori Loughlin), eventually becomes Jesse's girlfriend, and in the 1990s, his wife, adding a new dynamic to the household. The expanded family was important in the development in 1980s' comedic

The Cosby Show featured stories about a middle-class African American family. In the past, the television networks had produced few successful shows focusing on African Americans, and even fewer with a focus on African American families. (NBC/Photofest)

television, as the living arrangements were outside of what might have been considered traditional at the time. Stamos became a heartthrob among female teenage fans, and the always-cute Olsen twins (who alternated on the show to comply with child labor laws) were fan favorites until the show ceased in 1995.

The Cosby Show was a groundbreaking television show in the 1980s, as finally there was the chance for a show to feature an economically and socially flourishing African American family on television. The characters were not in a lower-income, struggling family, as in the 1970s hit show *Good Times*, and unlike *The Jeffersons*, which featured a husband with a successful business with a wife at home, both parents in *The Cosby Show* were successful professionals in their own right. Even more convincingly, the show was one of the highest-rated programs for all audiences in the 1980s, and it sat atop the ratings for five consecutive years.

The show was important in helping build a bridge between racial divisions and opening the door to shows that featured an all African American cast later in the decade. By 1984, Cosby had already enjoyed a good deal of success in his educational television program (and doctorate thesis project) *Fat Albert and the Cosby Kids*, which was broadcast from 1972 until 1985. *The Cosby Show* is about the Huxtables, an upper-middle-class family that lives in Brooklyn Heights, New York. Cosby plays Cliff Huxtable, an obstetrician who is married to attorney Clair (Phylicia Rashad). The Huxtables have five children: college student Sondra (Sabrina Le Beauf), teenagers Denise (Lisa Bonet) and Theo (Malcolm-Jamal Warner), preteen Vanessa (Tempestt Bledsoe), and the elementary-age Rudy (Keisha Knight Pulliam). As in most family shows, there are struggles as the kids mature (literally in front of the audience throughout the decade), with solid advice coming from their parents to teach them lessons about growing up.

Growing Pains was another family-focused show featuring two working professionals. Psychologist Jason Seaver (Alan Thicke) and his journalist wife, Maggie (Joanna Kerns), are raising four kids: Mike (Kirk Cameron), Ben (Jeremy Miller), Carol (Tracey Gold), and, by the fourth season, newborn Crissy (Ashley Johnson). Dr. Seaver conducts his practice from home while his wife works as a reporter. The children experience typical teenage problems, jealousy over love interests, school dances (with somewhat hackneyed plots like Mike accidentally making dates with two girls for the same night), and running for student body president. Jason would even struggle with the feeling that he was growing older, longing for the rock band of his youth. The show was highly rated in the first few seasons of the 1980s, but ratings declined over time before it finally was canceled in 1992.

Happy Days was a family-oriented show that flourished in the 1970s and lasted into the 1980s, but it took place in a much different period. Most fans recognize that in its original, more classic form, when the show was at its height, it focuses on a family in the 1950s, a cool, motorcycle-riding "greaser" who rents a small apartment above their garage, two teenage friends of the eldest child, and the struggles of teens who often hang out at a diner, Arnold's. In the 1980s, the eldest child, Richie Cunningham (Ron Howard), goes off to college, while his friend, Ralph Malph (Donnie Most), joins the army. Though the greaser, who is more sensitive than his persona, Fonzie (Henry Winkler), wants to admit, maintains a strong presence on the show into the 1980s, the show started to focus on Fonzie's nephew, Chachi (Scott Baio), and his relationship with the youngest Cunningham, Joanie (Erin Moran). A spin-off focusing on Chachi and Joanie was later created, to little success. The show was best when it was set in the 1950s; as it evolved into the 1960s, the show lost much of its appeal and luster. Baio would go on to star in *Charles in Charge* later in the decade but with mixed results.

Perfect Strangers focused on Larry Appleton (Mark Linn-Baker), a young man who had just moved into his first apartment in Chicago, and Baliki Bartokomus (Bronson Pinchot), his long-lost cousin from a fictional island in the Mediterranean,. Larry was looking forward to living alone, but he felt obliged to take in Baliki, whose knowledge of American culture was poor. The show, featuring two buddylike characters, was a solid performer in the ratings.

Both of the men work in a discount store for their landlord, "Twinkie" (Ernie Sabella), who does little more than berate the pair. In the third season, Larry becomes a newspaper reporter, allowing the pair to move to a nicer apartment. A new character, Harriett Winslow (Jo Marie Payton-France), is also introduced as an elevator operator in their building, along with her husband, Carl (Reginald VelJohnson); later, those two went on to their own spin-off series, *Family Matters*, which became a significant hit in the 1990s.

Married . . . with Children began in 1987 and had success in both the 1980s and the 1990s. The story line revolves around a dysfunctional family headed by Al Bundy (Ed O'Neill), a former high school football player who often relives his past glories to escape his miserable existence as a women's shoe salesman and his negative home life. He is married to Peg (Katey Sagal), who is interested in Al's affection, but with no relief in sight. Peg is the quintessential lazy housewife, far more interested in shopping than housework. The Bundys' attractive party-animal daughter Kelly (Christina Applegate) is the ditzy blonde, whose naïve lack of intelligence frequently puts her at odds with her father. The person in the house with the most intelligence, son Bud (David Faustino), has one primary mission in life—to sleep with a girl—but his own missteps keep him pining for affection. The Bundys also have neighbors, the Rhoades, who add another element of friction to the show. Wife Marcy (Amanda Bearse) is Peg's best friend and Al's complete opposite, an environmentalist and feminist whom he constantly belittles; and her husband is Steve (David Garrison), who is eager to get out from under the thumb of Marcy's rule and have the freedom that Al enjoys.

The Wonder Years premiered in 1988, with a different premise than other shows of its period. The show focuses on the reenactment of the childhood of Kevin Arnold (Fred Savage), a teenage boy growing up in the late 1960s, and a narrative of that period provided by the adult version of the boy (voiced by Daniel Stern). Kevin is going through many of the typical experiences of growing up, often featuring his best friend, Paul Pfeiffer, and the girl he is in love with, Winnie Cooper. He also struggles with his relationships with his older siblings, aggressive brother Wayne (Jason Hervey), who physically bullies Kevin, and hippie sister Karen (Olivia d'Abo), who clashes with their conservative father. The father, Jack Arnold (Dan Lauria), a proud Korean War Marine Corps veteran, works for a defense contractor, while homemaker mother Norma (Alley Mills) is beginning to exhibit feminist qualities that fully emerge in the late 1960s. The show was significant because its narrative viewpoint on the late 1960s and early 1970s from years later helped younger viewers understand the complications and difficulties of growing up as a teenage boy. Later in the series, Kevin and Winnie begin a relationship, which further enhances the story line.

In *Who's the Boss?*, New York advertising executive Angela Bower (Judith Light), a woman obsessed with her career, is seeking a live-in housekeeper to help in her home with her shy son, Jonathan (Danny Pintauro), and her mother, Mona (Katherine Helmond), who is infatuated with men and sex. Retired baseball player Tony Micelli (Tony Danza) moves from Brooklyn to Connecticut to take the job, bringing his own daughter, Samantha (Alyssa Milano), into the home. Tony's more relaxed persona is the perfect foil to Angela's high-strung personality. The interaction and chemistry between Angela and Tony made it seem to viewers that it would only be a matter of

time before they became romantically involved; however, that did not happen until the end of the decade. In the meantime, both would date others
(with somewhat of an extended relationship for Angela with Geoffrey Wells,
played by Robin Thomas). Later in the series, Angela opens her own advertising
firm, while Tony returns to college. Perhaps the show's greatest accomplish-
ment is that it helped to change the stereotyped roles of both genders in
the home: the woman was the primary provider and the man the domestic
backbone.

The Golden Girls was one of the unique comedies of the 1980s, as its story
lines were so much different from others on television. Four widowed or
divorced women were living in a house in Miami: substitute teacher Dorothy
Zbornak (Bea Arthur) and her mother, Sophia Petrillo (Estelle Getty); mid-
westerner Rose Nylund (Betty White); and southern belle Blanche Devereaux
(Rue McClanahan). All four of these actresses won Emmys at varying points
while the show was on the air.

Dorothy is bitter from her divorce from the womanizing Stan (Herb Edel-
man), who reenters her life at various points during the series. Sophia's husband,
Salvadore, had died years before, and Sophia is going through her retirement
years as a spunky, ridiculing roommate to all three of the other women, finding bits of romance along the way. Rose, naïve, not well educated, and always
nostalgic for her Norwegian-populated hometown of St. Olaf, Minnesota, is
widowed, yet she also finds love on occasion. Blanche is always with a different man, much to the mockery and scorn of the other three, but her relationships never work out—something she longs for. The banter between the four
is both comical and sensitive, bringing up issues that many women of their
age would go through, and the well-written and directed show became a fan
favorite.

Cheers, which debuted in 1982, established itself as one of the best-known
television shows of the decade. The characters either worked or were patrons
at a Boston bar of the same name, where "everyone knew your name." A former Boston Red Sox pitcher, Sam Malone (Ted Danson), is the bar owner and
bartender, not to mention resident womanizer. Sam bought the bar because
his alcoholic ways had essentially ended his playing career—an interesting
choice of career for an alcoholic, but it seems to work for him. The quick-
witted Diane Chambers (Shelley Long), an on-again, off-again love interest
for Sam, takes a job as a waitress at Cheers after being jilted by her professor
lover; she provides a sense of normalcy for the bar. Carla Tortelli (Rhea Perlman), another waitress, clearly does not take grief from Sam or any of the bar's
patrons and has a gaggle of badly behaved children. "Coach" Ernie Pantusso
(Nicholas Colasanto), former coach and present friend of Sam's, is a fellow
bartender.

Cliff Clavin (John Ratzenberger) is a postman; he, along with mostly unem-
ployed accountant Norm Peterson (George Wendt), are the resident barflies at
the end of the bar in most episodes, drinking beer and providing commentary
on the proceedings. In the third season, Dr. Frasier Crane (Kelsey Grammer)
begins a relationship with Diane. Pompous and uptight, Frasier the psychiatrist
ironically has trouble relating to the other patrons.

Cheers, featuring (left to right) Ted Danson, George Wendt, Woody Harrelson, and John Ratzenberger, as well as Rhea Perlman, Shelley Long, Kirstie Alley, and Kelsey Grammer, had a long run for most of the 1980s. Set in a Boston sports bar where "everybody knows your name," the on-and-off relationship between Sam Malone (Danson) and Diane Chambers (Shelley Long) was a source of tension and laughs in this workplace comedy. (NBC/ Photofest)

Ultimately, Diane agrees to marry Frasier, but at the last minute, she walks out on their wedding. On the rebound, Frasier moves back to his hometown, Seattle, and begins a new life (and a new series, *Frasier,* in the 1990s). Sam eventually sells the bar to a corporation before traveling around the world, and Rebecca Howe (Kristie Alley) becomes the new bar manager (and later, a new sparring partner for Sam). Sam begins to work at the bar again after his trip, which now includes new bartender Woody Boyd (Woody Harrelson).

Night Court is set in a courtroom, with a young judge, Harry T. Stone (Harry Anderson), presiding over the odd cases that one would expect to see in an overnight courtroom. Dan Fielding (John Larroquette) is the prosecutor, who stops at nothing to have sex with any woman that he can. Bull Shannon (Richard Moll), the very tall, physically imposing, and ultimately harmless bailiff, is always trying to expand his vocabulary by using new words in conversation. Despite his intimidating bulk, Bull is sensitive and very protective of Harry. Mac Robinson (Charles Robinson) is the court clerk, known for wearing cardigan sweaters. A variety of public defenders are on the show as well, including Liz Williams (Paula Kelly), Billie Young (Ellen Foley) and, eventually, Christine Sullivan (Markie Post), the love interest of Harry and the lust interest of Dan. The show was a top performer in the ratings during the latter half of the 1980s.

Murphy Brown emerged in 1988, and it became a staple in the 1990s. The title character (Candice Bergen) is a middle-aged reporter for a Washington-based TV news magazine. Brown, a recovering alcoholic, becomes sober after staying at the Betty Ford Center. Not drinking makes her irritable and stubborn, but her talent as a reporter, courageous enough to ask the tough questions, goes unquestioned by her friends and colleagues, especially when she is working at the White House (which was Republican in the 1980s). Her friend Corky Sherwood (Faith Ford), a former Miss America and Murphy's replacement while she is in rehab, is a sweet, bubbly, albeit ditzy character. The production staff includes a young, up-and-coming producer named Miles Silverberg (Grant Shaud), veteran coanchor Jim Dial (Charles Kimbrough), and her best friend, Frank Fontana (Joe Regalbuto), an investigative reporter who is undergoing therapy because of a troubled personal life. Though the Murphy Brown character was a perfect portrayal of the typical journalist in the late 1980s, the real magic of the show came through its political satire. The program continued throughout the 1990s, with Murphy Brown's role expanding to include being a single mother.

The Bob Newhart Show was an important staple of 1970s television, starring the eponymous comedian as psychologist Bob Hartley. In *Newhart*, which launched in 1982, he took on a new role. Writer Dick Loudon (Newhart) and his wife, Joanna (Mary Frann), leave New York City to take over a 200-year-old inn in Vermont. Dick ultimately also becomes the host of a television talk show, *Vermont Today*. George Utley (Tom Poston) works at the inn as the handyman, and Stephanie Vanderkellen (Julia Duffy), a rich girl cut off from her family's money, is a maid. Stephanie later begins dating, and then marries, the producer of Dick's television show, Michael Harris (Peter Scolari), and the two became a typical 1980s' yuppie couple. One of the show's more humorous running gags has to do with three brothers from the backwoods, Larry (William Sanderson), Darryl (Tony Papenfuss), and Darryl (John Voldstad); the two Darryls never speak (until the final episode, that is), while Larry is known for telling tales that on the surface might seem too big to be true but often are.

ACTION/DRAMA

The Dukes of Hazzard, which began in the 1970s but continued into the mid-1980s, followed the exploits of two brothers from rural Georgia, Bo and Luke Duke (John Schneider and Tom Wopat). The young men spend a lot of time avoiding local, good-old-boy, and corrupt law enforcement authorities in their customized muscle car, nicknamed the "General Lee," which is readily identifiable because of its Confederate battle flag. The show also features the boys' cousin, Daisy (Catherine Bach), who quickly became a 1980s' sex symbol, as well as their Uncle Jesse (Denver Pyle) and mechanic Cooter Davenport (Ben Jones). The boys are on probation for transporting moonshine that was illegally distilled by their uncle—a restriction that keeps them from possessing guns. Their solution to this problem is that they use bows and arrows, often with exploding tips. The corrupt county commissioner, Jefferson Davis "Boss" Hogg (Sorrell Booke), is always at the root of the boys' problems. Boss tends to participate in a variety of illegal activities, which he promptly blames on the boys. Other law enforcement officers, Sheriff Roscoe P. Coletrane (James Best) and deputies Enos Strate (Sonny Shroyer) and Cletus Hogg (Rick Hurst), are bumbling types that round out an unsophisticated bunch, which (somewhat unfairly) casts them as ill-educated folks from the backwoods.

The A-Team was popular from 1983 until 1987. The series is about a former Special Forces unit that has been disbanded, court-martialed, and sent to military prison for a crime they did not commit. The group escapes from the prison and is being hunted by the military. In the meantime, they drive around in a characteristic car and work as mercenaries for oppressed parties who need help from the true "good guys." The group improvises different parts of different weapons and vehicles to create a customized van for their needs. The group

Magnum, P.I. was a top television show in the 1980s. Thomas Magnum (Tom Selleck) was a Hawai'i-based private investigator who lived on the beachfront estate of his employer and drove a Ferrari while solving mysteries in locations many considered to be paradise. A source of frustration for Magnum was his relationship with Higgins (John Hillerman), the caretaker of the estate, who was ostensibly tasked with looking after Magnum, but frequently clashed with him with often humorous results. (CBS/Photofest)

is led by Lieutenant Colonel John "Hannibal" Smith (George Peppard), alongside pilot "Howling Mad" Murdock (Dwight Schultz); Lieutenant Templeton "Faceman" Peck (Dirk Benedict), a well-dressed smooth talker who cons people (or in the case of women, downright flirts with them) out of equipment or other goods; and the enforcer with a fear of flying, Sergeant First Class B. A. Baracus (Mr. "T"), a fan favorite who became one of the biggest celebrities of the 1980s because of this program and his previous appearance in *Rocky III* in 1982. One of the show's most appealing aspects was its action, often involving some type of explosion, car chase, fistfight, or other type of violent act; however, some critics looked down their noses at this type of writing. Preteen and teen boys were a sizeable portion of the show's audience, likely because of all the exciting action sequences.

Magnum P.I. was a top show in the early 1980s. Thomas Magnum (Tom Selleck) is a private investigator who lives in the guesthouse of a wealthy patron named Robin Masters, in what seems to be repayment for a past favor. Masters is never seen; he simply speaks on the phone to Magnum when necessary (in the voice of Orson Welles). Magnum is joined by Jonathan Higgins III (John Hillerman), a former British soldier who is the caretaker of the house and its amenities—in particular, a Ferrari.

Magnum's relationship with Higgins is for the most part strained; however, Magnum is allowed to use the Ferrari quite often to help solve crimes on the island of Oahu in Hawai'i. Magnum has two friends, both former Marines who served in Vietnam: T. C. Calvin (Roger E. Mosely), who runs a chartered helicopter company to take tourists on sightseeing flights, and Rick Wright (Larry Manetti), who owns a bar. Magnum solves cases, often for beautiful female clients, and as a result, his life seems to be spectacular in paradise, between the house, the car, and his career, which he enjoys on his own terms. Selleck became a sex symbol to many female viewers in the 1980s and was a well-known celebrity who had some success in films in the years after *Magnum P.I.* folded in 1988; he continues to be a television star to the present day.

Like Selleck, David Hasselhoff became one of the most identifiable male stars of the 1980s. In the setup to *Knight Rider*, billionaire Wilton Knight is developing a new organization to enhance law enforcement: the Foundation for Law and Government (FLAG). Hasselhoff's character, Michael, a former police detective, joins FLAG after Knight pays for Michael's lifesaving surgery, including plastic surgery for a gunshot to the face. At the time of his shooting, he was known as Michael Long, but he changes his name to go along with his new appearance and identity as Michael Knight. Knight becomes the new top agent for FLAG and is given a supercar, the Knight Industries Two Thousand (KITT), to help him with his new endeavor. KITT has artificial intelligence, and its original Trans Am body has been changed into an indestructible machine that can communicate with Michael.

Other prominent characters in the show are Devon Miles (Edward Mulhare), the director of FLAG, who gives Michael his missions, and Dr. Bonnie Barstow (Patricia McPherson), who programs KITT and is flirtatious with Michael, but the two never become a couple. The show was on for only four seasons, but it became popular with fans looking for nostalgia from the decade.

The Fall Guy featured another macho actor, Lee Majors. Majors had been a 1970s television staple on *The Six Million Dollar Man,* playing Steve Austin, "the bionic man." Majors's character in *The Fall Guy* was Colt Seavers, a stuntman in Hollywood who also has a secret life as a bounty hunter. As Seavers explained in the introduction for each show, the work of a stuntman is sporadic, so he makes extra money by finding people who have skipped bail in the U.S. Justice Department. His two sidekicks, Howie Munson (Douglas Barr) and Jody Banks (Heather Thomas), are also stunt performers. Because of their training, they can work with automobiles without getting hurt. Like *Knight Rider,* there is a prominent vehicle used in the course of the show—in this case, an elaborate GMC truck that can secrete weapons, withstand the punishment of fast car chases, and execute jumps that would be expected of a stunt vehicle. The premise of the show on the surface might seem somewhat absurd, but this show worked well because it was unique and also because Majors was already an identifiable hero for many audience members.

Airwolf was not focused on a car, but rather a helicopter that was involved in the Cold War of the 1980s. The helicopter was designed by Dr. Charles Henry Moffet (David Hemmings) for a special wing of the Central Intelligence Agency called The Firm. Moffet decides to turn the helicopter on the United States, so he hires a gang of henchmen to steal the helicopter to take it to Libya, which in real life was led by Muammar Gaddafi, a clear enemy of the United States at the time. The Firm is led by Michael "Archangel" Coldsmith-Briggs III (Alex Cord), who commissions test pilot Stringfellow "String" Hawke (Jan-Michael Vincent). Hawke has a brother who has been missing in action since the Vietnam War. Along with mentor Dominic Santini (Ernest Borgnine), Hawke recaptures the helicopter, but the team decides that they will not return it until they know what happened to Hawke's brother. Archangel then agrees that Hawke and Santini can keep the helicopter to perform espionage missions, both in the United States and abroad, for The Firm and provides protection from U.S. authorities who are trying to regain the helicopter. Although the story line was a perfect reflection in the Cold War setting of the period, the ratings were moderately successful for the first three seasons, and the show got canceled after the fourth.

The program *Riptide* featured three Vietnam war veterans working as private investigators in southern California. Murray "Boz" Bozinsky (Thom Bray) is proficient at computers, and his partners Nick Ryder (Joe Penny) and Cody Allen (Perry King) work the streets to solve cases for the firm. Like *Airwolf*, a helicopter is a prominent part of the story line, but *Riptide*'s helicopter was anything but a state-of-the-art machine. Indeed, the "Screaming Mimi" certainly had seen better days. *Riptide* did not last long (merely three seasons), but because the show was sophisticated, involved technology as *Airwolf* did, and was set in a sunny American location as in *Miami Vice*, it is curious that it was not more popular.

Another unique story line was found in a series that only lasted for three seasons: *The Greatest American Hero*. A teacher named Ralph Hinkley (William Katt) is coming back from a field trip in the desert when his bus breaks down. As he is walking through the desert, he meets Bill Maxwell (Robert Culp), an agent with the Federal Bureau of Investigation (FBI). The pair then encounters aliens, who give them a suitcase containing a red suit and instruction manual that will give the wearer superhuman powers that could be used to save the world. The suit only fits Ralph, and he begins to wear it while fighting crime. Ralph's girlfriend, Pam (Connie Sellecca), and Bill help Ralph in his new endeavor.

To make the scenario even more problematic, Ralph loses the instruction manual, so he is forced to experiment with how to use the suit, which often does not produce the expected results. The suit allows him to have extrasensory perception (ESP), the ability to run at high speeds, X-ray vision, precognition, the ability to blow air at high velocity, psychokinesis, and invulnerability to gunshots (in areas covered by the suit, anyway). One of the more memorable (albeit unexpected) features of the show was the theme song, "Believe It or Not," which went to No. 2 on the Billboard Top 200 chart.

Hill Street Blues was one of the most popular police shows of the 1980s. It is often considered a "police procedural," as the detectives were working to solve crimes throughout the course of each episode. The central characters in the series were Officer Bobby Hill (Michael Warren), who is the calm counter-weight to his more animated partner, Andrew "Cowboy" Renko (Charles Haid). On the surface, the show's format was part classic buddy relationship between these two characters and part classic police drama.

As an expansion of this principle, Edward Copeland remarked on his well-regarded blog (http://eddieonfilm.blogspot.com/2010/01/lets-not-be-that -careful-out-there.html) that *Hill Street Blues* "was the first to take the elements of a soap—large casts, continuing storylines, cliffhangers—and transfer them to a different setting. Instead of the standard relationship drama that you'd find on a soap, *Hill Street Blues* was the first to camouflage those aspects in a police story." Copeland is on solid ground here, as the cast was quite large and consistent though most of the episodes in the six-year series, and *Hill Street Blues* developed into the model for police shows on television (particularly ones based in New York) in the decades that followed. Other important characters included Captain Frank Furillo (Daniel J. Travanti), Sergeant Mick Belker (Bruce Weitz), Lieutenat Howard Hunter (James B. Sikking), Sergeant (later Lieutenant) Henry Goldblume (Joe Spano), Sergeant Lucy Bates (Betty Thomas), and public defender Joyce Davenport, Furillo's love interest (Veronica Hamel).

Miami Vice was another police show that was a fan favorite in the 1980s. The show was important because it established two top stars of the 1980s: Don Johnson, who played James "Sonny" Crockett, and Philip Michael Thomas, who played Ricardo "Rico" Tubbs. The show also made Jan Hammer, who composed the memorable theme song, well known among those outside the music community. *Miami Vice* differed from other shows of the period in that it embraced the current fashions of new wave (often presented in pastel colors to match the Art Deco scenery of Miami) and contributed to the trend of wearing a designer suit jacket over a T-shirt and light beard stubble (worn to great advantage by Johnson). The music included current hits by a wide variety of artists, ranging from U2 to Phil Collins, and Iron Maiden to Kate Bush, as well as music that was often electronic in nature. Cocaine use in the United States had risen in the 1980s, and a considerable amount of the drug was being smuggled into the country through Miami during this period. Storylines were isolated to just one episode, similar to other crime shows, but the focus on drug trafficking led to a seemingly endless supply of exciting stories. Other story lines highlighted the struggles against Cuban guerillas, prostitution, and anticommunist regimes in South America. The show, which lasted from 1983–1987, was a true reflection American society of the decade.

Matlock featured the beloved television veteran Andy Griffith as an expensive defense attorney named Ben Matlock. His standard fee was $100,000 for each case, with proceedings usually held in the Fulton Country courthouse near Atlanta. Matlock's method for winning most of his cases included extensive investigations of his own, where he would expose the true criminal on the stand at the end of the show, establishing his client's innocence à la Perry Mason. Despite his opulent fees, Matlock led a thrifty, homespun lifestyle, dressing in inexpensive suits and eating a steady diet of hot dogs. Early in the series, he was assisted by private investigator Tyler Hudson (Kene Holliday), but later, Hudson was replaced by former North Carolina deputy sheriff Conrad McMasters (Clarence Gilyard, Jr.) for the remainder of the series. The show was never a top ten hit, but it was a solid ratings performer throughout its ten-year run, which ended in 1995.

In the Heat of the Night, loosely based on the acclaimed 1967 film of the same name, featured television veteran Carroll O'Connor as Bill Gillespie, the Caucasian chief of police of the city of Sparta, Mississippi. He worked alongside African American chief investigator Virgil Tibbs (Howard E. Rollins, Jr.). As in the original movie, the racial relationship was important to this series, as Gillespie persuaded Tibbs to return to his hometown of Sparta from Philadelphia so there could be more African Americans on the force. Tibbs struggled with the attitudes that others had toward him, while Gillespie had trouble with Tibbs's own attitudes toward their small hometown. Working as a partnership proved effective, as they tackled tough problems of racism, AIDS, drugs, child abuse, and rape, among others that are usually addressed in the context of a television show set in a large city. Other prominent characters included Captain Bubba Skinner (Alan Autry), Officer Parker Williams (David Hart), Virgil's wife, Althea (Anne-Marie Johnson), Officer Parker Williams (David Hart), and Lieutenant Lonnie Jamison (played by O'Connor's own son, Hugh).

Cagney & Lacey differed from other police dramas, as it featured two female detectives. Throughout the show's run (1982–1988), one of the two lead actresses won an Emmy for six consecutive years—an impressive feat that has not been duplicated since. The partners had very different personal lives. Christine Cagney (Sharon Gless) was a single woman from an upper-class upbringing, who was chatty and outgoing, while Mary Beth Lacey (Tyne Daly) was clearly more reserved and dedicated to her husband and four children. Apart from the two main female characters, another of the show's appealing qualities was the fact that they had such contrasting personalities. Other members of the cast included the detectives' supervisor, Lieutenant Bert Samuels (Al Waxman), Mary Beth's husband, Harvey (John Karlen), and detectives Victor Isbecki (Martin Kove) and Mark Petrie (Carl Lumbry). The series ran from 1981–1988.

Simon & Simon featured two main characters similar to *Cagney & Lacey,* but the difference was that the two main characters, A. J. and Rick, were brothers who worked as private investigators. A. J. (Jameson Parker) was well educated and had a finer sense of refinement, dressing impeccably in suits and driving classic cars. Younger brother Rick (Gerald McRaney) was a Vietnam veteran who wore cowboy boots and drove four-wheel-drive trucks. Both had their own way of researching each case that came to their firm, and as such, their conflicts were the driving force of the series. Marcel "Downtown" Brown (Tim Reid) worked with the brothers to solve their mysteries; and Cecilia Simon (Mary Carver), their mother, was the steadying force in the boys' lives.

Murder, She Wrote, one of the longest-running television shows in history, lasting from 1984 until 1996, was widely watched in the 1980s and established Broadway and film star Angela Lansbury as a top television actress as well. Lansbury played Jessica Fletcher, a widowed, retired English teacher who had become a famous author, writing mystery novels during her golden years in the fictional little town of Cabot Cove, Maine. Many of the episodes took place in Cabot Cove, but many other times the mysteries would occur while Jessica was traveling to promote one of her books or visiting friends and family members. With each episode, she entered a murder investigation where a body would be found in some remote location, occasionally to the chagrin of the local law enforcement. Eventually, Jessica would put the pieces together for the officers to help bring the culprit to justice. There were not many recurring characters on the show, but the one who made the most appearances was Seth Hazlitt (William Windom), the local doctor and Jessica's friend. Other noteworthy characters included two sheriffs of Cabot Cove (Amos Tupper, played by Tom Bosley, and Mort Metzger, played by Ron Masak).

Hart to Hart featured an affluent husband and wife who find themselves brought into various criminal activities, and they acted as amateur detectives to help solve the cases (and occasionally, clear their own names). Jonathan (Robert Wagner) and Jennifer (Stefanie Powers) Hart were global jet-setters, with Jonathan as chief executive officer (CEO) of his company, Hart Industries, and Jennifer as an attractive freelance journalist. Since Jonathan was a corporate businessman, the crimes the duo was involved with might include theft, espionage, and usually murder as well. The couple had a butler/chauffeur/cook, Max (Lionel Stander), who occasionally got involved in their investigations. The most appealing quality in *Hart to Hart* was the openly affectionate relationship that they had—they seemed to never have a serious disagreement. The series ran from 1979 to 1984.

There were a variety of detective shows that featured a duo in the 1980s that had lesser degrees of success than *Hart to Hart* did. For instance, there was *Moonlighting,* which featured Maddie Hayes (Cybil Shepherd), a model who lost all of her fortune except for a house and a struggling private detective agency. The detective, David Addison (Bruce Willis), was a know-it-all wise guy who looked for Maddie to be not only the owner of the agency, but part of it. Agnes DiPesto (Allyce Beasley) was their receptionist, whose shtick was that she answered the phone in a rhyme. The show was a hit with viewers, but it lost momentum when Maddie and David's relationship became romantic—a marked contrast with the success of *Hart to Hart.*

Remington Steele featured a private investigator, Laura Holt (Stephanie Zimbalist), who was running her own agency but was not being taken seriously. So she invented a male partner—Remington Steele. But then a mysterious man (Pierce Brosnan) appeared, claiming to be Steele, and the two started solving crimes together. What was different about *Remington Steele* was that the episodes were narrated from Laura's point of view and often made direct reference to movies made in the film noir style from the 1940s and 1950s. As with *Moonlighting,* the relationship between the two leads began professionally and morphed into a romantic relationship over time.

Scarecrow and Mrs. King featured Lee "Scarecrow" Watson (Bruce Boxleitner), an agency operative who met Amanda King (Kate Jackson), a divorced woman in a train station, and gave her a package to hold. They became more familiar with each other, and Amanda decided to join the agency, first in a clerical capacity, then later as an agent herself. In later episodes, the two struck up a friendship, and eventually became romantically involved. Though it looked as if the two characters were to be married, Jackson became stricken with cancer, and the series ended prematurely.

Though not filled with much action, the (sometimes comedic) drama *Little House on the Prairie* was a family favorite that started in 1974 and ended in 1982. Based on the *Little House* series of books by Laura Ingalls Wilder, the show focused on the Ingalls family, who lived on a farm in the rural Minnesota town of Walnut Grove in the 1870s. Millworker Charles Ingalls (Michael Landon) was the patriarch of the family, married to Caroline (Karen Grassle), and their four daughters: Mary (Melissa Sue Anderson), Laura (Melissa Gilbert), Carrie (played by twin sisters Lindsey and Sidney Greenbush), and Grace (also played by twin sisters, Brenda and Wendi Turnbaugh). As the series developed throughout the 1970s, the family adopted three more children, Albert, Cassandra, and James, but they had only minor roles. Another family in the town that appeared in most episodes was the Olesons, whose patriarch Nels (Richard Bull) owned a local store and had a gossipy wife, Harriet (Katherine MacGregor), and two poorly behaved children, Willie (Jonathan Gilbert, brother of Melissa) and Nellie (Allison Arngrim). The struggles of small-town life in the late 19th century were explored, but the plot lines also included themes relevant to viewers of every generation, including racism, alcoholism, and adoption. Gilbert, Grassle, and especially Landon became iconic actors of the period, largely because of their popularity among the families who were fans of the show.

In the late 1960s, *Star Trek* became a significant hit on television, and it has remained a fan favorite into the 21st century. *Star Trek: The Next Generation,* a sort of sequel, appeared in 1987 and expanded on the themes pioneered in television science fiction. There is a significant difference between the shows—the 1987 version was set 100 years after the original, so it had different crew members played by different actors. The new crew flew around the galaxy in a new version of the starship *Enterprise.* The species of aliens that had been considered the enemy in the previous show, the Klingons, were now allies, while other species, the Borgs and the Romulans, emerged as new nemeses. The new cast helped make the series tremendously popular: Captain Jean-Luc Picard (Patrick Stewart), Commander William Riker (Jonathan Frakes), Lieutenant Commander Geordi La Forge (LeVar Burton), Lieutenant Commander Data (Brent Spiner), Counselor Deanna Troi (Marina Sirtis), Lieutenant Worf (Michael Dorn), and Dr. Beverly Crusher (Gates McFadden). With any science fiction film, there is a need to make the fantasy world of the future relatable to the time period in which the viewers are currently in, and like the original, *Star Trek: The Next Generation* did that for seven seasons.

Few shows in the late 1970s and early 1980s had the suspense of the prime-time soap opera *Dallas*, featuring the dysfunctional Ewing family. Starting in

1978, the series lasted throughout the 1980s and finally reached its end in 1991. The drama in the series revolved around Dallas-based oil tycoon J. R. Ewing (Larry Hagman), an unscrupulous character who was both a ruthless businessman as owner of Ewing Oil and a womanizing sleaze. J. R. was married to former beauty queen Sue Ellen (Linda Gray), who became an alcoholic after years of enduring her husband's shenanigans. Eventually, Sue Ellen moved into a separate bedroom before she and J. R. divorced in 1988. Cally Harper (Cathy Podewell) replaced Sue Ellen as J. R.'s second wife toward the end of the series.

J. R.'s younger brother, Bobby (Patrick Duffy), was also an oil baron, but his less aggressive and devious ways ultimately kept him from being as successful as his brother. Bobby was married to Pam Barnes (Victoria Principal), the daughter of Digger Barnes (whose brief appearances were in the 1970s), a nemesis of the Ewing family. Pam's brother, Cliff (Ken Kercheval), was the chair of Wentworth Tool and Dye and seemingly fixated on taking over Ewing Oil, which put him and J. R. at loggerheads. The matriarch for the Ewing family was Miss Ellie (Barbara Bel Geddes), J. R. and Bobby's mother; she grew to be a fan favorite thanks to a plot line that made her a breast cancer survivor. It seemed that the only person who did not seem to have a problem with J. R. Ewing was his mother. The immense hostility that he inspired in everyone else he encountered led to one of the most hyped media blitzes of the 1980s: the mystery of "Who shot J. R.?" In the third season finale, J. R. was shot by an unseen assailant, and the audience was forced to wait eight agonizing months before they found out who did it—Kristin (Mary Crosby), one of his mistresses, who was also pregnant with his child. Thanks to the way the creators exploited the suspense and stoked the publicity to maximum effect, that episode was the highest rated in television history at that time.

Knots Landing was another prime-time soap opera, a story that was spun off from *Dallas* and featured Gary Ewing (Ted Shackelford). Gary was J. R.'s alcoholic brother, who had moved to Knots Landing in California to begin a new, sober life. The start of that life introduced his neighbors Sid (Don Murray) and Karen Fairgate (Michele Lee), who owned Knots Landing Motors, a used car dealership. Sid eventually gave Gary a job as a vice president, but Gary resumed drinking, and his irrational behavior of his past returned. After meeting Sid's sister, Abby Cunningham (Donna Mills), Gary began an affair with her, and his marriage dissolved.

By this time, prime-time soaps were all the rage. Another popular entry in this genre was *Dynasty*, which, like *Dallas*, was based on a wealthy oil family. Based in Denver, the Carrington family was headed by Blake (John Forsythe) and his wife, Krystle (Linda Evans), who had been his secretary. Blake's previous wife, Alexis (Joan Collins), entered the series in the second season to wreak havoc on the family. Blake was completely dedicated to his oil company, Denver-Carrington, which meant that Krystle had to endure the poor treatment she received from Blake's daughter, Fallon (Pamela Sue Martin), a typical spoiled rich kid, with no support. Meanwhile, Steven, Blake's openly gay son, treated Krystle much better than he treated his sister, but his strained relationship with his father frustrated his ambitions to become the eventual head of the company. Alexis had her own company, ColbyCo, which she obtained after marrying the Carringtons' rival, Cecil Colby, right before his death. Tension between Krystle and Alexis, which often led to open combat, was a driving force behind the popularity of the series. Indeed, the show was one of the most popular dramas of the decade, reaching number one in the 1984–1985 season.

DAYTIME PROGRAMMING

Daytime television has been its own special genre of programming for decades; in particular, soap operas were frequently must-see television, typically watched by stay-at-home caregivers, particularly housewives. Romance and the shifting dynamics of relationships fueled the stories behind soap operas. *Dallas, Knots Landing,* and *Dynasty* merely took that formula and transferred it to nighttime. Though the viewership of daytime soaps could never be compared with the prime-time versions, the advertising dollars generated from such programming were significant.

The 1980s was the era where the "supercouple" developed into an integral part of the soap opera. The first supercouple to gain attention among mainstream viewers was Luke Spencer and Laura Webber (Anthony Geary and Genie Francis) on *General Hospital.* The publicity surrounding the couple's wedding was more aggressive than soap operas had been in the past, and that episode was among the most watched in the 1980s. Adding to the viewer interest was the controversial storyline—Laura fell in love with Luke after he had raped her. *General Hospital* also featured married doctors Alan and Monica Quartermaine (Stuart Damon and Leslie Charleson), and Frisco and Felicia Jones (Jack Wagner and Kristina Malandro) who were not only married on the show, but also in real life. *General Hospital*, which told stories about the Quartermaine and Spencer families, was the most popular soap opera of the decade. Distinguishing features of this soap were that there were episodes shot on location around the country, and that the show included some celebrity guest stars, most notably Elizabeth Taylor and Sammy Davis, Jr., who were fans of the show. The show's popularity in the 1980s was attributed largely to producer Gloria Monty. Monty received some criticism from the mainstream press for portraying rape insensitively as a plot line, but the show's supercouple concept helped change the entire soap opera landscape.

Days of Our Lives has been one of the longest-running soap operas in television history. In the 1980s, the story lines revolved around three families: the Hortons, the Bradys, and the DiMeras, residing in the fictional town of Salem in an unspecified U.S. state. *Days of Our Lives* had its own group of supercouples, especially Bo Brady and Hope Brady (Peter Reckell and Kristian Alfonso), which was established when Bo rode his motorcycle into town and saved Hope from marrying politician Larry Welch. Bo and Hope's relationship has withstood the many travails the show saw fit to throw at it for over three decades. Another story line involved the pairing of Shane and Kimberly Donovan (Charles Shaughnessy and Patsy Pease), which was ongoing throughout the 1980s, regardless of questions of legitimacy of Kimberly's children and perilous situations that Shane would have to save Kimberly from. Steve "Patch" Johnson and Kayla Brady (Stephen Nichols and Mary Beth Evans) started off in a very rocky relationship. Patch had come to Salem to avenge the loss of his eye in a fight to Bo (Kayla's brother), but soon he became the object of Kayla's affections. Though they did not get together immediately, Steve and Kayla became a couple after her marriage to Steve's brother, Jack, fell apart.

All My Children was one of the top soap operas of the 1980s. It starred Susan Lucci as Erica Kane and was set in the fictional East Coast suburb of Pine Valley. Among the top supercouples in *All My Children* were Greg Nelson and Jenny Gardner (Laurence Lau and Kim Delaney), who were on the show until 1984. Greg and Jenny went through multiple trials and tribulations, including when Jenny moved to New York with her best friend, Jesse Hubbard, without telling Greg; Greg's paralysis, which made him decide to break up with Jenny for her own sake; and later, his return to her after being miraculously cured. Jenny's boyfriend at the time, Tony, plotted to kill Greg, but the plan went awry, and tragically Jenny was killed instead.

Other supercouples from the show included Jesse and Angela "Angie" Hubbard (Darnell Williams and Debbie Morgan), the best friends of Greg and Jenny and the first African American supercouple; and Cliff Warner and Nina Cortlandt (Peter Bergman and Taylor Miller). When Williams left the show in 1988, the Jesse character was killed by a gunshot, and the show focused on Angie's grief and attempts to rebuild her life. All of these relationships were developed by producer Agnes Nixon, which helped make *All My Children* popular in the 1980s by focusing on the love stories of younger characters.

The Young and the Restless was another top soap opera in the 1980s, but this one did not feature a supercouple as part of its story line. The program, which began in 1973, focused on the affluent Brooks family and the blue-collar Foster clan. In the 1980s, new families were introduced, the Abbott and Williams families, and all the original characters were removed from the show except Jill Foster, who had married into the Abbott family. Four different actresses played Jill in the 1980s: Bond Gideon (1980), Deborah Adair (1980–1983, 1986), Melinda O. Fee (1984) and Jess Walton, who has portrayed her since 1987. When Foster was first introduced, she was a young manicurist, and she soon began a long-running feud with Katherine Chancellor (Jeanne Cooper). The feud between the two women began when Jill had an affair with Katherine's two husbands, first Phillip Chancellor II, in the 1970s, and then later in the 1980s, Rex Sterling (Quinn Redeker).

The Bold and the Beautiful emerged in 1987, telling the occasional cross-story with *The Young and the Restless,* and soon became a top-rated soap opera. The story line revolved around Forrester Creations, a family-owned fashion business based in Los Angeles. College sweethearts Eric and Stephanie Forrester (John McCook and Susan Flannery) headed the family; as often happens in soaps, they got married when Stephanie found herself pregnant. When the show started, the couple was middle aged, and Eric soon had an affair with an old girlfriend, Beth Henderson and abandoned Stephanie. Eric returned, however, when he realized that he had a deformed child (now 24 years old), who he thought had died at childbirth. Beth had a daughter named Brooke, who fell in love with Eric's son, Ridge, who was already engaged to another woman, Caroline Spencer.

Complicating the family dynamic was the relationship between brothers Ridge and Thorne Forrester. Thorne eventually was married to Caroline, and Brooke to Ridge. This particular soap opera has stayed on right up to the present day, as it has a dedicated fan base.

Another important aspect of daytime television is the game show. *The Price Is Right* was among the top game shows of the decade. Though not the original host, Bob Barker emceed the game show for 35 years starting in 1972. Chuck Woolery started off as the host of *Wheel of Fortune* in 1975, but he was replaced by Pat Sajak, who became the iconic host throughout the 1980s. Susan Stafford was the hostess for *Wheel of Fortune* until 1982, when she was replaced by Vanna White. White was the hostess throughout the rest of the decade, and both she and Sajak became wildly popular after the show was aired later on other networks in syndication. *Jeopardy* started in the 1960s and ran through the 1970s. Like *Wheel of Fortune*, its popularity expanded when the show went into syndication in the 1980s, featuring host Alex Trebek and narrator Johnny Gilbert. The most popular version of *Family Feud* was released on ABC, featuring Richard Dawson as host from 1976–1985. Toward the end of the decade, the show was reestablished on CBS with Ray Combs as host.

The 1980s began a shift in the future of television due to a number of programs that focused on their contestants' "real" lives, decades before reality television. Two game shows fit into that format in the 1980s: *Love Connection* and *The People's Court*. Chuck Woolery had moved from *Wheel of Fortune* to *Love Connection* when that show started in 1983, and he remained the host through the 1980s. Contestants would try to find a suitable dating partner by answering a series of questions, and then the new couple would go out on a date and then return to the show with a report on how it went. Often, the tales of the date did not go well, to hilarious effect. *The People's Court* was the first courtroom type of television show, where two parties would go in front of Judge Joseph Wapner to have him mediate a dispute. The judge's decision was not binding, but the success of the format led to the development of many similar shows in the 1990s, including *Judge Judy*.

The increase in the popularity of talk shows in the 1980s was important to the development of daytime television. *Donahue,* featuring Phil Donahue, was one of the first talk shows recorded in front of a live audience, where audience members would give their input about the subject of each episode. The show ran for 29 years and was the genesis for many successful shows that followed for the rest of the decade and into the next, such as *Sally Jesse Raphael, The Ricki Lake Show,* and most significantly, *Oprah.* Oprah Winfrey's talk show became one of the most influential in American television history, and its success made her one of the most powerful women in all of media. Both Donahue and Winfrey are discussed further in Chapter 9, "Game Changers."

Children's shows are among the most important shows in the daytime television format. Ever since its debut in the late 1960s, educators have regarded *Sesame Street* as one of the top children's programs. The show began on the independent educational network NET in 1969 and shortly afterward moved over to the national Public Broadcasting Station (PBS). Since the mid-1970s, the show has featured celebrity guests and a barrage of Muppets (cute puppet-like dolls invented by Jim Henson) that portray characters that were attractive to children (and eventually beloved). The Muppets go through scenes that help children with educational concepts such as writing, reading, and math, as well as interpersonal concepts to prepare them for attending school.

Cartoons are not traditionally seen as pillars of education, but the most popular ones in the 1980s included *He Man, Fraggle Rock, My Little Pony, Strawberry Shortcake, Adventures of The Gummi Bears, Adventures of Teddy Ruxpin, Alvin & the Chipmunks,* and longtime classics such as *Looney Tunes, The Flintstones,* and *Tom and Jerry.* The television audience was expanding, and there was a need for more information and more entertainment in the 1980s than ever before.

The Information Age through Network and Cable Television

As effective as the three major networks were at controlling most of the original programming on television in the 1980s, each was successful at creating and maintaining news programs that attracted audiences that were widely viewed and as popular as news shows are considered to be. The American Broadcasting Company (ABC) featured its flagship newscast, *World News Tonight,* anchored by Frank Reynolds until his death in 1983. Peter Jennings succeeded Reynolds and remained the anchor for the rest of the decade. A supplemental program, *Nightline,* hosted by Ted Koppel, extended new programming into late night. *Nightline* initially started in 1979 to cover the Iran hostage crisis (then named *The Iran Crisis—America Held Hostage*), but when the predicament ended in 1980, ABC continued the late-night program as *Nightline.* How *Nightline* differed from *World News Tonight* was that each episode focused on a specific topic. *ABC Primetime,* started in 1989 and hosted by Diane Sawyer and Sam Donaldson, was a live program that included a studio audience; and *20/20,* hosted by Hugh Downs, was a television magazine focused on in-depth human-interest stories. *This Week,* hosted by David Brinkley and broadcast on Sunday mornings, focused on political content and included a roundtable discussion format. ABC also had two successful morning programs, the best known being *Good Morning America.* Joan Lunden was a coanchor for that show during the entire 1980s, working with David Hartman until 1987 and Charles Gibson for the rest of the decade. The other early morning program, *ABC News This Morning,* was hosted by Steve Bell and Kathleen Sullivan.

The Columbia Broadcasting Service (CBS) was just as successful as ABC in the 1980s. The *CBS Evening News* was hosted in 1980 by the iconic Walter Cronkite, but Cronkite retired the next year and was replaced by Dan Rather. Rather had a few incidents in the 1980s where he exhibited very aggressive behavior. Examples included an on-air argument with Vice President George H. W. Bush about the Iran-Contra affair; and walking off the set when a U.S. Open tennis match went long and overran his program, which was to feature Pope John Paul II's visit to Miami. When the tennis match ended, two minutes into Rather's time slot, he could not be located for nearly ten minutes, and viewers were met with the dreaded "dead air"—a black screen.

CBS Morning News was an early-morning program that featured a revolving door of anchors throughout the decade, including Diane Sawyer, Bill Kurtis, Forrest Sawyer, and Faith Daniels. *The Morning Program* replaced the *Morning News* temporarily in 1987 to poor reviews and ratings, followed by *CBS This Morning*.

CBS Sunday Morning was a very popular weekend show hosted by Charles Kuralt; it included his "On the Road" segment, where he would travel around the country to do feature stories. In the 1980s, *Face the Nation*, a political interview show with multiple guests and a moderator, was introduced. George Herman hosted the show until 1983, and Lesley Stahl took over for the rest of the decade. Other programs that had fleeting success were an overnight program, *Nightwatch*, the news magazines *West 57th*, and *48 Hours*. More successful in the 1980s was one of the pinnacles of network news magazines, *60 Minutes*, which featured three long segments in which a reporter would present a news or feature story. The broadcast also regularly included "A Few Minutes with Andy Rooney," where the irascible commentator would give his opinion on matters both trivial and serious.

The National Broadcasting Company (NBC)'s flagship program, the *NBC Nightly News*, enjoyed popularity in the 1980s. At the start of the decade, three anchors rotated, but in 1982, Tom Brokaw took over, becoming the most successful news anchor for the rest of the decade. There was also a weekend version of the show with different hosts (Jessica Savitch, Connie Chung, and Bob Jamieson on Saturdays, and John Hart, Jane Pauley, and Chris Wallace on Sundays).

The *Today* show has been one of television's most respected morning shows for decades, with multiple hosts at any given point in time. In the 1980s, those hosts included Tom Brokaw, Jane Pauley, and Bryant Gumbel, with other on-air personalities including Gene Shalit (the movie reviewer), Willard Scott (the weatherman), and John Palmer (the news anchor). A weekend version, *Weekend Today*, started in 1987 and featured Maria Shriver and Boyd Matson as anchors, Al Roker as the weatherman, and Bill Macatee as the sports reporter. *Meet the Press*, also on the weekend, was a political talk show with a moderator and panel that competed with the other networks' similar programs (*This Week* and *Face the Nation*), most successfully when Bill Monroe hosted (which was until 1984). Two other programs, *News Overnight* and *News at Sunrise*, both struggled to hold their own against their competitors.

The Tonight Show is one of the longest-running shows in television history. In the 1980s, Johnny Carson was still the host; his tenure lasted from 1962 to 1992. Ed McMahon was Carson's announcer and sidekick, and Doc Severinsen led the show's band during the 1980s. Carson did an opening monologue and recurring skits, such as Carnac the Magnificent, a "mystic from the east," who would psychically know the answers to questions provided by McMahon; the Mighty Carson Art Players, who would perform funny bits and slapstick; and "Stump the Band." When his deadpanned responses were negatively received by the audience, Carson would remark, "May a rabid holy man bless your nether regions with a power tool!" or "May a diseased yak befriend your sister!" The guest list was extensive, including mostly actors and comedians, but on occasion, also sports figures, musicians, politicians, and even celebrity psychologist Dr. Joyce Brothers, a frequent and popular guest. In the late 1970s, Carson was involved in a legal battle with NBC, the result of which was that Carson's production company gained ownership of the show. This gave Carson a three-night workweek for most of the year (a guest host would work on Monday and a rerun would be shown on Tuesday). Common guest hosts included comedians Martin Mull, Bill Cosby, David Brenner, and especially Joan Rivers.

Starting in 1982, *Late Night with David Letterman* was broadcast right after *The Tonight Show* on NBC; hence the two programs were not competitors, and Letterman saw Carson as a mentor. The show was a great success throughout the decade. It was coproduced by Carson's production company, with stipulations that restricted who Letterman could have on the show (for instance, no performers who had already established a relationship with Carson), and an avoidance of similarities between the two shows, ranging from the band's instrumentation, to having a specific cohost, to the skits. This turned out to be a blessing for Letterman's show, as it became a hit with a younger audience base than the *Tonight Show,* with skits that would be considered too risqué for the more mainstream Carson. Paul Shaffer led the "World's Most Dangerous Band," made up of top session musicians from New York who would play music rooted in modern rock, R&B, and pop with some type of jazz/fusion influence. Recurring skits included the nightly "Top Ten List," "Stupid Human Tricks," "Stupid Pet Tricks," and "Viewer Mail." Another important difference between *Late Night* and *The Tonight Show* was that modern rock groups would perform on the show, often with Shaffer and one or more members of the band playing alongside the guest performer. Guests were often actors and musicians, and sometimes sports and political figures appeared as well.

Though Letterman featured comics as guests on his program, *Saturday Night Live (SNL)* did a better job of promoting and developing comedians than any other show in the 1980s. The show would rehearse throughout the week, cumulating in a live broadcast on Saturday night. It started in 1975, but the show went through somewhat of a slump in the early 1980s, as original creator Lorne Michaels left the show and his collaborator, Dick Ebersol, succeeded him but had a difficult time maintaining the show's passionate fan base. When Michaels returned, the ratings went back up, and the show is still on today.

The show has a core group of performers (originally known as the Not Ready for Prime Time Players, but later just an unnamed troupe); in the 1980s, prominent and popular members included Eddie Murphy, Joe Piscopo, Billy Crystal, and Martin Short. Each episode has a guest host, which may include actors, musicians, sports figures, and comedians, and a musical act that performs two or three songs during the 90-minute program. Some have hosted more than five times and are referred to as members of the "Five-Timers Club." Hosts who eclipsed this milestone in the 1980s include Elliott Gould, Paul Simon, and Chevy Chase (one of the original *SNL* performers); Tom Hanks and Candace Bergen joined the club shortly after the 1980s ended. There was a house band; Tom Malone served as music director until 1985, and then

G. E. Smith succeeded him for the rest of the decade. Some of the major recurring SNL skits, such as *Wayne's World* (two teenagers running a public-access show out of their basement), *Coneheads* (aliens visiting Earth) and *The Blues Brothers* (two blues musicians who performed on the show) were made into hit movies.

The most crucial developments in how entertainment was delivered and the new information age came by way of cable television. In the late 1970s, the United States became the first country to have cable television nationally; other countries would eventually adopt this format. Prior to the development of cable television, there were just three American channels (CBS, NBC, and ABC), each of which worked with producers on programs in a variety of genres, including comedy, all-day sports coverage on Saturday, and both day-time and prime-time soap operas and other dramas. Cable television, on the other hand, was able to host new channels that focused on specific types of programming, such as Ted Turner's Cable News Network (CNN), an early cable news network; the movie-dominated Home Box Office (HBO); and the sports-focused ESPN.

With all this, it was natural that a channel dedicated to music would be among the new formats. Music Television (or MTV, as it became widely known) featured videos of singers and bands performing their music. MTV's early programming featured promotional videos of singles that were used to expand an artist's or group's popularity to a national audience. In addition, the network featured full-length concerts. Performances of popular music on television had been occurring for years, of course; both the Beatles and Elvis Presley were shown on television on the *Ed Sullivan Show* in the 1950s and 1960s, and groups also had been featured on talk shows, such as the *Michael Douglas Show*, throughout the 1970s. Since the 1970s, groups had appeared on *American Bandstand* and rhythm and blues (R&B), and disco artists were featured on *Soul Train*. *Ed Sullivan* came on once a week, and both *American Bandstand* and *Soul Train* were weekly shows. However, there had been no avenue for broadcasting music 24 hours a day, and MTV filled that niche. In the late 1970s, the music video was taken to a new level; the typical MTV video was a short film, often featuring a story line that may or may not follow the lyrics from the song. Early artists included the Buggles, Pat Benatar, and Rod Stewart.

The new format was similar to radio, but with a host that performed the function of a disc jockey. MTV had five on-air hosts called "VJ's." The network wanted to make sure to have at least one VJ that could represent different demographics of the audience, as described by John Lack (Marks and Tannenbaum, 2011, 55): "We need a black person. We need a girl next door. We need a little sexy siren. We need a boy next door. And we need some hunky Italian-looking guy with curly hair. They all had roles to play." The idea was that MTV would be accessible to its audience, who were viewed as consumers. Companies would sell to these consumers, who would be inspired by audience-specific advertisements. In these early years, music videos were the only content, and the network would run specialized contests and events meant to appeal to a teen audience.

When MTV started, the channel was committed to playing album-oriented rock (AOR) bands, but then English "New Wave" bands like A Flock of Seagulls

Music Television (MTV) was an immensely popular and influential cable television channel in the 1980s, and the original video jockeys (VJ's) were an essential part of the programming. A diverse group, they were (left to right) Nina Blackwood, Mark Goodman, Alan Hunter, Martha Quinn, and J.J. Jackson. (Mark Weiss/WireImage/Getty Images)

and Duran Duran were added, largely because of their camera acumen and outrageous appearance. The artists saw MTV as a way of reaching a wider audience, and in a pioneering sense that would separate themselves from their predecessors. The approach could apply to all subgenres of pop and rock, R&B, hard rock, and later, heavy metal and rap as well.

Not everyone was enthusiastic about how everything changed toward the end of the decade. Mark Mothersbaugh (Marks and Tannenbaum, 2011, 240) claimed:

MTV changed the architecture of being an artist. In some good ways, because all of a sudden, bands were forced to think about images. Some of them were doing great films. The bad thing about MTV is, they decided early on that the most lucrative avenue was to let their palms be greased by record companies. They promoted whatever crap record companies put money into. It became a lot of mindless baby pictures. And it changed the way artists worked, because music got punished in the trade-off. There was a one-two punch: MTV was swiftly followed by CDs, and all of a sudden instead of a well-crafted album of songs, you had to put all your bets on one particular song, and that's what people saw or heard from you. The rest of the CD was filler. So MTV created the all-or-nothing syndrome in pop music.

However, this attitude was only one reason for the decline of the vinyl record in the 1980s, and singles have traditionally been the backbone of the recording industry for years. In fact, MTV's role in these developments was no different from the role of broadcast radio during the same period—it just added visuals to the mix.

Warner Communications bought MTV in the mid-1980s, staving off a takeover bid by MTV senior management. Warner Communications did not care for the staff's lackadaisical, relaxed, rock-and-roll attitude, and the people who had helped create the cultural phenomenon left the channel in droves. Marks and Tannenbaum (2011, 261) claimed that "as a result of that failure, and new management that didn't care for the staff's rock and roll attitude, many of the people who'd made MTV a cultural phenomenon began leaving as though the building was on fire." Nevertheless, hard rock and heavy metal were gaining a significant amount of viewer and play hours in the mid-1980s. Rock critic Deborah Frost wrote about how popular MTV was in September 1984: "suddenly, rock's most extreme fantasy genre looked bigger, brighter, more *fantastic* than ever before, and MTV is in the fantasy business (Marks and Tannenbaum, 2011, 331, italic in original)." This is ultimately what resulted in the "hair band" moniker that critics used against hard rock groups such as Poison, Bon Jovi, Mötley Crüe, and Dokken as the decade ended and entered the 1990s. Marks and Tannenbaum (2011, 436) noted that "no one was a bigger underdog than Guns n' Roses, five scuzzballs from LA whose caustic notion of hard rock had little to do with Poison or Bon Jovi. As with rap, MTV was afraid of the band. The network relented only after pressure from David Geffen, one of the titans of the record business, and ironically, Guns eventually became so prominent on MTV that the network hired a new VJ mostly because he came recommended by the band."

All the while, rap artists were having trouble getting recognition in the mid-1980s. Rapper Kool Moe Dee (Marks and Tannenbaum, 2011, 276) considered that "Ann Carli and Russell Simmons deserve credit for believing hip-hop artists should be treated like mainstream artists. We were aware that there was one video budget for an R&B or hip-hop act and another budget for a pop act. We had to fight to even have a video budget in our contract." However, rap artists became more prominent and as 1980s hard rock was declining, other types of music were being noticed. *The Cutting Edge* was a Sunday show that highlighted underground rock groups (often called "college," and later known as "alternative") such as R.E.M., the Red Hot Chili Peppers, and the Minutemen. Eventually, MTV created a show called *120 Minutes* to help cultivate those artists. Though broadcast at 1 a.m., it slowly gained momentum among teenagers who would be rock pioneers in the 1990s.

As important as MTV would be to the development of television for music, CNN would be for the development of news. In 1976, Ted Turner, who had taken over a successful outdoor billboard business, purchased WCEG, a television station in Atlanta. In time, he developed it into WTBS, one of the first

Ted Turner's Cable News Network (CNN) became a top news outlet in the 1980s and helped expand the reach of cable television in many American homes. Turner widened his influence in television entertainment via sports and classic movie channels. (Ted Thai/The LIFE Picture Collection/Getty Images)

satellite-distributed television channels, which he called a "superstation" due to its wide variety of programming. Within a few years, Turner was ready to launch CNN, which he did on June 1, 1980.

The channel was an instant success, featuring an interview with President Jimmy Carter as one of its first segments, and one of its first important news stories was the shooting of President Ronald Reagan less than a year later. The programming included up-to-the-minute news coverage, as well as individual shows such as *Moneyline*, a financial news program hosted by Lou Dobbs; and *Evans and Novak*, hosted by Rowland Evans and Robert Novak, a political discussion program similar to the the major networks' weekend political programs. As CNN's success grew, Turner developed a new network, CNN2, which became known as Headline News and would repeat the latest headlines every 30 minutes. The new, separate network allowed CNN to add even more specialized programs to its lineup, such as the late-night political discussion *Crossfire* and the very popular interview show *Larry King Live*, hosted by the veteran journalist. Later in the 1980s, CNN would run nonstop coverage of significant news stories on the large and small scale, such as the *Challenger* space shuttle disaster in 1986, and when 18-month-old Jessica McClure fell down a well in Texas (the "Baby Jessica" coverage of her ordeal and rescue helped redefine cable news). By the mid-1990s, CNN had competitors that used a similar format, but even into the 21st century, CNN remains a leader in news coverage.

ESPN, which dealt exclusively with sports events and features, changed the way that a specialized subject was broadcast, similar to CNN and MTV, although ESPN's impact was less dramatic during the 1980s. The channel started in Bristol, Connecticut, in 1979 with one main program: *SportsCenter*, which is still relevant today. The network began to obtain advertising arrangements with various companies, including Budweiser, and would provide coverage for two events that at the time were not major events in the sporting world: the NCAA men's basketball tournament, and the NFL draft. Both became hugely popular because of ESPN's coverage, which can be attributed in part to the personalities the network used. Former basketball coach Dick Vitale was animated and an instant draw for viewers of the new "March Madness" repackaging of the tournament. Mel Kiper joined as analyst for the NFL draft, and though he was often incorrect in his predictions, no one had scrutinized college players coming into the professional ranks before as he did, making the NFL draft one of the most followed events of the year. Chris Berman was the main sportscaster for *SportsCenter* and became one of the network's most identifiable personalities.

Later in the decade, the network started to broadcast NCAA football, and after ESPN was acquired by ABC, it obtained the leverage to broadcast professional football, hockey, baseball, and basketball as well. And as television was an important part of popular culture in the United States in the 1980s, the increasing popularity of American sports was important to television's reach and helped generate more advertising dollars than any previous decade. The next chapter discusses some of the most popular sports of the 1980s.

FURTHER READING

Abramson, Albert, and Christopher H. Sterling. *The History of Television, 1942–2000.* Jefferson, NC: McFarland and Company, Inc., 2003.

Castleman, Harry, and Walter J. Podrazik. *Watching TV: Eight Decades of American Television.* 3d ed. Syracuse, NY: Syracuse University Press, 2016.

Curtin, Michael, Jennifer Holt, Keith Sanson, and Kurt Sutter. *Distribution Revolution: Conversations About the Digital Future of Film and Television.* Berkeley, CA: University of California Press, 2014.

Edgerton, Gary. *The Columbia History of American Television.* New York: Columbia University Press, 2009.

Hilmes, Michelle, and Jason Jacobs. *The Television History Book.* London: British Film Institute, 2004.

Marks, Craig, and Rob Tannenbaum. *I Want My MTV.* New York: Dutton, 2011.

Williams, Raymond. *Television: Technology and Cultural Form.* 3d ed. London: Routledge, 2003.

CHAPTER 2

Sports

Sports was one of the most widely broadcast genres on television in the 1980s. Enormous television contracts were negotiated for each professional league, including football, baseball, basketball, and hockey, as well as collegiate teams playing Division I football and basketball in the National Collegiate Athletic Association (NCAA). By the end of the decade, the Super Bowl had become television's most anticipated event of the year. By its 17th season in 1986, ABC's *Monday Night Football* had become the longest-running prime-time series in the history of the network. Baseball, which had been the most popular sport in the United States for decades before the 1980s, lost a percentage of the overall television viewing audience and was succeeded in popularity by football. However, the overall audience grew considerably, so the viewership for baseball, in absolute numbers, did not necessarily shrink in the process.

College basketball, particularly through the NCAA tournament (known colloquially as "March Madness"), became a cultural phenomenon to the point that by the end of the decade, there were local contests (office pools, for example) to find out who picked the most winners in their bracket. Michael Jordan became an enormous cultural icon and helped transform the impact that athletes would have on commerce through advertising and endorsement deals. The Olympic Games were televised in 1980, 1984, and 1988, and for a few weeks, national pride was awakened within millions of people galvanized to support their Olympic athletes. In some cases, the Games were broadcast in the context of the Cold War with the Soviet Union. Even professional wrestling, considered largely regional before the 1980s, emerged with the rise of cable television. With golf, tennis, and boxing added to the mix, the television landscape changed greatly from the beginning to the end of the decade, with pro football leading the way.

PRO FOOTBALL

Before the 1980 season began, there were two controversies surrounding the presence of the National Football League in Los Angeles. The current Los Angeles team, the Rams, which had played in the historic Los Angeles Coliseum since 1946, had begun making arrangements to play in Anaheim, just over 25 miles away. Meanwhile, the Oakland Raiders, led by managing general partner Al Davis, became interested in moving into the Coliseum, as efforts to build a new stadium in Oakland were failing. The NFL did not support the Raiders' plan, however, and the team joined the Los Angeles Coliseum Commission in a lawsuit against the league. This battle continued throughout the 1980 season, and ironically, it was the Raiders who won the Super Bowl. At that point, the league's commissioner, Pete Rozelle, had to award the Vince Lombardi Trophy to Davis, even though the men were still battling each other in court.

From a business perspective, regular season attendance was higher than at any point in league history. In addition, television ratings in 1980 were the second highest in history (behind 1976), with each of the three major networks seeing higher ratings. These successful ratings helped give the league an advantage in negotiating a radio deal with CBS at the time. For $12 million, the league's regular season and postseason games would be broadcast by CBS exclusively.

The 1980s season, a year where Cleveland quarterback Brian Sipe won the Most Valuable Player (MVP) award, also marked the beginning of a new era of attention to player safety. For the first time, "personal fouls" could be called against players for swinging their helmet at an opponent, or otherwise striking them in the head, neck, or face during a play, regardless if the neck was the point of initial contact. This was an extension of the 1977 rule changes that disallowed a "head slap" by a defensive lineman, or the use of the hands on the defensive lineman's face by the offensive lineman. Some offensive and defensive linemen in the 1970s (notably, offensive lineman Conrad Dobler and defensive lineman Deacon Jones) practiced playing techniques that ultimately led to more concussions for players.

In 1981, there was a new, important rule: the banning of adhesives. In the 1970s, two Oakland Raiders became notorious for using an adhesive called "Stick-um" all over their uniforms so that the football would stick to their clothes, making it easier to catch and hold it. The adhesives ban was passed largely in response to that discovery. Other notable off-field issues in 1981 were the sale of the Denver Broncos to Canadian financier Edgar Kaiser, Jr., and the NFL reaching out to host recruits from historically black colleges and universities during training camp. Cincinnati quarterback Ken Anderson won the MVP Award for the year. The season ended with the San Francisco 49ers defeating the Cincinnati Bengals in Super Bowl XVI, the highest-rated game in televised sports history. San Francisco had endured years of poor showings, but the arrival of coach Bill Walsh and his new "West Coast Offense," as well as quarterback Joe Montana, started the 49ers on a run as one of the most successful teams in pro football in the 1980s. The West Coast offense was different from run-oriented offenses of the 1970s, where the former relied on short passes to open up the running game.

During the 1981 season, one game of note was a divisional playoff contest between the San Diego Chargers and the Miami Dolphins. In the second-longest game ever played, the Chargers' thrilling victory is considered by many to be one of the greatest ever played. Football's popularity continued to grow, with attendance records breaking the average of 60,000 fans per game, and 93.8 percent of stadiums being filled to capacity. The ABC and CBS television networks were also enjoying all-time-high ratings. A CBS Sports/*New York Times* poll showed that 48 percent of sports fans preferred football, while only 31 percent preferred baseball.

Before the 1982 season, the dispute among the Oakland Raiders, the Los Angeles Coliseum Commission, and the NFL went to trial. In May 1982, a jury ruled in favor of the Raiders, so the team was allowed to move to Los Angeles for the upcoming season. The NFL also signed a five-year contract with the major television networks, bringing in more money than ever before. The players, who knew of the agreement and thought they deserved a higher percentage of the stake, went on strike for 57 days (from the end of September until nearly the end of November), until they received a new Collective Bargaining Agreement. The NFL rookie draft was extended through 1992, and the veteran free-agent system was not changed; however, minimum salaries, training camp and postseason salaries, and medical and retirement benefits were all increased for the players. In addition, a severance-pay plan to assist players in their transition from football was introduced—the first in professional sports.

Because of the strike, the usual 16-game season was reduced to 9 games, and the league was organized into two tables by conference (the American Football Conference and National Football Conference), without divisions, to allow a 16-team, tournament-style playoff. The Washington Redskins defeated the Miami Dolphins in Super Bowl XVII. The game was the second-highest-rated live television program of all time, which meant that the NFL had the top 10 spots in the history of live television. Washington kicker Mark Moseley was voted as the 1982 season's MVP.

The year 1983 saw a few changes to the rules, and the divisions were restored to their 1981 format. The 1983 NFL draft was one of the strongest in league history, including future star quarterbacks John Elway (selected by the Baltimore Colts and then traded to the Denver Broncos, where he spent the rest of his playing career), Ken O'Brien (New York Jets), Tony Eason (New England Patriots), Todd Blackledge (Kansas City Chiefs), Jim Kelly (Buffalo Bills), and Dan Marino (Miami Dolphins). Elway, Kelly, and Marino would all enter the NFL Hall of Fame after their playing careers ended. The newly minted Los Angeles Raiders, led by running back Marcus Allen, won Super Bowl XVIII at the end of the season, and Washington quarterback Joe Theismann won the season's MVP award.

The biggest news in pro football in 1983 concerned an upstart league, the United States Football League (USFL), which would play in the spring when the NFL was not in session. The NFL had a longtime rule that college students were not eligible for the draft until the year that their collegiate class graduated, to encourage students to stay in school instead of moving to the professional ranks. However, the USFL allowed student-athletes to become eligible after their junior year—an important development for 1980s' collegiate sensation Herschel Walker. Walker had been the best player in college football since his freshman year (winning the Heisman Trophy and Maxwell Award in 1982), and the NFL was eagerly waiting for him to finish his four-year term at the University of Georgia. However, the financial payoff offered by the USFL led Walker to leave college and go professional in 1983, and he became one of the faces of the new league, helped in part by playing for the New Jersey Generals (owned by real-estate mogul and future U.S. president Donald Trump). Further, quarterback Jim Kelly had spurned the NFL's Buffalo Bills' offer to play for them so he could play in a warmer climate instead, for the USFL's Houston Gamblers. The USFL was deemed a success in its first year, raising concerns in the NFL about its ability to sign draft picks in the future.

A number of news stories grabbed headlines before the 1984 season. Two more college stars, Heisman Trophy winner Mike Rozier and Brigham Young quarterback Steve Young, opted to join the USFL instead of the NFL. Meanwhile, in the NFL, a new rule was adopted to quash excessive celebrations, which was inspired by the antics of New York Jet defensive end Mark Gastineau after he would tackle (or sack) the quarterback. There were ownership changes as well, as the Dallas Cowboys were sold to a new ownership group, and billionaire Alex Spanos bought the San Diego Chargers. The New York Jets moved to play games in the New York Giants' stadium in New Jersey. The biggest news, however, was the move of the Baltimore Colts to Indianapolis. The Colts' owner, inspired by the Raiders, moved after secretly negotiating with a group from Indianapolis; the team famously left in the middle of the night, using U-Haul trailers.

The San Francisco 49ers won Super Bowl XIX over the Miami Dolphins. President Ronald Reagan participated in the coin toss before the Super Bowl, right after taking the oath of office for his second term. Miami quarterback Dan Marino won the league's MVP award in 1984, at least in part because he set a new record for passing yardage and touchdowns in a season. Also of note was that Rams' running back Eric Dickerson eclipsed a new milestone, breaking the record for the amount of yards rushed for in a season; Redskins' wide receiver Art Monk caught 106 passes, a new high; and Chicago's Walter Payton broke the career rushing mark. According to a CBS Sports/*New York Times* survey, 53 percent of the nation's sports fans said they most enjoyed watching football, compared to only 18 percent for baseball. Attendance was at the second highest in league history, and the Super Bowl was widely watched in the United Kingdom and Italy.

Because of the popularity that the NFL was enjoying internationally, owners agreed to begin playing preseason games in England and Japan in 1985. That year also saw the sale of another team, the New Orleans Saints, to new owner Tom Benson. However, the big story of the 1985 season was the success of the Chicago Bears. The team, featuring coach Mike Ditka, future Hall of Fame running back Walter Payton, maverick quarterback Jim McMahon, rookie defensive tackle William "The Refrigerator" Perry, and a stifling defense led by coordinator Buddy Ryan, marched through the season with only one loss. That loss was on a *Monday Night Football* game against the Miami Dolphins, the only team that had achieved a perfect record (unbeaten and untied in the regular season, and undefeated in the playoffs up through the Super Bowl) in any season. It was the most widely watched prime-time football game in history.

The Bears became media celebrities, recording a rap song ("The Super Bowl Shuffle"), and McMahon was at odds with the league over messages that he would place on his headband, such as the last name of the league's commissioner, Pete Rozelle, or "Pluto," or his support of causes including Prisoners of War/Missing in Action, and juvenile diabetes. The 1985 Bears' defense, led by linebacker Mike Singletary, was considered one of the best of all time, shutting out both of their conference opponents in the playoffs. The Bears won Super Bowl XX against the New England Patriots in January by an overwhelming 46–10 victory. Raider running back Marcus Allen won the MVP award for the 1985 season. Ratings were higher than ever for all three networks, and a Louis Harris poll showed that pro football was the most popular sport in the country.

In 1986, a rule was passed to prohibit players from wearing items that carry personal messages or names of organizations of any type—a reaction to McMahon's behavior from the year before. That was also the year that NFL owners adopted the use of instant replay for the first time to help officials make accurate rulings on the field. In addition, the USFL had decided to move to the fall to compete directly with the NFL. After the USFL was unsuccessful in obtaining a television contract, they sued the NFL for antitrust violations. The court sided with the USFL, but it awarded them only $1 in damages, crushing the future of the league.

On the field, the NFL began to play preseason games internationally, with the first occurring at Wembley Stadium in London. The telecast was the most popular preseason game in history, and the fans (perhaps curious to see what this American football was all about) sold out the stadium. The New York Giants beat the Denver Broncos in Super Bowl XXI, their first NFL title game since 1956. The game was nearly as popular as the previous year's game, which was the highest-rated telecast in history. More than 100,000 spectators attended the game, which was held at the Rose Bowl in Pasadena, California. Giants' linebacker Lawrence Taylor won the season's MVP award for the 1986 season.

On March 15, 1987, the NFL entered into new agreements with the major television networks, as well as a three-year contract with the cable sports provider ESPN. The ESPN contract—the first that the league had with a cable company—included the rights to broadcast 13 games. The first game, Chicago at Miami, was the highest-rated sports program in basic cable history, but it was soon bettered by the Oakland Raiders–Dallas Cowboys game later in the season. However, another players' strike, which started after the second week, marred the season. Replacement players ("scabs," as they were often called) played in the games from weeks four through six before the union called off the strike. In addition, Rams' running back Eric Dickerson was holding out for a new contract, which ultimately led to a three-team trade that also involved the Buffalo Bills and the Indianapolis Colts. The Colts ended up winning their division that year thanks to Dickerson, but over the long term, the addition of Cornelius Bennett to the Buffalo team led to multiple Super Bowl appearances in the 1990s. 1987 was also the beginning of the short career for Heisman Trophy winner Bo Jackson. Jackson was originally drafted by the Tampa Bay Buccaneers in 1986. Jackson was also playing college baseball at the same time. After Jackson went to a meeting and had a pre-draft physical with the Buccaneers, he was stripped of his eligibility in college baseball, even though he claimed that he was told he would not lose the eligibility. In protest against the Buccaneers, Jackson played professional baseball with the Kansas City Royals in the 1986 organization instead, and was reentered into the 1987 draft. Jackson, a running back selected by the Los Angeles Raiders, was often paired with future Hall of Fame running back Marcus Allen in the offensive backfield. Jackson's story became one of the most popular in 1987, and because of his ability to excel at both sports, he would soon become one of America's most loved athletes. The Washington Redskins defeated the Denver Broncos in Super Bowl XXII, its second championship of the 1980s. Denver quarterback John Elway received the season's MVP award.

In 1988, the NFL approved a move by the Cardinals from St. Louis to Phoenix; the team called itself the Phoenix Cardinals before finally adopting the name Arizona Cardinals in 1994. The rookie draft, now called the Annual Selection Meeting, was broadcast on cable television over a two-day period for the first time. The ratings were higher than expected. In the years since, cable television coverage of the NFL draft has made it one of the year's fan-favorite events. The San Francisco 49ers won Super Bowl XXIII over the Cincinnati Bengals, 20–16. It was considered one of the most exciting Super Bowl games to date, as John Taylor caught the winning pass with just 34 seconds left in the fourth quarter. Taylor's catch followed a series of important catches by Hall of Fame wide receiver (and game MVP award winner) Jerry Rice. Cincinnati quarterback Boomer Esiason won the season's MVP award. The 1988 season also saw the retirement of Dallas Cowboy coach Tom Landry, who had led the team to multiple championship games throughout the 1960s, 1970s, and 1980s.

The 1989 off-season included another important retirement, one of NFL commissioner Pete Rozelle. Rozelle's impact on the popularity of football in the United States cannot be understated. In his almost 30-year tenure, he successfully protected the league against challenges from upstart leagues in both the 1960s (the American Football League) and the 1980s (the USFL); he was a key player in negotiating lucrative contracts with both the main networks and cable television that placed football at the top of the sporting world by the mid-1980s; and he helped popularize the Super Bowl as the most important television event in the United States—by the 1990s, it would be the most important event globally. Paul Tagliabue, an attorney with the league office, eventually succeeded him.

Also in the 1989 off-season was the purchase of the Dallas Cowboys by Jerry Jones, who would go on to be one of the most influential (and controversial)

As commissioner of the National Football League for nearly thirty years, Pete Rozelle's impact on professional football was profound. Rozelle led the league through labor strikes on its way to international success, as football became the most popular sport in the United States and the Super Bowl became the most-watched television event throughout the 1980s and the years that followed. (Jerry Coli/Dreamstime.com)

owners in the league for the next 25 years. In addition, the owners enhanced previous policies against anabolic steroids and masking agents, as it had become clear through research that their use was affecting the long-term health of the players, both physically and, as discovered later, mentally.

A new free agent system, Plan B, was implemented that allowed more freedom for players with expiring contracts to leave their teams, while providing some type of protection for the team itself. In addition, a new development league was founded, the World League of American Football, that would have teams based internationally. Rosters included fringe players on the rosters of some NFL teams, and other players hoping for a chance to play in the NFL by impressing personnel staff looking for undiscovered talent. In October, Art Shell became the first African American head football coach when he joined the Los Angeles Raiders. Owner Al Davis was widely praised for the long-overdue move. San Francisco defeated Denver in Super Bowl XXIV, making them one of only two teams (the Pittsburgh Steelers was the other) to win four Super Bowl titles. San Francisco's Joe Montana won the MVP award for the season.

During this decade, even as pro football became the most important sport in the United States, college football was also expanding its reach because of its media presence.

COLLEGE FOOTBALL

In the 1980s, college football, governed by the NCAA, became an important part of the broadcast sports landscape. The bowl season was (and remains) the highlight of the year, as it helps determine the national champion. In the 1980s, the NCAA teams from the biggest and most competitive schools (called Division I-A) was divided into regional conferences, with some schools participating on an independent basis. The top teams of the major conferences had agreements to appear in specific bowl games, many of which were long standing. The writers for the Associated Press (AP) voted for the national champion (though there was also another poll, voted on by coaches, that was not as respected as the AP's), and it was customary that if a top team won its bowl game, they would retain their position at the end. There was not an automatic championship game, however, so if the true top two teams in the country were not scheduled to meet all year, there was no guarantee they would meet in a bowl game at the end of the season. The amount of money that the schools would receive was tied into the ever-increasing television contracts for the bowl. The top five teams usually included those that had won an important bowl or were top teams that lost to another top team. In addition, there was more interest in the broadcast of the Heisman Trophy presentation, given to the top player in college football. This section focuses on the results of the top five teams and Heisman winners for each year in the 1980s.

The 1980 NCAA football season was distinguished by two running backs: George Rogers, from the University of South Carolina; and Herschel Walker, from the University of Georgia. Rogers led the Gamecocks to an 8–3 record and won the Heisman Trophy for the year. Walker, a freshman, led the Bulldogs to the No. 1 ranking at the end of the year, capped by a Sugar Bowl win over Notre Dame, and finished third in the voting for the Heisman Trophy (rare for a first-year player). The other finalists for the Heisman in 1980 were quarterback Mark Herrmann (Purdue University), Jim McMahon (Brigham Young University), and defensive end Hugh Green. Green helped lead the University of Pittsburgh (Pitt) to the No. 2 ranking at the end of the season, and his team won the Gator Bowl against South Carolina. Alongside Green were running back Randy McMillan and tackle Mark May, just three of a dozen Panthers drafted by the NFL in 1981. Finishing third in the rankings was the University of Oklahoma, who had just two losses and won the Big Eight Conference, beating Florida State in the Orange Bowl. Florida State also lost just two games, one to Pittsburgh and the other to the University of Miami, en route to finishing fifth. Oklahoma State, also with just two losses, finished fourth, and featured J. C. Watts as its quarterback.

In 1981, the undefeated Clemson captured the Atlantic Coast Conference crown and the national title after defeating Nebraska in the Orange Bowl. Nebraska was crippled in the bowl games by the loss of their starting quarterback, Turner Gill, and Clemson featured a strong defense led by defensive back Terry Kennard and linebacker Jeff Davis, as well as the youngest coach to win a national championship, Denny Ford, who was just 34. Clemson was a complete surprise, as they had not been ranked at all before the season and entered the rankings only after a surprise third-week upset of Georgia, then ranked No. 4. Texas, led by defensive lineman Kenneth Sims, captured the No. 2 ranking after a close win over Alabama in the Cotton Bowl. Pennsylvania State University (Penn State) captured the third spot in the ranking with its win over the University of Southern California (USC) in the Fiesta Bowl. Pitt got ranked fourth thanks to its win over Georgia in the Sugar Bowl, and the top five was rounded out with Southern Methodist University (SMU), who did not have a bowl game because of an NCAA suspension (the SMU football program was found to have had violations in recruiting practices). USC running back Marcus Allen, who rushed for over 2,300 yards, won the Heisman Trophy over Herschel Walker and Jim McMahon (finalists from the previous year) and new finalists Dan Marino from Pitt and Art Schlichter from The Ohio State University.

Penn State, led by quarterback Todd Blackledge, won their first national championship during the 1982 season after beating Georgia 27–23 in the Sugar Bowl. With that loss, the previously top-ranked Georgia dropped to fourth position. SMU, led by the "Pony Express" (running backs Eric Dickerson and Craig James), came back from their postseason suspension to win the Cotton Bowl and a place as the second-ranked team at the end of the year. Nebraska narrowly won the Orange Bowl to earn the third ranking, while the University of California at Los Angeles (UCLA) won the Rose Bowl to place fifth. Georgia's Herschel Walker, who had been dominating many of his opponents during his first two years in college and was a Heisman finalist twice, finally won the honor in 1982 over finalists Stanford quarterback John Elway, Dickerson, Michigan wide receiver Anthony Carter, and Nebraska center Dave Rimington. Rimington was such a dominant lineman during his career that the annual award for the top center now bears his name. Elway was the only one of the finalists who was not on a team that went to a bowl game; his season highlight was an upset win over Washington, ranked No. 2 in the nation at the time. The season was particularly important in that it was the final season of coaching for Alabama legend Paul "Bear" Bryant, who coached for 38 seasons. He died only 28 days after retiring.

The Miami Hurricanes won the 1983 national championship by beating Nebraska 31–30 in one of the most legendary games played on a college football field. Nebraska, top ranked and led by Heisman winner Mike Rozier, scored with less than one minute remaining to bring them within one point. Tom Osborne, the Nebraska coach, wanted to win the game rather than settle for a tie by just kicking the extra point, so he attempted to score a two-point conversion, which failed. Miami had been a resurgent team since Howard Schnellenberger took over as coach in 1979, but with this win, Miami won the first of its three national championships in the 1980s. Miami had entered the game ranked No. 5, but with upset losses by Illinois, Texas, and Michigan (who lost a close game to Auburn in the Sugar Bowl), voters elevated Miami to the top position. Nebraska held onto second place in the ranking. Auburn, led by sophomore running back Bo Jackson, placed third, followed by Georgia and Texas. Rozier was the clear winner for the Heisman; fellow finalists included quarterback Doug Flutie (Boston College), quarterback Turner Gill (Nebraska), safety Terry Hoage (Georgia), and quarterback Steve Young (Brigham Young University).

Young's replacement the following year, Robbie Bosco, would guide Brigham Young to the national championship. Brigham Young was in the Western Athletic Conference in 1984, and there was no agreement for an automatic bid to a bowl against a top opponent (they won the Holiday Bowl against an unranked Michigan team). The rest of the top five were second-ranked Washington (who beat the previous No. 2-ranked Oklahoma in the Orange Bowl), third-ranked Florida (who would not play in a bowl game that year because of NCAA recruiting violations), fourth-ranked Nebraska (who won the Sugar Bowl), and fifth-ranked Boston College (who won the Cotton Bowl behind Heisman Trophy winner Flutie). Flutie won the Heisman by a significant margin over the other finalists: running back Keith Byars of Ohio State, Bosco, Miami quarterback Bernie Kosar, and Texas Christian University running back Kenneth Davis. Though Flutie had received some attention the previous season in the Heisman race, he became the talk of college football on the Friday after Thanksgiving that year. In front of a large television audience and from his team's own 22-yard line, Flutie threw a 48-yard Hail Mary victory pass in the waning seconds against Miami.

In 1985, Oklahoma rebounded from their disappointing loss in the previous year's bowl game by beating previously top-ranked Penn State in the Orange Bowl, which elevated them to the top spot. Oklahoma had been ranked third, but the second-ranked Miami lost to Tennessee in the Sugar Bowl. After the bowls concluded, the top five were Oklahoma, Michigan (who had won the Fiesta Bowl), Penn State, Tennessee, and Florida, who was again banned from postseason play. Running back Bo Jackson of Auburn won the Heisman in 1985, beating finalists Iowa quarterback Chuck Long, Michigan State running back Lorenzo White, Miami quarterback Vinny Testaverde, and the previous year's finalist Robbie Bosco.

Penn State won the national championship the following year with a victory over Miami in the Fiesta Bowl, even though Miami had a superb season, finishing no lower than second the entire time. Penn State ranked second after beating Alabama in week seven, and they managed to stay there for most of the rest of the 1986 regular season, largely because of a stifling defense that took them to an undefeated season. Oklahoma gained the third position after humiliating Arkansas in the Orange Bowl, Arizona State gained the fourth position after beating previously ranked No. 4 Michigan in the Rose Bowl, and Nebraska became the fifth-ranked team after beating the previously fifth-ranked Louisiana State University (LSU) in the Sugar Bowl. Vinny Testaverde won the Heisman over running back Paul Palmer (Texas Christian); quarterback Jim Harbaugh (Michigan); controversial linebacker Brian Bosworth (Oklahoma), who was vocal in criticizing the NCAA and was well known for his outrageous hairstyle; and running back/cornerback Gordie Lockbaum (with Holy Cross, from Division I-AA).

In 1987, Miami won the national title by beating Oklahoma in the Orange Bowl, which pitted the top two teams in the country against each other. Florida State played Nebraska in the Fiesta Bowl, and with the Oklahoma loss, moved to the No. 2 ranking, with Oklahoma finishing third. Syracuse maintained their No. 4 ranking, even though they had tied with Auburn in the Sugar Bowl. LSU had a convincing win over South Carolina in the Gator Bowl, which moved them to the fifth spot. The 1987 Heisman was won by the electrifying wide receiver Tim Brown, who, though he played for 17th-ranked Notre Dame, dazzled fans throughout the country with his receiving, kicking, and punt-returning skills. Brown was the first wide receiver to win the Heisman Trophy. Other finalists included quarterback Don McPherson (Syracuse), running back Craig Hayward (Pittsburgh), 1985 finalist Lorenzo White, and 1986 finalist Gordie Lockbaum.

The 1988 season is when Notre Dame returned to prominence, with an undefeated season and a win over West Virginia in the Fiesta Bowl. Miami ended up ranked second after their convincing victory over Nebraska in the Orange Bowl. Florida State finished third by winning the Sugar Bowl, and Michigan, with a surprising win over fifth-ranked USC in the Rose Bowl, came in fourth. West Virginia, after losing in the Fiesta Bowl, ended up fifth. Running back Barry Sanders from Oklahoma State University won the Heisman Trophy over four quarterback finalists: Rodney Peete (USC), Troy Aikman (UCLA), Steve Walsh (Miami), and Major Harris (West Virginia).

The decade ended with the 1989 Miami Hurricanes winning the national championship. Miami won the Sugar Bowl (on January 1, 1990) over Alabama. The Hurricanes were the second-ranked team in the country, but moved to the top spot with Colorado's loss to Notre Dame in the Orange Bowl. Notre Dame moved into the second spot, largely because of the exciting receiving, kicking, and punt returning by wide receiver Raghib "Rocket" Ismail. Florida State ranked third after their crushing defeat of Nebraska in the Fiesta Bowl. Colorado was an unexpected No. 1 finisher in the regular season, but they had a particular (if unfortunate) motivation: their quarterback, Sal Aunese, had been diagnosed with stomach cancer the previous February and died at the beginning of the season, and the team dedicated the entire 1989 season to their fallen comrade. Their loss pushed Colorado to fourth place. Tennessee moved into the fifth spot after winning the Cotton Bowl. Andre Ware, who broke numerous passing records as a member of the University of Houston's run-and-shoot style offense, won the last Heisman Trophy of the 1980s, beating out running back Anthony Thompson (Indiana University), quarterback Tony Rice (Notre Dame), quarterback Darian Hagan (Colorado), and quarterback Major Harris, a finalist for the second year in a row.

Among the biggest college football stories of 1989, as well as the entire decade, was the announcement of an agreement between NBC and Notre Dame in which the network agreed to broadcast the university's games for six years for $30 million. Although conferences and the NCAA had negotiated contracts with networks in the past, this marked the first occasion where an individual university had made an agreement with a network on its own.

BASEBALL

The Philadelphia Phillies, from the National League, won the World Series in 1980 in six games over the Kansas City Royals, with third baseman Mike Schmidt named as the MVP. It was the first World Series for the Phillies since the team's founding in 1882. Phillies' fans had endured years of frustration, but the team finally rewarded their patience. Led by rookie manager Dallas Green and fueled by pitcher Steve Carlton's 24 wins, Schmidt's 48 home runs, and Pete Rose's overall contributions, the Phillies eked out a win in their division over the Montreal Expos (by one game), and then defeated the Houston Astros for the pennant. Meanwhile, the Royals were capturing the American League pennant over the New York Yankees. The New York Yankees had been one of the strongest teams all year. Yankee owner George Steinbrenner had reacquired star Reggie Jackson, who hit 41 home runs; coupled with Tommy John's 22 wins as a pitcher, it is easy to see why they would have been tough to beat. Indeed, many sportswriters considered that the Royals would have less difficulty with the Phillies than with the Yankees, but of course, that didn't quite work out. Schmidt also won the MVP in the National League, while Kansas City Royal third baseman George Brett did the same for the American League.

The 1981 season was one of the most difficult in recent memory for Major League Baseball. A strike by the Major League Baseball Players Association had crippled the league. An incredible 713 games were not played, nearly $100 million in player salaries were not paid, and there were no ticket, broadcast, or concession dollars either. After the strike ended at the end of July, the season was split into two halves, with an extra round of playoff games. The teams leading their divisions' prestrike standings were called the "first-half" winners, and a similar designation was given to the "second-half" winners. Then, the two winners would play each other in a best-of-five series to determine the champion for each division. If they turned out to be the same team, then a second-place team would go into the playoffs too. Finally, the eventual winners would play in the division series for the pennant. The teams most adversely affected by this structure were the ones who were in a close second place before the strike, such as the Cincinnati Reds, and then didn't get to the playoffs because they didn't win in the second half.

In the American League East, the New York Yankees and the Milwaukee Brewers faced each other, with the Yankees winning. The Oakland Athletics played the Royals in the West, with the Athletics winning. The Yankees and Athletics played each other for the league championship, putting the Yankees into the World Series. In the National League, the Phillies and Montreal Expos played for the East title, with the Expos victorious; and the Los Angeles Dodgers defeated the Houston Astros in the West. The Dodgers, featuring a 20-year-old pitcher from Mexico named Fernando Valenzuela, made it to the World Series against the Yankees and emerged victorious. To put a final, farcical touch on the ridiculous season, Steinbrenner held a press conference after the World Series to apologize to the people of New York for his team's poor play against the Dodgers. Milwaukee's Rollie Fingers won the American League MVP award, and Philadelphia's Mike Schmidt won the National League for the second year in a row.

By the time 1982 came around, everyone affiliated with baseball just wanted to have a nice, normal season as usual. The National League champions, the St. Louis Cardinals, won the World Series over the American League champions, the Milwaukee Brewers in a tightly contested series; Milwaukee got out to a 3–2 lead and needed to win only one of the last two games, but they fell short. The Cardinals had made a couple of great off-season moves, landing Lonnie Smith and Ozzie Smith (no relation), who helped propel the team to the top despite having the fewest home runs in the league. Similar to the World Series, the divisions and the American League divisional playoffs were competitive, going down to the final weekend of play. Milwaukee's shortstop Robin Yount won the American League MVP award, while Atlanta's outfielder Dale Murphy won the National League MVP.

The 1983 season went relatively smoothly again, with the exception of one incident. Yankees manager Billy Martin accused Royals' star George Brett of using pine tar more than 18 inches from the knob on the bat right after he put the Royals ahead with a home run. Ultimately, the umpires called Brett out, ending the game in the Yankees' favor, but the league later reversed the decision and the final inning of the game was replayed (and the Royals ultimately prevailed). The Pine Tar incident was one of the most widely talked about events of the year, though it affected neither team's ability to get to the playoffs (for more about this, see Chapter 8, "Controversies"). The Orioles, sparked by the MVP year of its shortstop, Cal Ripken, Jr., and the White Sox met in the American League Championship series, with the Orioles coming out on top. Ripken's performance that year was one of the best of his 21-year, Hall of Fame career. The National League champion was the Phillies, who defeated the Dodgers for the pennant only to lose to the Orioles in the World Series. Dale Murphy was the National League MVP.

The 1984 season started with considerable attention focused on the Detroit Tigers, who won their first 11 games, and by late May, was far in front of the rest of the American League East at 35–5. Managed by Sparky Anderson, the Tigers had obtained a couple of players before the season who would help the team solidify into a strong unit, including first baseman Dave Bergman and relief pitcher Willie Hernandez, the latter winning the American League MVP for 1984. Another big story started in the summer, as the Chicago Cubs, baseball's perennial also-rans who had not won anything significant since 1945, went on a tear. Led by Ryan Sandberg, who won the National League MVP, the Cubs went on to win the National League East. The Cubs started the National League Championship series strong, winning the first two, but they were disappointed yet again—the San Diego Padres won three straight to earn a spot in the World Series. The Tigers had little trouble with the Royals in the American League series, taking it 3–0, and with the Padres, winning the World Series 4–1.

By 1985, more trouble was looming between the owners and players. A strike that began in August threatened the season, but cooler heads in both camps prevailed, and only two games were lost. In a further complication, Curtis Strong, a former caterer for the Phillies, was put on trial for selling cocaine to baseball players. A number of players came forward and testified that they had indeed purchased the drug from Strong, resulting in his conviction.

Fortunately, there was baseball to be played to distract the fans from the trial. The season highlight was the World Series between two Missouri teams, the Royals and the Cardinals, which became known as the "I-70 series." The Cardinals had won a tight, 3-game race with the Mets for the National League East title, while their opponent in the National League championship, the Dodgers, won their division by 5.5 games. Nevertheless, the Cardinals beat the Dodgers four games to two. The Royals narrowly won the American League West division, and played the Toronto Blue Jays for the right to face the Cardinals. The Royals, led by George Brett, eventually beat the Cardinals in a series that went a full seven games. The Yankees' first baseman Don Mattingly won the American League MVP title, while Cardinal outfielder Willie McGee won the National League MVP.

The 1986 season saw four teams emerge as clear leaders of their divisions at the beginning of October: the New York Mets, the Houston Astros, the Boston Red Sox, and the California Angels. In the American League Championship series, the Red Sox were beaten in a squeaker of a fifth game by the Angels (4–3 in 11 innings) to fall behind three games to one. The next day, up against the wall and trailing going into the ninth, the Red Sox came back to go ahead 6–5; the Angels tied the game in the bottom of the ninth, but the Sox eked out a 7–6 win, again in 11 innings. Then the Sox won the next two games decisively to get to the World Series. The series between the Mets and Astros included several extra-inning games that racheted up the tension, and the Mets prevailed in seven games. The Mets were shocked to lose their first two home games in the World Series, but as with their championship series, the lead swayed back and forth. During the sixth game, leading the Mets three games to two, it seemed like the Red Sox would win the series—they took a two-run lead into the 10th inning—but first baseman Bill Buckner bobbled his attempt to field a ground ball. It dribbled between his legs, enabling Mets' infielder Ray Knight to score the winning run. Boston would go on to lose Game 7 too, breaking the hearts of many Red Sox fans, who had been without a World Series win since 1918. Mike Schmidt won the National League MVP in 1986.

The powerhouse teams of the early 1980s were beginning to lose their grip on the league by the mid- to late 1980s. The 1987 season was a year that saw players hit a significant number of home runs, highlighted by Mark McGwire and Andre Dawson, each of whom hit 49. That was also the year that a new team emerged at the top of the American League: the Minnesota Twins. This season also saw the decline of three of the previous year's championship series' participants: the Mets, the Astros, and the Angels. The Twins won the American League West and battled the Detroit Tigers, who had narrowly won the East by outlasting the Toronto Blue Jays. The Cardinals won the National League pennant over the San Francisco Giants, but in the World Series, the Twins outlasted them, winning their first championship since the team moved to Minnesota (they had won the World Series as the Washington Senators in 1929). Two outfielders won the MVP that year: Toronto's George Bell in the American League and the Chicago Cubs' Andre Dawson in the National League.

In 1988, the Los Angeles Dodgers had become a formidable force, in part because of the pitching of Orel Hershiser. He pitched 59 straight scoreless innings, a new record, and ended the season with six straight shutouts. Not only that, but free agent Kirk Gibson brought intensity and power hitting to the team; he was the MVP of the National League in 1987. The Dodgers won their National League West division and beat the New York Mets (who had won the East) to get to the World Series. The American League champions, the Athletics, led by power hitter and MVP Jose Canseco, had outplayed the East-winning Boston Red Sox to take the pennant. Gibson continued to be a rallying point for the Dodgers even though he was suffering with injuries to both legs—in his first and only plate appearance in the World Series, he hit a pinch-hit, walk-off home run in the first game, and the Dodgers eventually triumphed in five games.

The 1989 season was dominated by headlines, some momentous, some scandalous. First, Bart Giamatti became the new commissioner of baseball on April 1, and initially, he was warmly received as a proponent of the game. Soon after, however, Giamatti began an investigation of Pete Rose, a legendary player and, at the time, current manager for the Cincinnati Reds. It was revealed that Rose had a gambling problem and would frequently bet on sports. Unfortunately, that included baseball games—possibly even Reds games. Rose sued the league in the hope of keeping Giamatti from ruling on the situation, but the gambit failed: in late August, the commissioner banned Rose from the league for life, which Rose grudgingly accepted. As of today, Rose remains banned, and this has kept him from being elected to the Baseball Hall of Fame, something his record would otherwise merit. Tragically, Giamatti died nine days after the suspension (no commissioner had such a short tenure). The World Series pitted two teams from the San Francisco Bay Area against each other: the National League's Giants, including MVP Brian Mitchell, and the American League's Oakland Athletics. Both teams had won their respective championship series 4–1 (the Giants over the Cubs in the National League, and the Athletics over the Blue Jays in the American League). While game three was going on in San Francisco's Candlestick Park, a significant earthquake hit the area. There were no casualties of attendees or participants in the game or significant damage to the stadium itself, but dozens in the area died, causing new commissioner Fay Vincent to postpone the series for 10 days. Then the series continued, and the Athletics swept the Giants in four games. Robin Yount captured the American World Series MVP. Baseball had experienced some turmoil in the 1980s and lost some of its popularity in the sporting world, replaced partially by pro and college basketball.

PROFESSIONAL AND COLLEGE BASKETBALL

Professional basketball became more popular in the 1980s because of a new generation of star players who helped establish rivalries between just a few teams that dominated the sport for the entire decade. One of those stars was Magic Johnson of the Los Angeles Lakers. Johnson had played point guard for Michigan State University, which unexpectedly won the NCAA tournament in Johnson's freshman year; after two years, he left school to join the NBA. In the 1979–1980 season, Johnson's first with the team, the Lakers won the NBA championship. Johnson's playing style was more energetic than teams and fans were used to, and his fellow players followed his example in subsequent years. Johnson's teammate, Kareem Abdul-Jabbar, won the MVP award for the season.

At the beginning of the decade, two changes to the game itself occurred that were important to its development. First, the three-point shot was adopted, and second, rims were redesigned to allow them to collapse easier so that backboards would not shatter (as Darryl Dawkins had done twice during the 1979 season, resulting in a lengthy game delay each time and leading to the act being penalized). The 1980 season was also the rookie season for Boston Celtics forward Larry Bird (who was named rookie of the year), and he and Johnson went on to have a friendly rivalry throughout the decade.

Earvin "Magic" Johnson was one of the more formidable forces in professional basketball throughout the 1980s. Johnson led the Los Angeles Lakers to five NBA championships, and won the league's MVP award three times. (Jerry Coli/Dreamstime.com)

Bird led the Celtics to the NBA championship in the 1980–1981 season over the Houston Rockets, who had eliminated the defending champion Lakers in the first round of the playoffs. Bird, alongside fellow starters Robert Parish, Cedric Maxwell, Chris Ford, and Nate Archibald, tied with the Philadelphia 76ers for first place in their division during the 1980–1981 regular season, but the Celtics came out on top in the tiebreaker, so they enjoyed home court advantage throughout the playoffs. Julius "Dr. J" Erving, the 76ers' forward who had been one of the league's most popular players since the 1970s, was named MVP. Other veterans led important statistical categories, such as Artis Gilmore (field goal percentage), Adrian Dantley (points per game), Moses Malone (rebounds per game), and Kareem Abdul-Jabbar and Dennis Johnson (All-NBA first team selections). The game was beginning to turn toward the younger players, though, as Magic Johnson lead the league in the percentage of steals. The 1980–1981 season also marked the debut of the Dallas Mavericks.

The 1981–1982 season featured the 76ers against the Lakers in the NBA Finals. Magic Johnson, though still quite young (just shy of his 23rd birthday at the end of the season), powered the Lakers to a second championship and was the MVP of the series. This season was also the first for Pat Riley as the coach of the Lakers, which would become a formidable team for the rest of the decade. Houston forward Moses Malone, who led the league in rebounds, won the MVP award for the season, even though Houston was eliminated early in the playoffs. Bird was featured on the All-NBA team alongside older veterans, and Buck Williams was the rookie of the year.

Malone was traded to the 76ers the following season, and now that his significant rebounding skills were coupled with Julius Erving's heroics, the 76ers won their division, their conference, and eventually the championship for the 1982–1983 season, prevailing over the Lakers. The 76ers lost only 17 games that year and lost only 1 game in the three series in which they participated during the playoffs. The season also marked the arrival of some top rookies, including James Worthy (Lakers), Dominique Wilkins (Atlanta Hawks), Terry Cummings (San Diego Clippers), and Quintin Dailey (Chicago Bulls). Alex English led the league in scoring and was considered the franchise player for the Denver Nuggets during the 1980s. Magic Johnson was now the league leader in assists, while Larry Bird earned a place on the All-NBA team again. With Malone out of Houston, the Rockets quickly became the league's worst team.

The Rockets were rewarded for their poor showing with the top pick in the 1983–1984 draft, choosing Ralph Sampson. Sampson was one of the most heralded players to come from the NCAA in nearly two decades, and he earned rookie accolades while playing on a poor team. The playoff field was expanded to eight seeds in each conference for the first time, a format that has remained for over 30 years. Larry Bird's Celtics won the championship over Magic Johnson's Lakers; the series was among the classic meetings of the two teams during the decade. It went to seven games, with the Celtics winning the decisive game 111–102. The season also marked the beginning of David Stern's tenure as league commissioner, a position that he would keep for 30 years. Stern significantly contributed to the overall popularity of the sport among a larger percentage of the mainstream audience, and he helped build a stronger core fan base. The season also saw the emergence of third-year player Isaiah Thomas as a top player in the league; Thomas would lead the Detroit Pistons for the rest of the decade.

In the 1984–1985 season, the Clipper franchise moved from San Diego to Los Angeles. Having two NBA teams in the same city was not common until this happened. This was one of the most important seasons in NBA history, for it marked the debut of the superstar Michael Jordan. Jordan, a star at the University of North Carolina, actually was not the first pick in the draft (Kentucky's Sam Bowie, who had a shortened, injury-filled career, was the first pick), but he soon became one of the league's most exciting players and a main fan draw. Jordan was the only rookie to lead the league in four statistical categories (points, assists, rebounds, and steals per game). Other notable rookies who played in the 1984–1985 season included Charles Barkley, John Stockton, and Hakeem Olajuwon. Olajuwon became paired with Ralph Sampson on the Houston Rockets, and the two were nicknamed the "Twin Towers" by fans. The Lakers, led by the seemingly ageless Kareem Abdul-Jabbar, won the championship over the Boston Celtics in another magnificent series, this time prevailing in game 6.

The next year, 1985–1986, saw the Celtics regain the NBA title, this time against the Houston Rockets and their "Twin Towers." This was one of only two times that a team from the Western Conference other than the Lakers went to the NBA Finals during the decade (both by the Rockets). The Celtics were tremendous on their home court; throughout the whole season, they lost only one home game—the best record in this category in league history. Larry Bird was the MVP, in part because of his league-leading free throw percentage. Magic Johnson led the league in assists for the first time in two years. Michael Jordan, who won in the category the year before, was injured with a broken foot for most of the season. In 1985, a new development, the NBA draft lottery was instituted, which allowed nonplayoff teams to have a random chance at one of the first three picks of the draft, as opposed to the last-place team automatically getting first pick. The New York Knicks came out on top in the lottery, and they selected Patrick Ewing, a celebrated player from Georgetown University, with the first pick.

The Lakers, still led by Magic Johnson, regained the championship, winning the 1986–1987 series over the Celtics. This began what is commonly called the "Golden Era" of the NBA, with a full complement of stars at the height of their careers—not only the ones noted so far in this section, but also Karl Malone, Clyde Drexler, Dennis Rodman, and Joe Dumars. Many of the statistical leaders in the early part of the decade continued to lead the league in specific categories, such as Michael Jordan (points), Charles Barkley (rebounds), Magic Johnson (assists), and Larry Bird (free throw percentage).

The 1986–1987 season was marked by a celebration of the career of Julius Erving, who retired at the end of the year. But it was also marred by the death of Len Bias; the promising forward, who was picked second in the draft by the Celtics, died of a cocaine-related heart condition at a party shortly afterward. As a result, the league decided to adopt a stronger antidrug policy. Bias's death was among the most talked-about sports stories of the year, not only by sportswriters but also the national mainstream media. In addition, the Kansas City Kings relocated to Sacramento during the season.

Before the 1987–1988 season began, new franchises were awarded to Orlando, Charlotte, Minneapolis, and Miami to begin play over the following two years. A new mark was set for individual accomplishments this season, as Michael Jordan became the first in league history to win the scoring title and the defensive player of the year award. David "the Admiral" Robinson, the first NBA player to be drafted from the U.S. Naval Academy, was selected in the first round by the San Antonio Spurs, but his military commitment prevented him from playing for two years. The 1987–1988 season was highlighted by the Lakers winning yet another championship, this time over the Detroit Pistons, but not until they survived a tough, seven-game playoff win over Utah and Dallas. James Worthy had emerged as a power player for the Lakers, joining Johnson and Kareem Abdul-Jabbar to become a formidable force.

The Pistons, led by Joe Dumars and Isaiah Thomas, prevailed in a rematch against the Lakers in the championship of the 1988–1989 season. Michael Jordan continued to cement himself among the top players ever with statistical honors, including leading the lead in points per game. Jordan also won a playoff game that year with a dramatic final shot, later known as "The Shot," over the Cleveland Cavaliers. However, the Chicago Bulls teams that he had been playing on had not been advancing very far into the playoffs for a few years, largely because of the fierce, physical defense by Detroit when they would play each other (the two teams were in the same conference). The Lakers, on the other hand, had little competition in the Western Conference, not losing a single playoff game until the Pistons swept them in the finals. The season also marked the retirement of Kareem Abdul-Jabbar.

In the final season of the decade, 1989–1990, the Pistons repeated as champions, this time against the Portland Trail Blazers, ending the Lakers' dominance of the Western Conference, though the Lakers were seeded first in the playoffs. Robinson came into the league during this season as well, and his presence helped turn around the San Antonio Spurs dramatically. In addition to Robertson's magnificent debut, Tim Hardaway and Vlade Divac enjoyed stellar rookie campaigns during the year. Michael Jordan again won the scoring title, and Dennis Rodman was selected as the defensive player of the year. Hakeem Olajuwon led the league in both rebounds and shots blocked per game, but the Rockets did not advance far into the playoffs.

In addition, just as the 1980s were important to the popularity of professional basketball, the sport made its highest jump in popularity during the 1990s, largely because of Michael Jordan and the dominance of the Chicago Bulls. Jordan, already legendary because of his college career at the University of North Carolina, achieved a level of fame from both his stellar play in the pros and his wide-ranging endorsements, which fueled a newly emerging national passion for both pro and college basketball.

The highlight of the 1979–1980 NCAA basketball season was the first championship for Denny Crum, the coach for the University of Louisville. Guard Darrell Griffith, who helped popularize the dunk with basketball fans in the 1980s, led the Cardinals to victory. Sophomore Mark Aguirre was the consensus top basketball player of the 1979–1980 season, though his DePaul University team failed to advance deep into the NCAA tournament. In 1980, Aguirre was selected to play on the U.S. Olympic basketball team. Among the most talked-about players that year were freshman sensation Ralph Sampson at the University of Virginia and Joe Berry Carroll at Purdue University, who was picked first in the following season's NBA draft. The 1980–1981 season championship was won by Indiana University, who had Isaiah Thomas as their star point guard, denying the championship to the University of South Carolina and their legendary coach, Dean Smith. Seniors Danny Ainge of Brigham Young University and Steve Johnson of Oregon State joined Sampson, Isaiah Thomas, and Aguirre on the 1981 All-American team.

The 1981–1982 was the season when Smith finally won his first championship (after 20 years coaching the Tar Heels), led by a top-flight starting squad, including Sam Perkins, James Worthy, Kenny Black, Matt Doherty, and a freshman sensation named Michael Jordan. North Carolina defeated Georgetown in a tight game during the season by a last-second shot by Jordan. Georgetown was led by freshman marvel Patrick Ewing, and their coach, John Thompson, became the first African American to coach a team into the Final Four.

Controversy did mark the season, though, as the University of San Francisco suspended their basketball program because of illegal payments by a booster to guard Quintin Dailey. A new role change was implemented that changed the jump ball, used to determine possession in the college ranks, to a possession arrow, where each team would alternate instances.

In 1982–1983, another North Carolina–based team, North Carolina State University, won the national championship over the favored University of Houston. The championship game came to a dramatic conclusion on a dunk made in the final seconds by Lorenzo Charles, guarded by Houston's Hakeem Olajuwon (nicknamed "Phi Slamma Jama" by the fans and media at the time). North Carolina State was led by Jim Valvano, an impassioned coach and a favorite of both fans and his peers. Valvano would pass away a decade later from cancer, but his legacy lives on through a foundation dedicated to cancer research.

The 1983–1984 NCAA basketball championship was won by Georgetown, led by Patrick Ewing and John Thompson, over Olajuwon's University of Houston team. The season marked the end of Michael Jordan's college career, and Jordan joined North Carolina teammate Sam Perkins, Ewing, Olajuwon, and Wayman Tisdale on the All-American team that year. Houston had a tightly contested semifinal game against Virginia, while Georgetown was a more decisive winner over Kentucky.

For the first time, the 1984–1985 tournament was expanded to 64 teams in four regional divisions. What was unusual about the 1985 Final Four was that three of the four teams hailed from the Big East Conference: Villanova, Georgetown, and St. John's. The fourth member, Memphis State, was later asked to vacate their spot in the tournament for using ineligible players. Villanova, featuring forward Ed Pickney and coached by P.J. Carlesimo, defeated Thompson and Ewing's Georgetown team in the championship game. The 1984–1985 All-American team included Ewing, Wayman Tisdale, Chris Mullin, Xavier McDaniel, and Keith Lee, and that marked the last year that Ewing would play college basketball.

The University of Louisville won the NCAA championship in the 1985–1986 over Duke. Kansas and the surprising LSU joined Louisville and Duke in the Final Four. Pervis Ellison lifted coach Denny Crum's Louisville team over Mike Krzyzewski's Duke team; Krzyzewski was coaching in the national championship for the first time, which began a string of making it to the Final Four 7 of the next 11 years. The 1985–1986 All-American team included Len Bias, Steve Alford, Walter Berry, Johnny Dawkins, and Kenny Walker. The 1986–1987 title game, between Indiana and Syracuse, was close right to the very end, with Indiana's Keith Smart scoring the winning shot in the final seconds. The semifinalists included the University of Nevada–Las Vegas, coached by the colorful Jerry Tarkanian, and an unexpected "Cinderella" team from Providence College, coached by Rick Pitino. Pitino became one of the most sought-after coaches in basketball in the next decade. The 1986–1987 All-American team comprised Steve Alford, David Robinson, Danny Manning, Kenny Smith, and Reggie Williams.

The University of Kansas team, coached by Larry Brown, won the 1987–1988 National Championship over Oklahoma, led by Billy Tubbs. Kansas, featuring Danny Manning, was widely expected to lose to Oklahoma, a rival from the Big Eight Conference. The semifinalists included Duke and Arizona, and the strong performance by the latter kicked off a period of success not seen in their history. The All-American 1987–1988 team included Manning, Sean Elliott, Hershey Hawkins, Gary Grant, and J. R. Reid.

The University of Michigan, which started the season under coach Bill Frieder, won the national championship in the 1988–1989 season. But prior to the start of the tournament, assistant coach Steve Fisher took over for Freider after the latter accepted the head coaching job at Arizona State University. Glen Rice, who established many of the school's all-time records while he played there, was the key to Michigan's success. Former Villanova player P.J. Carlesimo had become the coach at Seton Hall University, which made it through to the championship game, where they lost to Michigan. Other Final Four participants included Duke and Illinois. The 1988–1989 All-American team included Chris Jackson, Sherman Douglas, Sean Elliott, Danny Ferry, and Stacey King.

The final season of the decade, 1989–1990, was the year that Jerry Tarkanian led the University of Nevada–Las Vegas to their first championship, over Duke. Other Final Four semifinalists included Arkansas and Georgia Tech, the latter appearing in their first Final Four. Just before the tournament, Loyola Marymount University, based in Los Angeles, suffered the untimely death of its star player, Hank Gathers, of a heart condition. Gathers's teammate and lifelong friend, Bo Kimble, shot his first free throw in every game during the tournament with his left hand in honor of the left-handed Gathers. Loyola Marymount quickly became a fan favorite in the tournament, and the team went as far as the "Elite Eight" round. The 1989–1990 All-American team included Chris Jackson, Derrick Coleman, Larry Johnson, Gary Payton, and Lionel Simmons. The 1980s was a decade in which basketball, both professional and college, became a top draw for audiences. In addition, the decade saw the unexpected rise in the popularity of professional hockey.

PROFESSIONAL HOCKEY

Professional hockey has been a prominent element of Canadian sports culture since the early years of the 20th century and gradually became popular in the United States as well throughout the rest of the century. Bobby Orr, Bobby Hull, and Gordie Howe were among the most popular players before the 1980s. Throughout the 1980s, the top fan favorite was Wayne Gretzky. Gretzky, a Canadian, entered the National Hockey League (NHL) when his World Hockey Association (WHA) team, the Edmonton Oilers, joined the NHL along with three other teams (the Hartford Whalers, Winnipeg Jets, and Quebec Nordiques) when the two leagues merged in 1979. Gretzky was one of the most celebrated amateur hockey players in history, and the fact that a WHA team (the Indianapolis Racers) was appealing enough for Gretzky to sign with as a teenager was to the credit of the upstart league. The WHA's seven-year run against the NHL in the 1970s proved that it was major competition, which may well have been a factor in the merger. The merger was so important that hockey legend Howe, who had left the NHL in the early 1970s to play in the startup WHA league, decided to return for an incredible 35th season, at over 50 years of age, to play for the Whalers.

With Gretzky now in the NHL, compounded with the unexpected victory by the American team in the 1980 Olympics (discussed in the section "The Olympic Games," later in this chapter), professional hockey began to receive more attention in the United States. With the merger of the two leagues, 18- and 19-year-old players could be drafted into the NHL for the first time. The 1979–1980 season included a number of rookies who would go on to have such prolific, distinguished careers that they were inducted into the Pro Hockey Hall of Fame.

The Philadelphia Flyers had a tremendous run in the 1979–1980 regular season, winning an incredible 35 games without a loss en route to winning the league's Patrick division and the season championship. The Buffalo Sabres won the Adams division, Montreal Canadiens won the Norris, and the Chicago Black Hawks won the Smythe. Gretzky was tied with Marcel Dionne (of the Los Angeles Kings) as the league's leading scorer, and he would go on to win the MVP award. After expanding from a 12-team playoff to a 16-team playoff (to accommodate the additional teams), the New York Islanders, the fifth seed, defeated the Flyers four games to two to win the Stanley Cup. The championship marked the beginning of a successful era in Islanders history, as stars Mike Bossy and Bryan Trottier led the team to a string of four straight Stanley Cup championships.

In addition to winning their second straight Stanley Cup, the Islanders won the season championship in 1980–1981 over the Minnesota North Stars. Gretzky won his second MVP award, broke the season record for assists (109), and was the league's top scorer. The Islanders won the Patrick division, and the other division winners included the Buffalo Sabres (Adams), Montreal Canadiens (Norris), and the St. Louis Blues (Smythe). The Islanders' right wing Mike Bossy became only the second person in NHL history to score 50 goals in his first 50 games.

The Islanders enjoyed similar success in the 1981–1982 season, winning both the season title and the Stanley Cup (this time over the Vancouver Canucks). En route to their success, the Islanders won 15 straight games, a record at the time. Gretzky soared to new heights as well, scoring 50 goals in just his first 39 games, setting a record for goals in a season (92), and tying the assist record that he had achieved the previous year (120). Even though Gretzky was achieving personal milestones, the Edmonton Oilers were still having trouble getting to the playoffs (though they won the Smythe division that season). The league underwent realignment before the 1981–1982 season to try to save on travel costs, which affected who won each division because some of the more talented teams were moved into divisions based on geography; the other winners were the Islanders (Patrick), Minnesota North Stars (Norris), and the Montreal Canadiens (Adams).

The 1982–1983 season saw the Oilers finally get to the Stanley Cup championship, where they met the persistent Islanders. The Oilers had only lost one game in the playoffs before facing the Islanders, who were helped by the New Your Rangers eliminating the Philadelphia Flyers, who won the Patrick division decisively (a full 10 points ahead of the Islanders), in the first round. The other division winners were the Boston Bruins (Adams—and also won the regular season title), Chicago Blackhawks (Norris), and the Oilers (Smythe). One unique aspect of the 1982–1983 season was that it was the first to include all seven Canadian teams in the playoffs. As in previous years, Gretzky was the leading scorer in the league.

The Oilers finally won the Stanley Cup in the 1983–1984 season, with the help of both Gretzky and his teammate Mark Messier. Gretzky set another significant record as well, as he scored a point in each of the first 51 games that season en route to winning the Smythe division and the season championship. Other division winners included the North Stars (Norris), the Islanders (Patrick), and the Bruins (Adams).

The Oilers won the Stanley Cup the following season for the second straight year, beating the Flyers four games to one, but the Flyers won the season championship. Division leaders included the Oilers (Smythe), Flyers (Patrick), Blues (Norris), and the Canadiens (Adams). Gretzky again led the league in scoring, and in 1984–1985, the second-highest scorer was his teammate, Jari Kurri, which definitely made the Oilers a force to be reckoned with throughout the season. The 1984 draft also marked the arrival of Mario Lemieux to the Pittsburgh Penguins, for which he would play his entire career.

In 1985–1986, the Oilers won the season championship (and the accompanying President's Trophy, which was introduced for the first time to recognize the team with the best record), but the Montreal Canadiens won the Stanley Cup for the first time that decade, beating the Calgary Flames. The division winners included the Oilers (Smythe), the Black Hawks (Norris), the Flyers (Patrick), and for the first time in the 1980s, the Quebec Nordiques (Adams), who were in the same division as the Canadians. Of the division winners, only the Oilers would survive the first round of the playoffs, and they were themselves eliminated in the second round. As in other years, Gretzky was the league's leading scorer.

In 1986–1987, the Oilers rebounded to retake the Stanley Cup and win the President's Trophy, the Smythe division, and the Clarence Campbell conference, once again because of Gretzky. The division winners included the Blues (Norris), the Flyers (Patrick) and the Whalers (Adams).

In 1987–1988, the Oilers won another Stanley Cup, losing only two games in the playoffs, but the President's Trophy was captured by the Calgary Flames. The division winners were Calgary (Smythe), Detroit (Norris), the Canadiens (Adams), and the Islanders (Patrick). The Boston Bruins won the Prince of Wales conference. Of particular significance is the record of the Los Angeles Kings, who finished fourth in 1987–1988 in the Smythe division, behind Calgary, Edmonton, and Winnipeg. This fact is notable because of the unexpected trade of Gretzky to the Kings during the 1988 off-season, which resulted in a dramatic turnaround for the Kings the next season.

Though Gretzky's arrival did not immediately result in a championship for his new team, the landscape of the league changed in the 1988–1989 season.

Gretzky won the MVP in 1989, but Mario Lemieux became the top scorer. Calgary won the President's Trophy and Stanley Cup; they had to beat the Montreal Canadiens (the winner of the Prince of Wales conference and the Adams division) in the final. The 1989–1990 season saw the Boston Bruins winning the President's Trophy, and Gretzky returned to his place as the top scorer. However, the Stanley Cup winners were the Oilers yet again, with Mark Messier as MVP (in a close vote against Boston's Ray Bourque). Hockey has always taken a back seat to football, baseball, and basketball in the United States, but for a brief period during the Winter Olympics in 1980, hockey was *the* sport to talk about.

THE OLYMPIC GAMES

There were six Olympic Games scheduled in the 1980s (Winter and Summer, held in 1980, 1984, and 1988), but political disagreements made an impact on them—most specifically, on who would participate in them in any given year. This was because of the frosty relationship between the United States and the Soviet Union and their respective allies, which ultimately led each country to decline to participate in one of the Games.

The decade started with the XIII Olympic Winter Games in Lake Placid, New York, and both countries participated. The highlight of the Games was an ice hockey semifinal between the United States and the Soviet Union, which was important to fans in both countries because of the existing Cold War tensions. The U.S. team was made of college players, and most hockey experts did not give the Americans much of a chance in the tournament. Shockingly, the Americans beat the Soviets (in the so-called Miracle on Ice), and then went on to defeat Finland in the gold medal game (the Soviets won the bronze medal by besting Sweden). Regardless of that upset, the Soviets won the most gold medals for the Games (10), while East Germany won the most medals in total (23). Another notable American gold medalist was Eric Heiden, who won the 500 m, 1000 m, 1500 m, 5000 m, and 10,000 m speed-skating events. The American team won only four silver medals (two by Leah Poulos-Mueller in 500 m and 1000 m speed-skating events; one apiece by Phil Mahre in the slalom event and Linda Fratianne in women's figure skating) and two bronze (Charles Tickner in men's figure skating and Beth Heiden in the 3000 m speed-skating event).

It was before the Games of the XXII Olympiad, held in the summer of 1980 in Moscow, that political tensions began to increase. U.S. president Jimmy Carter led a coalition of 65 countries in a boycott of the Games as a protest of the Soviet Union's invasion of Afghanistan. The countries that ultimately participated included the communist, Soviet-bloc countries of Eastern Europe and Cuba, but some individual participants from Western countries were represented by the Olympic flag instead of their own. The Western countries held their own event in Philadelphia, the Liberty Bell Classic, which was not widely covered on television.

In response to the 1980 boycott, the Soviet Union boycotted the 1984 Summer Olympics in Los Angeles. Also, 14 other Soviet-bloc countries declined to participate, as did Libya and Iran, who had strained political relationships

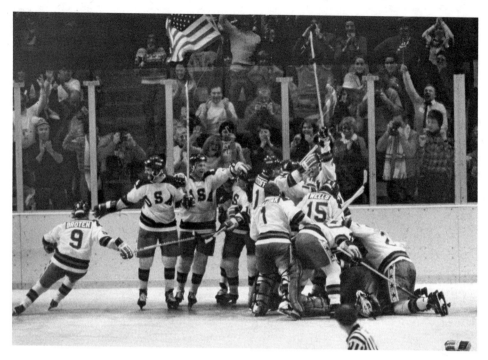

The Soviet hockey team, who were the defending gold medal champions, were highly favored against the young American hockey team in the semifinal game of the 1980 Lake Placid Olympics. Called the "Miracle on Ice," the Americans surprised the Soviets, defeating them by a score of 4–3. Considering the tension between both countries during the Cold War, the victory was particularly symbolic to many American fans who preferred the victory over the Olympic final, in which the U.S. defeated Finland to win the gold medal. (AP Photo)

with the United States at the time. However, some American and Russian athletes later participated in the 1986 Goodwill Games in Moscow, as the Cold War was slowly beginning to thaw.

The American highlights from the 1984 Summer Games included a gold medal in men's basketball and an impressive showing by track and field star Carl Lewis, who won four gold medals in the 100 m, 200 m, 4×100 m relay, and long jump. A controversial incident involved the American runner Mary Decker, who was competing in the 3000 m race and was heavily favored to win, and Zola Budd, a South African running for Great Britain. Budd collided with Decker, causing her to fall, and while neither won, the controversy overshadowed the win by Romanian Maricica Puica. Though Decker blamed Budd for the collision in a press conference after the race, the officials concluded that there had been no intentional infraction. Regardless, Budd received aggressive media attention and even death threats. American gymnast Mary Lou Retton became the darling of the Olympics, as she was the first gymnast outside Eastern Europe to win a gold medal in the all-around competition. The diminutive Retton (four feet, nine inches tall) had recently recovered from a knee operation, but she came back to win five medals.

Fortunately, the 1984 XIV Olympic Winter Games in Sarajevo, Yugoslavia, was held without a boycott by either side. For the United States, the main gold medalists were Scott Hamilton (men's figure skating), Debbie Armstrong (women's giant slalom), Bill Johnson (men's downhill alpine skiing), and Phil Mahre (men's slalom); and there were four other silver medalists among the Americans. East Germany won the most gold medals (9), and the Soviet Union won the most medals in total (25).

The 1988 Olympics were also devoid of political controversy. The XV Olympic Winter Games, held in Calgary, had full participation, including the Soviet Union, who won the most medals in total (29) and the most gold medals (11). The United States fared poorly in the Winter Games, winning only six medals, with only two gold (Brian Boitano in men's figure skating and Bonnie Blair in women's 500 m speed skating). But the United States had better results in the Summer Olympic Games, held from mid-September to early October (despite the name) in Seoul, South Korea. Americans won 94 medals, including 36 golds. Janet Evans, a 17-year-old swimmer, was the biggest individual winner, with three medals (women's 400 m individual medley and 400 m and 800 m freestyle). Other notable individual medals were won by Carl Lewis (100 m and long jump), Florence Griffith-Joyner (100 m and 200 m), Jackie Joyner-Kersee (women's long jump and heptathlon), Greg Louganis (men's springboard diving and men's platform diving), and Matt Biondi (50 m and 100 m men's freestyle swimming). Biondi also contributed to U.S. gold medals in three more swimming events, the men's 4×100 m and 4×200 m freestyle relays and the 4×100 m medley relay. These Games would be the last ones in which East Germany and the Soviet Union would participate, as Germany unified in 1990 and the Soviet Union dissolved in 1991.

INDIVIDUAL SPORTS: GOLF AND TENNIS

Golf and tennis has had a more limited fan base than team sports or ones played for national pride, such as the Olympics. One primary champion ruled the landscape of professional golf in the 1980s: Tom Watson. Watson developed a reputation as an assertive player who could adapt to weather conditions whenever needed. Watson's 19 wins in the 1980s, 5 of which were in major tournaments (the Masters in 1981, the U.S. Open in 1982, and the Open Championship in 1980, 1982, and 1983), put him head and shoulders above his competitors. The U.S. Open victory was of significant personal importance, as he beat Jack Nicklaus on an incredible 17th-hole chip that is part of golf legend. Watson was also the PGA Player of the Year in 1980, 1982, and 1984. Though Watson was considered the "money leader" (the player who made the most money on the tour because of the final results in each contest) in the 1980 and 1984 PGA tours, Watson began to slump, not winning his next tour event until 1987.

Spaniard Seve Ballesteros had seven PGA tour wins, including four majors (the Masters in 1980 and 1983 and the British Open in 1984 and 1988). Ballesteros was also proficient in Europe, winning over 50 tournaments. He was largely considered something of a prodigy (he turned professional at just 16 years old), and he soon developed a flamboyant playing style. He was a member of the 1985 Ryder Cup team that ended the United States' 28-year dominance of the biannual contest. But health issues led Ballesteros to retire early in the late 1990s, and he passed away from cancer in 2008.

The decade also saw success by a number of golfers who were so beloved that they were given nicknames by their fans. One of these was Jack Nicklaus (the "Golden Bear"), one of the most prominent and recognizable golfers of the 1960s and 1970s. He struggled in 1980, finishing in the top 10 just four times in 14 events, but he won the PGA Championship and the U.S. Open. But he enjoyed more success the rest of the decade, with seven more appearances in the top 10 at major championships. Nicklaus had a tremendous year in 1986, where he set a record for 18 wins in a year and won the Masters tournament at 46 years of age. Australian Greg Norman was another fan favorite in the 1980s. Nicknamed "the Shark," Norman, a consistent performer during the decade, won eight tournaments on the PGA tour, including the Open Championship (often called the British Open) in 1986. He placed second in another four major tournaments in the 1980s. Other notable golfers in the 1980s included Lee Trevino, Bernhard Langer, Sandy Lyle, Ray Floyd, Larry Nelson, Curtis Strange, Nick Faldo, and Tom Kite.

The LPGA, the women's professional golf league, generally has not received the same amount of media attention as the men's tour. However, it did feature some strong golfers in the 1980s, particularly JoAnne Carner and Pat Bradley. In 1981, Carner had a banner year—she won the USGA Bob Jones, Vare, and LPGA Player of the Year awards. During the decade, she had 50 LPGA tour wins and 2 major tournament wins: the Women's PGA Championship (1982) and ANA Inspiration (1989).

As for Bradley, she had the most wins in the LPGA in both 1983 and 1986, and in the latter year, she also was named the Female Player of the Year by the Golf Writers Association of America (GWAA), was the LPGA Player of the Year, and won the Vare Trophy. Bradley had 18 wins during the 1980s, including six majors: the U.S. Women's Open (1981), ANA Inspiration (1986), the Women's PGA Championship (1986), and the du Maurier Classic (1980, 1985, and 1986). There were other female golfers of note as well, such as Amy Alcott; Alcott had 21 LPGA Tour wins, including three majors (the U.S. Women's Open in 1980 and the ANA Inspiration in 1983 and 1988), and also won the Vare Trophy in 1980. Another leading player was Betsy King, who was named the GWAA Female Player of the Year in 1987 and 1989, won the Vare in 1987, and earned the LPGA Player of the Year award in 1984 and 1989. King had 20 wins, including 2 majors (ANA Inspiration and the U.S. Women's Open). Nancy Lopez won the Women's PGA Championship twice, in 1985 and 1989, and the U.S. Women's Open in 1989. Beth Daniel finished second in three events in the 1980s and was a fan favorite.

The popularity of tennis was advanced through the impact of a group of distinguished stars in the 1980s. Swede Bjorn Borg was one of the most successful tennis pros in the sport's history. He helped bring tennis into the mainstream during the 1970s, and he was a key player in the early part of the 1980s. Borg earned a total of 11 Grand Slam singles titles—5 at Wimbledon and 6 at the French Open (where he was the most dominant—he lost only one match at the tournament in his entire career). He surprisingly announced his retirement in January 1983, at the age of 26.

Borg had two major American rivals: Jimmy Connors and John McEnroe. Connors, like Borg, began competing in Grand Slam events in the 1970s, and his rivalry with Borg during that time helped popularize the sport. His two-handed backhand gave him a great service return, and his playing style was aggressive and powerful. In his career, Connors won eight Grand Slam singles titles (five at the U.S. Open, two at Wimbledon, and one at the Australian Open). His last Grand Slam victory was at the U.S. Open in 1983. Connors was popular throughout his career, actively trying to excite the fans about the action on the court. But he was also famous for his fiery persona and on-court antics, especially for arguing with officials and wielding his racket in suggestive ways.

A younger player, John McEnroe, became a rival to both Borg and Connors. McEnroe had a strong ability to volley, but what he became notorious for was his behavior and attitude on the court, especially toward the officials. When a call went against him, he often would launch a loud, vocal tirade against the umpire; one particular phrase of his, "You cannot be serious," became so well known among tennis fans and the mainstream public that it was parodied in popular programs in Britain (and McEnroe ultimately used it as the title of his autobiography). McEnroe won seven Grand Slam singles titles—four at the U.S. Open and three at Wimbledon—and he had even more success in the doubles (winning nine Grand Slams in men's doubles and one in mixed doubles).

McEnroe had a major rival in the Czech player Ivan Lendl, who moved to the United States in 1981 and became an American citizen in 1992. He was considered a member of the newer generation of tennis players in the 1980s who established a sense of physical power when he played. Lendl's topspin serve made him a force to be reckoned with, and it helped him win eight Grand Slam events between 1984 and 1990, including three U.S. Opens, two Australian Opens, three French Opens, and two Wimbledon championships. By that time, Borg had retired, Connors and McEnroe were beginning to slow, and Lendl and his contemporaries were playing with more power. Therefore, Lendl tore through the singles ranks, with few players that could compete consistently with him; he ended up with one of the top winning percentages in professional tennis.

Boris Becker was one of those few players. Becker, a German, won six Grand Slam tournaments in his career, but one of his most noteworthy achievements is that he won his first one, Wimbledon, at just 17 years of age. His other Grand Slam tournament wins include two more Wimbledon championships, two Australian Opens (both in the 1990s), two French Opens, and one U.S. Open. Like Lendl, Becker had strength that the older players could not match, especially his powerful serve, which earned him the nickname "Boom Boom." As with McEnroe and Connors, Becker was vocal on the court, but the target for his tirades was not the umpire, but rather himself. He would berate himself in front of the crowd when playing poorly, and on occasion, he would smash his tennis racket.

Another Swedish player, Stefan Edberg, was a key Becker rival. Edberg won six Grand Slam events, including two Wimbledon championships, two U.S. Opens, and two Australian Opens. Edberg was noted for using the serve and volley technique, in which he would run toward the net to pick off his opponent's service return (often for a winner). This technique relies more on speed than power in the serve. He was also known for his one-handed backhand, a less powerful, yet still difficult shot to defend.

On the women's side, the world of tennis saw the rise of a new generation of players who had some similar attributes to their game as their male counterparts. Chris Evert (known as Chris Evert-Lloyd for most of the 1980s) had a thrilling career spanning the 1970s into the mid-1980s, winning 18 Grand Slam titles (six U.S. Opens, three Wimbledon championships, two Australian Opens, and seven French Opens). She still holds the record for the most French Open wins by a woman. Evert was known for her powerful two-handed backhand stroke, as well as having a precise manner of serving, a consistent and crafty baseline style, and a steely calm under pressure.

Martina Navratilova was Evert's main tennis court rival, as well as being her close friend off the court. Originally from Czechoslovakia, Navratilova became a U.S. citizen in 1981. Her style featured the serve and volley, which proved so effective for her that she was only the second player in modern tennis (after Evert) to win 1,000 matches. Like Evert, she won 18 Grand Slam titles: two French Opens, three Australian Opens, nine Wimbledon championships (a record that still stands), and four U.S. Opens. Navratilova's playing style was aggressive and attacking, and she had considerable power. She was also the only player in tennis history to hold the world's No. 1 ranking in tennis in both singles and doubles over 200 weeks. In fact, for five consecutive years and seven total, she was ranked No. 1 in singles at the end of the year, making her one of the best players not only in the 1980s, but of all time.

Steffi Graf emerged as one of the top tennis players in the late 1980s. She won the French Open in 1987, but she came on strong the next year: In 1988, she accomplished what become known as the "Golden Slam" in singles, winning all four Grand Slam tournaments in a single year (called the Grand Slam) and the gold medal in the 1988 Olympics. No player has come close to doing that in the almost 30 years since. By the end of her impressive career, which continued well into the 1990s, Graf had won the second most championships at Wimbledon (7), behind Navratilova, and won 21 Grand Slams—more than any other player, male or female—including six French Opens, four Australian Opens and five U.S. Opens. The efforts of Evert, Navratilova, and Graf helped bring further attention to women's tennis, even though the three were the only truly dominant players in the 1980s.

BOXING AND PROFESSIONAL WRESTLING

When the 1970s ended, boxing featured a strong individual who appealed to many fringe fans of the sport: Muhammad Ali. Ali had retired as the heavyweight champion in 1979, but he decided to try to win the title again by fighting Larry Holmes in 1980. Ali lost the bout, but it was marred by controversy.

Due to a number of health issues in the months leading up to the fight, Ali had to go to the hospital, and many felt that he was actually not fit to box but was only fighting to pay back promoter Don King for paying for Ali's hospital bills. Throughout the decade, King would go on to be one of boxing's most polarizing figures, developing fame for himself as the sport's top promoter while the legends of the 1970s that he helped promote, both Ali and Joe Frazier, were replaced by a younger field of heavyweight fighters. Tim Witherspoon won the heavyweight title twice in the 1980s, but he had difficulty defending the title for extended periods. Michael Spinks won the World Boxing Commission (WBC) title by defeating Dwight Muhammad Qawi in 1982, and eventually he won the other two major boxing titles, World Boxing Association (WBA) and International Boxing Federation (IBF), by defeating Larry Holmes in 1985. Spinks had some formidable opponents challenging him for his title, and he lost it to Mike Tyson in 1988.

Tyson was the most dynamic and feared fighter of the 1980s. He turned professional at age 18 in 1985 and become an unbeatable force for the rest of the decade. He won 12 of his first 19 fights by knockout, and the WBA, WBC, and IBF titles from Spinks at merely 20 years of age. He was selected to be featured in a Nintendo video game, *Mike Tyson's Punch Out*, which expanded his popularity beyond the dedicated boxing fan base into the mainstream. However, Tyson was a troubled soul, coming from a difficult background in Peeksville, New York. King and Bill Clayton, who took over managing Tyson after his longtime trainer, mentor, and father figure Cus D'Amato died in 1985, controlled his affairs. By 1990, Tyson had lost his fire and passion, and he also lost his title in a stunning upset to largely unknown Buster Douglas. He later went to prison for rape, and after reemerging, had trouble sustaining a top career. He was the heavyweight of the decade, and the heavyweight title has always held a special spot in the hearts of boxing fans.

Other weight classes featured a number of noteworthy boxers during the decade. The middleweight class featured "Marvelous" Marvin Hagler, who held the title for more than six years in the 1980s, the longest term in history. Thomas "The Hitman" Hearns won titles in four different weight classes and had one of the most proficient knockout percentages in history. Sugar Ray Leonard was one of the top fighters of the decade, competing in five weight classes, and also was a fan favorite. His most famous win was over Roberto Duran, whose exclamation during the fight, "No mas!" (Spanish for "no more"), became a slang term throughout the country. Carlos "Sugar" de León won the cruiserweight belt twice in the 1980s, and Ray "Boom Boom" Mancini was a fan favorite in the lightweight category in the mid-1980s. Boxing in all the weight classes was reaching unprecedented levels of popularity, especially in weight classes below heavyweight.

Another type of fighting gained popularity in the 1980s: professional wrestling. Professional wrestling taped from live matches in regional circuits unified by the National Wrestling Alliance (NWA) had been broadcast on television for decades prior to the 1980s. Many sports fans felt that it was less legitimate than others, however, and the fan base was limited. In the 1980s, the sport was expanded. Vince McMahon, Sr., a promoter in the northeastern part of the

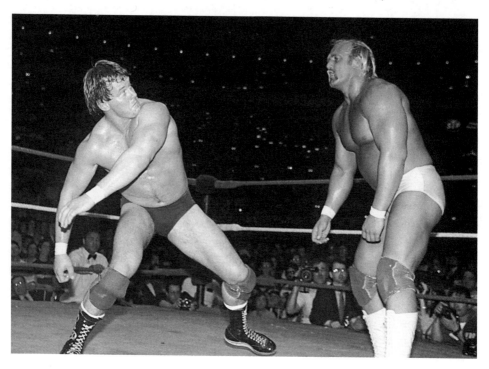

The World Wrestling Federation, led by Vince McMahon, became popular in the 1980s. Hulk Hogan (right) shown in a match with "Rowdy" Roddy Piper, became a recognizable figure, not just in the wrestling world, but in the wider popular culture as a whole. (Globe Photos/ZUMA Press Inc./Alamy Stock Photo)

country, left the NWA and started his own group, the World Wrestling Federation (WWF). He sold the WWF to his son, Vince Jr., in the early 1980s, and the younger McMahon immediately decided to sell videotapes outside the region, lessening the impact of the regional tours. He then purchased Georgia Championship Wrestling, which had purchased a time slot on WTBS, known as TBS Superstation outside Georgia. This move allowed the WWF to go national. In short, the emergence of cable television allowed WWF to become a national spectacle.

To increase the sport's exposure, McMahon signed several prominent wrestlers, most notably Hulk Hogan, "Rowdy" Roddy Piper, Jesse "The Body" Ventura, Dusty Rhodes, Ricky "The Dragon" Steamboat, and Jake "The Snake" Roberts, as well as tag teams such as the Hart Foundation, Powers of Pain, Demolition, and the Rockers. Helping popularize the WWF was its association with pop star Cyndi Lauper, who asked her manager, Lou Albano, to be in her music video for "Girls Just Want to Have Fun," and then the pair appeared on WWF.

McMahon's biggest gamble was the development of *WrestleMania*, broadcast on closed-circuit television from Madison Square Garden. Lauper and Mr. T (who played the villainous boxer Clubber Lang in *Rocky III*; see Chapter 4, "Film") were brought on board to help publicize the event, which was being billed as the "Super Bowl" of Wrestling. *WrestleMania* was a success, cementing a role for professional wrestling in mainstream U.S. society. It was followed by a 1985 pay-per-view event, *The Wrestling Classic,* broadcast from the Rosemont Horizon in Chicago, which featured Junkyard Dog and Randy Savage. Even *Sports Illustrated* featured Hulk Hogan on one of its covers in 1987, and that issue became a top seller. A new weekly series, *WWF Championship Wrestling,* was featured on syndicated television.

WrestleMania 2, a pay-per-view event in 1986, continued the success of the series. It featured a steel-cage match with Hulk Hogan vs. King Kong Bundy and a boxing match with Mr. T vs. Rowdy Roddy Piper. The event was unique in that it was broadcast from three venues (Nassau Veterans Memorial Coliseum on Long Island, Los Angeles Memorial Arena, and Rosemont Horizon in Chicago). The series became even more popular with the debut of *WrestleMania III,* held in the Pontiac Silverdome, home of the Detroit Lions football team and even the site of some Super Bowls. Over 90,000 spectators attended the event, which featured Hulk Hogan and Andre the Giant, and that alone focused the general public's attention on professional wrestling. A rematch, *WrestleMania IV,* was held at the Atlantic City Convention Hall the next year, followed by the final such event of the 1980s, *WrestleMania V* at Trump Plaza in Atlantic City.

A competitor eventually emerged to challenge the booming WWF. Toward the end of the decade, a regional promotion company, Jim Crockett Promotions, was purchased by cable TV mogul Ted Turner and renamed World Championship Wrestling (WCW). WWF (which later became known as WWE) and WCW would be rivals throughout the 1990s. Nevertheless, the simple notion that a sport that had been so regional, and often marginalized, at the beginning of the decade could become so popular within 10 years illustrates how sports in the 1980s became more popular than ever because of advances in television technology.

FURTHER READING

Crepeau, Richard C. *NFL Football: A History of America's New National Pastime.* Champaign, IL: University of Illinois Press, 2014.

King, Chris. *Boxing: The Greatest Fighters of the 20th Century.* London: Lorenz Books, 2013.

MacCambridge, Michael, and Dan Jenkins, eds. *ESPN College Football Encyclopedia: The Complete History of the Game.* Bristol, CT: ESPN, 2005.

McFarlane, Brian. *Brian McFarlane's History of Hockey.* Urbana, IL: Sagamore Publishing, 1997.

Shoals, Bethleham, and Jacob Weinstein. *FreeDarko Presents: The Undisputed Guide to Pro Basketball History.* New York: Bloomsbury, 2010.

Vecsey, George. *Baseball: A History of America's Favorite Game.* New York: Modern Library/Random House, 2008.

CHAPTER 3

Music

The 1980s was one of the most important decades in the development of popular music in all of the 20th century, rivaled only by the 1950s. The main reason for this is that the majority of popular music became focused primarily on a single new medium: music television. Clearly, the artists benefited, but it is important to note that the whole music industry changed beginning in the 1980s because of the rise of music television. Some thought that people who made music videos "drew a specific type of characters, brave and hard men and women bent on exploration and merriment, people whose personalities—and appetites, especially for drugs—often rivaled those of the bands whose videos they made. In short, pirates, lunatics, outcasts, misfits, iconoclasts, and barbarians" (Tannebaum and Marks, 2012, 186). This sentiment indicated that an overall change in attitude toward popular music was evolving, and the way that audiences accepted those changes affected which artists became popular during the decade.

POP MUSIC

Michael Jackson was one of the first artists to enjoy the benefits that the new medium offered. He had already established a career as a child performer through the late 1960s and early 1970s, and at the beginning of the 1980s, he was just entering his 20s. After working with producer Quincy Jones on a movie adaptation of the Broadway musical *The Wiz* in 1978, Jackson began collaborating with Jones on a regular basis. Jones's arranging and producing, coupled with Jackson's incomparable musicality, resulted in the hit album *Off the Wall* in 1979 and two massively popular albums in the 1980s, *Thriller* (1982) and *Bad* (1987). *Thriller* became (and remains) the top-selling album of all time, and Jackson was catapulted to megastardom as the most famous performer in the world. Seven of the nine songs on the album were top 10 singles—a feat unheard of before or since. Jackson's performances were deliberate, to the point where his vocals almost pushed the energetic music along, complementing the driving bass and guitar lines that fueled it.

Jackson's videos were embraced enthusiastically by the MTV cable channel, with "Beat It" and especially "Billie Jean" in near-constant rotation. Other songs from the album were released as videos as well, but most notable was the video for the title track—at 13 minutes, it was more like a mini-movie, and it was released to great fanfare. *Bad* was a musical extension of the writing style found on Jackson's groundbreaking *Thriller* but in a more mature style. Jackson, who had grown up in the media spotlight, wanted to use his appeal to help hungry, less fortunate Africans, so he wrote a song with Lionel Richie for a charity album, *USA for Africa*, whose proceeds went towards famine relief in Africa. Released

Michael Jackson recorded the best-selling album of all time, *Thriller* (1982), which spawned numerous top singles. Jackson had a substantial career as a performer in his youth and teen years and became a controversial public figure in the years that followed the album's release. (AP Photo/Doug Pizac)

as a single in 1985, "We Are the World" featured a slew of artists from the pop world (billed as the supergroup USA for Africa), including Jackson, Richie, Bruce Springsteen, Cyndi Lauper, Billy Joel, Ray Charles, Tina Turner, Paul Simon, Diana Ross, and Bob Dylan, among many others. It was a huge No. 1 hit, raising over $60 million for its cause; its success inspired a string of other charitable albums and singles in the 1980s that stretched across multiple genres.

Like Jackson, Prince (born Prince Rogers Nelson) came from a background in 1970s pop. He played all the instruments on many of his early recordings, making him a musical machine that understood every element of the creation process, evocative of Stevie Wonder's 1970s career. In addition, like Jackson, Prince received attention from a number of hit music videos. Some of those videos were for songs from a movie, *Purple Rain* (1984), which starred Prince and featured him in several extended concert sequences. Inspired by events in his own life, Prince wrote the storyline and the songs and produced the album as well. The movie and its accompanying soundtrack marked Prince's commercial and creative peak. The title track was a rhythm and blues (R&B)

Madonna has always embraced the visual aspects of entertainment, via music videos or erotic stage shows, that could be used to enhance her recordings. Though she has generated a good deal of controversy in her career, Madonna's consistent change of both musical and visual style has made her a fan favorite for decades. (AP Photo)

version of a power ballad that could equal those of Prince's hard rock counterparts of the era, such as Bon Jovi and Mötley Crüe. Both genres had songs with accessible lyrics and melodies over subdued verse sections, married with grandiose choruses and melodic guitar solos.

A number of Prince's songs featured sexually suggestive lyrics on occasion; for example, "Darling Nikki," which contained openly risqué references, inspired Tipper Gore to found the Parents Music Resource Center in the late 1980s. Prince did not enjoy the same level of success as a recording artist during the rest of the decade; however, he consistently released moderately successful and often critically appreciated albums. *Around the World in a Day* (1985) and *Parade* (1986), each featured one successful single, and the albums *Sign o' the Times* (1987) and *Lovesexy* (1989) were very well reviewed, though they were not commercial hits.

Madonna (born Madonna Louise Ciccone) differed from both Michael Jackson and Prince, in that her visual impact was as much a part of her success as her music. The Michigan native moved to New York to work as a professional dancer for Pearl Lange and Alvin Ailey, and she was encouraged by DJ John "Jellybean" Benitez to sing. Under Benitez's guidance, Madonna's recordings became favorites of the New York dance club scene, and she eventually signed with Sire Records. Madonna's self-titled 1984 debut featured two hit singles, "Borderline" and "Lucky Star." In these videos, Madonna wore jewelry featuring a cross, lace tops, leather corsets, skirts over capri pants, and fishnet stockings, contrasting religion and sex. Teenage girls mimicked her style, sparking a national fashion trend. Her videos and fashion impact would be widely important within the new visually based medium of MTV.

It would be a mistake to consider Madonna the first female artist to mesh a strong visual image with her musical talent; Olivia Newton-John, Pat Benatar, and Deborah Harry of Blondie immediately come to mind as examples of singers who did just that in the late 1970s. But Madonna took it to a whole other level via the medium of the music video. She became a new breed of pop star and in the process, forever changed the way that pop artists were marketed.

Madonna's second album, *Like a Virgin* (1985), featured four top-five singles (including the title track, which sat at No. 1 for six weeks), and her third album, *True Blue* (1986), had three No. 1 singles. Both albums demonstrated the artist's expanded approach to dance music. Her fourth album, *Like a Prayer* (1989), continued her tradition of pushing the boundaries by addressing uncomfortable topics in her songs. The video for "Like a Prayer" evoked racial and religious issues, with an underlying questioning of her own power as a woman. By the time this fourth album was released, Madonna had cemented herself as a popular music icon.

The new wave group the Go-Go's—one of the first all-girl bands to release chart-topping records—emerged a few years before Madonna, but they had a less dramatic impact. Their first album, *Beauty and the Beat* (1981), was a wide commercial success with a younger, female audience. The album's second single "We Got the Beat," was highlighted in a video that showed the performers having fun around Hollywood before cumulating in a live performance at the end.

Like the Go-Go's, Cyndi Lauper focused on having fun with both her music and her public image. Her first single, which stated as much in its title, made her a huge pop star. "Girls Just Want to Have Fun," with its feminist message and iconic video, reached No. 2 as a single and made Lauper a unique presence on MTV. It also helped to propel her debut album, *She's So Unusual* (1984), to the top of the record charts. Her popularity was further cemented by her first No. 1 hit, a ballad called "Time After Time," a significantly successful pop ballad.

Whitney Houston had a number of family connections in the music industry—her mother, Cissy Houston; her aunt, Dionne Warwick; and her godmother, Aretha Franklin. She may have had a leg up with music insiders, but her stunning beauty and soaring vocals made her a superstar. She was singing in a nightclub alongside her mother when she caught the eye of the legendary Arista Records executive Clive Davis. Convinced that she had what it took to be a pop sensation, Davis signed her to a record contract. *Whitney Houston*, released in 1985, was the first debut album (and the first by a solo female artist) to produce three No. 1 singles, including the immensely popular "Greatest Love of All." Her second album, *Whitney* (1987), had four No. 1 singles—an astounding number for any album.

Houston may have known a few people in the music industry, but few artists could claim as strong a family connection as Janet Jackson. Raised in the famous showbiz family, the 10-year-old Janet joined her brothers, the Jackson 5, to perform on the variety show *The Jacksons* in the mid-1970s. She briefly abandoned music to take acting roles in television shows like *Good Times* in the 1970s and *Diff'rent Strokes* in the early 1980s, but then she decided to focus on making records. By 1986, Jackson had risen to the top of both the R&B and pop charts with her album *Control*, which included five top-five singles. For her, music was at the forefront of her image, not dancing or sexuality—a stark contrast from Madonna.

Yet, for most singers in the 1980s, dancing was an essential element of being a pop sensation. Jackson's choreographer, Paula Abdul, helped solidify the trend of dancing in music videos as essential to the genre's development. Although Abdul had little background in singing, she funded her own demo recording, with the goal of becoming a pop vocalist/dancer in the image of the stars she was working with. Abdul's first album, *Forever Your Girl* (1988), rose to the No. 1 position on the *Billboard* Hot 100 chart and stayed there for 62 weeks.

In addition to Michael Jackson, many male artists who had successful careers in the 1970s transitioned smoothly into the 1980s. Rick James's concept album *Street Songs* (1981), including his hit "Super Freak" with the members of the Temptations on backing vocals, was seen as the highlight of his crossover success. The Commodores featured both a funky sound and top ballads written and sung by their lead vocalist, Lionel Richie. Richie embarked on a solo career in 1982 with a self-titled release and a ballad, "Truly," which became a commercial success and set the tone for his more successful endeavors during the decade. His follow-up, *Can't Slow Down* (1983), featured both a midtempo hit, "All Night Long," and a ballad, "Hello," highlighting his versatility.

The 1980s was the decade that saw the emergence of a new type of group: the "boy band." New Edition, formed in the late 1970s in Boston, was one of the first of these. The teenage, all–African American group was discovered by Maurice Starr, who produced their debut album, *Candy Girl* (1983). After Starr guided the group to sign a more financially lucrative contract with MCA Records, they released another hit album, *New Edition* (1984), with two successful singles. Following the ouster of Bobby Brown, the group added Johnny Gill as lead singer and released *Heartbreak* in 1988, featuring a more mature sound.

After splitting with the New Edition, Starr sought a replacement, forming New Kids on the Block with five white teenage boys. New Kids on the Block would become one of the decade's greatest successes with preteen fans eager to buy not only the group's music, but also merchandise emblazoned with the members' likenesses. In the meantime, Brown went on to succeed on his own. His second solo album, *Don't Be Cruel* (1988), on which he worked with producers L.A. Reid and Babyface, as well as producer Teddy Riley, included his signature song, the No. 1 "My Prerogative."

Riley's production approach came to be described as "new jack swing," a term coined by scriptwriter Barry Michael Cooper in a magazine article. Riley had initially used this style on Keith Sweat's debut album, *Make It Last Forever* (1987). New jack swing saturated much of urban popular music in the late 1980s and early 1990s. Before its emergence, much urban music of the 1980s was divided into two types. The first, melodic pop, used synthesizers, and the main percussive beats were provided by a group including a drummer, a bassist, and often a guitarist; Prince used this type of instrumentation in many of his 1980s hits. The other genre, rap music, took most of its accompaniment from sampling records and playing figures on drum machines sequenced by musical instrument digital interface (MIDI), a form of electronic music. New jack swing combined both approaches into a single, unified style, particularly employing a sequenced "swing beat" that pushed the rhythm of the song forward.

Riley led two more groups to popularity in the late 1980s and into the 1990s, not only as the producer, but also as a performer. Riley's first group, Guy, put out a self-titled debut in 1988, consisting of five singles that helped establish the new jack swing style. The group's follow-up album, *The Future* (1990), included the single "Let's Chill." Riley's second group, BLACKstreet, was initially not as successful as Guy; however, their second album, *Another Level* (1996), featured "No Diggity," a collaboration with hip hop star Dr. Dre. Other producers used the style as well, notably Jimmy Jam and Terry Lewis on Janet Jackson's *Rhythm Nation 1814* album in late 1989, and Babyface and L.A. Reid on Whitney Houston's *I'm Your Baby Tonight* about a year later. Clearly, new jack swing would not have been such an enduring influence without the success of New Edition's members.

R&B was not limited to just African American performers, however. Often compared to white R&B/soul (aka "blue-eyed soul") performers of the 1960s such as the Rascals and Lonnie Mack, Darryl Hall and John Oates formed a group that achieved notable success in the early to mid-1980s. The duo had modest success before the 1980s, notably with their 1977 hit "Rich Girl" and 1981's *Private Eyes* album, but they shifted to a more synthesized sound with the albums that they released in the middle of the decade. Their "rock and soul" approach became even more modern, as its synthesizers were idiomatic of the new wave movement of the 1980s.

The Cuban group Miami Sound Machine, featuring vocalist Gloria Estéfan and led by her husband, guitarist/producer Emilio Estéfan, was largely influenced by the Latin/Cuban music that has permeated the Miami music scene for decades. Their Latin roots meshed successfully with dance music in the 1985 hit "Congo," and once they renamed themselves Gloria Estéfan and the Miami Sound Machine, they released the hit album *Let It Loose* in 1987, featuring the dance hit "Rhythm Is Gonna Get You" and the soulful ballad "Anything for You." Gloria Estéfan became known for her sincere, sultry voice, and in the late 1980s she launched a successful solo career that lasted well into the 1990s.

British groups had a strong presence on MTV. The Police and U2, two British groups with some type of punk influence, were successful on MTV, and they often used both guitars and synthesizers hand in hand to define their style. Duran Duran emerged in 1981 with an eponymous debut album, but were regulars on American MTV with the success of their album *Seven and the Ragged Tiger* (1983) that featured "The Reflex." Though the punk scene inspired Bow Wow Wow's visual appearance, their minor hit "I Want Candy," was clearly based in guitar pop. Others such as Thomas Dolby, Howard Jones, Adam and the Ants, A Flock of Seagulls, and ABC also achieved success with a heavier concentration of synthesizer use. Tears for Fears enjoyed a greater degree of success with two important songs that defined the middle of the decade, "Shout" and "Everybody Wants to Rule the World."

Culture Club's music was influenced by Reggae, particularly with their hits "Do You Really Want to Hurt Me" (*Kissing to be Clever*, 1982) and "Karma Chameleon." Made up of only two musicians, vocalist Annie Lennox and guitarist/keyboardist David Stewart, the Eurythmics's music was heavy on synthesizer use joined with R&B influenced vocals. Wham! was a duo in the manner of the Eurythmics, featuring vocalist George Michael and guitarist/ keyboardist Andrew Ridgeley, and achieved a higher degree of success in America than either the Eurythmics or Culture Club. Both performers and the accompanying dancers and musicians in the video for "Wake Me Up Before You Go-Go" wore shirts with words "Choose Life" emblazoned on the front. The shirts became a fashion trend. Genesis's original lead singer, Peter Gabriel, left the group in the late 1970s. Phil Collins, the group's drummer, began to sing for the group, and by 1981, released a very successful studio album, *Face Value*. Genesis, left with Collins and two original members bassist/ guitarist Mike Rutherford and keyboardist Tony Banks, released additional recordings independently. Similar to Genesis, Yes also had personnel changes from their original, classic memberships. Yes achieved widespread success with their 1983 album, *90125*. Played consistently on MTV, both groups were performing with newer MIDI electronic music technology. Though not American, groups in this section were widely played on MTV in the United States.

An important development in pop music was the emergence and mainstreaming of rap. Although it began the decade mainly on the streets of New York City, by the end of the 1980s, it had become one of the top genres in popular music. When music was played at block parties in New York, the disc jockey (DJ) supplied banter while changing records. Over time, the DJ would hire a master of ceremonies (MC), who would rhythmically talk ("rap") over the music. The DJ started to use two turntables, in the manner of a radio station or disco club; as a result, the party moved forward seamlessly and eventually the MC came to be seen as a performer in his own right. (Rap was almost exclusively male at the time, though some female artists emerged, as discussed later in the chapter.)

Early rap pioneers such as DJ Kool Herc and Grandmaster Flash used the turntable as a kind of musical instrument. Grandmaster Flash moved the record by hand instead of having the turntable move it, which allowed him to control the tempo of the music. In addition, he began pushing the record back and forth; with this technique, he could play specific musical phrases repeatedly and, when done more aggressively, even create an innovative effect, scratching. The technique gained attention through Grandmaster Flash's most successful album, *The Message* (1982), featuring the title track. He started to use five MCs; one of them, Kurtis Blow, had rap's first certified gold record, "The Breaks (Part I)," in 1980. In addition to Grandmaster Flash's solid approach, Blow's lyrics highlighted the plight of the inner-city youth. It was at this point that the MC became the focus and the DJ became the accompanist, which changed the dynamic of the genre.

Two independent music veterans from Sugar Hill Records, Joe and Sylvia Robinson, went to a party and heard guests rapping along with instrumental sections on disco records. They assembled a few of these rappers in a recording

Run-D.M.C helped make rap music a part of the larger popular music landscape and was one of the top rap artists of the 1980s. Their collaboration with rock band Aerosmith acted as a bridge between two seemingly disparate genres, and their sense of fashion helped influence a generation of fans. (AP Photo/Wilbur Funches)

studio to perform over "Good Times," a disco hit for Chic. The group, under the name The Sugarhill Gang, released the record as the 1979 song "Rapper's Delight," the first rap hit to make the top 40. Encouraged by this success, Joe and Sylvia Robinson, the heads of Sugar Hill Records, began to release other records, most notably Grandmaster Flash and the Furious Five's "The Message" (1982).

Following the lead of Sugar Hill Records, a New York–based club promoter/artist manager and a New York University student interested in rap music formed Def Jam Records. Russell Simmons, the promoter, concentrated on the business aspects for the independent record label, and the student, Rick Rubin, focused on the music. The musicians that Simmons managed included Kurtis Blow and Run-D.M.C., a group that included his brother, Joseph "Run" Simmons. Early on, both Simmons and Rubin wanted to succeed by emulating the model of 1960s' Motown: Music traditionally made by African American performers would be cultivated and marketed to white audiences as crossover hits.

Run-D.M.C. differed from other artists, as the group featured a DJ with two rappers rather than one. Their debut, *Run-D.M.C.* (1984), highlighted a style less reliant on 1970s' funk and disco and more in line with 1980s' MIDI technology. Visually, the group also differed from postdisco artists, abandoning the bright clothing of that era in favor of being more authentic and "street." The performers sported workout jumpsuits and Adidas shoes without laces (prisoners were not allowed to have laces in their shoes, as the authorities thought that they might try to hang themselves with them). This signaled to their fans that this style of music was idiomatic of the 1980s and should be considered a new breed for a new generation.

In 1985, Run-D.M.C. had been rapping in rehearsal over the instrumental break from "Walk This Way," one of Aerosmith's biggest hits in the 1970s, and Rubin got the idea of recording it. The new version of "Walk This Way," featuring Aerosmith's Steven Tyler and Joe Perry, was widely accepted by whites as well as blacks, and it was the first rap single to be a top 5 hit. Run-D.M.C. had made it as a crossover rap group.

Run-D.M.C. helped their record company, Def Jam, become one of the more recognizable labels in the mid 1980s. The label's goal to find artists who could appeal to white suburban listeners was furthered by their signing of the Beastie Boys. The Beastie Boys had been a punk group dabbling in rap when Rubin discovered them in 1984. The group began to incorporate even more rap into their music, and the three core members released *Licensed to Ill* in 1986.

LL Cool J's R&B take on rap, demonstrated by his 1987 hit "I Need Love," made it even more palatable to a white audience. Working with Def Jam producer Rubin, LL Cool J released *Radio* in 1985; the title track has been identified as one of the first rap songs to use a conventional pop song structure. This is an important point, as the approach helped make the new genre easier for the mainstream pop audience to understand. Salt-N-Pepa, which became one of the few female rap groups to achieve national popularity, would also use the pop song structure. Their debut album, *Hot, Cool, & Vicious* (1986), achieved limited success with the song "Tramp." Included on the flip side of "Tramp," however, was the song "Push It," and that became the group's biggest hit.

With rap now a cultural powerhouse, its lyrical content was beginning to expand. Though their career was brief, 2 Live Crew's album *As Nasty as They Wanna Be* (1989) and their song "Me So Horny" helped put the new trends in rap in the context of sex. Group leader Luther Campbell was aligning with ghetto-style DJs, who helped develop the Miami bass sound that revolved around a Roland TR-808 drum machine and samples from comedy albums. Boogie Down Productions (BDP), led by KRS-One (aka Kris Parker), came to the forefront of using rap lyrics to critique America's social and political framework and explain the harsh reality of urban life, especially in the Bronx, where they lived. An important point of influence with BDP was that they were one of the first groups to challenge another group over authenticity. The Bronx-based BDP's feud with Juice Crew, a group led by Marley Marl, was referred to as the "bridge wars" when it was implied that the Queensbridge area was the birthplace of hip hop music in the Juice Crew's 1985 song "The Bridge," a "B side" of the single "Beat Biter."

Influenced by BDP and Run-D.M.C., Public Enemy became a leader of the new hip hop movement. The group started to gain acclaim with the release of *It Takes a Nation of Millions to Hold Us Back* (1988), featuring "Don't Believe the Hype" and "Black Steel in the Hour of Chaos." Their next album, *Fear of a*

Black Planet (1990), spoke of African American empowerment in its main hit, "Fight the Power." The abrasively named N.W.A. (Niggaz with Attitude) was the first successful gangsta rap group to emerge from the Los Angeles area. As different as L.A.'s inner city is from New York, the lyrical content reflected an equal contrast.

Easy-E (born Eric Wright) was a drug dealer as a teenager, and met Steve Yano, a swap meet record salesman. Yano introduced Wright to one of the best-known club DJs, Andre Young (better known as Dr. Dre). Wright and Dre began putting out records that reflected the lifestyle in their rough neighborhood. Cheo Horari Coker (Light, 1999, 253) stated that Dre wanted "to combine the profane and sexually provocative humor of Richard Pryor and Dolemite with the lurid, nihilistic violence of Al Pacino's *Scarface*." Thanks to the help of a white businessman, Jerry Heller, the group eventually signed with Priority Records.

Similar to N.W.A., Compton-based Ice-T (Tracey Morrow) released his first album, *Rhyme Pays*, in 1987. Lyrically, Ice-T describes the lifestyle of a drug dealer in "I'm Your Pusher" (*Album Power*, 1988), featuring a sample of 1970s' soul artist Curtis Mayfield's "Pusherman." His approach became associated with a West Coast rapping style, and by the mid-1990s, a stylistic and philosophical difference between West Coast rappers and East Coast rappers became the focal point of the rap community. However, hip hop was not the only music to emerge from the Los Angeles area in the 1980s. Earlier in the decade, Hollywood was saturated with hard rock music.

HARD ROCK AND HEAVY METAL

Since emerging in the 1970s, hard rock has received scrutiny from critics and parents alike. Its popularity was fueled by the emergence of MTV, similar to the way that pop music expanded in the 1980s. Hard rock's rise eventually opened the door for heavy metal to become accepted by mainstream rock fans by the end of the decade.

The hard rock style of the 1980s actually began before the decade, with the release of Van Halen's eponymous debut record in 1978. Lead guitarist Eddie Van Halen quickly made his reputation as an innovative virtuoso guitarist, while frontman David Lee Roth was more of an entertainer, with bravado and a sexually charged swagger, than a vocalist. *Van Halen* featured the singles "Running with the Devil," "Jamie's Cryin'," and a remake of the Kinks' "You Really Got Me," which cracked the top 40, as well as "Eruption," an instrumental featuring a guitar solo from Eddie Van Halen. The latter established Van Halen as leader of the 1980s' style of guitarist, discussed later in this chapter, largely because it included new guitar techniques not seen in the commercial realm, especially two-handed slurs (aka tapping).

Their music, coupled with their dynamic videos (like the one for "Jump," the group's only No. 1 hit, from the chart-topping *1984* album), made Van Halen one of the most emulated groups of the 1980s. During this period, Roth influenced a generation of musicians and fans. Eventually, Roth left Van Halen to go solo, putting out a few records with a "supergroup" of hard rock veterans in 1985; Van Halen hired songwriter Sammy Hagar to replace him. Hagar's songwriting was a better fit for the direction of the band in the mid-1980s, and the group continued to have wide commercial success through the early 1990s, but most serious Van Halen fans prefer the Roth years, largely because of nostalgia for the period.

Quiet Riot was one of the most popular of Van Halen's peers without recording contracts in the Los Angeles rock scene. The group was led in the late 1970s by singer Kevin Dubrow and guitarist Randy Rhoads, and it differed from Van Halen in that Quiet Riot had the musical style of a glamorous hard rock band—which was a large reason for their early inability to get a record deal. After Rhoads left to join the band backing former Black Sabbath singer Ozzy Osbourne, Quiet Riot had little impact on the Hollywood scene. Rhoads went from strong pop-hard-rock–based guitarist in Quiet Riot to classically influenced heavy metal guitar hero with Osbourne.

Rhoads was the first hard-rock guitarist in the 1980s to use elements of classical music in his songs and solos; he would eventually become one of the most influential guitarists of the decade. The group Black Sabbath shared a common characteristic with Van Halen: a controversial and charismatic lead singer and a virtuoso guitarist. Osbourne's shock-based reputation differed from Roth's sexual prowess, though—he favored outrageous actions such as biting the heads off of doves or bats (which may or may not have been still alive at the time), drinking to ridiculous excess, and even going so far as to defecate on the Alamo Cenotaph, a Texas monument (for which he was arrested and fined $40); however, the national press widely announced that he had urinated on the actual Alamo. Rhoads became a cult guitar hero largely because of his dedication to his instrument and interest in classical guitar. Unfortunately, an airplane accident took Rhoads's life at age 26 after only two commercial releases; his career was sadly brief, but it solidified him as an important hard rock guitarist of the decade.

As Rhoads's reputation grew, fans began to show some interest in his former band. Quiet Riot became an immediate sensation with their videos "Metal Health (Bang Your Head)" and the cover of English glam-rock group Slade's 1970s' hit "Cum on Feel the Noize" (which played almost constantly on MTV). As the first group to emerge from the Hollywood scene with any success in the early 1980s, major record companies began to look around for "the next Quiet Riot"—a tribute to how important it was to the genre's development during the 1980s.

Osbourne continued to have success following Rhoads's death, though on a different scale. His career became very popular in the late 1980s and thrived well into the first decade of the 21st century. Osbourne's most popular songs, including "Crazy Train," "Over the Mountain," and "Flying High Again," were written with bassist Bob Daisley while Rhoads was still alive. Osbourne began to make videos for the new MTV format for singles from the albums *Bark at the Moon* (1984) and *The Ultimate Sin* (1987), which featured Southern California guitarist Jake E. Lee. Following these was *No Rest for the Wicked* (1988), with then New Jersey–based guitarist Zakk Wylde. As a result of the latter, Osbourne became reestablished as a heavy metal vocalist, gaining respect from younger fans, and Wylde enjoyed an eventful career with Osbourne into the first decade of the 21st century.

Osbourne helped raise the profile of Los Angeles–based Mötley Crüe by making them Black Sabbath's opening act on tour in the early 1980s, and "the Crüe," as they were affectionately known, became one of the most popular groups of the decade as a result. Mötley Crüe's debut album, *Too Fast for Love*, was recorded for an independent label as the band emerged from the Hollywood scene in 1981 and then was released to the mainstream public after they signed with Elektra Records the next year. The first album they recorded for major label release, *Shout at the Devil*, sparked controversy because of its title, but it boasted two significant rock radio hits.

Mötley Crüe helped popularize the hard rock power ballad. Often exploring emotional subjects, power ballads exposed aggressive hard rockers as "hard on the outside, soft on the inside" young men. Some groups had put out power ballads before, such as Journey's "Faithfully" (from *Escape*, 1980), but Journey was much softer stylistically, while Mötley Crüe had a harder edge. As a result, female fans became even more attracted to the "bad boys with good hearts."

"Home Sweet Home" (from *Theater of Pain*, 1985), featuring Tommy Lee playing drums and piano and lyrics about a band returning home after a long tour, fueled Mötley Crüe's mainstream success. Almost every hard rock band in the 1980s wrote a power ballad in the years that followed. Most of Mötley Crüe's music videos, featuring the group in concert, reflected the American society's love of excess. They employed explosive devices in their stage shows more than groups had done before, and their scantily clad female backing vocalists flouted conservative attitudes about sex.

With Mötley Crüe's success came other Hollywood groups. Ratt formed in Los Angeles in 1981, and their two-guitar lineup differed from other one-guitar groups from Hollywood in the 1980s. This allowed Ratt to have the full sound commonly heard in a heavy metal group, along with harmony guitar parts that softened the hard rock melodies. Shortly after the group became popular on MTV, guitarist Warren DeMartini became a hero to young guitarists reading guitar magazines. He was joined by bandmates Robbin Crosby (who served as co-lead guitarist, though he was more of a rhythm guitarist), bassist Juan Croucier (who was also in Dokken at the time), and drummer Bobby Blotzer.

Ratt singer Stephen Pearcy's abrasive vocal tone gave legitimacy to a heavy metal crowd—one that, at least in the early 1980s, blurred the lines between hard rock and heavy metal. Thanks to the strong, loud production by record producer Beau Hill, the band had a sound not seen in most rock groups at the time. Hill's production, especially for Ratt, incorporated large sounding drums and simulated room "reverb." Producers such as Hill, while recording albums, incorporated the loud sound of cheering crowds to make it seem as though these groups were performing live in an arena. The group had four albums whose singles were accompanied by hit videos, but most of their record sales were for the first two, *Out of the Cellar* (1984) and *Invasion of Your Privacy* (1985).

Dokken had their own guitar hero in George Lynch, who was a solo guitarist for most of his tenure in the band. Though not as commercially successful

Bon Jovi (vocalist Jon Bon Jovi, left, with bassist Alec John Such) became one of the most popular hard rock groups of the 1980s, following the release of their multiplatinum record *Slippery When Wet* (1986). With catchy songs and strong performances, Bon Jovi continued to have success through the latter half of the decade. (AP Photo/Gary Gershoff/Media-Punch/IPX)

as Ratt, Dokken made an impact on the MTV establishment by putting out a great number of music videos throughout the mid-1980s. Two albums released at the beginning of their career, *Breaking the Chains* (1983) and *Tooth and Nail* (1984), received moderate attention from hard rock fans. The group achieved their pinnacle with videos from 1985's *Under Lock and Key*, including "In These Dreams" and "The Hunter."

Dokken had two stylistic traits that were enduring to fans. First, the clean vocal timbre of Don Dokken meshed well with moderately aggressive hard rock and even better with the ballads that were beginning to become a large part of the 1980s' landscape. Second, the powerful backing vocals of Jeff Pilson added polish to the group's overall sound. Many guitarists responded to the group's work since they were fans of Lynch. Beginning with Eddie Van Halen at the start of the decade, virtuoso guitarists became an important element of the hard rock style, and Lynch was one of the benefactors of the interest in "guitar heroes" during the 1980s.

New Jersey–based Bon Jovi was one of the top-selling groups of the late 1980s. Named after lead vocalist Jon Bon Jovi, the group's first two albums had only marginal success before they broke through with the classic hard rock album *Slippery When Wet* (1986). A number of videos, including "You

Give Love a Bad Name" and "Livin' on a Prayer" showcasing the charismatic Jon Bon Jovi, was in regular rotation on MTV, fueling the album's rise on the charts.

One reason why Bon Jovi's music was so popular was because their songs had accessible themes and lyrics. For example, "Livin' on a Prayer" narrated a story about a young couple trying to survive in America against all odds and proclaimed their faith that if they stay strong, they will make it together. Bon Jovi was American music that young adults, male and female, could understand. Jon Bon Jovi's poster-boy good looks, guitarist Richie Sambora's catchy and accomplished playing, and a strong rhythmic section helped catapult Bon Jovi to a high level of commercial success. MTV was the primary promotional vehicle for Bon Jovi; the channel showcased the band's videos highlighting their live performances and tours, and the members assumed the persona of traveling cowboy, especially in the lyrics of "Dead or Alive." The group strengthened their following with another popular album, *New Jersey*, in 1989.

Poison, a group that formed in western Pennsylvania but found success after they went to California and joined the Hollywood rock scene, was vilified by the genre's critics, even while the band was at the height of its commercial popularity. One reason was that the group wore feminine makeup and displayed outrageous behavior on and off stage, and in music videos—a style that can be characterized as "glam hard rock." Over a period of many years, hard rock and heavy metal had developed a reputation for being dangerous music that the mainstream did not understand; but Poison was far more dangerous in the eyes of their opponents. Many critics questioned why grown men would wear makeup in such a "girly" (or even "queer") way. Poison remained popular after they softened their makeup use and started to write in minor keys more frequently on *Open Up and Say Aaah!* (1988).

In marked contrast was Sacramento–based Tesla. While Poison represented the glamorous Los Angeles scene of the mid-1980s, Tesla's music and persona were seen as more authentic. Tesla represented the everyman, personifying the cowboy mentality that Bon Jovi pioneered but on a more genuine level. Tesla, whose style was influenced by the Beatles, southern rock, and the blues, found a perfect niche for itself in its antiglamour. They were quick to proclaim their authenticity, stating that their albums featured "No Machines." Their first album, *Mechanical Resonance* (1984), boasted the popular singles "Modern-Day Cowboy" and "Little Suzi." Tesla's follow-up album, *The Great Radio Controversy* (1988), featured blues-based slide guitar singles and lighter, acoustic-infused songs that reinforced their roots-based version of hard rock. In the perfect stroke of authenticity, Tesla was the first rock group to release an all-acoustic album titled *Five Man Acoustical Jam* in 1990, a few years before any alternative artist did an unplugged album.

Guns 'N' Roses lacked the glam songwriting and makeup of Poison, preferring a heavier use of blues tonality that was more in the vein of the Rolling Stones and Aerosmith. The band blazed the way to a new thread of hard rock, known as "sleaze rock." High-energy shows had become necessary among groups in the hard rock genre, and Guns 'N' Roses took over where Poison left off. Because of the high-energy shows of groups in hard rock, hard rock artists translated to an MTV viewership well. However, Guns 'N' Roses developed a reckless reputation. The energy from Guns 'N' Roses largely emanated from lead vocalist Axl Rose; his lyrics about drug use and the Hollywood scene, coupled with an openness about his drug and alcohol habits, made him an instant rock star in the eyes of American fans. Though the group was not initially featured on MTV, once the single "Welcome to the Jungle" (from *Appetite for Destruction,* 1987) was released, its video went into frequent rotation. The success of the group changed the complete landscape of 1980s' hard rock.

Guns 'N' Roses was the best example of a complementary two-guitar sleaze rock band in the 1980s (other similar groups who emerged from the Hollywood scene during this period included Faster Pussycat and L.A. Guns). Their two-guitar setup was different from other Hollywood groups such as Van Halen, Poison, and Quiet Riot. In Guns 'N' Roses, Slash was the charismatic and respected lead guitarist, while rhythm guitarist Izzy Stradlin was the musical glue holding the band together. Stradlin's steady role as a rhythm guitarist coupled with his quiet personality was important, as the band's music was true to the personas of the group members, including Rose's, as if no one knew when disaster was going to strike. The danger inherent in their members was an appealing characteristic to the group's fans. Their debut album, *Appetite for Destruction,* featured songs such as "Welcome to the Jungle," and "She's So Easy," which were in stark contrast to the glam hard rock of Bon Jovi and Poison. Rather, the lyrics and visual image of the group were symbolic of the chaotic music scene in Hollywood in the 1980s.

And as popular as Bon Jovi and Poison power ballads ("Never Say Goodbye" and "Every Rose Has Its Thorn," respectively) were, Guns 'N' Roses' approach to their own power ballad, "Sweet Child 'o Mine," had a definitive raw style that separated them from other hard rock groups of the era. Musicians flocked to the Hollywood area in the hope of finding stardom for themselves, and the whole situation was rampant with drugs and sex.

Skid Row, a heavy metal group led by Sebastian Bach, had two successful albums during the 1980s, with aggressive chord progressions that fit into much of the music of the late 1980s. The eponymous first release included the hits "Youth Gone Wild" and the power ballad "I Remember You." By the end of the 1980s, groups that had been considered underground often were enjoying the same kind of success as sleaze hard rock bands. These groups followed the heavy metal approach, either via thoughtful lyrical content that questioned the government and its excessive policies during the 1980s' administrations or through excessively heavy metal that came to be called "thrash metal."

Starting in Los Angeles in the early 1980s, Metallica was influenced by the heaviest bands in the new wave of British heavy metal. But it was much heavier than any other American band in the early 1980s; the group played only sporadically, but it was considered part of the Hollywood scene. At one point, Metallica was looking for a new bassist; the man they picked, Cliff Burton, insisted that the group relocate to San Francisco, and they wanted Burton so much that they agreed. Metallica was very comfortable with the decision, though, as they were already feeling that they did not fit in well with their less aggressive compatriots such as Mötley Crüe and Ratt. The band released four albums that afforded them an increasing level of popularity, bringing them into the mainstream by the early 1990s. Over time, Metallica became the standard for heavy metal groups.

Metallica guitarist Dave Mustaine left the band to form Megadeth in 1983, which was initially popular in the underground metal scene. Mustaine's lyrical content on *Peace Sells but Who's Buyin'?* (1986) contained politically charged commentary, specifically in the album's title track, "Peace Sells." With the addition of Shrapnel school guitarist Marty Friedman for the albums that followed, Megadeth's music became more virtuosic than noisy, which started them on their way to widespread acceptance. Megadeth capped the end of the decade by joining the "Clash of the Titans," the first major all-thrash tour, with Anthrax and Slayer. The tour was considered to be a multiheadliner, as the three groups alternated time slots.

The New York group Anthrax was part of the underground metal scene along with Metallica, but they did not achieve the same amount of success. Anthrax's popularity expanded when Joey Belladonna became the lead singer in 1984; his vocal range, which was wider than his thrash metal contemporaries, and soaring singing style made the group accessible to a hard rock audience while maintaining their thrash roots. Anthrax ultimately became well known for their merge of rap and metal, working with rap artist Public Enemy on "Bring the Noise." Initially, Anthrax's members switched instruments on their own rap song, "I'm the Man," in an attempt to infuse humor into their live shows. In the 1980s, rap fusion was more of a novelty, but this approach was important for bands as they entered the 1990s. However, Anthrax also sang about daily struggles of members of the metal culture ("Caught in a Mosh") and racism ("Indians"). The group seemed to have the ability to have fun and not focus on serious subjects in the way that Metallica and Megadeth did.

Slayer differed from Anthrax in many ways, to the point where it might seem that a thrash musical characteristic might be the only common element. They were different from other American bands of the era in that they tried, in the words of Colin Larkin (2006, vol. 7, 520), "to play at breakneck speed with amazing technical precision." Their fast playing style exhibited a hardcore punk influence, and the songs they have released throughout their career focused on such bleak topics as serial killers, the Holocaust, and war. Slayer's music was the main influence on extreme metal (via its riffs) and black metal (via more aggressive vocals) that emerged in the 1990s. Nevertheless, a message critical of Christianity was a difficult one to deliver to a mainstream audience, so Slayer always lacked the popular success that Metallica, Megadeth, and Anthrax enjoyed. The fans the band has are furiously loyal, sticking with the group throughout their history, regardless of the ebb and flow of the genre's popularity. Though heavy metal and hard rock were important elements of 1980s rock, American mainstream rock also continued to have great success throughout the decade.

ROCK

In the 1980s, mainstream hard rock and heavy metal videos rose to the top of MTV's playlists However, other rock styles continued to make impressions on the American popular music landscape as well. Bruce Springsteen, whose music offered colorful and resonant descriptions of various aspects of American life, had a well-established career in the 1970s, and his success continued in the 1980s. He released two albums with working-class themes, *The River* (1980) and *Nebraska* (1982), before his most popular release of the decade, *Born in the U.S.A.* (1984). (The album's title track, a fiery criticism of how the U.S. government and citizens shunned Vietnam veterans, was wrongly interpreted by many—including President Ronald Reagan—as a patriotic anthem.) The biggest hit of the album (indeed, of Springsteen's entire career to date), "Dancing in the Dark," featured a synthesizer, one of the more common developments of 1980s' musical technology.

John Cougar Mellencamp was another example of a heartland rocker. Throughout his career, from its beginnings in the 1970s to the present, his songs have focused on topics that resonate with many Americans: living in a small town, the struggles of the working man, and realistic depictions of romantic relationships. It was with his sixth album, *American Fool* (1982), with hits such as "Jack and Diane" and "Hurts So Good," that he began to achieve success. That was also the last album that he made under the name "John Cougar"; he added Mellencamp, his given last name, for *Uh-Huh* (1983). His follow up album, *Scarecrow* (1985), is thought to be his most classic by many of his fans.

Tom Petty and the Heartbreakers started in the 1970s, as Springsteen had, and released three commercially successful albums in that same decade. The group's 1985 album *Southern Accents* contains some different stylistic touches; however, *Hard Promises* (1981), *Long After Dark* (1982), and *Let Me Up (I've Had Enough)* (1987), Petty's other 1980s' releases with the Heartbreakers, were commercial successes rooted in the down-home style that they were most comfortable with. Petty's personal creative highlight in the 1980s was his solo album *Full Moon Fever* (1989). The Georgia Satellites were a minor 1980s' success in the heartland rock vein, primarily with their eponymous album, which featured the smash hit "Keep Your Hands to Yourself."

Two older styles, rockabilly and electric blues, gained some mainstream recognition in the 1980s. The Stray Cats were a rockabilly group from Long Island, New York, led by vocalist and guitarist Brian Setzer. The music and appearance of the Cats aligned with 1950s' styles in their only U.S. release, *Built for Speed* (1982); but despite the success of that album, the group disbanded. Electric blues gained mainstream acceptance because of the popularity of Stevie Ray Vaughan. His albums *Texas Flood* (1983), *Couldn't Stand the Weather* (1984), *Soul to Soul* (1986), and *In Step* (1988) enjoyed both commercial and critical acclaim. After beating a battle with alcohol and drug addiction, Vaughn tragically died in a helicopter accident in 1990. Robert Cray was also vital to the blues revival in the 1980s, though his approach was more traditional than Vaughn's. Cray's first two albums, both on the noted blues label Hightone, received attention from the blues community but less from the general public. His greatest mainstream success came with his third release, *Strong Persuader* (1986).

Bruce Hornsby and the Range formed in 1984. Their first hit, the title track to *The Way It Is* (1986), was a socially charged song discussing the 1960s' civil rights movement. Also included on the album were the singles "Mandolin Rain" and "Every Little Kiss," both of which fused pop writing with some jazz and bluegrass influences. The band 38 Special was among the leaders (if not *the* leader) of southern rock in the early to mid-1980s. Its stylistic influence appears to be Lynyrd Skynyrd, which may or may not be surprising—Donnie Van Zant, the lead singer/guitarist of 38 Special, is the brother of Ronnie Van Zant of Lynyrd Skynyrd. What set 38 Special apart, however, was a glossy rock sound typical of 1980s' production.

Billy Joel was considered one of the new breed of American singer/song-writers in the late 1970s, and he was another artist who successfully transitioned to the MTV format. Though his "Pressure" video featured an ultramodern style that received ample airplay on MTV, he also created some songs (and videos) in a 1960s' style with an R&B influence. Joel's albums reflected producer Phil Ramone's knowledge of earlier production styles and received a modern recording treatment that made his songs seem relevant to contemporary listeners despite their throwback approach; this was most notable on Joel's 1983 release *An Innocent Man*. Thus, even though MTV was readily enjoyed by a teenage generation in the 1980s, groups and artists were also reacting to older influences, making their mark on the network by appealing to an older demographic. MTV during the 1980s was not just for teens; the network was marketed with a "music first" mentality.

In the 1980s, Don Henley, a former member of the 1970s country-rock band the Eagles, released modern representations of synthesizer-based pop rock of the period. 1982's *I Can't Hold Back* featured the largely successful "Dirty Laundry." Shortly after the song's release, he sang on "Leather and Lace," a duet with Stevie Nicks from her 1981 album *Bella Donna*. Nicks was a member of Fleetwood Mac at the same time that Henley was with the Eagles in the 1970s, and she enjoyed similar fantastic success. How Nicks differs from Henley, though, is that her solo success came while her 1970s' group was still together in the 1980s, although Fleetwood Mac's recording schedule had slowed during the decade. Fleetwood Mac released *Mirage* in 1982, with a few hits such as "Gypsy" and "Hold Me." However, dissention among band members led to a long period of inactivity before the group released *Tango in the Night* in 1997.

Toto was a group made of session musicians who performed on 1970s' recordings for Steely Dan, Boz Scaggs, and Seals and Crofts. Guitarist Steve Lukather and keyboardist David Pasich have led the group over most of their career. Toto's greatest success came in 1982 with the release of *Toto IV*, which eventually netted them six Grammy awards, including record of the year for 1983 (for the single "Rosanna"). Their 1980s' albums that followed, *Isolation* (1984), *Fahrenheit* (1986), and *The Seventh One* (1988), were less well received than *Toto IV*.

The J. Giles Band was another 1970s' group that did not gain a large amount of success until releasing 1980s' material. In 1980, the group released *Love Stinks*, and the title track made the top 40. Their follow-up, *Freeze Frame*, included two very successful singles: "Centerfold" and the title track. Kenny Loggins had experienced significant success as a member of the rock duo Loggins and Messina in the 1970s; in the 1980s, some of his songs were featured on movie soundtracks (*Top Gun* and *Footloose*) and became top 10 hits.

Arena rock veterans Styx, Foreigner, and Journey were active during this decade as well. Styx was a popular 1970s' group who had a large degree of success in the early 1980s, largely because of two albums: *Paradise Theater* (1981) and *Kilroy Was Here* (1983). They were considered concept albums, as each one focused on a central idea. Foreigner had success in the 1970s with their album *Head Games*, but their highlight came with the immensely successful *4* (1981); on this album, hard rock producer Robert John "Mutt" Lange brought a modern 1980s' sound to the group. After a brief hiatus, the group returned with a less aggressive *Agent Provocateur* (1984) album, which—with songs that were softer in tone—was clearly marketed to an older audience. The song "I Want to Know What Love Is" was featured in the group's first music video, but the largely teenage viewers of MTV did not find its style relevant.

Journey had a consistent career throughout the 1970s and was considered among the leaders of arena rock, but the success of their 1982 album *Escape*, including new keyboardist Jonathan Cain, brought the group to the forefront of 1980s' rock. Its follow-up, *Frontiers*, also experienced great success, fueled by the success of the ballad "Faithfully." Both of Journey's albums in the early 1980s were released before MTV rose to prominence; hence, they did not make videos at that time. Similar to Foreigner, Journey took a hiatus before releasing an album that brought some commercial success, *Raised on Radio* (1986). Though they did put out videos for the singles on that album, the MTV demographic was not the same as their core fan base, so they did not enjoy the widespread impact that their hard rock counterparts did.

Like Journey, Boston was another group that debuted in the 1970s and also released an album in the 1980s. It had had two very successful albums in the late 1970s, *Boston* (1976) and *Don't Look Back* (1978), which naturally made their record company eager for a follow-up; but the band did not agree. After lawsuits from the record company that spanned a six-year period, *Third Stage* (1986) was released with a good degree of commercial success. However, like Foreigner and Journey, the band's mature core audience preferred their rock with less edge, exemplified by the hit "Amanda." The song went to No. 1 on the charts, but since it was not seen as appealing to a younger audience, a video was not made for it.

Another supergroup from the Boston area, Aerosmith, began and flourished in the 1970s, and its success continued into the 1980s. However, their career could not have been more dramatically different from Boston's. In the 1970s, Aerosmith, billed as "the Bad Boys of Hard Rock," was musically rooted in the blues influence of the Rolling Stones. The group's success in the early part of the 1980s was limited because of their drug and personality conflicts, but their fortunes changed as the members became sober. Their new clear way of thinking led to the release of two successful albums in the late 1980s: *Permanent Vacation* (1987) and *Pump* (1989). Both albums' successful singles delivered the group to a new set of younger fans, with the help of videos with sexy young actresses as the focal point (including Liv Tyler, the daughter of Aerosmith lead singer Steven Tyler, and Alicia Silverstone).

Heart, originally from Seattle and featuring sisters Ann and Nancy Wilson, had received considerable attention as a hard rock group in the 1970s, but personnel changes led to a change in the group's fortunes in the 1980s. In 1984, Ann recorded "Almost Paradise," a duet with Mike Reno, the lead singer of the Canadian hard rock group Loverboy, that became a hit (probably helped by its being on the *Footloose* movie soundtrack). The success of this ballad encouraged Heart to bring in outside writers to make their music, which brought it a new pop sound. The two albums that resulted from this development, *Heart* (1985) and *Bad Animals* (1987), became two of the group's biggest successes. However, Heart's mainstream popularity ebbed in the years that followed.

Cheap Trick and Jefferson Starship, like Heart, were 1970s' groups that began to bring in the talents of outside songwriters after doing all their songwriting themselves. Cheap Trick's career in the 1970s was highlighted by a live version of their "I Want You to Want Me" that appeared on their *Cheap Trick at Budokan* album (1978), recorded in Japan. The band's largely successful 1987 album, *Lap of Luxury*, featured outside writers Bob Mitchell and Nick Graham ("The Flame"), Jon Lind and Jim Scott ("No Mercy"), and Diane Warren ("Ghost Town"). Jefferson Airplane had enjoyed a strong career throughout the late 1960s and 1970s. They changed their name to Jefferson Starship, but they lacked support from fans under their new identity until their 1985 album *Knee Deep in the Hoopla* was released, with four top singles (including the No. 1 "We Built This City"). Both of these groups succumbed to the urge to put out a slick pop hit to achieve mainstream success but at the risk of alienating their core audience.

Rick Springfield's musical style was rooted in pop rock. Originally from Australia, Springfield moved to Los Angeles for a music and acting career at age 18. His music career was highlighted by the album *Working Class Dog* (1981). Billy Squier emerged around the same time, and gained recognition in the 1980s because of the success of three albums: *Don't Say No* (1981), *Changes in Motion* (1982), and *Signs of Life* (1984). *Don't Say No* featured his most successful hit, "The Stroke," which comments on how the music industry takes advantage of musicians. However, his follow-up album, *Signs of Life*, featured a pop-sounding single "Rock Me Tonite." The song received extensive airplay on MTV, but his pink-and-white, pop-based attire, forced dance moves, and pop production alienated many in his rock audience, and his popularity sank quickly. Sammy Hagar had a comparable career to Springfield in the early 1980s before he joined the hard rock group Van Halen in 1985 (as discussed earlier). As with Squier and Springfield, it was in the 1980s that Hagar started to gain some mainstream attention. Hagar's first significant solo success was with his 1981 album *Standing Hampton*, followed by *Three Lock Box* (1983) and *VOA* (1984), which included his most popular song, "I Can't Drive 55."

Female performers who emerged in the late 1970s carried their success into the early part of the decade as well. For instance, Pat Benatar flourished in the 1980s, producing a string of major albums that included *Crimes of Passion* (1980), *Precious Time* (1981), *Get Nervous* (1982), *Tropico* (1984), and *Seven the Hard Way* (1985). Joan Jett, the lead singer of the Blackhearts, saw her career expand considerably with the release of the band's second album, *I Love Rock and Roll* (1982), which became a considerable hit (fueled by the megahit title track). Their subsequent releases, *Album* (1983), *Glorious Results of a Misspent Youth* (1984), and *Good Music* (1986), did not enjoy comparable success. However, *Up Your Alley* (1988) returned them to mainstream prominence because of the success of the single "I Hate Myself for Loving You."

Night Ranger was a hard rock group from San Francisco that formed in the late 1970s but reached its pinnacle in the 1980s. Their first album, *Dawn Patrol*, was released in 1983 with one hit, "Don't Tell Me You Love Me." The group's real success came with their next album, *Midnight Madness* (1984), which contained three hit singles (including its best-known song, "Sister Christian"). Night Ranger's fourth album, *Seven Wishes* (1985), spawned two more hits, but the group's fortunes declined with two less successful albums in the 1980s, *Big Life* (1987) and *Man in Motion* (1988).

Huey Lewis and the News began to release albums in 1980, but they were well-seasoned members of the San Francisco rock scene in the 1970s. Though their eponymous first album was not well received, the group started to gain success on their second album, *Picture This* (1982). However, the group's next album, *Sports* (1983), proved to be the highlight of the band's career, with four hit singles. REO Speedwagon's career exploded in 1980 with their very successful album *Hi Infidelity*, which included three major singles. Their follow-up album, *Good Trouble* (1982), was a top seller as well, with the hits "Keep the Fire Burnin'" and "Sweet Time." Their final important album, *Wheels Are Turnin'* (1984), featured the hit "Can't Fight This Feeling" and marked the last big seller of the group's career. Survivor released their second album, *Premonition*, in 1981, with little success short of the single "Poor Man's Son." Fortunately, actor Sylvester Stallone was a fan of the song and asked the group to write a similar song for the soundtrack of his upcoming movie, *Rocky III*. The result, "Eye of the Tiger" was an instant success, and the band featured it as the title track for a full album in 1982.

MTV was not restricted to just American artists, of course; though the channel featured many successful artists from the United States, the influence of British pop groups cannot be ignored. New wave music was a version of pop that evolved from the punk scene in Britain in the late 1970s. The Police were one of the most important groups in the early 1980s—they had plenty of fans even without MTV exposure, but the new medium brought them even more success. U2's approach to making music in the 1980s followed a similar formula: solid songwriting with introspective lyrical content and thick guitar soundscapes provided by the group's lead guitarist (The Edge).

Genesis had success in the progressive community during the 1970s, but as a whole, the progressive rock movement did not enjoy widespread popularity. Two albums solidified the band's popularity during the 1980s: 1981's *Abacab* and 1986's *Invisible Touch*. Each album contained a title track released as a single that helped fuel a great number of sales. In between these two albums were solo albums released by Phil Collins (the band's vocalist and drummer) and Mike Rutherford (guitarist and bassist). Collins's *Face Value* (1981) and *No Jacket Required* (1985) were both immense hits, featuring a pop feel that was a departure from the Genesis sound. Similarly, Rutherford's *Mike and the Mechanics* (1986) was a far cry from Genesis. Collins's predecessor in Genesis, Peter Gabriel, released the album *So* in 1986, and it enjoyed tremendous success, largely because of two songs heavily played on MTV (the hit "Sledgehammer" had a particularly innovative video featuring claymation).

Devo was important to the development of new wave, and although they had only one hit, that song, "Whip It" (from *Freedom of Choice*, 1980), introduced the heavily synthesized sound to a wider audience. The Cars, playing in a style of rock that was closer to new wave than their contemporaries, had a number of hits in the late 1970s. Then, in the 1980s, the group had two successful albums, *Shake It Up* (1981) and *Heartbeat City* (1984). The latter featured songs that became staples in the early days of MTV, including "You Might Think" and "Drive."

Talking Heads were a new wave band that emerged out of the 1970s New York punk scene. A major influence on the new wave groups that followed, they achieved commercial success with their 1983 release *Speaking in Tongues*, and their documentary and live concert, *Stop Making Sense*. 'Til Tuesday was an American new wave group with only limited success, primarily with their 1985 album *Voices Carry*, fueled by the frequent play on MTV of the title track's video. Mr. Mister was a pop rock group that bordered on new wave; their second album, *Welcome to the Real World* (1985), was a great success. The Romantics first started to attract mainstream attention with their single "What I Like About You," from the first full-length, eponymous release 1980, and they reached their commercial peak in 1983 with the *In Heat* album. Oingo Boingo was a new wave group that started in the 1970s. The title track of their first full-length album, *Only a Lad* (1981), became a staple on the playlists on KROQ, a Los Angeles–based new wave station. The single started to receive limited underground success nationally soon after. The group placed a number of songs on soundtracks of teen-oriented films, such as *Weird Science* (1985) and *Fast Times at Ridgemont High* (1982).

Universities have been the home of many of America's most eclectic elements of society—both faculty and students. Towns where the focus of the community is dominated by the local university are often called "college towns," and in the 1980s, music called "college rock" developed in these areas. In the 1980s, new wave, punk, and folk were the central influence for the independent music scene. In addition, college radio stations and independent record labels prided themselves on their eclectic content that set them apart from the more corporate national music scene. Each entity maintained a sense of independence, disaffection, and on occasion, satire. Athens, Georgia, home of the University of Georgia, is a perfect example of a college town, and it was an early locus of college music.

The group that emerged from that scene first was the B-52s, who became a college favorite in the 1980s. The main dynamic of this group is that they had one male lead singer, Fred Schneider, counteracted by two female lead vocalists, Kate Pierson and Cindy Wilson, often singing in harmony. Their fun atmosphere was similar to that of Oingo Boingo. In addition to their music, the B-52s had a unique stage persona early in their career, featuring 1950s' style and beehive hairdos by the female vocalists. The group signed with an independent record company, and with the underground success of the single "Rock Lobster," they were awarded a contract with Warner Brothers. Their eponymous debut (1979) included a rerecorded version of "Rock Lobster" and unusual instrumentation; in addition to drums, guitar, bass, organ, and percussion, other instruments played by the group included toy piano, walkie-talkies, and smoke alarms. The B-52s put out three other albums, *Studio Album* (1981), *Whammy!* (1983), and *Bouncing Off the Satellites* (1985), but none of them achieved the underground success of their earlier ones. At the end of the decade, the B-52s released *Cosmic Thing*. This brought the underground, college rock, new wave sound into the mainstream, setting a new attitude toward what type of music would be accessible to and accepted by mainstream listeners in the years to follow.

One of the most enduring groups of the college rock scene was one of the subgenre's originators: Athens-based R.E.M. Their impact was so great that the music they helped pioneer, now called "alternative" by the rock community, had replaced hard rock and heavy metal as the predominant type of mainstream rock by the early 1990s. Simon Reynolds (2005, 392) considered that "after post punk's demystification and new pop's schematics, it felt liberating to listen to music rooted in mystical awe and blessed-out surrender." *Murmur* (1983), *Reckoning* (1984), *Fables of the Reconstruction* (1985), and *Life's Rich Pageant* (1986), followed, each of which sold well later in R.E.M.'s career, but not initially because the singles from the albums did not meet with much success.

Punk enjoyed its greatest impact in the late 1970s, but its influence extended into the next decade, too. For instance, Social Distortion was a prominent punk group from Orange County, California. With the popularity of their first full-length album, *Mommy's Little Monster* (1982), this band was one of the first punk groups to appear on MTV. Following a lengthy battle with drugs by singer Mike Ness, they released their second album, *Prison Bound* (1988), in a more aggressive, hardcore style of punk. This disc also marked the beginnings of a country-influenced style of punk, eventually known as "cowpunk."

Black Flag, led by guitarist Greg Ginn, was a hardcore punk band signed to the independent label SST, and a part of the first wave of American West Coast punk rock. Ginn, like many other punk artists in the late 1970s, was not a fan of "stupid" rock music; he "considered it just trying to interject some kind of legitimacy into making three-minute pop commercials basically" (Azerrad, 2002, 143). As a rebellion against the rock music that Ginn disdained, the group featured short songs, often lasting approximately 1 minute, throughout their career. The Minutemen released their first EP, *Paranoid Time,* in 1980, which was produced by Black Flag's Ginn. The group's first full-length album, *The Punch Line* (1981), kept the attitude that came to exemplify early hardcore punk: its 18 songs totaled only 15 minutes, averaging under 1 minute in length.

Sonic Youth, based in New York, would be an important musical influence on the iconic group Nirvana in the 1990s. After signing with Neutral Records for the release of an EP, *Confusion Is Sex,* the group moved to Homestead Records. Their album *Bad Moon Rising* (1985) was a political commentary on current state of American politics. It used experimental devices inspired by classical composer John Cage and became part of the new noise rock approach to creating sonic landscapes in punk.

Bad Brains became one of the strongest influences on groups who performed in the 1990s, including Fishbone, 311, No Doubt, and Sublime. The group's style fluctuated between hardcore punk and reggae. Like Bad Brains, Minor Threat was based in Washington D.C., but a big difference with Minor Threat that set it apart from others in the punk scene is that it advocated refraining from the use of alcohol or drugs in its songs, such as "Straight Edge," from their eponymous debut EP. A second EP, *In My Eyes,* followed; both EPs featured short songs, not much more than a minute long, similar to Bad Brains, Black Flag, and the Minutemen. The Replacements merged influences of 1970s hard rock with aspects of early English punk bands, including the Clash, the Damned, and the Jam; they signed with the independent label Twin/Tone and put out two albums that attracted attention in the underground punk scene: *Sorry Ma, Forgot to Take Out the Trash* (1981) and *Stink* (1982), before releasing *Hootenanny* in 1983. The widespread reputation that the Replacements developed nationally via their 1984 album, *Let It Be,* led to a major label contract with Sire Records. Subsequent albums received critical acclaim and attracted attention from the underground music scene, while being ignored by the mainstream.

The Pixies only existed for a few years in the late 1980s, but their impact on groups of the 1990s was dramatic. Nirvana singer/songwriter Kurt Cobain remarked to *Rolling Stone* writer David Fricke (January 27, 1994) that when he was writing songs for his own albums, he was "trying to write the ultimate pop song. I was basically trying to rip off the Pixies." He added, "when I heard the Pixies for the first time, I connected with that band so heavily I should have been in that band" (http://www.rollingstone.com/music/news/kurt-cobain-the-rolling-stone-interview-19940127). Bad Religion, led by vocalist Greg Graffin and guitarist Brett Gurewitz, released their first album (*How Could Hell Be Any Worse?*) on Gurewitz's own Epitaph Records in 1982. Not only did the group enjoy strong support in the underground music scene, Epitaph became one of the more respected independent punk rock labels in the next decade.

COUNTRY

In the 1980s, country music went through a number of transitions that distinguished the music from the beginning and end of the decade. Some country artists from the 1970s, including what was called "outlaw country," continued into the 1980s, and many of them transitioned to a pop country style spearheaded by an unexpected development: Hollywood productions began to feature country music and artists that changed the landscape of the genre's mainstream success, such as *Urban Cowboy* (1980, starring John Travolta) and *Hard Country* (1981, starring Kim Basinger). Solo female performers began to enjoy more popularity during the decade, as did vocal-based groups emerging from a gospel tradition. By the middle of the decade, a traditionalist approach came back into fashion, and bluegrass-influenced artists began to gain mainstream popularity as well. By the end of the decade, groups that were created as country groups, including a number of family-based ensembles, began to make their mark on the American music landscape. In short, the decade was filled with high and low points that showed that by the decade's end, country music was as strong as ever, ready to make another run at mainstream acceptance.

Barbara Mandrell was an important force in the emergence of urban country in the mid-1970s. Her crossover hits "Sleeping Single in a Double Bed" and "(If Loving You Is Wrong) I Don't Want to Be Right" (both from *Moods*, 1978) helped open the doors for the female artists that came after. And she had several hit albums in the 1980s too, including *Love Is Fair* (1980), *In Black and White* (1982), *Spun Gold* (1983), and *Meant for Each Other* (1984). In early 1980, women held all of the top-five positions on the Billboard Country Singles chart for the first time. Each of the featured artists had had success in earlier decades, especially the 1970s: Crystal Gayle ("It's Like We Never Said Goodbye"), Dottie West ("A Lesson In Leavin'"), Debby Boone ("Are You on the Road to Lovin' Me Again"), Emmylou Harris ("Beneath Still Waters"), and Tammy Wynette ("Two Story House," a duet with George Jones). Crystal Gayle had enjoyed some mainstream success in 1977 with her enormous hit "Don't It Make My Brown Eyes Blue." The crossover success in the 1970s by both Mandrell and Gayle at least partly helped bring country music into the pop mainstream. Gayle's 1980s' success did not match her 1970s' accomplishments, but she still was well received among country fans in the 1980s. Gayle released *Hollywood, Tennessee* (1981), an album that was a deliberate attempt to appeal to both the pop style, with side A (aka "Hollywood") featuring pop stylings, and more traditional country songs on the B side (aka "Tennessee"). This is a key indicator that Gayle wanted to straddle both the traditional and pop country worlds. Many years later, the pop country singer Shania Twain picked up on her idea in her 2002 release, *Up!*

Emmylou Harris performed and recorded throughout the 1970s, frequently performing in duets with various country artists. Her 1979 release *Blue Kentucky Girl*, which featured contributions by Dolly Parton and Linda Ronstadt, was the pinnacle of her 1970s' period. Rooted in a traditional country sound, the album became the springboard for her 1980 release *Roses in the Snow*, which presented a marked contrast to the "urban cowboy" sound that was becoming the industry standard. Harris started to gain crossover recognition in 1981, with a cover of the Chordettes 1950s' hit, "Mr. Sandman" (from the *Evangeline* album) that made it into the top-40, and followed that up with *White Shoes* in

1983 and *The Ballad of Sally Rose* in 1985. Then, in 1987, she had her biggest success with the *Trio* album, which featured Harris alongside Parton and Ronstadt; the record was eventually nominated for the record of the year Grammy (won by U2 for the *Joshua Tree*). Her last significant release of the 1980s, the gospel collection, *Angel Band,* was released the same year. Where Gayle and Harris enjoyed careers into the 1980s, Dottie West, Debby Boone, and Tammy Wynette were at a high point in their careers in the legendary week discussed earlier.

After a few uneventful albums in the late 1970s, Charly McClain gained recognition early in the next decade with her first successful single, the title track to *Who's Cheatin' Who* (1980). She followed that up with the album *Surround Me with Love* (1981), featuring three hits. That same year, she was featured in a special documentary on the HBO cable network, *So You Want to Be a Star,* which portrayed the singer's life while on tour. McClain's next two albums, *Too Good to Hurry* (1982) and *Paradise* (1983), each featured a hit single: "Fly to Your Love" and a widely popular duet with Mickey Gilley, "Paradise Tonight." McClain and Gilley were so pleased with that song's success that they released an album of duets, *It Takes Believers* (1984). McClain's following solo album, *The Woman in Me* (1983), was received with only limited success. After releasing a somewhat disappointing self-titled follow-up album in 1984, she returned to the upper echelon of the country charts with *Radio Heart* (1985). Her success declined after 1986 with the rise of pop-influenced country.

Pop/urban country became a new trend in 1980s' popular music, a backlash against the disco that suffused the pop music scene in the late 1970s, and provided a perfect transition out of the decade. The 1980s was a period where the film industry and country music would become more aligned, starting with the 1980 movie *Urban Cowboy*, starring John Travolta. Its soundtrack included musicians both in and out of the Nashville world: the Eagles, Jimmy Buffett, Joe Walsh, Bonnie Raitt, Dan Fogelberg, Boz Skaggs, Linda Ronstadt, and J. D. Souther. The central location of the movie was Gilley's, a bar owned by mid-level 1970s' country artist Mickey Gilley.

The success of the movie was also a boon to Gilley's career, as it introduced him to a mainstream audience. His cover of "Stand by Me" was a true crossover hit, making both the country and top 40 pop chart. The impact that the movie had on Gilley's recording career resulted in hits from his own album, released the same year. Gilley's follow-up albums, *You Don't Know Me* (1981), and *Put Your Dreams Away* (1983), also received much attention from country listeners. By the mid-1980s, the excitement for Gilley's music, stoked by the success of the *Urban Cowboy* movie, had diminished, but Hollywood's interest in country music continued.

Another key country artist who made an impact on mainstream audiences through movie work was Dolly Parton, who enjoyed a long and historic career in both the country and pop areas. Parton started her career by appearing on *The Porter Wagoner Show* in 1967, a long-running variety show with definitive country flair, and continued to experience critical and commercial success through the 1970s. During the next decade, she also began to make feature films that further featured her country music and brought it to the mainstream public. For example, the eponymous theme song from the 1980 film *9 to 5*, in which she starred with Lily Tomlin and Jane Fonda, went to No. 1 on both the pop and country charts. Additionally, the song was featured on her album *9 to 5 and Odd Jobs* (1980). To solidify her status as a true crossover pop country artist, Parton rerecorded her song "I Will Always Love You" for the soundtrack on another of her movies, *The Best Little Whorehouse in Texas* (1982). She was also featured in *Rhinestone* (1984), where she performed two hits on the film's soundtrack.

By the mid-1980s, Parton had appeared on television and film many times, including Christmas specials. In addition, she became a cultural icon through her flashy fashion sense and platinum blonde hairdo, though Parton has taken her criticism in stride, further cementing her status as authentic country royalty. Pam Wilson (Tichi, 1998, 98) added that Parton "fashioned her star image to accentuate her ample, voluptuously overflowing body, particularly her large breasts, a body image that she has embellished with shiny costumes and an exaggeratedly sculpted blond wig." Thus, for good or ill, few could forget who she was. She also founded the Dollywood theme park in 1986, located in Pigeon Forge, Tennessee, which remains a popular tourist attraction today.

Parton recorded a lot of her own original material in the 1970s, including the first version of "I Will Always Love You," from her 1977 album *Here You Come Again*, which became a significant hit for Whitney Houston in 1992. However, some of her hits during the 1980s were written by others, such as "Starting Over Again" (Donna Summer) and her smash duet with Kenny Rogers, "Islands in the Stream" (the Bee Gees). Her original hits in the 1980s were clearly focused toward crossover success, but she returned to her country roots in her 1982 album, *Heartbreak Express*. Parton also had success on the albums *Real Love* (1985) and *White Limozeen* (1989), as well as the 1987 album *Trio*, with Linda Ronstadt and Emmylou Harris.

Parton's one-time duet partner, Kenny Rogers, had a well-established career at the end of the 1970s, particularly with his 1978 album, *The Gambler*. Throughout the early and mid-1980s, Rogers collaborated with pop writers and producers that exposed him to an even wider audience. Lionel Richie, a pop artist who started with the funk and R&B group the Commodores in the 1970s, produced the single "Lady," which was released on its own, without an album. Moreover, Richie produced Rogers's 1981 album *Share Your Love*. Albums released by Rogers later in the decade included *Love Will Turn You Around* (1982) and *We've Got Tonight* (1983), the last of which included a fan favorite, "You Are So Beautiful," recorded originally by Billy Preston in 1974 and most notably by Joe Cocker in 1975. Another hit song from that latter album was the title track, Rogers's first collaboration with producer David Foster, who later worked with Whitney Houston and Celine Dion. The Bee Gees contributed some songs to Rogers's follow-up album, *What About Me?* Foster returned to the studio with Rogers in 1985 to perform on *Heart of the Matter*, an album produced by George Martin, the Beatles' legendary producer. Although this was a No. 1 country album, it marked the beginning of the decline in Rogers's mainstream popularity, in part because of a new trend that focused on newer country artists.

Juice Newton had moderate success in the 1970s, but her third album, *Juice* (1981), marked the beginning of a newfound popularity in pop country. Four songs effectively allowed her to make the crossover, especially the No. 4 "Angel of the Morning"; the MTV hit "Queen of Hearts" made her an important country artist at the beginning of the decade. This early part of her career helped introduce her, and country music in general, to the MTV audience. Newton maintained her popularity with singles from her following album, *Quiet Lies* (1982), but her next two albums moved further from her country roots, as she began to adopt a sound more rooted in rock, a stylistic change that struggled to win audience recognition. Newton made a comeback in 1985 by returning to her country style on her album *Old Flame.*

Eddie Rabbitt reached commercial pop country success a couple of years before Newton, as he had four hit albums in the 1970s, including the title track to the movie *Every Which Way But Loose,* which jump-started his pop career. He achieved even greater success with his next album, *Horizon* (1980), which featured the immensely popular "I Love a Rainy Night."

Rosanne Cash started the decade with a debut album, *Right or Wrong* (1980), with three successful singles. Her popularity soared with the release of *Seven Year Ache* (1981), featuring "My Baby Thinks He's a Train" and "Blue Moon with a Heartache," as well as the title track, which received considerable crossover attention. Her subsequent albums, *Somewhere in the Stars* (1982) and the pop-influenced *Rhythm & Romance* (1985) and *King's Record Shop* (1987), also were well received, and she released a greatest hits album in 1989 (*Hits 1979–1989*) that got onto the top-10 country chart. Janie Fricke differed from Cash in that she concentrated on recording ballads that would get to the top of the country charts rather than the pop charts. By 1981, the plan worked, placing two ballads in high positions of the singles charts. This began a lucrative period in Fricke's career, with two hits from *Sleeping with Your Memory* (1981) and four from *It Ain't Easy* (1984). Eventually, she began to gain attention with up-tempo songs, continuing her stream of success with the albums *Love Lies* (1983) and *The First Word in Memory* (1984), the latter with the single "Your Heart's Not in It." Fricke released *Somebody Else's Fire* in 1985 and *Black & White,* featuring the hit "Always Have, Always Will" in 1986. Her subsequent albums later in the decade failed to enjoy the same level of success.

Although the majority of country artists have been solo singers performing material written by professional songwriters, there were also a number of country groups during the 1980s. These groups are generally divided into two categories: vocal groups, commonly quartets, influenced by sacred music; and string bands leaning toward the bluegrass tradition. The Oak Ridge Boys were one of the most successful of the former in the 1970s, and they also had some success into the mid-1980s. While the group had focused on gospel music since they began in the mid-1940s, the Oak Ridge Boys switched to a secular emphasis in the 1970s, with some success. Their most famous song, "Elvira," was released in 1980, and its success made their sixth album, *Fancy Free,* the commercial pinnacle of their career. The album also featured the title track as a single. Their following albums, *Bobbie Sue* (1982) and *American Made* (1983), were crossover successes as well, and the title track of the latter was used in a

Miller beer advertisement, exposing the group (and vocal country groups in general) to an even greater mainstream audience. Their string of hits continued with *Deliver* (1983) and *Step On Out* (1985).

The Statler Brothers followed a path similar in their career to the Oak Ridge Boys. The group formed in the 1950s, released albums to critical acclaim throughout the 1970s, and maintained their fan base via strong-selling releases through the 1980s. The group released *10th Anniversary* (1980), *Years Ago* (1981), *The Legend Goes On* (1982), *Today* (1983), *Atlanta Blue* (1984), *Pardners in Rhyme* (1985), *Four for the Show* (1986), and *Maple Street Memories* (1987). However, by the end of the decade, they too were swept up in the changes that were occurring in the Nashville music industry that favored younger artists.

Alabama came from the same type of background as the Oak Ridge Boys and the Statler Brothers, but they had little success with any of the music they released in the 1970s. However, their career exploded in the 1980s, as they recorded no less than 27 No. 1 singles throughout the decade. *My Home's in Alabama* (1980) began the stream of top-selling albums, followed by *Feels So Right* (1981) and *Mountain Music* (1982). In the mid-1980s, Alabama took full advantage of the new country music video channels Country Music Television (CMT) and The Nashville Network (TNN) to gain a firm hold as the most popular country artist of the decade. *The Closer You Get* (1983), *Roll On* (1984), *40 Hour Week* (1985), *Seasons* (1986), *The Touch* (1987), and *Southern Star* (1988) continued their hold on the charts.

Nashville record producer Tim DuBois and Scott Hendricks created Restless Heart in 1984 to record songs that they had been writing, in a style that Colin Larkin (2006, 860) described as "a latter day Eagles." Eventually, the group (which was still nameless at that time) signed to RCA Records on the strength of their music. Restless Heart released their self-titled debut album with four singles, followed by the albums *Wheels* (1986) and *Big Dreams in a Small Town*, (1988) both featuring hit singles. In contrast to Restless Heart, Sawyer Brown did not emerge from the Nashville music scene, but rather suburban Orlando. They had won the 1980s reality talent show competition *Star Search,* which led to a contract with Curb Records. They put out three albums that were commercial hits: *Sawyer Brown* (1985), *Somewhere in the Night* (1987), and *The Boys Are Back* (1989).

In a 1985 *New York Times* article, "Nashville Sound: Blues for Country Music," Robert Palmer discussed what he considered was the current state of country music. It took a very negative tone, focusing on the pop country of the early 1980s and ignoring any new country. As a result, the article revitalized the country music industry by bringing attention to newer artists. The cable channels TNN and CMT helped raise the profile of several attractive performers, including Randy Travis and John Schneider, an actor on *The Dukes of Hazzard*. Ultimately, Travis and other artists were signed by younger industry executives, who were reacting to what was perceived as a bland mainstream popularity that artists were achieving via the general public's acceptance of urban country.

This neotraditionalism looked to the established leaders of old country music, such as Hank Williams, Jr., Ernest Tubb, and Kitty Wells, for inspiration.

The mid-1980s became a time where country music embraced its older roots. Classic country material, as well as carefully crafted vocal delivery, helped bring neotraditionalism to the forefront of country music in this period. This type of music became very popular during the 1980s and 1990s, but with time, a pop-rock approach to country became more favorable. Essentially, there were two types of neotraditionalists in the early 1980s: the cowboy with a rugged sex appeal, and the mountain man who came from a bluegrass background but had the performance skills of the best side musicians in both the studio and live performances. George Strait became the best example of the former in the 1980s and Ricky Skaggs the latter.

George Strait released the album *Strait from the Heart* in 1982, which produced more No. 1 songs than any album in country music history and included his first one, "Fool-Hearted Memory." The 1980s were also the time when the music business in Nashville started to be run by outsiders (namely, executives from Los Angeles and New York City). As a result, younger artists were promoted more than older, established artists, giving Nashville a new sound, and eventually, established artists such as Dolly Parton, Johnny Cash, and Ernest Tubb saw their contracts dropped. When Strait emerged, his record company encouraged him to embrace the pop country look that had been popular in the earlier part of the decade, but he wanted to maintain a traditional country music and visual style. His music featured swing and two-step rhythms (the latter popularized in line-dancing bars) and love ballads. One way that Strait differed from pop country artists is that he shunned media attention; also, compared to a 1970s' outlaw country artist, his song topics were less vulgar than the older honky-tonk approach. As a result, Strait had a slick quality shared by many 1980s' pop artists.

Randy Travis came from the same neotraditionalist background as Strait, demonstrated especially on his 1986 album *Storms of Life*, the first debut country album to sell one million copies. Like Strait, Travis lacked the hard-drinking, honky-tonk elements of outlaw country artists, but unlike Strait, he personified a traditional country style. Travis's biggest hit, "Forever and Ever, Amen," was on his next album, *Always and Forever* (1987). He continued in the neotraditionalist style on *Old 8x10* (1988) and his last album during the 1980s, *No Holdin' Back* (1989).

In the first two years of the decade, John Anderson released three albums, *John Anderson, John Anderson 2*, and *I Just Came Home to Count the Memories*, but without a great deal of sustainable success. But the title track of his fourth album, *Wild & Blue* (1982), became a No. 1 country hit, and another song, "Swingin'," enabled him to gain moderate popularity for the first time in the country mainstream. Anderson's neotraditionalist sound has what Kingsbury (1998, 13) has described as "a distinct and modern quality while remaining firmly rooted in the honky-tonk music styles of the 1950s." Ricky Van Shelton released his debut album, *Wild-Eyed Dream*, in 1987, with a style influenced by rockabilly. His follow-up albums, *Loving Proof* (1988) and *RVS III* (1990), each spawned successful singles in the beginning of the 1990s.

Reba McEntire took longer than some artists to have a No. 1 hit. She had released six albums with her old label from 1976 until 1983 on Mercury Records that often featured McEntire singing ballads, but she only started to find success with her second album for MCA Records. *My Kind of Country* (1984) featured the hits "How Blue" and "Somebody Should Leave." Her turnaround was fueled in part by how she and her music were produced (with songs that were more upbeat, with fewer ballads) and marketed (with a new record company, MCA). Her *Best of Reba McEntire* album, featuring an upbeat on the song "Can't Even Get the Blues," resulted in McEntire's first No. 1 hit. The albums that followed made McEntire the most popular female country recording artist of the decade. She released two albums in 1986, *Whoever's in New England* and *What Am I Gonna Do About You*, followed by *The Last One to Know* (1987), featuring the hits "Love Will Find Its Way to You," as well as the title track. One common thread in her music was that she wrote from a scorned woman's perspective, which made it easier for the influx of female country artists in the 1990s, including Shania Twain and Faith Hill.

Steve Wariner released his debut album, *Down in Tennessee*, in 1978, but the country public met the album with a lukewarm response. He then released a series of singles on their own (i.e., not on full albums) before he finally got the chance to reestablish himself as a promising artist. It came via his self-titled album (1980), which included three hit singles, while his next album, *Midnight Fire* (1983), had two highlighted singles, "Midnight Fire" and "Lonely Women Make Good Lovers." Wariner's true pinnacle period began when he released *One Good Night Deserves Another* (1984), which featured top singles. His success continued with *Life's Highway* (1986), *It's a Crazy World* (1987), and *I Should Be with You* (1988), and *I Got Dreams* (1989) ended his run of mainstream success that made him among the most popular country artists of the 1980s.

Earl Thomas Conley started recording for the independent label GRT Records and released a few singles in the early 1970s, but he failed to gain traction in the industry. Eventually, he signed a new record contract with Warner Brothers and put out singles from his debut *Blue Pearl* (1979), but still with little fanfare. However, *Fire and Smoke* (1981) kicked off a series of accomplished albums that included *Somewhere Between Right and Wrong* (1982) and the top-selling *Don't Make It Easy For Me* (1983). Conley also released *Water* (1984) and a greatest hits album in 1985 that also included two new hits. He released *Too Many Times* (1986), which featured a surprise appearance by Anita Pointer of the R&B/pop group the Pointer Sisters for the duet on the title track. That No. 2 country hit ultimately led Conley to an appearance on the TV show *Soul Train*, making him the only country artist to be featured on this show geared to the African American community. Conley's final album of the decade, *The Heart of It All* (1988), featured four hit singles.

The historical significance of bluegrass has established it as a traditionalist style in country. Bluegrass, in the words of Neil Rosenberg (1985, 3), is "music in which singers accompany themselves with acoustic rather than electric instruments, using the fiddle, mandolin, guitar, five-string banjo, Dobro and bass." This opinion stands on solid ground, as by using acoustic instrumentation, this music is among the most authentic of all genres, not just country music. Lester Flatt, Earl Scruggs, and the Foggy Mountain Boys were a bluegrass group that performed from the mid-1940s until the 1970s. The group's influence was given a 1980s' twist with the addition of Ricky Skaggs, who focused on becoming a top bluegrass guitarist in the Flatt and Scruggs tradition as he grew up in Kentucky. After years of performing with Emmylou Harris, the multitalented instrumentalist released an album that highlighted his bluegrass influence, *Waitin' for the Sun to Shine* (1981). This album represented the beginning of a period of popularity that lasted throughout the 1980s. Skaggs followed up with *Highways and Heartaches* (1982), *Don't Cheat in Our Hometown* (1983), *Country Boy* (1984), *Love's Gonna Get Ya!* (1986), *Comin' Home to Stay* (1987), and *Kentucky Thunder* (1989). All of his albums feature a more traditional sound than that of the pop country artists that saturated the record charts. As a result, Skaggs kept an element of old country, now known as "neo-traditionalist" as described previously, before country listeners. Skaggs has claimed on his website that legendary guitarist and producer Chet Atkins had even gone as far as to claim that Skaggs was "single-handedly saving country music."

Patty Loveless came from an Appalachian and honky-tonk influence but incorporated rockabilly for a different type of sound. This approach was likely because of her extensive touring as a country rock performer in the bar circuit during the 1970s. Although Loveless initially left her home in Kentucky for Nashville in the 1970s and had been working steadily since then, she returned from her touring in 1986 and convinced her brother, Roger Ramey, to record a demo to reintroduce her to record company executives. Loveless initially focused on releasing singles; after her single "I Did" started to make headway on country radio, her record company rewarded her with a new contract to release full albums. Her self-titled debut (1986), *If My Heart Had Windows* (1987), and *Honky Tonk Angel* (1988) each included top singles. Kathy Mattea was influenced by folk music and southern California country rock rather than just bluegrass as Loveless was, but her use of an acoustic guitar also gave her music a mountain style.

The new, younger record company executives that came from outside Nashville wanted to make country artists more appealing to rock fans. Steve Earle was one of these artists, though his style could certainly be considered as fitting into the neotraditionalist vein. Earle started as a songwriter in Nashville, releasing some rockabilly-influenced recordings, including *Guitar Town* (1986) and *Exit O* (1987), but did not gain significant mainstream attention until the mid-1990s after a period of drug-fueled strife in his personal life.

Dwight Yoakam represented the new style of country that was sought after by these new executives—a genre that embraced older, traditional country symbols, including clothes and lifestyle, including cowboy hats, boots, jeans, women, whiskey, and hard living. Yoakum's *Guitars, Cadillacs, Etc., Etc.* (1986) contributed to the rise of neotraditionalism. On his album, *Hillbilly Deluxe* (1988), the honky tonk scenario is particularly important for his neotraditionalist image, as a honky tonk tavern is often seen as a drinking location for a hypermasculine patron. Yoakum's first No. 1 hits came from *Buenas Noches from A Lonely Room* (1988), including a duet with Bakersfield country legend Buck Owens that further endeared him to a neotraditionalist audience. Yoakum had some success in the 1990s, but his only No. 1 hits were in the 1980s.

Chuck Morris, a music industry insider, discovered North Dakota native Paulette Carlson in Nashville; he established a group that featured her called Highway 101. The group had some success in the 1980s, beginning with four singles from their debut album (*Highway 101*, 1987), followed by their second album, also self-titled. Three singles came from their third album, *Paint the Town* (1989). After the release of a greatest hits album in 1990, Carlson left the band, leading to the group's demise. Following Highway 101's lead, other groups emerged in the mid- to late 1980s, each with a background in rock music. Shenandoah released their debut album in 1987, featuring two singles. It was in 1989 that they became established as an important country group, as their second album *The Road Not Taken* featured six successful singles.

Family ensembles were also emerging in the late 1980s. Sweethearts of the Rodeo, featuring sisters Janice and Christine Oliver, hailed from Los Angeles, and they experienced a rapid rise and fall. Named for the 1968 album by the rock group the Byrds, Sweethearts of the Rodeo released their self-titled debut album in 1986; their next album, *One Time, One Night*, marked the end of their popularity, though they released two more albums after that. Featuring lead singer Naomi Judd and her daughter Wynonna, who also sang lead, but played the guitar and harmonica as well, the Judds were one of the most successful groups of the 1980s, with 14 No. 1 hits between 1984 and 1991, when Naomi retired because of complications with hepatitis C. The Judds' style was rooted in neotraditionalism; their first album included "traditional country harmony singing, and the arrangements emphasized acoustic instruments without too much clutter" (Carlin, 2010, 210). The duo's debut, *Wynonna & Naomi* (1983), achieved moderate acclaim, but their true run of success began with their 1984 album *Why Not Me*. The group's follow-ups, *Rockin' with the Rhythm* (1985) and *Heartland* (1987), featured four more successful singles each. They followed up that album with a 1988 greatest hits album, *River of Time* (1989), and *Love Can Build a Bridge* (1990), each of which also had successful singles. Yet, as effective and numerous as these vocal groups were, a smaller portion of artists in the bluegrass tradition made important contributions to the country style of the period.

NEW YORK MUSICALS

The music theater landscape has largely been associated with the Broadway circuit in New York City, with only select performances by a touring company that would visit the rest of the country, unlike the music in other areas (such as Nashville for country, and Hollywood for hard rock in the 1980s). There are financial limitations that restrict the amount of touring that a company can undertake, and even when a production has sufficient financial backing, its touring goes only to the largest cities, so its audiences are often limited to those who can afford the high ticket prices. This discussion will primarily include groups performing in New York City, both on and off Broadway.

Ethan Morddan (2004, 210) opined that musical theater's golden age ended in the 1970s, and the composers during that age "knew what people were. They knew life." In this context, Morddan was referring to real-life situations, in contrast to the writers in the 1980s, who were influenced by pop music, politics, language, and ideas. The strength of a musical has always been its story, referred to as the *book*. The book was important even before the 1980s; the creators of the classic musicals (like Rodgers and Hammerstein) relied on a strong story in the tradition of the operatic librettist, who traditionally wrote a compelling story while the composer wrote music that supported it. Jessica Sternfeld (2006, 3) has noted that the mega-musical was "not just big inside the theater; it is big outside it as well. New megamusicals, especially in the 1980s, were cultural events marketed with unprecedented force." Sternfeld is correct; this new, all-encompassing entertainment package, sold to those outside the usual audience, suited these productions from the 1980s well. As the focus on the entertainment aspect of the musical moved toward the elaborate and theatrical, with the high level of excess demanded by 1980s audiences, it is not surprising that composers wanted to reinvent ideas from the classics to help counter the weak stories (such as for *Into the Light* and *Bring Back Birdie*) that had emerged in the years prior.

Written by Harry Warren and Al Dubin, *42nd Street* offered songs that were known to many in the audience, such as "We're in the Money" and "42nd Street." This comforting familiarity made the musical more accessible than newer productions. The release of *42nd Street* made obvious that in the years just before this, live musicals had been gradually scaling back their productions. The sheer size of *42nd Street* marked a return to the broad productions established on Broadway years before. Another success of the early 1980s was *Barnum* (which opened at the St. James Theatre in 1980). The book, by Mark Bramble, focused on the legendary 19th-century showman P. T. Barnum. Highlighting the music was the unconventional staging by Joe Layton, which featured circus acrobats on stage performing *while* singing—quite a difficult feat.

Given the level of success of *42nd Street*, it seemed fitting that another musical used an existing work of art as its inspiration: *Cats* This was among the most popular musicals on Broadway in the 1980s and ran for 18 years (for a while, it was the longest-running musical in history). It provided a showcase for music by Andrew Lloyd Webber, lyrics that Tim Rice based on poems in T. S. Eliot's *Old Possum's Book of Practical Cats*, and additional lyrics by Trevor Nunn. Whereas *Cats* featured an impressive dance troupe, *Starlight Express* (premiering on Broadway in 1987) took stage movement to a whole new level: the entire cast performed on roller skates. Because of the skating, the action had great energy and took on a revue feel. A similar characteristic with *Cats* is that each story lacked much of a central plot. One important way that *Starlight Express* differed from *Cats*, however, was its approach. For that show, Webber aimed for a tone firmly rooted not in pop opera, but with popular music of the last half of the 20th century.

From then on, the budgets for musicals, including those by Webber, soared to astronomical heights. Derived from Gaston Leroux's novel *Le Fantôme de l'*

Opéra, *The Phantom of the Opera* had a budget of $8 million, so financial success was more important (and more difficult) to achieve than ever before. Webber's musical undertaking for *Phantom* differed from his other works, in that the melodies were more adventurous.

But this show was about more than the music. One important element that contributed to the high budget came at the climax of the first act, when a chandelier crashes to the stage. Highly effective in an era where excess was practically a given, the chandelier effect seemed to have more of an impact than any of the music. *Phantom of the Opera* epitomized excess—and found great profit in doing so (in fact, it supplanted *Cats* as the longest-running musical in 2006, and continues to run to this day). It became apparent that opulent visual effects were worth the investment. The higher prices that patrons were charged could easily be seen in the elaborate set, costumes, and effects—audiences clearly seemed to feel the satisfaction of getting value for their ticket price.

Many theatergoers during this decade were not consistent fans of Broadway, but rather visitors to New York who were willing—nay, eager—to pay as much as $50 for a single ticket. This price was astronomical compared to previous prices. For example, during the 1977–1978 season, a theater patron could view *The Act* from the most expensive seat for a mere $25. By the end of the decade, however, the top ticket price was $100 for *Miss Saigon* (1989), another megamusical. The break-even point for *Miss Saigon*, as established by the show's producer, Cameron Mackintosh, eclipsed $10 million—$2 million more than *Phantom of the Opera*. *Les Miserables* (which opened at the Broadway Theater in 1987) continued the 1980s' tradition of looking to the past for a musical's story. Originally written in the late 19th century by dramatist/poet Victor Hugo, the story chronicles the lives of French characters over 20 years following Napoleon Bonaparte's final defeat and subsequent fall from power.

As musical theater became more mainstream on Broadway, the appeal of going to see a show became a priority to patrons beyond the seasoned theater fan. As a result, these new audiences flocked to theaters in search of spectacle, glitz, and bombast. In turn, producers backed these kinds of shows, investing far more money in their budgets than they ever had in the past. Eventually, though, the audience realized that spectacle alone does not always make a show great, and by the end of the decade, a number of ill-received "busts" were scattered along Broadway.

FURTHER READING

Azerrad, M. *Our Band Could Be Your Life.* Boston: Back Bay Books, 2001.

Bordman, G. *American Musical Theatre,* 2d ed. New York: Oxford University Press, 1992.

Buckley, D. *R.E.M.: Fiction: An Alternative Biography.* London: Virgin Books, 2002.

Cantwell, R. *Bluegrass Breakdown: The Making of the Old Southern Sound.* New York: Da Capo Press, 1992.

Carlin, R. *Country Music.* New York: Routledge, 2003.

Ching, B. *Wrong's What I Do Best.* New York: Oxford University Press, 2001.

Chivers, C. J. *Van Halen Encyclopedia.* Lincoln, NE: IUniverse, 2001.

Cobb, W. *To the Break of Dawn: A Freestyle on the Hip Hop Aesthetic.* New York: New York University Press, 2006.

Fricke, D. (January 27, 1994). "Kurt Cobain, The Rolling Stone Interview: Success Doesn't Suck." Accessed April 4, 2017, from http://www.rollingstone.com/music/news/kurt-cobain-the-rolling-stone-interview-19940127.

Fox, P. *Natural Acts.* Ann Arbor, MI: University of Michigan Press, 2009.

Ganzl, K. *Encyclopedia of Music Theater.* 2d ed. New York: Schirmer, 2001.

Garafalo, R. *Rockin' Out.* 5th ed. Upper Saddle River, NJ: Pearson, 2011.

George-Warren, H., P. Romanowski, and J. Pareles. *The Rolling Stone Encyclopedia of Rock & Roll (Revised and Updated for the 21st Century).* New York: Fireside, 2001.

Hess, M., ed. *Hip Hop in America: A Regional Guide.* Santa Barbara, CA: Greenwood Press, 2010.

Keyes, C. *Rap Music and Street Consciousness.* Urbana, IL: University of Illinois Press, 2004.

Kingsbury, P. *The Encyclopedia of Country Music.* New York: Oxford University Press, 1998.

Kulkarni, N. *Hip Hop: Bring the Noise.* New York: Thunder's Mouth Press, 2004.

Larkin, C., ed. *The Encyclopedia of Popular Music, Fourth Edition.* New York: Oxford, 2006.

Light, A. *The Vibe History of Hip Hop.* New York: Three Rivers Press, 1999.

Tannebaum, R., and C. Marks. *I Want My MTV.* New York: Plume, 2012.

Morddan, E. *The Happiest Corpse I've Ever Seen.* Hampshire, UK: Palgrave Macmillan, 2004.

Reynolds, S. *Rip It Up and Start Again: Postpunk 1978–1984.* Upper Saddle River, NJ: Pearson/Penguin Books, 2005.

Rosenberg, N. *Bluegrass.* Urbana, IL: University of Illinois Press, 1985.

Sternfeld, J. *The Megamusical.* Bloomington, IN: Indiana University Press, 2006.

Tichi, C., ed. *Reading Country Music.* Durham, NC: Duke University Press, 1998.

CHAPTER 4

Film

Feature films have been one of the most impactful areas of popular culture for decades. They have the ability to transform viewers back or forward in time, into different worlds they have not seen before, or to act as a chronicle of situations that are relevant to a generation of viewers. The movies made during the 1980s, for a 1980s' audience, also enable today's viewers to transport themselves virtually (if only temporarily) to an era of their past that was not initially made as a historical statement. So long as there are moving pictures that are synchronized with dialogue, music, and sound effects, the ability of filmmakers to tell compelling stories is endless. The films of the 1980s have the potential to be among the classics of the genre, but more importantly, they also serve as a statement of the mentality of American society during that decade.

ACTION/CRIME/GANGSTER

Top Gun was a significant box office success after its 1986 release, generating $270 million in revenue in theaters and an additional $50 million in sales for home video, while it cost only $17.5 million to produce. The film also marked the commercial rise of Tom Cruise, who, as Maverick, is an undisciplined pilot at the Fighter Weapons School at Miramar, the facility where the best pilots are trained to be "Top Guns." Alongside co-pilot Goose (Anthony Edwards), Maverick is one of the competitive pilots looking for statistical success of virtual "kills" over rival pilot "Iceman" (Val Kilmer). Along the way, Maverick falls in love with his flight instructor, Charlie (Kelly McGillis). Tragically, Maverick kills Goose in an airplane crash during a training exercise; however, Maverick pulls his discipline together and graduates from the school. He eventually gets into a dogfight with the Russians (which he wins, of course). Critics such as Jürgen Muller (1994, 418) remarked that the film featured a "flimsy and cliché-ridden story," where Cruise was the "perfect combination of seclusion and aggression, a character whose physical make-up seems to crave action and military posturing." The film, as well as its successful soundtrack, was a neat fit for the political climate of the 1980s, when the United States was at the height of the Cold War with the Soviet Union.

Predator (1987) featured Arnold Schwarzenegger as the leader of a Special Forces team whose mission is to save hostages from Central American guerrilla fighters. What seemed to be a simple rescue mission soon becomes a fight between an alien-type creature, the Predator, and the Special Forces. The Predator is armed with a plasma-powered cannon, an experimental weapon that uses plasma, and not chemicals, as the means of launching a heavy projectile via high voltage. The film featured actors known for their physiques, including Schwarzenegger (as Dutch

Tom Cruise became one of the most popular actors of the 1980s with films such as *The Outsiders* (1983), as Maverick (pictured here) in *Top Gun* (1986), and *Rain Man* (1988). Cruise has continued to be a successful film star well into the 21st century. (Paramount Pictures/Photofest)

Schaefer), Carl Weathers (as George Dillon), and former professional wrestler Jesse Ventura (as Blaine Cooper). Elpidia Carrillo is Anna, a female guerilla who can fight right alongside the men. The special effects and makeup played a central role in the effectiveness of the film. Although the plot of the film is somewhat lacking, the action and excitement between the Predator and the Special Forces led to three sequels.

Rocky III (1982) and *Rocky IV* (1985) continued the series of films about a Philadelphia boxer, Rocky Balboa (Sylvester Stallone), which began in the late 1970s. Unlike the first two films, where Rocky was a struggling fighter, *Rocky III* highlights him as the heavyweight champion of the world, with considerable money, who has been fighting soft opponents. After initially agreeing to retire, Rocky is challenged by the up-and-comer Clubber Lang (Mr. T), who overpowers each opponent. After Rocky loses his fight to Lang, he undergoes a total transformation to become the fighter he once was. The reinvention is because of his new trainer, his former opponent Apollo Creed (Carl Weathers), who coaches him to regain what he describes as the "Eye of the Tiger." The attitude of redeeming yourself by working hard parallels 1980s' society; and another significant aspect of the movie is that it is the African American from the streets of Los Angeles who helps bring the Caucasian back to his own working-class roots. The two work together, reinforcing the biracial buddy vibe that developed in the 1980s' films. *Rocky IV* gives the series a different storyline, with a new antagonist, Ivan Drago (Dolph Lundgren), arriving from the Soviet Union. Drago, engineered to be a 6'5" fighting machine by the Soviet government, initially comes to the United States to fight Creed in an exhibition. After Drago kills Creed in the ring, Rocky travels to Drago's homeland and refocuses his training to fight Drago to avenge the loss of his friend. Since the Cold War was a significant part of the 1980s, the storyline of a U.S. hero against the evil Soviet was easily and readily digestible by American moviegoers. However, Rocky remarks at the end of the film how change and understanding are important to both countries and him personally.

Stallone was featured in a mildly successful war film, *Escape to Victory* (1981), but the release of *First Blood* (1982) really established Stallone as something other than Rocky Balboa. Stallone played the iconic character of John Rambo, a Vietnam veteran and Special Forces fighter, a hard-bodied defender of values of democracy and family against hostile enemies in Third World countries. As Rambo goes to visit an old Vietnam comrade dying of cancer in the Pacific Northwest, he is arrested for vagrancy. As the police mistreat him, he begins to have flashbacks to his Vietnam experiences, breaks away after beating a police-man, and then starts to fight with law enforcement authorities. Rambo is an antihero—the flip side of the Rocky character—but audiences related to him anyway.

As in the *Rocky* series, Stallone became indelibly associated with the charac-ter, and he did a number of sequels, including *Rambo: First Blood II* (1985) and *Rambo III* (1986). *Rambo: First Blood II* shifts from Rambo being sought after by the authorities, as in the first movie, to him becoming a government operative trying to rescue prisoners of war (POWs) left behind in Vietnam. Though directed to avoid confrontation by his superior, the inevitable occurs, and Rambo fights both Vietnamese and Soviet soldiers throughout the conflict. Eventually, he confronts his superior about hiding the truth of the POWs' fate from the public. *Rambo III* features the hero fighting in Afghanistan at the request of a former superior, Colonel Samuel Trautman (Richard Crenna). Trautman is eventually captured, and Rambo saves his friend. Through the success of these films, Stallone became a true Hollywood star. His physique and persona as a strong, resilient achiever made him a fan favorite.

Die Hard (1988) was another hit that featured a strong male lead and spawned several successful sequels. In that sense, *Die Hard* was similar to the *Rocky* films, *Lethal Weapon,* and *48 Hrs.* In the opinion of Chris Jordan (2003, 70) these films were "about strong and honest working-class white men who restore a culture of classlessness by vanquishing corrupt and greedy aristo-crats who threaten meritocracy, even though the characterization of them as natural aristocrats simultaneously defines them as champions of individual rights." What separated the film's star, Bruce Willis, from actors in similar films was his sensitivity and vulnerability, which ultimately won over people who didn't usually care to watch action movies. Willis plays John McClane, a New York Police Department (NYPD) officer trying to save attendees of a corporate Christmas party (including his own estranged wife and children), who have been taken hostage by terrorists. The head terrorist, Hans Gruber (Alan Rickman), is interested in stealing gold and securities stored in Nakatomi Plaza, owned by the party's host, the Nakatomi Corporation. The contrast between the well-spoken, erudite (or even snobby) German terrorist and the everyman cop enhanced McClane's appeal; he was even more heroic in that he had to take on the terrorists by himself—which enhanced his sex appeal, too.

Lethal Weapon (1987) and its successor, *Lethal Weapon 2* (1989), featured a strong central character similar to McClane, in the somewhat reckless cop Martin Riggs (Mel Gibson). However, the dynamic between Gibson and fellow cop/family man Roger Murtaugh (Danny Glover) was even more interesting. Glover, an African American, and the Caucasian Gibson are paired up in the first movie, where they investigate a suicide/possible homicide of a daughter of one of Murtaugh's friends from the times that he was in the Special Forces. The daughter, Amanda, had fallen into a life of drugs and prostitution before her death. In the sequel, *Lethal Weapon 2*, the partners work to catch a gang of South African criminals (during the time of apartheid—see the introduction to this book for more on that issue) who operate a money-laundering enterprise through the South African consulate in the United States. Murtaugh also jokes about Riggs's sexual abilities as a Caucasian even as he defends him against shooters. The biracial relationship of the two buddies highlights not only the ways that they work together, but also the role that each character plays (the African American as the responsible one, in this case) during the movie. Murtaugh, a father of three, is interested in preserving life, while Riggs, who we learn is troubled by the accidental death of his wife, is quick to pull a gun on their enemies. In a plot twist, the partners learn that the root of the problem lies in a drug-smuggling operation founded by a special unit during the Vietnam War. Both partners become the target of the smugglers, and the banter between the two highlights their buddy relationship as they work together to save each other. Like many action films, *Lethal Weapon* and *Lethal Weapon 2* featured many explosions and chase scenes that became staples of the 1980s.

The Untouchables (1986) pits a team of policemen against the legendary gangster Al Capone (Robert De Niro) in a thriller loosely based on real life. Department of Prohibition agent Eliot Ness (Kevin Costner) and policeman Jim Malone (Sean Connery), working alongside George Stone (Andy Garcia) and Oscar Wallace (Charles Martin Smith) against the Prohibition-era gangsters in Chicago, run into obstacles trying to tame the mob's illegal activities. The group starts to gain a reputation for their ability to fight the gangsters, and the press nickname them "the Untouchables." Malone interrogates Capone's accountant in a ruthless manner, to the point of shooting the body of another gangster that had already been killed in order to intimidate him.

Capone henchman Frank Nitti (Billy Drago) infiltrates the police station, eventually killing Wallace and George in an elevator; in a final sadistic touch, he writes "touchable" in blood next to the bodies. This event causes Ness to confront a mocking Capone; however, they only manage to catch up with him through an investigation of his tax records, which revealed that he had not filed for a number of years. That technicality allows Capone to be arrested. Nitti goes to Capone's trial, armed with a handgun, and tries to escape after Ness identifies him as Malone's killer. Ultimately, Capone is convicted and given an 11-year sentence for tax evasion.

Few gangster movies before the 1982 release of *Scarface* had such an intense level of violence. The movie was significantly more violent than earlier popular gangster movies, such as *The Godfather* and its sequel, *The Godfather, Part II.* The central character in the *Godfather* series is an immigrant from Italy, the main character in *Scarface* is a Cuban immigrant, and both are criminals; however, the similarities stop there. Tony Montana (Al Pacino, who also starred in the *Godfather* films) is an aggressive drug lord, whose violent actions in the final scene of the movie are what make the film so memorable. A remake of Howard Hawks's 1932 version of the story, *Scarface: Shame of a Nation*, this version, set in Miami, highlights the desire for money and power that was typical of the 1980s. In the age of "just say no," Montana's drug-driven life drove him out of control; unlike the *Godfather* series, this film was not about family, but the love of excess. What complicates his actions is that he ultimately destroys everything that he truly cares about, including the family and the wealth that he acquired.

Highlander (1986) tells the tale of immortals who have been fighting since the 16th century. The conflicts begin in Scotland, with a disagreement between the clans McLeod and Fraser. The Clan Fraser decides to kill the main McLeod member, Connor (Christopher Lambert), by hiring a mercenary called the Kurgan (Clancy Brown), who becomes Connor's enemy for centuries. Connor assumes aliases, fakes his own death (multiple times), and then takes the identities of his dead children, who died as infants. The immortals must keep fighting until the loser is decapitated, century after century, until the last one standing receives "the Prize," the ability to control humans via slavery.

The film moves back and forth in time between 1985 and the 16th century. The immortal Juan-Sanchez Villa-Lobos Ramirez (Sean Connery) meets with McLeod to convince him that no one should win the Prize, or else humanity will enter a dark period. The action starts in 1985 with a fight at the beginning of the film in a parking garage, with the immortal Iman Fasil. Policewoman Brenda Wyatt (Roxanne Hart) investigates the fight; Wyatt is familiar with the type of sword that Fasil used. Wyatt befriends McLeod, and after she discovers McLeod's immortality, they become romantically involved. Kurgan kidnaps Wyatt in order to get access to McLeod. Within time, McLeod and Kurgan fight to win the Prize. *Highlander* differed from other fantasy films, either before or of the time, by switching between the 16th century and the present day, with characters wearing period-specific attire in each era.

Once Upon a Time in America (1983) is another film that chronicles a story over many years, though in this case, it is not two periods in two centuries, but rather three distinct periods in time over a few decades. The central character, David "Noodles" Aaronson (Robert De Niro), is a poor, Jewish teenager. He is part of a gang in 1920s-era New York City, the first part of the chronological story. Noodles and his three friends work for an older boy, Bugsy, but after meeting Max Bercovicz (James Woods), Noodles is convinced to join him in their own venture, selling liquor on the black market during Prohibition. This starts a long friendship/partnership. Bugsy does not like the idea, as he is being cut out of the profits, so he kills the youngest member of Noodles's new gang. As Noodles tries to exact revenge, he stabs a policeman and goes to prison for 10 years. Upon his release, Noodles, now an adult, rejoins his former gang. Their escapades, which make up the second chronological part of the film, have broadened to include robbery, prostitution, and alcohol smuggling. Eventually, Max and Noodles's relationship sours. The third period of the chronological story shows Noodles later in life, reminiscing about the old days while struggling with an opium habit. In the words of Jürgen Muller (223), *Once Upon a Time in America* is "not just a tale of friendship or a homage to classic gangster movies, it also sheds light on the dark side of the American Dream." The characters are not overtly violent, as in *Scarface,* nor are they passionate about family, as seen in the *Godfather* series. Rather, they are hardened businessmen in an illegal trade.

The Karate Kid (1984) featured a teenager who had just moved to California from New Jersey to live with his mother in a small apartment. After the teen, Daniel LaRusso (Ralph Macchio), starts to flirt with Ali Mills (Elisabeth Shue), he is bullied by the girl's boyfriend, Johnny Lawrence (William Zabka). Johnny practices Cobra Kai, an aggressive form of karate, under the mentorship of John Kreese (Martin Kove). When Johnny and his Cobra Kai gang assault Daniel, Kesuke Miyagi (Pat Morita), the handyman in Daniel's apartment building, rescues him, fighting off the five attackers in an impressive display of karate. Daniel then asks Mr. Miyagi to train him. When Miyagi confronts Kreese to try to stop his gang from harassing Daniel, Kreese responds that Daniel needs to prove he can beat his students. Mr. Miyagi responds with a challenge: Daniel will participate in an upcoming karate tournament against Johnny and his teammates. If Daniel should win, the bullies will agree to stop harassing him. The unspoken part of that deal is that if he loses or fails to show up, both Mr. Miyagi and Daniel will be tormented by the gang. Mr. Miyagi proceeds to teach Daniel karate, as well as becoming his mentor in general. Chris Jordan (2003, 67) considered that "*The Karate Kid* focuses on underdogs who achieve class transcendence through their redemptive embrace of a culture considered exotic as it is removed from typical Caucasian culture." The younger apprentice looks to the elder Asian mentor for wisdom and training. In time, Daniel becomes an expert in karate, even learning a pose called the Crane, which helps him win the tournament (and he gets the girl, too).

Batman (1989) features the fabled comic book character, whose wealthy parents were killed when he was a child, so he was raised by his family's butler. When he grows up, he becomes a hero who commits his life to fighting crime in Gotham City. *Batman* had also been a very successful television show in the late 1960s (which was rerun frequently throughout the 1970s); but thanks to the storytelling of director Tim Burton, the movie version as a whole more resembled a futuristic comic book with live actors than it did the rather campy show. In this version, Michael Keaton plays the billionaire Bruce Wayne, whose alter ego is the famed superhero. Batman's exploits (and eventually Bruce Wayne himself) attract the interest of photojournalist Vicki Vale (Kim Basinger).

Jürgen Muller (1994, 186) remarked that *Batman* "tells the story of a duel between two quasi-schizophrenic characters," being Batman and the Joker. We learn in the movie that as a superhero, Batman is untouchable and impenetrable; but on the other hand, the same man is also the neurotic Bruce Wayne, who relies on his butler and friend, Alfred (Michael Gough), for every important decision. The Joker, embodied in a tour-de-force performance by the legendary Jack Nicholson, is the villain to Batman's hero. He had a tragic origin story as well—as a normal (if criminal) man, he fell into a vat of chemicals, which marked him with a permanent, sadistic grin. That turned him from an ordinary crook into a supercriminal. He fancies himself an artist, or even something of a Robin Hood to the citizens of Gotham City, but unfortunately he is also a megalomaniac with a vendetta against Batman. What ties this tale together is the music performed and written by pop star Prince for the movie soundtrack. The film also marks another rise up the Hollywood pecking order for the composer of the film score, former Oingo Boingo singer and songwriter Danny Elfman. The music delivered by both artists, as well as Burton's distinctive directing style, give *Batman* a late 1980s' vibe that took the film beyond just being part of an already established franchise.

The Blues Brothers became a cult hit in the 1980s, starring two comics well known from *Saturday Night Live*, Dan Aykroyd and John Belushi. The comedians played the characters on *SNL* three times before they hit the big screen. As Elwood Blues and his brother, the recently paroled Jake, the duo embark on "a mission from God" to save the orphanage they grew up in from foreclosure. Their solution is to reunite their blues band to earn enough money to pay the orphanage's outstanding tax obligation, so they start traveling the country to round up their former bandmates. The police are in hot pursuit (among other things, Elwood, who is driving them around, has a suspended license) and so are a variety of unsavory characters, including a mystery woman bent on killing them (Carrie Fisher), a Nazi gang, and a country band. The re-formed group finally finds their way to the Daley Center in Chicago, where they perform, and a record company executive offers them a contract. A portion of that money goes to pay the tax bill, but then the two are finally arrested and taken back to jail. The movie was somewhat successful commercially, but its enduring value is as a cult classic. The 1980s was filled with such cult movies, including many science fiction films.

SCIENCE FICTION AND ADVENTURE

Any discussion about science fiction in the 1980s should start with the most popular cult classic series of movies ever released, the *Star Wars* series. Though the original *Star Wars* movie was released in 1977, the two subsequent movies released in the 1980s have become significant in the history of filmmaking. The first of the two, *The Empire Strikes Back* (1980), brought a few unexpected twists and turns from the original movie. The hero of the first film, Luke Skywalker (Mark Hamill), and the rebel force that he leads have hidden from the Empire on the frozen planet of Hoth. He is joined by maverick pilot Han Solo (Harrison Ford) and the princess he saved in the first film, Leia Organa (Carrie Fisher). Meanwhile, their nemesis Darth Vader has been searching the galaxy for the rebels. The Empire forces invade Hoth, forcing the rebels to flee. Han and Leia leave in Solo's ship, the *Millennium Falcon*, along with Han's sidekick, Chewbacca, and two of Luke's trusted droids, C-3P0 (Anthony Daniels) and R2-D2 (Kenny Baker). Meanwhile, Luke leaves for Dagobah to meet Yoda, a Jedi master, for training so he can fulfill his destiny as a Jedi knight.

After working with Yoda for a while, Luke sees a vision of his friends in danger, so he leaves his training prematurely to save them from Vader. Han has been captured and is being used as bait to lure Luke to Vader. Han is eventually turned over to a bounty hunter. Luke confronts Vader, and in the midst of the fight, Vader informs him that he is Luke's father. The rebels escape and begin their quest to save Han; nevertheless, the movie ends on a grim note.

The follow-up film, *Return of the Jedi* (1983), begins with Leia coming to see Jabba the Hut. Jabba had hired the bounty hunter to find Han, who owed him smuggling money. Leia has come to negotiate for Han's release. When her bid fails, Luke comes to do the same, using his Jedi designation to try to sway Jabba's mind. After defeating Jabba's Rancor, a monster that Jabba uses to eat his enemies, Han, Leia, and Luke are taken to the desert, where they are to be fed to another monster, the Sarlacc, but they finally escape. Luke returns to Dagobah, where he is visited by the spirit of his mentor, Obi-won Kenobi, who confirms that Luke is indeed Vader's son. Yoda informs him that to complete the training, he must confront Vader again.

Han and Leia rejoin the rebels and discover that another version of the deadly Death Star, a weapon/space station that can implode a complete planet (and which they had blown up in the first *Star Wars* film), is being constructed and they must band together to destroy it again. A safety field that is emitted from the moon of Endor protects the space station. The trio goes to release the field so that the rest of the rebel force can attack it when it is unprotected, and they are successful. Luke surrenders to Vader as the rebels battle with the Empire to destroy the space station. Vader and Luke battle in front of the evil Emperor, who commands Luke to kill his father after he cuts off Vader's hand. Luke refuses, prompting the powerful emperor to attack him, but Vader steps in to save him. Vader's injuries are too severe, and he dies.

E.T. The Extra Terrestrial was one of the decade's most beloved movies. Coproduced and directed by Steven Spielberg, the central focus is the relationship between an alien and Elliott (Henry Thomas), a 10-year-old boy. The alien is left on Earth by his fellow aliens. Elliott discovers the alien in his family's shed, where the boy uses candy to coax the creature into the house and hides him in the closet. Elliott stays home from school the next day, and his younger sister, Gertie (Drew Barrymore), meets the alien. The following day, the alien, nicknamed E.T., remains at the house with Gertie, watching *Sesame*

Harrison Ford, shown here as Indiana Jones in *Raiders of the Lost Ark* (1981), became a top box office draw in the 1980s. In addition to starring in two films as Indiana Jones, Harrison's other significant films during the decade included the final chapter in the original *Star Wars* trilogy, *Return of the Jedi* (1983), as well as *Blade Runner* (1982) and *Witness* (1985). (Paramount Pictures/Photofest)

Street with her; from the show, E.T. learns enough English that he can communicate with Elliott. Whatever the alien does, such as drinking beer, affects Elliott (causing the boy to be drunk at school).

Elliott learns later that day that E.T. wants to "phone home" to reconnect with his fellow aliens. On Halloween, Elliott, Gertie, and their older brother, Michael, sneak E.T. out of the house so that he can communicate with the aliens via a device made out of an umbrella, a coffee can, and a Speak & Spell handheld computer game/trainer. The next morning, E.T. is gone from the house, and after finding him, they discover him near death. Because of their intense physical connection, as E.T. is nearing death, so is Elliott. Government workers come to the house and quarantine the two to save them; however, it seems that E.T. is sacrificing his own life so Elliott can recuperate. After E.T. dies, and Elliott survives but is distraught, E.T. begins to rejuvenate himself before making the journey to his home planet with his alien friends.

Raiders of the Lost Ark (1981) introduced audiences to Henry "Indiana" Jones (Harrison Ford), an archeology professor and adventurer in search of historic artifacts. In the 1930s, the U.S. government approaches Jones because they have learned that the Nazis are trying to find the Ark of the Covenant, which is the vessel in which the Ten Commandments were transported according to the Bible. The government does not know why the Nazis would want such an artifact so intensely, but they are nevertheless concerned. Jones tells him a legend that the possessor of the Ark will be able to harness an immense amount of physical power, so they determine that the Nazis cannot be allowed to get their hands on it. Jones travels to Nepal to reconnect with Marion (Karen Allen), an old girlfriend who is the daughter of his mentor, the one man who would know the ark's whereabouts. The Nazis soon arrive, asking for similar information. Marion has an artifact of her father's that will lead to the ark. An imprint of the artifact, which is believed to give the true location of the ark, is burned onto a Nazi henchman's hand, but Marion and Jones keep the true one. They head to the Middle East. The duo discovers the Nazis furiously excavating land for the ark, but the Nazis have the wrong location since they do not have the actual artifact. Jones and his men find the ark, but the Nazis quickly get it from them, and Jones and Marion are taken prisoner. The Nazis decide to bring the ark back to Berlin, but on the way, it is shown to a large group of them, and it wreaks its true power and devastation upon them.

Two follow-up movies from the series were made in the 1980s. The second film, *Indiana Jones and the Temple of Doom* (1984), takes place in a whole new setting—first Shanghai, and then India. Jones goes to India with a young boy named Short Round (Jonathan Ke Quan) and a showgirl he had met in Shanghai, Willie Scott (Kate Capshaw). In India, they discover that a village has had their mysterious stones, not to mention all its children, taken from them. They approach the child emperor for information and discover that the children have been taken to work as slaves in the mission of finding the last of the stones, now known to be the Tankari stones. Jones now becomes fixated on having the children returned, and after a series of further adventures, succeeds. The third installment, *Indiana Jones and the Last Crusade* (1989), features Sean Connery as Jones's father. The bickering between the two as they look for the legendary Holy Grail adds a new twist to the movie series.

One of the most beloved science fiction/comedy films of the 1980s is *Back to the Future* (1985). Jürgen Muller (1994, 330) "interpreted the title of the film as the secret agenda of Reagan's retrogressive belief in progress." Teenager Marty McFly (Michael J. Fox) has befriended Doc Brown (Christopher Lloyd), an eccentric scientist who is building a time machine out of a DeLorean sports car. The scientist needed to obtain plutonium in order to power the time machine, so he double-crossed some terrorists to get some. But they find him just as he is showing Marty how the time machine works. During the confrontation with the terrorists, Marty is accidentally sent back to 1955 in the DeLorean. While there, he meets his mother and father (now teenagers themselves, of course). He also tracks down the young Doc Brown, and after convincing him that Marty is indeed from the future, he and Doc try to figure out how to send him back to his own time. Meanwhile, though, Marty's mother has fallen in love with him—a complication in itself—and Doc realizes that if Marty's own parents do not fall in love and marry, then Marty will not exist. Marty tries to ensure that his parents do get together, while Doc schemes to find a way to generate enough energy to send the machine, and Marty, back to the future. At one point, the scientist

Christopher Lloyd (as Dr. Emmett Brown, left) and Michael J. Fox (as Marty McFly) starred in *Back to the Future* (1985), one of the decade's most popular films and a favorite of movie fans to this day. Fox was able to make the transition from successful television star to successful movie star largely because of the film's popularity. (Universal Pictures/Photofest)

asks Marty who the president is in 1985 and cannot believe it when Marty tells him it is Ronald Reagan, the star of *Bedtime for Bonzo*, released in 1951. There are many comic elements to the story, but there is also an urgency behind Marty's mission to unite his parents before he disappears from history. Throughout the movie, he keeps checking a picture of him and his brother and sister; in a poignant touch, they are slowly fading from the image. Everything works out in the end, though, and Marty goes back to 1985—but amazingly, the lives of his parents and siblings (not to mention himself) have vastly improved thanks to the things that Marty did while he was in the 1950s.

Audiences who grew up in both eras were fans of the film. As a result, naturally, a number of sequels to *Back to the Future* were released throughout the decade. However, they were far less successful than the original, perhaps because the subsequent tales were less compelling.

While *Back to the Future* used special effects to make a story become magical, *Blade Runner* (1982) exploited them to the fullest in a predigital production stage. The film took ideas from the Lucas *Star Wars* films and added them to action, violence, and a science fiction story based in 2019. Los Angeles has become an industrial wasteland, where the streets, in the words of Jürgen Muller (1994, 146), were "home to an exotic blend of races, while whites are housed in forbidding, monolithic skyscrapers. Everyone who can afford it has relocated to one of the 'off world colonies.'" On other planets, the Tyrell

Corporation uses humanoids called "replicants" to work as laborers, but these beings are not allowed to come to Earth. When they do, former policemen called Blade Runners pursue and "retire" (i.e., kill) them. Complicating the situation is that the humanoids and the Blade Runners are physically indistinguishable. The way they identify them is to ask them questions that would elicit emotional responses (to which replicants respond differently than humans). One of these Blade Runners is Rick Deckard (Harrison Ford), who is being asked to hunt down four replicants coming to Los Angeles from another planet. It is believed that the four only have four years left to live and are coming to Earth to find a way to prolong their lives. The four are led by the evil Roy Batty (Rutger Hauer), who has the compassion of a human regardless of his android identity. Roy confronts and kills his creator, Eldon Tyrell (Joe Turkel). The action and effects in the film powerfully influenced other science fiction/action films to follow.

The Terminator (1984) was one of the most important movies of the decade, as it established a new benchmark for how a male action hero was portrayed in a science fiction film (and, ultimately, how audiences embraced the genre and special effects as a whole). A cyborg (Arnold Schwarzenegger) has been sent to 1984 Los Angeles from the future, programmed to kill a young woman named Sarah Connor (Linda Hamilton). As portrayed in the movie, the future has become quite complicated, as a defense computer network named Skynet has learned from its programming to instigate a nuclear holocaust and overpower the humans of Earth. Connor has been targeted because she is pregnant with a boy who, if he is allowed to be born, will become the leader of a resistance against the Skynet machines in the mid-21st century. Kyle Reese, a resistance fighter also from the future, arrives to protect Connor from the assassin. Skynet has sent the Terminator back since he is a killer without conscience. The cyborg appears to be human, but it is really a killing machine with a sophisticated mechanical eye. Bullets have no effect on him, since he is a machine, and when he is damaged, he has the ability to repair himself; all these characteristics make him a formidable murderer. The appearance of the cyborg Terminator, including sunglasses, fit well with 1980s' American society.

The Terminator spends most of the movie chasing Connor and Reese, with Reese doing battle with the machine. The level of action and special effects in the movie, the work of director James Cameron, was considerable. *The Terminator* solidified Schwarzenegger's career as a top movie star and established Cameron as a top director.

Aliens (1986) was the sequel to the successful 1979 release of *Alien*. Both films star Sigourney Weaver as Ellen Ripley; in the 1986 sequel, she had been adrift in space for over 50 years after she lost her ship and crew in the first movie. The company she had worked for, Weyland-Yutani Corporation, had colonized the planet, establishing an energy plant where her earlier encounter occurred. However, the colony has gone dark, losing touch with the home company. A project manager named Carter Burke (Paul Reiser) was skeptical of Ripley's claims about a killer alien, so he, an android named Bishop, and a group of heavily armed Marines are sent to the planet to investigate why the company and colony had lost communication, and Ripley accompanies them.

Upon arriving, the team finds an apparently deserted planet; however, they soon find a young girl named Newt (Carrie Henn), who has been hiding after the Aliens occupied the complex. The aliens are living in an underground city, full of soldiers and workers. There is also a "uterus machine," which lays eggs out of which will hatch future aliens. In the city, the team finds the missing human colonists, who have been placed in cocoons to serve as human incubators for the alien eggs. Ripley and Newt are among the last survivors, who battle the Alien queen, and in the end they escape with their lives.

Ripley is one of the only female action heroes of the decade, and playing her transformed Weaver's career (she received an Oscar nomination as Best Actress for this part). Director James Cameron had just finished *The Terminator*, to great fanfare, and his work with Weaver on this film changed her from the victim of a horror film (the original *Alien*) to an action hero on par with any male counterpart.

Robocop (1987) is set in the future, but not too far ahead, so audiences in the 1980s could find it relatable. In the movie, prisons are now privatized, and Detroit, newly minted as "Delta City," has become a crime haven that has caused the city's residents to flee. To counteract the crime problem, a private firm, Omni Consumer Products (OCP), is brought in to try to reestablish order. OCP's initial plan is to have a droid police officer roam the streets, but the droid kills a board member at its initial demonstration. As a replacement, a cyborg design is incorporated. Alex Murphy (Peter Weller), a rookie cop, is shot by Clarence Boddicker (Kurtwood Smith) and is assumed dead by most, including Murphy's family. Murphy undergoes a number of complex procedures that turn him into a cyborg. The new Robocop becomes a force on the streets, alongside his partner Anne Lewis (Nancy Allen); he has four directives: serve the public trust, protect the innocent, uphold the law, and—as viewers find out—not take action against an OCP executive. Murphy later catches Bodddicker, but he learns that Boddicker has forged an alliance with OCP president Dick Jones (Ronny Cox), so he is unable to kill either Jones or Boddicker. The film represents how the future could evolve: into a world where mankind's old approaches are taken over by new technology, and where society has to be aware of privatized media control and surveillance. Throughout the film, the Robocop struggles with finding his way back to his former, fully human emotional self.

The *Mad Max* series of films (1979's original *Mad Max* and *Mad Max 2—The Road Warrior*, released in 1981), starring Mel Gibson, were box office successes. The Earth is portrayed as a postapocalyptic wasteland in both. The third entry in the series, *Mad Max Beyond Thunderdome* (1985), sheds the low-budget quality of the earlier two films and remolds itself into a more traditional action thriller featuring the central Mad Max character as heroic and less vengeful following the murder of his wife and child than he had been in the earlier two films. When the movie opens, Mad Max is traveling by camel across the desert of Australia. He is attacked and robbed of all his possessions, so he treks to Bartertown on foot. Bartertown, the central area of commerce (as its name indicates), is a rough city that that restricts visitors on the basis of whether they are carrying goods for sale. Mad Max makes a deal with the city's ruler, Aunty

Entity (played by pop music icon Tina Turner, who had begun her musical comeback the previous year) that she will replace his possessions if he defeats her enemies: a dwarf known as "Master" and his giant bodyguard, "Blaster." Master controls Bartertown's power supply, and the defeat that Aunty Entity wants is for Mad Max to defeat Blaster in a battle in the Thunderdome, an arena stocked with fences and weapons for the contestants to use. Max overpowers the giant enemy but takes pity on him and refuses to kill him. Aunty Entity retaliates by banishing Max to the desert, where he discovers a tribe of children traveling. Though pursued by Aunty Entity, he serves as their hero, trying to lead them to Tomorrow-morrow Land.

The 1980s also included several more entries in the *James Bond* series. The British secret agent had become a legend of film beginning in the 1960s, and the Bond films of this decade continued that success. The decade featured six films in the series, five of which were produced by a Canadian production company known as Eon. In the first three, *For Your Eyes Only* (1981), *Octopussy* (1983), and *A View to a Kill* (1985), Roger Moore played the superspy. The later two, *The Living Daylights* (1987) and *License to Kill* (1989), featured Timothy Dalton. Joining the Eon films was one produced by Taliafilm, *Never Say Never Again* (1983), a remake of the 1960s-era *Thunderball* starring the original Bond, Sean Connery. The title of the remake was attributed to a vow that Connery made after *Diamonds Are Forever* in 1971 that he would never play the character again.

All of the films followed a familiar framework: Bond as the agent 007, fighting international criminals while romancing beautiful women and having his martinis "shaken not stirred," in accordance with the original novels written by Ian Fleming. The main thread that made all six films so successful during this decade is that they had more realistic settings that audiences found plausible, as opposed to some of the more fantastic plots and settings of the 1960s' and 1970s' Bond movies.

While the *James Bond* series has been enjoyed for many years by multiple generations of filmgoers, other adventure movies are considered typical products of the 1980s. *Stand by Me* (1986) was an adventure film with tragic undertones that might seem geared toward children because of its teenage cast, but it was warmly embraced by adults. This was largely because of the nostalgic nature of the film, which featured an adult narrator remembering events from his youth in 1959, the first time he saw a dead human being at the age of "12 or 13." It is the story of four boys who run the gamut of characters: Chris (River Phoenix), a kid from the wrong side of the tracks; Teddy (Corey Feldman), a boy obsessed with the Army because his father took part in the Normandy invasion during World War II; Vern (Jerry O'Connell), overweight and frequently picked on; and Gordie, the narrator as a child, who has a vivid imagination and likes to write stories.

The movie is based on a short story, *The Body,* by Stephen King (probably best known for his horror stories, discussed later in this chapter and also in Chapter 5, "Literature"). The boys hear that a body of another teen is in the woods, and they decide that they need to find it for themselves, possibly to gain some type of heroic accolades (or at least attention). Though the story of

Stand by Me centers on different interpretations of death, it is not a horror film; rather, death becomes a thread that ties together the adventures of the boys: looking for a dead body of another boy; Gordie's brother Dennis, whose recent death Gordie and his family are still coming to terms with, often at Gordie's expense; the four boys confronting an oncoming train on a railway bridge high above a river, outrunning the train to save their own lives; and a pistol that Chris has stolen from his father. The tale is framed as a coming-of-age story, but ultimately, the audience learns that Gordie is telling the story because he just learned that his friend Chris has died.

The Goonies (1985) is an adventure film geared toward children that featured a group of preteen boys who live in Oregon. Their families are collectively facing the potential demolition of their home because a country club is expanding near them, and the boys decide to get together for one final time. As in *Stand by Me*, the group featured widely varying characters who could be related to by a wider audience: optimist Mikey Walsh (Sean Astin), his older brother Brand (Josh Brolin), chatty "Mouth" (Corey Feldman), overweight "Chunk" (Jeff Cohen), and the intelligent "Data" (Jonathan Quan). After looking into the Walshes' attic, the group finds a 17th-century treasure map and coin and information about how a pirate named One-Eyed Willy had lost treasure in the area. They decide to search for the treasure, but they run into the Fratellis, a family of criminals, in an abandoned restaurant at the place where the map directs them. The Fratellis leave the restaurant, and the children decide to investigate. They discover the family is coordinating a counterfeit operation. When the Fratellis return, the boys escape through the tunnel (without Chunk, as he is too large) and experience adventures while looking for the treasure that resemble those in *Raiders of the Lost Ark*.

COMEDY

The previous section discussed science fiction and adventure films, particularly ones in the *Star Wars* series, as well as *Alien*. A humorous parody of these is Mel Brooks's *Spaceballs* (1987), which featured some of the top comedians of the 1980s: John Candy (Barfolomew), Dom DeLuise (Pizza the Hut), Joan Rivers (Dot Matrix), Rick Moranis (Lord Dark Helmet), and Brooks himself as President Skoob and Yogurt. Bill Pullman and John Hurt, usually known for dramatic roles, were cast as Captain Lone Starr and Kane, respectively. Certainly silly, the movie helps solidify the popularity of the aforementioned science fiction films through its parody treatment.

Equally as mindless is *Bill and Ted's Excellent Adventure* (1989), featuring two "slacker" high school students, Bill (Alex Winter) and Ted (Keanu Reeves). In the future (2688), these two were known as the Two Great Ones, who had inspired a utopian society via their music. They ask Rufus (comedian George Carlin) to travel back in time to ensure that the boys receive an A+ on their history report to keep them, and their band, together for the sake of future society. After the two teens come from the future to convince their younger versions to listen to Rufus, they travel with him through time, bringing historic figures such as Billy the Kid, Socrates, Princess Elizabeth I of England (and her fictional sister, Princess Joanna), Sigmund Freud, Genghis Khan, Ludwig van Beethoven, Joan of Arc, and Abraham Lincoln into their telephone booth time machine to the present day to help with the report. Two sequels followed *Bill and Ted's Excellent Adventure* in the 1990s.

In *Beetlejuice* (1988), a comedic fantasy directed by Tim Burton, a family has moved into a new house following the death of a young couple (Alec Baldwin and Geena Davis), who find that they are doomed to haunt their former home for 125 years. The new family includes a boorish father and superficial mother, and the ghost couple are appalled to see how they are redecorating their home, turning it into a display of tasteless modern art. The daughter, Lydia (Winona Ryder), is a "goth" (a darker member of the alternative punk movement who wears black makeup and clothes) who can see the ghost couple. Although they like Lydia, the ghost couple decides that they will need to scare the new family out of the house, but they have no luck. So they decide to enlist the assistance of an intolerable spirit named Betelgeuse (pronounced "Beetlejuice"), played by Michael Keaton.

Burton (discussed in the previous section for directing *Batman*) had also made a name for himself directing the cult classic *Pee-Wee's Big Adventure* in 1985, which featured offbeat, imaginative sets and costumes. *Beetlejuice* follows a similar approach, as that film offered stop motion, puppetry, prosthetic makeup, and replacement animation (where a number of puppets are used to change the action or emotion of a specific character), enhancing the story with ghosts that vary greatly in physical appearance. *Beetlejuice*'s use of visual effects was a key reason for Burton's selection as the director for *Batman* the following year.

Ghostbusters (1984) features three of the most popular comedians of the early 1980s: Bill Murray (as Dr. Peter Venkman), Dan Aykroyd (as Dr. Raymond Stantz) and Harold Ramis (as Dr. Egon Spangler). The story revolves around a team of paranormal academic researchers that had been dismissed by their university for their activities. In turn, the trio moves into private practice as ghost exterminators. Their services are sorely needed in New York City, which is seeing a marked increase in ghost activity (demonstrated by a liberal use of special effects). The trio becomes famous (or maybe infamous would be a better word) for their exploits, capturing and storing the ghosts in their specially designed devices. In time, the Ghostbusters are ordered to release their ghosts for environmental reasons, making the city more chaotic.

Making their task more difficult is that an accountant (Rick Moranis) has fallen for his beautiful neighbor (Sigourney Weaver), and both of them find themselves possessed by the ghosts in what turns out to be an orchestrated plan to release a bevy of evil spirits (including, in one of the most indelible images from the movie, a "Stay-Puft marshmallow man") into the whole world. Fueled by Murray's snappy one-liners and the give and take among him, Aykroyd, and Ramis, the comedic situations abound, and the movie became one of the funniest of all time. Underlying its cinematic success was its cultural success, marked by the hit title track, written and recorded by Ray Parker, Jr., and a number of tie-in toys.

Though not nearly as successful as *Ghostbusters*, *Gremlins* was another popular sci-fi comedy. A man looking for an unusual gift for his son buys a small, exotic creature called a Mogwai from a Chinese store. It is an adorable pet, but it comes with very specific instructions: Never expose it to bright light (especially sunlight, which will kill it), never let it touch water (that will cause it to multiply), and most important, no matter how much it cries or begs, never feed it after midnight. The inevitable occurs: The Mogwai is exposed to water and fed after midnight by accident, and more are created. However, the new ones soon become mischievous reptiles and cause havoc to anyone and everywhere that they can throughout the city. The movie became a favorite with both young viewers and their parents.

Tootsie (1982) was certainly a favorite among adults. Actor Michael Dorsey (Dustin Hoffman) is having trouble finding regular employment as an actor, largely because he is so difficult to work with that he has a terrible reputation in the industry. To counter that, he impulsively decides to audition for a (female) role on a soap opera as an actress named Dorothy Michaels. He (she?) lands the role and develops a new reputation as a career-driven actress. She begins to improvise in the middle of shooting to avoid love scenes and to develop her character on the show. Dorothy is seen as a strong woman and gains fans in the women's movement.

She becomes best girlfriends with Julie (Jessica Lange), her costar— unfortunately, at the same time Michael has fallen in love with Julie. Meanwhile, Julie's own father falls for Dorothy. Finally, at a live taping of an episode, Michael comes clean on his identity, shocking the millions viewing the show on television. In the end, Michael's stunt gets him a lot of publicity, and although Julie is furious at his deception, she comes to forgive him, and they begin a different kind of relationship. One of the keys of *Tootsie*'s success is that it examines accepted gender roles and highlights some of the chauvinistic problems that permeate American society.

Beverly Hills Cop (1984) features African American detective Axel Foley (Eddie Murphy), a police officer in Detroit. An old ex-con friend, Mickey, comes to visit Foley from Beverly Hills but is soon gunned down during his Detroit visit. Against the orders of his superiors, Foley goes to Beverly Hills to find the killer. In his investigation, he goes to Mickey's former employer, an art dealer. He discovers that the art dealer is engaging in drug smuggling, and after his bodyguards throw Foley through a window, Foley is the one who gets arrested by the Beverly Hills police. He winds up befriending a white detective on the force, Rosewood (Judge Reinhold).

The movie shows the contradiction between a black cop from struggling Detroit and the white police force in affluent Beverly Hills, but the audience finds themselves cheering for Foley as he tries unconventional ways to solve the case. Rosewood is eager to help, and his own sergeant (John Ashton) follows along to keep Rosewood out of any trouble that might come Foley's way. Foley's unconventional approach to solving the case is brought to life by the versatility of Murphy, who by 1984 had become one of the top comics in the country.

Airplane! is a parody of the airplane disaster movies of the 1950s (*Zero Hour*) and 1970s (the *Airport* series, including *Airport 1975* and *Airport '77*). Produced and directed by the team of Jim Abrahams, David Zucker, and Jerry Zucker, the driving forces behind the *Police Squad!* television series, this movie took the same frenetic, slapsticky, pun-laden approach to its jokes. Traumatized war veteran Ted Striker (Robert Hays) has a problem: His flight attendant girlfriend Elaine (Julie Hagerty) has left him. Despite his fear of flying (and drinking problem—he keeps sloshing water into his face), Striker musters the strength to board a plane in an attempt to win her back. The two pilots suffer from food poisoning and become unable to fly the plane. The crew tries to engage the autopilot, which in the movie's case is a large inflatable doll. Though the doll can fly the plane, it cannot land it, and Striker reluctantly agrees to take the controls via encouragement of his former commanding officer (and nemesis), Captain Kramer.

Crocodile Dundee became one of the top-grossing films of 1986. Mick "Crocodile" Dundee (Paul Hogan) is a crocodile hunter who is in charge of a safari business in the Australian outback. A journalist from New York, Sue Charlton (Linda Kozlowski), arrives to interview Dundee. The macho Australian, who subdues a water buffalo, dances with Aborigines, and can kill a snake with his bare hands, soon intrigues Sue. She decides that she can survive the outback alone, and armed with Dundee's gun, sets off to see if she can. Dundee trails behind, eventually saving her from a crocodile. In return, Sue invites Dundee to New York City, where he experiences culture shock from his first visit to a big city. He defends her from an attempted robbery, with the assailant using a knife much smaller than Dundee's. The tale becomes more complicated as they begin to fall for each other in the big city, and Sue must choose between Dundee and another man who has asked her to marry him.

Police Academy (1984) started a successful series that lasted until the mid-1990s. The original movie is centered around a town with a shortage of police officers, and the city has agreed to relax their requirements to include just about anyone from the town into the academy. The misfits who show up at the police academy are wide ranging: Carey Mahoney (Steve Guttenberg) is forced into service as an alternative to jail time. Karen Thompson (Kim Cattrall) is a socialite who wants to dress "like a man" in her police uniform. George Martin (Andrew Rubin) is a Hispanic ladies' man. Other recruits include Larvell Jones (Michael Winslow), who can make interesting sound effects with his voice; a man obsessed with guns, Eugene Tackleberry (David Graf); an overweight man, Leslie Barbara (Donovan Scott), who has the unusual problem of having two female names; and strongman Moses Hightower (played by former NFL star Bubba Smith). Their trainer, Thaddeus Harris (G. W. Bailey), tries to make the cadets' lives so difficult that they quit; but nothing is ever that easy.

Who Framed Roger Rabbit (1988) was a charming cartoon marketed to children, but with undertones that adults could appreciate; the plot pits cartoon actors like Daffy Duck, Bugs Bunny, and Donald Duck, residing in Toontown, against the studio stars in the late 1940s. The human studio boss, R. K. Maroon (Alan Tilvern), has concerns about his main "toon" actor, Roger Rabbit, who is having trouble concentrating on his work. To discover the reason for Roger's lack of dedication on the set, Maroon hires the human private investigator Eddie Valiente (Bob Hoskins) to see if Roger's beautiful and sexy cartoon wife, Jessica Rabbit, has been having an affair. Eddie has a visceral hatred of toons, largely because years earlier, a toon killed his brother, with whom he had founded the detective agency but he takes the case because he needs the money.

After Roger and Eddie discover that Roger's wife has been playing patty cake with Marvin Acme, the cartoon gag supplier, Acme is mysteriously found dead and his will, which determines the fate of Toontown, is missing. Roger and Jessica now become suspects, and the race is on to try to find the true killer (and the will), while running into mishaps along the way. *Who Framed Roger Rabbit* was certainly not the first time that cartoon characters and live actors were featured side by side on screen, but the technology used in the 1980s was more sophisticated and seamless than in earlier films.

Another popular, completely animated film, *The Little Mermaid* (1989), is based on Hans Christian Anderson's 19th-century fairy tale. The central character, Ariel, is a mermaid infatuated with humans, collecting their items that have been dropped into the sea. She dreams of walking on land, and most urgently, about a prince named Eric, who pilots a ship above the surface. Ariel's father, King Triton, wants the 16-year-old mermaid to ignore humans, since interactions between merpeople and humans are forbidden.

One day, a storm wrecks Eric's ship, and Ariel saves him by pulling him out of the water onto the shore. Eric remembers Ariel's singing voice. So she can become human, Ariel makes a deal with the evil sea witch/octopus Ursula, in which she will be human for three days if she sacrifices her voice. In those three days, Ariel needs to find a way for Eric to kiss her; if she fails, she becomes Ursula's slave for eternity. *The Little Mermaid* became Disney's most important cartoon movie in many years, breathing new life into the medium that had struggled in previous years and reestablishing the studio's place in animation.

An important part of 1980s' American popular culture consisted of movies that focused on teenagers. One of the first of these was *Fast Times at Ridgemont High* (1982). Written by Cameron Crowe and directed by Amy Heckerling, it set the standard for how hit teenage movies were to be made. Elizabeth Traube (1992, 158) noted that Heckerling "demonstrated her skill at playing with generic formulas" in the movie, while Robin Wood (1986) noted that the film undercuts the conventional sexism of the typical high school coming-of-age story.

Sophomore Stacy Hamilton (Jennifer Jason Leigh) is interested in Mark Ratner (Brian Backer), but she is shy and innocent. Stacy receives advice from senior Linda Barrett (Phoebe Cates) on how to snare Ratner through sex, but when Stacy tries to pursue him, he shies away from the encounter. But she eventually succeeds with Ratner's best friend, Mike Damone (Robert Romanus). Stacy's older brother, Brad (Judge Reinhold), is having trouble finding a job that suits him, but he eventually becomes the manager of a convenience store after preventing a robbery. Another student at Ridgemont High is the stoned surfer Jeff Spicoli (Sean Penn), who has an ongoing dispute with his teacher, Mr. Hand (Ray Walston). The teacher, however, gives him a concentrated tutoring session so that Spicoli can graduate with the rest of the class. The sex-themed movie featured a number of teen actors who went on to successful careers throughout the 1980s and even beyond (including Leigh, Cates, Penn, and Reinhold).

Although Chapter 9, "Game Changers," will provide more detail on the impact that John Hughes had on the movie industry, the movies he made in the 1980s should be discussed to at least some degree here. Hughes's first movie for teens was *Sixteen Candles* (1984), which started the trend for a specific type of teen-focused movie throughout the decade. Samantha (Sam) Baker (Molly Ringwald) is a sophomore approaching her 16th birthday, but she is largely ignored because of a pending wedding for her older sister. Not only that, but both sets of grandparents are staying at

The Breakfast Club (1985) became one of the most popular films among teenagers in the 1980s. The stars of the film were all core members of the "Brat Pack," a group of young actors that were featured in a variety of films geared towards teens throughout the decade. (Universal Pictures/Photofest)

their house, and one of them has also brought along a foreign exchange student named Long Duk Dong (Gedde Wantanabe).

Sam is obsessed with senior Jake Ryan, who has learned about her infatuation because he found a sex quiz that Sam took, revealing her virginity and her desire to give it to Jake. The geeky Ted (Anthony Michael Hall) is equally crazy about Sam. At a dance, Ted makes a bet with his friends that he can attract Sam. He attempts to dance with her, and eventually, they talk in an auto shop. Ted convinces her to give him her undergarments so he can win the bet with his friends, and she obliges. However, he and the two fellow geeks charge admission for other boys to see the underwear in a bathroom. Jake hosts a party at his house, and eventually Jake looks for Sam in the yearbook. Jake starts to inquire to Ted about her, and Ted vouches for Sam's love of Jake. As the film ends, Jake and Sam share a kiss—and a birthday cake.

Ringwald and Hall were cast together in the more successful movie, *The Breakfast Club* (1985), which became a cult favorite largely because audiences can relate directly to one or more of the characters. Five teenagers are serving an eight-hour school detention on Saturday, and they come from disparate backgrounds: rebellious John Bender (Judd Nelson), athletic Andrew Clarke (Emilio Estevez), intelligent/nerdy Brian Johnson (Hall), gothesque outcast Allison Reynolds (Ally Sheedy), and spoiled and entitled Claire Standish (Ringwald). During the day, the characters reveal their own individual secrets, including the fact that they all have problems with their parents. John comes from an abusive home, where both he and his mother are verbally and physically mistreated by his father. Andrew has trouble making decisions on his own and is pushed mercilessly by his father to excel as a wrestler. Brian's parents apply enormous pressure on him to get good grades, to the point that Brian has attempted suicide. As for Allison, her parents are so focused on their own issues that they ignore her completely, and she must resort to lying constantly for attention. Claire is often used as a pawn during fights between her parents, and while she is popular, her friends are also pressuring her to lose her virginity.

The students have different reasons for being in detention in the first place. Chris Jordan (2003, 137) suggests that the therapeutic culture of the support group is an antidote for the dehumanizing environment of the public high school, in which tracks of achievement follow corporate goals of efficiency and functionality by funneling individuals into class-circumscribed job paths, an essential part of the movie. In the course of the day, these distinct individuals become friendly (and even romantic sometimes) with each other, which shows viewers that while different kinds of people have their own struggles, they share similar obstacles and can find common ground on which to help and support each other.

Weird Science (1985) had a science fiction slant as well—the plot featured two nerdy boys who are chastened by two other, cooler teenage boys who date girls that they are attracted to. The nerds then go home to create a virtual, "perfect" girl using their computer, electricity, and a doll. Their creation, which they call Lisa, has the ability to conjure up desirable cars for the teens to drive (namely, a Porsche and a Cadillac) with the intention of irritating the cool teens that had bullied them.

Ferris Bueller's Day Off (1986), also directed by Hughes, is arguably one of the most important movies of the decade, not only because it was such a smash at the time, but also because of the long-term cult following it developed. As the postmodern hero of a teen comedy, Ferris (Matthew Broderick) decides that he wants to skip school, to simply enjoy life as a teen on a beautiful sunny day. The problem is that he has missed eight school days already, and if he skips once more, he will have to repeat his senior year. Through a series of clever ruses, Ferris convinces his parents and the school that he is sick at home. During his day out (part of which he spends in Chicago, enjoying the sights), Ferris must avoid his school principal to make sure he is not caught.

Ferris brings his girlfriend Sloane and his best friend Cameron along for the ride, taking Cameron's father's prized possession—a Ferrari. He dines at a swanky restaurant, visits the Art Institute of Chicago, and in one of the movie's highlights, joins a parade through the streets, lip-synching to the Beatles version of the 1950s' pop classic "Twist and Shout." It seems that Ferris can get away with whatever he wants, and always seems to find a way to keep from getting caught (even breaking into the school's computer to change his attendance records). With another actor, Ferris could have come off as smarmy and insufferable, but Matthew Broderick's charm and good humor make the character lovable.

Elizabeth Traube (1992, 79) added that "with its self-conscious, ironic attitude toward the events it narrates, the film reflects a tendency of contemporary mass culture to appropriate 'high' cultural forms." Chris Jordan (2003, 139) goes further by stating, "the condemnation of hard work as a means of upward mobility is explicit in the ridicule of Rooney, Ferris' high school principal. Tight-lipped and humorless, Rooney personifies an outmoded and repressive system of authoritarian control. Juxtaposed with the stuffy principal is the skillfully manipulative Ferris, who matriculates the scholastic bureaucracy on the basis of his careful management of appearances and a breezy, blank superficiality." Teenagers have been critical of the culture of their parents' generation for decades, but with the expansion of technology, music, and youth culture on television (especially MTV), and an energetic filmmaker such as Hughes, the time was ripe for a slew of teenage-focused movies that have since taken on a cult status among teens (and former teens) in the decades that have followed.

While *Pretty in Pink* (1986) does not have the cult status of *Ferris Bueller's Day Off*, it was an important film in the teen-sex realm. Ringwald, the star of other Hughes classics, returns in *Pretty in Pink* as Andie Walsh, who is infatuated with Blane McDonough (Andrew McCarthy). Andie comes from a blue-collar family, while Blane's family is more affluent. She works at a record store and is friendly with her boss, Iona (Annie Potts). Blane's friends harass Andie and her best friend, particularly John "Duckie" Dale (Jon Cryer), to keep Andie away from Blane. Duckie is secretly in love with Andie and is not happy about Andie and Blane's impending date.

As Andie doesn't want Blane to learn about her home life, she resists letting him take her home but eventually succumbs when Blane asks her to the prom. Andie's father buys her a pink dress from a thrift shop, and when pressed, finally admits to Andie that he has not been going to a full-time job after all. Though Blane begins to distance himself from Andie thanks to pressure by his friend Steff (who has his own crush on Andie), she goes to the prom in a dress that Iona helped modify from the original pink one from her father.

Although there were certainly dramatic elements in each of the teen movies described in this section, there were less comedic teen movies in the 1980s as well.

DRAMA

The "Brat Pack" moniker (a twist on the "Rat Pack" label given to Frank Sinatra, Dean Martin, Sammy Davis, Jr., and other entertainers in the 1960s) was largely applied to the actors in the highly successful *St. Elmo's Fire* (1985), a drama focused on a group of young people. Though the movie is not based on teenagers, the characters are having a tough time adjusting to their new adult responsibilities. Seven former classmates have recently graduated from Georgetown University, and their lives are somewhat intertwined. Alec Newberry (Judd Nelson), a professional with aspirations in politics, is dating an architect, Leslie Hunter (Ally Sheedy). Although Alec and Leslie live together, Leslie is looking to establish herself before she commits to marrying Alec, which causes Alec to act out in a fling with a saleswoman. Kirby Keger (Emilio Estevez) is studying law in graduate school, works as a waiter at a local bar, St. Elmo's, and is rooming with Kevin Dolenz (Andrew McCarthy), who wants to become a writer. Kirby is dating Dale Biberman (Andie MacDowell), a doctor that he knew in college, and is smitten with her. As Kevin is single and seemingly uninterested in changing his status, the friends in the group begin to speculate that he is gay. Wendy Bemish (Mare Winningham) comes from a wealthy family, works in a social services job, and has somewhat of a meek and sheltered life. Billy Hicks (Rob Lowe), on the other hand, is married with a child, but instead of devoting himself to his responsibilities, he is more focused on playing saxophone in bar bands and reliving his easygoing fraternity days. Wendy is in love with Billy, and the two eventually have sex. Jules (Demi Moore) is a banker who spends more money than she earns and is sexually promiscuous; her other six friends are worried about her.

The Outsiders (1983), directed by Francis Ford Coppola, was another film whose cast was given the "Brat Pack" designation. Its cast included many stars who would go on to success later in the 1980s, including C. Thomas Howell (Ponyboy Curtis), Matt Dillon (Dallas Winston), Ralph Macchio (Johnny Cade), Patrick Swayze (Darrel Curtis), Rob Lowe (Sodapop Curtis), Emilio Estevez (Two-Bit), and Tom Cruise (Steve Randle). The plot revolves around a gang called the Greasers. The Greasers have a rival gang, the Socs, with upper-middle-class teens.

The Socs members confront Ponyboy and Johnny because they caught them talking to the Socs' girlfriends the night before. In the scuffle, Johnny stabs one of the Socs, killing him. The two hide from the authorities in a church. After leaving to get some food, they return to find the church on fire. The two save several children who are trapped inside, but the authorities still charge Johnny for the stabbing. The Greasers and Socs fight in a rumble again, with the Greasers coming out on top. Dallas has trouble coping after Johnny dies in the hospital of the burns he incurred rescuing the children, so he robs a grocery store before the police shoot and kill him as well.

Terms of Endearment (1983) was one of the most critically acclaimed movies of the 1980s, starring Shirley MacLaine, Debra Winger, and Jack Nicholson. The movie chronicles the relationship between Aurora Greenway (Shirley MacLaine) and her daughter Emma (Debra Winger), from infancy through the loss of Aurora's husband. Eventually, the story reaches an important apex when Emma decides to move out of their home to marry Flap Watson (Jeff Daniels). Aurora disapproves and boycotts the wedding. Flap becomes a struggling English professor in Iowa, and he and Emma have two children. By the time Emma is pregnant a third time, her marriage has become strained because of Flap's infidelities. She responds by embarking on her own affair with Sam Burns (John Lithgow). Meanwhile, Aurora's own love life takes an unexpected turn when she starts a passionate relationship with Garrett Breedlove (Jack Nicholson), who is a retired astronaut and alcoholic.

Emma returns to her mother in Houston after she discovers that her husband is having an affair with a graduate student, Janice (Kate Charleson). Garrett decides to end his relationship with Aurora shortly afterward, and Emma returns to Iowa to save her own marriage. What seems to be a new start for Emma and Flap is his appointment to a new academic position in Nebraska. Emma ends the relationship with Sam and moves with Flap, but then she discovers that Janice is a student at the university in Nebraska. At a doctor's appointment for her daughter, the doctor notices that there are lumps in Emma's armpit, later diagnosed as cancer. Flap and Aurora go to Emma's bedside to support her and face difficult decisions about the future of the children as Emma deteriorates and eventually dies.

Ordinary People (1980), another critically acclaimed film, marked the directorial debut of veteran actor Robert Redford. The movie focuses on an upper-middle-class family whose elder son has tragically died in a boating accident, and whose other son, Conrad (Timothy Hutton), is in a mental institution after a failed suicide attempt. After Conrad's release, he comes under the care of a psychiatrist, Dr. Berger (Judd Hirsch). Conrad's father, Calvin (Donald Sutherland), is trying to be strong for his son and reconnect with him, but his mother, Beth (Mary Tyler Moore), feels resentment toward Conrad for the suicide attempt, and he in turn resents her because she seemed to love his brother more than him. Conrad starts to date a girl, Jeannine (Elizabeth McGovern), which helps his outlook, but he is still aloof from most of the people in his life, especially his mother. Calvin tries to mediate his strained relationship with Conrad, which progressively gets worse. Conrad finally confronts the truth about what happened to his brother and his relationship with his mother, and is able to make progress, while Beth leaves the family behind.

Dirty Dancing (1987) was an unexpected commercial success, and its soundtrack was also a best seller. When the film opens, Frances "Baby" Houseman (Jennifer Grey) is planning to start college at Mount Holyoke College in the fall of 1963. But before enrolling, she and her upper-class family visit the Catskills on vacation. She meets Johnny (Patrick Swayze), the dance instructor who works at the resort. Elizabeth Traube (1992, 183) considered that as the male lead, Johnny was the "sweet but none-too-bright youth whom the movies present as an appropriate match for intelligent and ambitious young women." After seeing a party that featured "dirty dancing" to rock music, she asks Johnny to introduce her to the style. Johnny helps Baby mature to womanhood as they dance together, The interplay between a working-class man and middle-class girl created an intrigue that was embraced by female audiences. Penny Johnson (Cynthia Rhodes), Johnny's regular dance partner, finds that she is pregnant by Robbie Gould, an arrogant, womanizing waiter at the resort. Feeling sorry for Penny, Baby helps pay for her illegal abortion, bringing them closer. She also fills in for Penny as Johnny's dance partner.

When the abortion runs into complications, Baby brings her physician father (Jerry Orbach) to help, but he believes that Johnny is responsible for the pregnancy and forbids Baby to have contact with Johnny. After Johnny is accused of stealing a wallet from a guest, Baby serves as his alibi, claiming that they were together the night of the incident. Jürgen Muller (1994, 45) remarked that the movie "defines its male and female leads in terms of fashion by resituating the angst-ridden, rough guy loner and constrained middle-class girl within the generic context of a Fred Astaire and Ginger Rogers musical." *Dirty Dancing* simultaneously defines Johnny as the rebel and Baby as the prom queen. Johnny is fired from the resort, and Baby's family learns of their relationship. After Robbie admits that he was responsible for Penny's pregnancy, Baby's father is willing to accept Johnny.

Footloose (1984) was based on a real-life story that occurred in the small, religious community of Elmore City, Oklahoma (called Bomont in the movie). Ren McCormick (Kevin Bacon), a high-schooler from Chicago, moves to Bomont, and he is surprised to find out that Bomont forbids both dancing and rock music. He also meets Ariel Moore (Lori Singer), a rebellious girl who is the daughter of the controlling pastor of the town and has an abusive boyfriend, Chuck Cranston (Jim Youngs). Chuck challenges Ren to a game of chicken with tractors, and the city boy wins. Ren expresses interest in Ariel, and although she is fond of him, her father disapproves. Further complicating Ren's position is that he has decided to lead the rest of his classmates against the city council to try to get the dancing ban repealed in time for the senior prom; he quotes Scripture to claim that the Bible actually promotes dancing. Not all critics were fond of the movie, as Chris Jordan (2003, 101) criticizes the way that Ren dances, in a style based on gymnastics and acrobatics rather than dance steps. But the real struggle explored by *Footloose* is pop culture versus the ultraconservative and religious mentality found in many rural areas.

Field of Dreams (1989) features Ray Kinsella (Kevin Costner), who had had a strained relationship with his late father, who had been a huge baseball fan. Kinsella hears a voice that says, "If you build it, he will come," which prompts him to build a baseball field on his farm in Iowa. The Kinsellas are in financial trouble, and by clearing part of his land for the field, Ray might actually lose his farm; he builds it anyway. His wife, Annie (Amy Madigan), does not believe that Ray really heard a voice, but she lets Ray go ahead with his plan. Ray travels to Boston to meet with a black, radical, 1960s' author, Terence Mann (James Earl Jones), of whom Ray was a fan when he was a student. This is what Chris Jordan (2003, 89) describes as a "white everyman's redemption under the tutelage of a black surrogate father figure." When the two arrive at the baseball field in Iowa, Ray's father's baseball heroes appear to come out of the cornfield to play a game on the field. In this way, *Field of Dreams* is more than a movie about baseball and a father/son relationship, as it was made during the farm crisis in the 1980s that changed traditional gender relationships. Mann gives a speech that shows how relationships and differences, regardless of race, political position, and even father/son conflicts, can be mended by baseball. At the end, Ray plays catch with his deceased father on the field, and cars start to arrive, fulfilling the prophecy that he heard in the first place: "If you build it, they will come."

Fatal Attraction (1987) is a psychological thriller that filled men with anxiety because of its subject matter and effective delivery. Dan Gallagher (Michael Douglas) is an attorney who lives in Manhattan with his wife and daughter. Dan meets Alex Forrest (Glenn Close), a book editor, and has an affair with her when his family leaves town for the weekend. Dan wants the affair to end there, but Alex has other ideas. Dan goes to Alex's house to convince her to leave him alone, and Alex responds by slitting her wrists in a suicide attempt. He responds sympathetically, which she sees as encouragement and interest; so she begins to show up at events that he is attending. She asks him to go to a play with her, and he declines. After instructing his secretary to not take calls from Alex, Alex begins to call his home. The Gallaghers' apartment is for sale, so Alex goes there, pretending to be a potential buyer, meeting Dan's wife, Beth (Anne Archer).

Alex is not deterred, even as Dan moves his family outside the city. She stalks him in a parking lot and pours acid on his car. Alex even breaks into the Gallagher home, killing the daughter's pet rabbit and leaving it in a pot of boiling water on the stove as a shock tactic. It is then that Dan tells Beth of the affair, and she demands that he leave. Beth calls Alex threatening her, in which Alex responds by picking up the Gallaghers' daughter from school and taking her to an amusement park without her parents' knowledge or permission. Beth frantically drives around searching for her daughter, finally getting into an automobile accident. Dan then attacks Alex in her apartment, but leaves without doing her serious damage. The police start to search for Alex, who has arrived at the family home, attacking Beth before Dan shows up; he tries to drown her, but she lunges at them. Finally, Beth shoots her dead.

Rain Man (1988), starring Dustin Hoffman and Tom Cruise, received four Academy Awards. Charlie Babbitt (Cruise), a Lamborghini dealer, and his girlfriend, Susanna (Valeria Golina), are traveling from Los Angeles to Ohio to settle the estate of his recently deceased father. Charlie had thought that he would be the principal heir, but he finds that although he will get a classic Lamborghini, most of the rest of the estate will be going to take care of Raymond (Hoffman), his autistic brother, who is living in an institution. This comes as a shock to him, since he did not even know he had a brother.

Charlie decides to discharge Raymond from the institution and sue for custody in an attempt to gain control of the inheritance. Raymond refuses to fly to California, which prompts Charlie to drive them across the country. Raymond has the ability to compute numbers at an amazing rate, and Charlie begins to remember his brother from his early childhood, when he called him "Rain Man." Charlie runs into financial trouble with his Lamborghini business, so he takes a detour to Las Vegas, hoping they can win at the blackjack tables, thanks to Raymond's amazing abilities. Charlie eventually realizes how much he loves his brother and becomes less concerned about the settlement.

War Games (1983) was the perfect movie for the 1980s, being set during a particularly tense period in the Cold War. David Lightman (Matthew

Broderick) is a teenage computer enthusiast. His skills are such that he is able to hack into his high school's computer system to change grades for himself and one of his classmates, Jennifer Mack (Ally Sheedy), and dial every phone number in his town to find an unreleased video game for his computer. What he finds instead is a top-secret computer, the War Operation Plan Response (WORP), a government war simulator that mimics possible outcomes of a nuclear war with the Soviet Union. Lightman starts a model on the assumption that it is a game called Global Thermonuclear War, but the military believes that it is a real interaction with the Soviet Union and begins to prepare to respond to an attack, nearly causing a war. David is eventually arrested for the security breach; he escapes from FBI custody with Jennifer and seeks out Stephen Falken (John Wood), the computer's designer. David talks Falken into going to the North American Aerospace Defense Command (NORAD) to stop the computer sequence. However, they first have to convince the U.S. military that the country is not really under attack; then they have to stop the computer from launching the missiles itself. They do this by "teaching" it the concept of a no-win scenario. What is also curious to note is how Broderick's character in *War Games* compares to his character in *Ferris Bueller's Day Off*: though both characters are very smart teenagers who break into a computer, the *War Games* character, David, has more remorse than Ferris.

HISTORICAL DRAMA/WAR

Chariots of Fire is a historical British film that had considerable box office success in the United States. The story features two runners, a Scottish Christian and an English Jew, who run for different reasons. The Scot, Eric Liddell (Ian Charleson), runs to glorify God, whereas the Englishman, Harold Abrahams (Ben Cross), runs to combat prejudice. Both ultimately disappoint the people closest to them while concentrating on their running careers: Abrahams is in love with a professional singer, Sybil (Alice Krige), but neglects her, while Liddell, who was raised by missionary parents in China, is planning on returning to China to work as a missionary. Liddell has come under criticism from his sister Jennie (Cheryl Campbell) on the whole idea of running. Liddell beats Abrahams in their first race, prompting Abrahams to begin to work with a coach, though his Cambridge University professors try to discourage him from pursuing this. The criticism becomes more aggressive when he misses a prayer meeting.

Both Liddell and Abrahams are accepted to represent the British team in the 1924 Olympics. Liddell receives international attention for refusing to run on the Sabbath in the 100 m; however, he runs in the 400 m the following Thursday in place of a teammate, Lord Andrew Lindsey (Nigel Havers), and medals. Abrahams runs in the 100 m, winning gold. The two runners' great success drives the British track team to a great showing at the Olympics. Although it takes some liberties with the facts, the story is well told, with portions in slow motion, close-ups of the runners themselves, and an award-winning soundtrack by Vangelis, that adds to the dramatic effect.

This film reinforces the struggle between personal feelings and national pride.

Gandhi (1982) is another well-received historical drama from Britain; recounting the life of the legendary Indian spiritual leader, the movie earned nine Academy Awards, including best picture and best actor. Mahatma Gandhi (Ben Kingsley) wielded a powerful influence over wide-ranging groups of people; his self-sacrifice and commitment to nonviolent protest, including fasting to protest the fighting between Hindus and Muslims in India and Pakistan, were effective in stopping the conflicts. He was outspoken against British colonial power and encouraged his followers to make salt from seawater to help them achieve economic independence. The British imprisoned Gandhi for years, and he was murdered by a Hindu nationalist in 1948. Gandhi's efforts largely led to the British leaving India, even though he did not succeed in quelling the violence that occurred between the Hindus and Muslims while both groups were trying to decide on the direction of the former colony. The movie tells Gandhi's story through flashbacks of his life, including an incident where Gandhi is removed from an "all-white" section in South Africa, his strict family life, his politics, and his religious tolerance. Critics and audiences alike universally applauded the film.

Amadeus (1984) was a tremendously successful movie, receiving eight Academy Awards. Largely a historical comedy adapted (albeit loosely) from the life of the 18th-century composer Wolfgang Amadeus Mozart, it focuses mainly on Mozart's adult life. Much has been written about Mozart's prowess as a child prodigy as both a performer and a composer, so this was a refreshing departure. Mozart (Tom Hulce) is the obvious, though very misunderstood, genius, driven by external factors that make simple existence difficult. Mozart is not polite to the upper echelons of Vienna society with whom he interacts; instead, he is rather rude and vulgar. He thumbs his nose at high society, always joking and behaving in an extravagant manner. He is also struggling with alcohol addiction and living beyond his means, even though he has a doting wife (Elizabeth Berridge) and children at home.

The story of Amadeus is told through the recollections of the Italian composer Antonio Salieri (F. Murray Abraham), languishing in a mental institution at the end of his life. Although Salieri has risen to a high position in the court as the royal composer, he is angry and bitter because he knows that his music is not as good as Mozart's. Considering Mozart his rival, he does everything he can to undermine him to the royal court and finally plots to trick Mozart into composing a piece that Salieri would take credit for. The work ends up being Mozart's *Requiem*, or mass for the dead; but he works so hard on composing it, along with his other responsibilities, that his health fails, and he ultimately dies.

La Bamba (1987) focuses on another, less famous, musician. Mexican-American Ritchie Valenzuela (known as Ritchie Valens professionally, and played by Lou Diamond Phillips in the film) was one of the rising stars in the early years of rock and roll. He is struggling with a number of issues: he is dating Donna Ludwig (Danielle von Zerwick), a Caucasian girl from his high school, and Donna's parents are unhappy about the relationship.

Ritchie also is suffering from a strained relationship with his older half-brother, Bob Morales (Esai Morales), who not only has a drinking problem but also is increasingly jealous of Ritchie's musical success. In spite of this, Bob plays an important role in his half-brother's musical develoment by going with him to Tijuana, where he first hears the traditional Mexican song, "La Bamba," which he later made into a hit. After a while, he made it so big that he toured with top acts like Buddy Holly and the Crickets and The Big Bopper. Valens had always had a fear of flying, which may have been an omen: on February 3, 1959, he was killed in a plane crash along with Holly and The Big Bopper.

The Last Emperor (1987) tells the story of Pu Yi, the final Chinese emperor. Pu Yi is appointed to the throne at age 3 in 1908, shortly after his predecessor's murder. The young emperor (Richard Vuu) is forced to live in the Forbidden City and restrict his visits with his family. Pu Yi is reliant on the royal advisors; however, he is unaware that there is movement toward a more modern Chinese society outside of the Forbidden City's walls. Scotsman Reginald Johnson (Peter O'Toole) is his tutor, who eventually does the nearly unthinkable: presenting the teen emperor (now played by Tao Wu) with a bicycle, which blurred the lines between monarch and commoner. As an adult, Pu Yi is forced from power and looks to the Japanese for protection. As Japan invades China, Pu Yi is expected to return to the throne, which he does under Japanese influence. When communists take over the country, though, he is arrested as a war criminal and convicted. Only after a decade does he receive a pardon, and he becomes a simple gardener. The story is tragic in that a sheltered boy chooses the wrong allies along the way, but the heartbreaking tale is skillfully reinforced by the realistic imagery (this was the first movie allowed to be filmed within the actual Forbidden City).

Dead Poets Society (1989) is a story of a group of boys studying at an elite prep school, Welton Academy, in the late 1950s. At the start of the school year, a new English teacher and Welton alum, John Keating (Robin Williams), arrives at the academy. Boys who attend school at Welton at this time include Neil Perry (Robert Sean Leonard), who excels academically but wants to be an actor, and Todd Anderson (Ethan Hawke), a shy newcomer to Welton. The two become roommates, and with a number of their friends, take Keating's English class. Keating is an inspirational and controversial figure, having the boys rip the introduction that explains a quantitative system of evaluating poetry out of the book, favoring a more improvisational approach to interpreting literature; he also urges them to "carpe diem" (seize the day). As a Welton alum, Keating takes the boys through a historical gallery, with pictures of students who have passed through the hallowed halls in the previous decades. Throughout, the headmaster, Gale Nolan (Norman Lloyd), is dubious of Keating and his teaching style.

The boys eventually discover that Keating was a member of a club called the Dead Poets Society, and they decide to start a new club where they can meet in secret to explore poetry the way Keating has taught them. Neil begins to take up acting, but he hides this from his parents (especially his father, who prefers that he attend medical school). Todd becomes less shy, and with

Keating's guidance, composes a poem on the spot in front of the class. However, a member of the group, Charlie Deaton, publishes an editorial in the school newspaper asking the all-boys school to begin to admit girls. This infuriates the headmaster, who is beginning to consider Keating the root of the problem of these rebellious boys. Neil eventually confronts his father, revealing his passion for acting. After the father attends a production that Neil is performing in, he informs Neil that he is to forget about acting, and indeed, that he has been transferred to military school to better prepare for Harvard University and medical school. Devastated, Neil commits suicide, and the school dismisses Keating because they blame him for the tragedy. The boys look toward Keating as a father figure that they can relate to, and end up learning some important life lessons. The movie was well received by its audience (mainly teenagers, many of whom had trouble relating to their own parents).

Out of Africa (1985) was another highly acclaimed film, winning seven Academy Awards. In this story, based on the life of the writer Isak Dinesen, Karen Dinesen (Meryl Streep) moves to British East Africa (now Kenya) from Denmark in 1913 to marry a Swedish baron, Bror Blixen (Klaus Maria Brandauer), for status and convenience. They intend to start a dairy farm, but then they open a coffee plantation instead. While in Africa, Karen falls in love with the area and also with a big-game hunter, Denys Finch Hatton (Robert Redford). Her husband proceeds to have multiple affairs and ends up infecting Karen with syphilis. Karen returns to Denmark for treatment, but she is drawn back to Africa years later. Her marriage and the coffee plantation both fail, but at the same time, she becomes more involved with Denys. Denys moves in with Karen, but their attitudes on lifestyle and commitment differ greatly. Their relationship falls apart, and Karen sells her possessions. The tragic love affair among Denys, Karen, and Africa is an emotional powerhouse that drives the film. Denys fears losing the area, as it is slated to become the new colony of Kenya; his relationship with the land, and the freedom he enjoys, are both something that Karen respects, though they make having a relationship with him impossible. Denys meets with her one last time before she is to move to Mombasa, and he agrees to fly her there. However, he is killed in a plane crash before he can, so Karen must move alone. She returns to Denmark and never sees Africa again, but she continues to write about it, so it lives on for her.

Driving Miss Daisy (1989) is a story of an elderly, white Jewish widow "Miss Daisy" Werthan (Jessica Tandy), who lives in Atlanta in the late 1940s with her African American housekeeper Idella (Esther Rolle). After Miss Daisy has a car accident, her son hires Hoke Colburn (Morgan Freeman) to be her chauffeur. Initially, she is resistant, but over time she warms up to him and even teaches him to read. As Idella later dies, Hoke becomes more involved with helping in the house. The film is a powerful statement on prejudice toward African Americans and Jews in the mid-1940s (even within Miss Daisy herself). Hoke drives her to a dinner where Dr. Martin Luther King, Jr., is speaking, but she only invites him to actually come to the dinner with her at the last minute; insulted by her rudeness, he refuses and decides to just sit in the car listening to the speech on the radio. By 1971, Miss Daisy, in a nursing home with dementia, finally reveals to Hoke that she truly considers him a friend—perhaps her only one.

Two movies set in the World War II era received critical attention in the 1980s. The first, *Das Boot* (The Boat), is a historical film about a crew stationed on a German submarine during World War II, told from the point of view of Leutnant Werner (Herbert Grönemeyer). Before embarking on their mission, the crew spends time in a French bar. Led by the submarine commander (Jürgen Prochnow), affectionately known as the "old man," the crew knows that their chances of survival are poor even as they are leaving the French port of La Rochelle. Within days, the crew finds themselves in their first battle, where they experience depth charges for the first time.

In the weeks that follow, the submarine and crew are battered by an aggressive Atlantic storm. The crew members encounter another British convoy, and they sink two ships. However, the submarine dives lower than typically allowed for that type of vessel. They incur heavy damage, but after resurfacing, they finish off a British tanker. The young crew watches the crew of a British tanker diving into the sea as their ship burns. The submarine returns to France for Christmas, but the crew's respite is short lived—they are ordered to go to Italy through the treacherous Strait of Gibraltar, heavily patrolled by the Allies. After replenishing supplies and fuel in Spain, the boat continues on its mission. However, it is spotted by the British, who force it toward the African coast. The vessel sinks, landing on a sea shelf. After extensive repairs, the submarine limps back to La Rochelle. Many of the crew members are wounded, and a good number of them die of their injuries, including the "old man."

The other critically acclaimed World War II movie was *Empire of the Sun* (1987), directed by Steven Spielberg. It chronicles the struggles of Jaime, a boy from a wealthy British family who is living in Shanghai, China during the war. The Japanese bomb and take over the city, and Jamie gets separated from his parents in the ensuing chaos. Though the boy returns to their home as his mother instructs him, he eventually runs out of food and leaves the house for town. He meets Basie, an older American con man who sells items for cash with his friend, Frank. After the pair unsuccessfully try to sell Jamie's teeth, Jamie brings them back to his house, promising to give them some things to sell. When they arrive, they find that Japanese troops have taken over the house, and both Basie and Jamie (now known as Jim) are taken prisoner. Jim helps Basie recover from his injuries as they languish in the Lunghua Civilian Assembly Center. Eventually, they are moved to the Soochow Creek Center, where Jim creates a trading network among the inmates and even the captors. Jim has come under the mentorship of the camp's British doctor, Dr. Rawlins, who is beaten after Rawlins tries to stop the destruction of the camp's medical facilities by the Japanese in response to a B-29 raid. Jim befriends a young Japanese pilot, and continues his relationship with Basie. Basie offers to help Jim find his parents at the end of the war, but Jim decides to continue searching on his own. Eventually, he is reunited with them.

Two movies set in the Vietnam era, both receiving strong critical acclaim, were released in the 1980s. *Platoon* (1986) was the first war movie directed by a

Vietnam War veteran (Oliver Stone), and it was based on some of his own experiences. Chris Taylor (Charlie Sheen), a privileged college dropout, has volunteered to serve in the U.S. army; unsurprisingly, he finds the conditions harsh, but he quickly begins to respect the more experienced veterans. The North Vietnamese attacks Taylor's unit shortly after he passed his night watch to another solider; that man fell asleep at his post, but it was Taylor who got blamed. Taylor is injured and hospitalized for a few days. Upon his return, he eventually befriends a group of men in the unit led by Sergeant Elias (Willem Dafoe), who relax and smoke marijuana together in a private bunker, while a more conservative group of soldiers led by Sergeant Barnes (Tom Berenger) plays cards next door.

On patrol, the unit finds that a fellow solider has been tied to a post and mutilated, causing Barnes to act irrationally toward the residents of a village as he tries to get information from them; in his attempts to intimidate them, he shoots the chief's wife and threatens his daughter. Elias arrives and, horrified by Barnes's action, gets in a fistfight with him. Their captain informs the soldiers that he will court-martial anyone who he finds has killed illegally, prompting Barnes to shoot Elias on patrol later and blame his death on the enemy. Convinced that Barnes is responsible for Elias's death, Taylor attacks him. Barnes and Taylor's relationship deteriorates further from then on, and after Taylor's second injury following an air strike, he returns to the United States. The film is effective in noting not only the complicated relationship between the soldiers during the war, but also the fact that they have lost focus on who the real enemy truly is. *Platoon* is an antiwar movie in many ways.

Stanley Kubrick's *Full Metal Jacket* (1987) was another Vietnam movie to make a significant impact, but it took a very different approach than *Platoon*. Its viewpoint is more abstract. The story is told from the perspective of Private Joker (Matthew Modine), who is instructed by the abrasive Sergeant Hartman (R. Lee Ermey) to watch over Private First Class Leonard Lawrence (Vincent D'Onofrio). Lawrence, nicknamed "Gomer Pyle" after the bumbling marine from the 1960s television show, is unstable. Though he does improve somewhat under Joker's care, he eventually kills Hartman before turning his gun on himself.

The second half of the film focuses on Joker's assignment in Vietnam. Joker is eventually promoted to the rank of sergeant and becomes a reporter for the military magazine *Stars and Stripes*, writing positive articles to keep up morale. His unit enters the town of Hue, where an unseen sniper is picking off the Americans one at a time. Their squad leader is killed, and a solider from boot camp, Robert "Cowboy" Evans (Arliss Howard), becomes the new leader. Eventually, Joker finds the sniper, and it turns out to be a teenage girl. His gun jams, preventing him from killing her as he intends, but his photographer partner shoots her without killing her. The girl begs to be killed, and it is up to the soldiers to decide the girl's fate. The group decides that Joker, with limited combat experience, should shoot her himself, and he reluctantly does.

HORROR

The Shining (1980) is a psychological and supernatural thriller made from the smash hit novel from Stephen King, which established him as one of the most important horror writers of the 1980s. Jack Torrance (Jack Nicholson), a struggling writer, arrives at a hotel in the Colorado mountains because he has been hired to serve as its winter caretaker from November until May. He is excited to take the position because he is a struggling writer, and he thinks that the quiet off-season environment of the hotel will break his writer's block. But the hotel manager tells Jack some discomfiting information: the previous caretaker killed his family and committed suicide. When Jack's wife, Wendy (Shelly Duval), and son, Danny (Danny Lloyd), arrive at the hotel, the chef communicates telepathically with Danny, telling him more about the hotel's negative past. In particular, he warns him to stay away from Room 237. He also tells Danny that the boy also has this telepathic ability, which he calls the "shining." Danny has a vision of blood oozing from an elevator door, frightening him.

After a couple of months, during which Jack begins to act strangely, Danny finally gets the courage to go in Room 237. Later, the audience learns that a woman attacked him in the room. Jack is still having trouble writing, and his wife finds him asleep at his typewriter, screaming. He explains that he had a dream that he had killed his family. Jack, a teetotaler, meets a ghost of a bartender, who serves him bourbon. In the ballroom, he sees the vision of ghosts, one of which urges him to kill his family. Jack loses his sanity and begins to hunt his family; but in the end, Danny tricks him into the hotel's hedge maze, and Jack gets lost and freezes to death. *The Shining* initially received a somewhat cold reception, both critically and commercially, but over time it has become one of the most most acclaimed horror films of all time.

The release of *Poltergeist* (1982) kicked off a successful film series. Co-written and produced by Steven Spielberg, it was a major success. The Freeling family has moved into a California housing development where there is a demon communicating with the youngest daughter, Carol Anne (Heather O'Rourke), via a television set (she proclaims its presence by the eerie phrase, "They're here . . ."). Intent on spiriting her away, the demon convinces Carol Anne to enter the light through a portal in her closet. The rest of the action focuses on bringing the little girl back from the demon's dimension. The first sequel, *Poltergeist II* (1986), provides more information about the demon, a 19th-century religious fanatic named Henry Kane, who led followers into believing the end of the world was imminent. The demon possesses Carol Anne, and his fellow spirits harass the family again, only to be helped by an Indian shaman who dispels them.

Films in the *Friday the 13th* series were significantly popular in the 1980s and became known as "slasher movies." In the initial movie in the series (released in 1980), a young boy named Jason died at a summer camp years before, and according to his mother, it was because the counselors assigned to supervise Jason ignored him while they were having sex. The mother is the villain of the movie, who intends to keep the camp closed—by killing any camp counselors unfortunate enough to come there. The other films in the series center around the grown Jason, who has morphed into a killing machine. It looked as though Jason was killed at the end of *Friday the 13th Part 2* (1981), but he returns in *Friday the 13th Part III* (1982), the first movie in which he starts wearing the hockey mask (taken from one of his victims); the mask becomes his trademark for the rest of the series. *Friday the 13th: The Final Chapter* (1984) picks up where the last left movie off, and Jason is finally killed. The film series continues with *Friday the 13th: A New Beginning,* in which a new killer is so terrified by the thought of Jason that he is institutionalized and takes on the Jason persona himself. In *Friday the 13th Part VI: Jason Lives, Friday the 13th Part VII: The New Blood,* and *Friday the 13th Part VIII: Jason Takes Manhattan,* Jason keeps getting resurrected. The specifics of the movie plots are generally less important than the nonstop mayhem that ensues, mostly on unsuspecting teenage victims. The series has continued into the 21st century.

The *Nightmare on Elm Street* series met with similar success as its compatriot, the *Friday the 13th* series. The first movie, *A Nightmare on Elm Street* (1984), introduced Freddie Krueger (Robert Englund), a child killer who comes back from the grave (after being burned to death by the parents of some of his victims) to pursue and slaughter teenagers in their dreams. In the first film, Krueger focuses on Nancy Thompson (Heather Langenkamp) and her friends on Elm Street. Nancy defeats Krueger by taking him out of the dream world, eliminating his ability to kill. The second movie in the series, *A Nightmare on Elm Street 2, Freddy's Revenge* (1985), finds Krueger possessing Jesse Walsh, whose family has moved into the Thompsons' house (from the first movie), and using his body to do the killing. *A Nightmare on Elm Street 3: Dream Warriors* (1987) revisits the children on Elm Street, who combine their dream powers to defeat Krueger for the last time, burying his bones. But in these movies, the killer is never really dead: in *A Nightmare on Elm Street 4: The Dream Master* (1988), Krueger is accidentally released from his grave, and a new character, Alice (Lisa Wilcox), works to defeat him with the help of the Dream Master. The last movie from the series to be released in the 1980s, *A Nightmare on Elm Street 5: The Dream Child* (1989), takes a new plot direction, with Krueger resurrecting himself via Alice's unborn baby. Like *Friday the 13th,* the movies from the series have continued into the 21st century.

Child's Play (1988) spawned another successful horror series, but only one of the films was released in the 1980s. Like *A Nightmare on Elm Street* and *Friday the 13th, Child's Play* featured a central villain who became part of popular culture—a doll named Chucky. Chucky, a serial killer, is shot by the police; he tries to avoid the afterlife via a voodoo ritual, but he becomes trapped in a doll's body. The doll winds up in the hands of a boy named Andy, and Chucky's goal is to possess Andy so he can rejoin the living. After a complicated series of events, Chucky gets burned up—but the door is left open for his return.

The Lost Boys (1987) features two brothers and their mother (Dianne West), who moved to California from Arizona. The brothers learn that there is a pattern of missing people in the area. The older brother, Michael (Jason Patric), meets with a local girl, Star (Jami Gertz), whose boyfriend, David (Kiefer Sutherland), is part of a gang. David tries to get Michael to join their gang by drinking what he thinks is wine, but it is actually blood. Two younger local boys warn Sam

(Corey Haim), the younger brother, to be careful, as there are vampires in the town. Michael begins to thirst for blood and attacks Sam's dog, but the dog fights him off. After the incident, and not seeing his brother's reflection in a mirror, Sam realizes then that Michael is turning into a vampire. Michael begins to realize this, confides in Star (who is a half-vampire looking to become fully human again), and takes Sam's two friends to the lair, as they are vampire hunters.

The 1980s included a variety of additional horror films that received limited commercial success when compared to the aforementioned films. *Children of the Corn* (1984) was another film series that launched in the 1980s but whose sequels did not occur until the 1990s. Based on a Stephen King short story, the tale focuses on the children of a small town in Nebraska struggling with a poor crop of corn. The children follow a child preacher who invokes a supernatural being and directs them to kill all the adults in the town to improve the harvest.

The Evil Dead (1981) started a series whose first film was about five college students vacationing in a remote area who become possessed by the Book of the Dead. A follow-up, *The Evil Dead II* (1987), continues the story, and the franchise expanded in the 1990s and into the 21st century. *Fright Night* (1985) and its sequel, *Fright Night II* (1988), feature a young man named Charley Brewster. In the first film, he discovers that his neighbor is a vampire and enlists a local TV host to help destroy the monster. The second film in the series continues Brewster's exploits as a vampire hunter. *The Thing* (1982), directed by the legendary John Carpenter, remakes the 1951 classic, whose protagonist is an otherworldly Alaskan malamute in the Antarctic. *Pumpkinhead* (1988) was the first of a series that found most of its success on video, featuring a monstrous, demonic beast. *The Fog* (1980) is about a mysterious fog that entraps a group of sailors who had died in a shipwreck 100 years before. *Hellraiser* (1987), based on a series of horror novels by Clive Barker, kicked off a series of horror flicks that features the evil Cenobite Pinhead, one of a group of villains in a puzzle box.

Feature films were some of the most provocative stories of the 1980s. In the next chapter, the impact of the story in literature, as was as other book releases, are highlighted.

FURTHER READING

Curtin, Michael, Jennifer Holt, Keith Sanson, and Kurt Sutter. *Distribution Revolution: Conversations About the Digital Future of Film and Television.* Berkeley, CA: University of California Press, 2014.

Jordan, Chris. *Movies and the Reagan Presidency.* Westport, CT: Praeger, 2003.

Muller, Jürgen, ed. *Movies of the 80s.* Cologne, Germany: Taschen, 1994.

Traube, Elizabeth. *Dreaming Identities.* Boulder, CO: Westview Press, 1992.

Wexman, Virginia Wright. *Creating the Couple.* Princeton, NJ: Princeton University Press, 1993.

Wexman, Virginia Wright. *A History of Film,* 7th ed. New York: Pearson, 2009.

Wood, Robin. *Hollywood from Vietnam to Reagan.* New York: Columbia University Press, 1986.

CHAPTER 5

Literature

As mechanized means of delivering media through television, recorded music, and movies became more prevalent in the 1980s, to the outsider, it might seem that the written word would fail to make an impact on American society. This is a misguided view, as printed literature via books, magazines, and newspapers provides a different type of intimate transfer of stories, information, self-help, and general entertainment that mechanized vehicles simply cannot provide. There were changes in newspaper readership from a mostly regional approach (however, it is always wise to acknowledge the national impact of *The New York Times*) to the emergence of *USA Today*, a national newspaper with a wide readership. The number of magazines increased significantly, to the point that there was a journal for nearly every topic imaginable, from sports to regional interests, to music and business advice, to more traditional weeklies such as *People, Time,* and *U.S. News and World Report*.

However, this chapter will focus only on books. As it would be impossible to give a synopsis of every important book released in the 1980s, or even the majority of them, this chapter will identify many of the important authors in various genres and provide a synopsis of one or more of their books, in order to examine how their writings fit into the context of the 1980s. Some authors who had a wider impact on the 1980s' book industry will have more synopses than others.

FICTION

A discussion of fictional writing in the 1980s must include the works of Stephen King. The Maine-based King produced a consistent string of best sellers throughout the 1980s, and his popularity cemented him as one of the decade's top writers. Many of his books and short stories also were adapted into films, including *Firestarter* (1980), *Cujo* (1981), *Christine* (1983), *Pet Sematary* (1983),

Stephen King is an American author who wrote many of the top horror novels of the 1980s. Many successful film adaptations have been made from his novels, including *The Shining* (1980), *The Dead Zone* (1983), and *Stand by Me* (1986). (AP Photo/HS)

Cycle of the Werewolf (1983), *Misery* (1987), and *The Running Man* (1984), the latter written under the pseudonym Richard Bachman. Nevertheless, for dedicated Stephen King fans, his books were always more important than his films.

One of his lesser known, but quite acclaimed, works was *The Talisman* (1984), co-written with Peter Straub. It tells the story of Jack Parker, who discovers an alternate universe called the Territories, inhabited by "twinners" whose population is parallel to American society. Jack discovers the Territories while trying to find the Talisman, a crystal that can save his mother, who is dying of cancer. Jack's "twin" in the alternate universe died, so he can "flip" back and forth between the two worlds, and that assists him in his quest for the Talisman. He finds that the queen of the Territories is the "twin" of his mother and is also dying. He is helped along the way by a wolf companion who accompanies him on his journeys.

It (1986) was one of King's most terrifying books and a fan favorite. The central character is an evil force known as "It," which can take a number of forms, primarily a fiendish clown named Pennywise. The force frightens seven children by addressing their deepest fears. Starting in the 1950s, a child moves into Derry, Maine, and befriends a group of boys (and one girl) known as the Losers after a spate of bullying by another group of boys. The members of the Losers come across It, who is responsible for killing a number of children, and slay the monster. Two of the bullies chase the Losers and are killed in the process, leaving the blame on their leader, Henry. Many years later, the Losers, all but one of whom live out of town, learn that It has returned to Derry and is back to its murderous ways. So they come back to their hometown and regroup to do battle with It for the last time.

In *The Tommyknockers* (1987), writer Bobbi Anderson discovers an alien spacecraft in the woods of rural Maine. It releases an invisible gas that transforms humans into aliens and gives them a higher level of intelligence through

Tom Clancy's novels set during the Cold War were some of the most popular books published in the 1980s. Film versions of his stories were produced in the 1990s, highlighted by *The Hunt for Red October* (1990) and *Patriot Games* (1992). (AP Photo/Carlos Osorio)

a process of "becoming" one with the spacecraft. Anderson's friend, James Eric "Gard" Gardner, is invulnerable to the gas, as he has a metal plate in his head because of a childhood skiing accident. Gard sees the transformation in the townsfolk and tries to stop the cycle by going into the ship. King's other noteworthy releases during the 1980s include *The Dark Tower* (1982) and *Dark Tower II* (1987), *The Dark Half* (1989), and *Roadwork* (1981), as well as the short-story collections *Different Seasons* (1982) and *Skeleton Crew* (1985). He also wrote under the pseudonym Richard Bachman, with that name on the initial releases for *Thinner* (1984) and *The Bachman Books* (1985, including *The Running Man*, which was made into a movie in 1987). King's impact on pop culture via his books, especially the ones that were made into movies, is discussed in more detail in Chapter 9, "Game Changers."

Tom Clancy was another prolific writer, specializing in storylines revolving around the Cold War, which meshed perfectly with the 1980s. His first book, *The Hunt for Red October* (1984), was a significant success, and it was made into a major motion picture as well in 1990. Jack Ryan, an analyst for the Central Intelligence Agency (CIA) who specializes in the Soviet intelligence and military, is contacted because Marko Ramius, a well-known Soviet naval captain, has gone missing along with the Soviet's most advanced ballistic missile submarine on its maiden launch. After the launch, a letter from Ramius is delivered to a Soviet politician, explaining that he intends to defect to the United States. The Soviets want to ensure that they find Ramius, his hand-picked and collaborative officers, and the submarine before the U.S. Navy does. Eventually, the Soviets reach out to the United States to try to hunt down and kill Ramius, using an excuse of a possible nuclear attack as the reason to do so. Thanks to a hunch by Navy analyist Jack Ryan, the U.S. government concludes that Ramius might wish to defect to the United States with the submarine. Clancy's second book, *Red Storm Rising* (1986), chronicles the war between the Soviet Union and allies of the North Atlantic Treaty Organization (NATO). Further books from Clancy in the 1980s, *Patriot Games* (1987), *The Cardinal of the Kremlin* (1988), and *Clear and Present Danger* (1989), continue the adventures of Ryan, either thwarting the assassination of members of the English royal family, intrigue with the Soviet KGB, or covert operations against Colombian drug lords.

Similar to Clancy, Frederick Forsyth wrote storylines that fit well with the Cold War concerns of the 1980s. Forsyth, an Englishman, released his first novel in 1971; among his top novels in the 1980s were *The Devil's Alternative* (1980), *Emeka* (1982), and *The Negotiator* (1989). He also published a collection of short stories, *No Comebacks* (1982). Forsyth was perhaps best known for *The Fourth Protocol* (1984), in which a thief breaks into an apartment of a British government official and discovers secret documents showing that the official is a traitor. The Soviet General Secretary has devised "Plan Aurora," which would place the Labour government in power in the upcoming election in Britain. The idea would be that the new prime minister would adopt a Marxist position, disassociating itself with the United States and NATO. John Preston, a British officer, is investigating the documents to discover the goal of the plan. Meanwhile, a Soviet spy enters the United Kingdom, collecting packages brought there from abroad that will assist in implementing the plan. Preston confronts one of the couriers, who commits suicide; under an inspection of a backpack, three metal disks are discovered, one of which is polonium, used to make an atomic weapon. Since the delivery is occurring via courier, the plan is now in violation of the Fourth Protocol, which was adopted in a nuclear control treaty in 1968. Preston continues his search for couriers to help thwart the Soviet plan, which ultimately fails. The book was adapted into a motion picture in 1987, starring Michael Caine and Pierce Brosnan.

John le Carré (the pen name for David John Moore Cornwell) was also prolific, writing many stories set against the backdrop of the Cold War. Cornwell had been a secret agent for the British government in his youth, which gave him insight into his writing. Toward the end of his government career, Cornwell began to write spy stories, and British government regulations compelled him to adopt a pseudonym. As le Carré, he wrote three books in the 1980s. *The Little Drummer Girl* (1983) is concerned with the Israeli and Palestinian conflict, while *A Perfect Spy* (1986) chronicles the story of a spy as he begins his career (this story is believed to be autobiographical). *The Russia House* (1989) was not only a successful novel but also a 1990 box office hit starring Sean Connery and Michelle Pfeiffer. In this story, Bartholomew Scott "Barley" Blair, a British book publisher, attends two book fairs in Russia, and he is approached by a beautiful Russian woman, Katya, who hopes that Barley will publish her friend Yakov's manuscript. She gives the manuscript to Barley's agent, who finds that it contains Soviet intelligence and forwards it to the British authorities in the "Russia House," the segment of the British government focusing on the Soviet Union. Barley is then contacted by the British government, where he agrees to ask Yakov about the accuracy of the contents. Barley meets with Yakov, knowing that he is likely bugged by the KGB, and focuses on finding a way for Katya, with whom he has embarked on an affair, to defect to the West.

Like le Carré, Robert Ludlum wrote thrillers about espionage. He began publishing novels in the early 1970s, and by the 1980s, he had released 11 novels. His first one that appeared in the 1980s, the tremendously successful *The Bourne Identity* (1980), introduces Jason Bourne, a spy who has survived an attack in the Mediterranean Sea but emerges with amnesia. The protagonist figures out that his name is Bourne because of a microchip embedded into his hip that allows him to access a bank account in Zurich that allegedly belongs to him. Bourne meets an economist named Marie St. Jacques, and the pair dodges attackers on their way to Paris to learn more about Bourne's past. In time, he discovers that his real name is David Webb.

The book is the first in a trilogy featuring Bourne; the second in the series, *The Bourne Supremacy* (1986), became another best-seller. After recovering from his injuries in the first book, Bourne begins to teach at a Maine university and is now married to Marie. The U.S. government learns that Sheng Chou Yang, a warmongering communist, is coming into power in China, and that there is an imposter using the Jason Bourne persona to kill rampantly. The government decides that Bourne should be enlisted to go to China to remove the official from his position and eliminate the imposter. To convince him to do so, the government kidnaps Marie, and Bourne goes to China to rescue her. The third book in the series, *The Bourne Ultimatum,* was released in 1990. Other major novels outside the *Bourne* series that sold well for Ludlum include *The Parsifal Mosaic* (1982), *The Aquitaine Progression* (1984), and *The Icarus Agenda* (1988).

Alice Walker began publishing books in the 1970s, including *The Third Life of Grange Copeland* (1970) and *Meridian* (1976). But it was in the 1980s that her widely acclaimed and probably best-known work, *The Color Purple* (1982), brought her to the attention of a mainstream audience. Employing African American vernacular in its language, the book explored the complexities and liberation of its female characters, including the main character, an abused, uneducated girl named Celie. Celie has been impregnated twice by Alphonso, the man she believes is her father (but who is actually her stepfather). She lives with her younger sister, Nettie, and her mother. Celie's children are given up for adoption. The mother dies, and a man simply named "Mister" comes to the family to marry the younger sister. But Alphonso offers Celie instead, who helps raise Mister's children. The children and Mister treat her poorly initially, but Celie begins to bring order to the home. Nettie runs away and moves in with Celie, and after Mister makes advances on Nettie, she leaves. Nettie writes letters to Celie in an attempt to keep in touch with her; however, Celie never receives them because Mister hides them from her.

Mister's children grow to adulthood, one of whom is Harpo, who becomes romantically involved with the self-assured Sofia. Though Harpo is aggressive with Sofia and tries to control her in the way that Mister does Celie, she fights back against this treatment. Sofia becomes a friend and inspiration for Celie. Mister then brings into the home a mistress, Shug, an ailing lounge singer. Celie helps nurse Shug back to health, becoming infatuated with her in the process. The two women become close friends, and Shug gives Celie the letters from Nettie, which reveal that two missionaries with whom Nettie has been working have adopted Celie's two children. Celie also learns from the letters that Alphonso is her stepfather.

The rest of the story continues to chronicle the relationships in Celie's life, particularly through the empowerment of the female characters, including Celie herself. *The Temple of My Familiar* (1989) is Walker's only other novel released during this decade; however, she also released other critically acclaimed works, *You Can't Keep A Good Woman Down* (1982), a short-story collection exploring the empowerment of women; *In Search of Our Mothers' Gardens: Womanist Prose* (1983), a collection of Walker's writings since the 1960s; *To Hell With Dying* (1988), a children's book; and a book of poetry, *Horses Make a Landscape Look More Beautiful* (1985).

John Jakes, like Alice Walker, had an intimate way of using historical settings to tell fictional stories that are relevant to contemporary readers. Jakes has been writing novels since the mid-1950s, and he received critical acclaim in the 1970s for his eight-book series about the Kent family that commemorated the bicentennial in 1976. Three of those eight books, *The Bastard*, *The Rebels*, and *The Seekers*, were adapted into television miniseries or movies in the 1970s and attracted a wide audience. Jakes wrote a trilogy based on the Civil War in the 1980s, starting with *North and South* (1982). The protagonists are two young men who attend the U.S. Military Academy at West Point in the early 1840s: Orry Main, from South Carolina, and George Hazzard, from Pennsylvania. Though they have political differences, they forge a strong bond. After completing their studies, the pair is sent to Mexico to fight in the Mexican-American War. Orry is injured in the war, and his arm is amputated, while George, who had met a girl in Texas on the way to the war, continues to serve in the military. Orry's sister, Brett, becomes romantically involved with George's brother, Billy. Orry plans to visit George in Pennsylvania, and his sister persuades him to bring her along. Brett continues to St. Louis, where Billy is stationed. Their train is detained in Harper's Ferry by John Brown's men, whose raid in 1859 helped accelerate the beginning of the Civil War. The book ends before the start of the war, but the next book in the series, *Love and War* (1984), continues the story through the war, and *Heaven and Hell* (1987) details these characters' lives during the early years of Reconstruction. Jakes also released *California Gold* (1989), whose protagonist is seeking his fortune 30 years after the beginning of the Gold Rush.

Louis L'Amour also uses historical settings in his books, and the majority of his novels focus on the American West of the 19th century. He started to release westerns (which he preferred to the term "frontier stories") in the 1950s, but he continued to produce books into the 1980s. Indeed, he was quite prolific, releasing two novels a year before his death in 1988. Among his best sellers were *The Lonesome Gods* (1983) and *Jubal Sackett* (1985). Released in 1987, *Last of the Breed* marked a departure from the typical western plot, in that the story is set during the Cold War. The protagonist is Major Joe Mack, an Air Force pilot working with a new, experimental aircraft over the Soviet Union. He has an accident and is captured by the Soviets. After escaping, he treks back toward the West. He begins to move through the Siberian woods to the Bering Strait and relies on Indian survival skills to complete his journey, all while being pursued by a Siberian native familiar with the area.

Ken Follett was another author using historical backgrounds for his works. A Welsh writer, he began releasing books in the 1970s, and his 1978 spy thriller *Eye of the Needle* brought him his greatest degree of commercial success. In the 1980s, however, Follett continued his streak of best-selling spy stories, including *The Key to Rebecca* (1980) and *Lie Down with Lions* (1986). *The Man from St. Petersburg* (1982) was set in the early 1910s. The Russian government was discussing naval strategy with the United Kingdom, and Czar Nicholas II sent his nephew, Prince Alexei, for talks with England's Lord Stephen Walden. Conveniently, Walden is married to Lydia, a distant relative of the Russian royal family. Meanwhile, a Russian anarchist, Feliks, is eager to assassinate the prince to destabilize the relationship between the two countries. Although he is initially unsuccessful, he contacts Lydia, his former girlfriend, for information that might help him in his mission. In the process, Feliks meets Lydia's daughter Charlotte, and they discover that Charlotte is actually Feliks's daughter, not Stephen's. Charlotte eventually provides the information that her father, Feliks, needs as he seeks out Alexei. Feliks succeeds in killing Alexei by setting the prince's home ablaze, but he also kills Charlotte in the process. Follett produced two additional best sellers, *On Wings of Eagles* (1983) and *Pillars of the Earth* (1989).

James A. Michener was a major author in the 1980s, releasing the best sellers *The Covenant* (1980), *Space* (1982), and *Journey* (1989), as well as a number of popular historical stories about fictional characters who interact with real-life figures in specific settings, including *Poland* (1983), *Alaska* (1988), *Caribbean* (1989), and *Texas* (1985). *Texas* was Michener's magnum opus, and it was a tremendous success, selling over one million copies. The book tells stories in the lives of five families: the Garzas, the Quimpers, the Macnabs, the Cobbs, and the Rusks. A member of each family serves on a task force for the governor, who wants to establish what children should learn for the sesquicentennial of Texas's statehood, a careful approach by the book's author to intertwine the family histories in one story and in the context of Texas history. The Garzas' story starts in the 16th century; the patriarch of this family a Mexican father and Spanish mother. The Quimpers, led by a matriarch, have come from Kentucky and Tennessee. The Macnabs, a Scotch-Irish family, have moved to Texas from Britain. The Cobbs, a Southern family, moved to Texas after the Civil War, and the Rusks made their fortune in the oil trade. Each story pieces together the overall history of the state in an imaginative manner.

Danielle Steele is one of the most popular authors in American literary history. Since the early 1970s, she has been amazingly prolific, and in the 1980s alone, she released 23 novels. Her best sellers in the 1980s include *Changes* (1983), *Full Circle* (1984), *Secrets* (1985), *Family Album* (1985), *Wanderlust* (1986), *Fine Things* (1987), *Zoya* (1988), *Star* (1989), and *Daddy* (1989). *Kaleidoscope*

(1987) features Sam and Arthur, soldiers in World War II who became very close friends. Both get married, and Sam later commits murder-suicide with his wife, leaving three daughters. Arthur arranges for Sam's sister to adopt Hilary, the eldest daughter, and helps place the two younger ones with new families. Hilary's home life is terrible, and she suffers from negligence and abuse from her new family. As she grows up, she seeks out Arthur, expecting that he will know where her sisters are. Unaware of the sisters' whereabouts, Arthur hires John Chapman, a private investigator, to find them for a reunion with Hilary toward the end of Arthur's life.

Jackie Collins is another novelist who found success in the 1980s. A native of England who relocated to Los Angeles, Collins released her first novel in the late 1960s, and she had success throughout the 1970s. In 1981, she released *Chances*, the first of two novels in the Santangelo series, which explored the lives of members from a New York–based, Italian American gangster family. Collins continued the saga with *Lucky* in 1985, and eight more novels in the series were released in the decades to follow. Inspired by living in Hollywood, Collins also wrote two best sellers, *Hollywood Wives* (1983), which became a television miniseries in 1985, its follow-up *Hollywood Husbands* (1986), and *Rock Star* (1988). The characters in *Hollywood Wives* are all trying to make their way in various areas of show business in Hollywood. Elaine Conti is married to movie star Ross, who is finding that his career in Hollywood is fading. Angel Hudson is married to aspiring actor Buddy. Montana Gray, an ambitious prospective screenwriter, is married to British director Neil. The tales of these women give readers an account of how the privileged in Beverly Hills live, including shopping, wearing glamorous clothes and jewels, eating, and socializing.

Judith Krantz became a top romance novelist with her release of *Scruples* in 1978. She continued to put out best sellers in the 1980s, including *Princess Daisy* (1980), *Mistral's Daughter,* (1982), and *Till We Meet Again* (1986), each of which became adapted as television miniseries. Krantz's most popular book, *I'll Take Manhattan* (1986), features protagonist Maxi Amberville, an ambitious 29-year-old three-time divorcée who is working in her late father's magazine publishing company. Maxi is wealthy, living in Trump Tower, and enjoying the best things in life. In her quest for even more success, she becomes the editor-in-chief of *Buttons and Bows (B&B)* magazine, which develops into the top fashion magazine in the United States. Along the way, Maxi experiences both love and heartache, while hanging on to what she has, even though her widowed mother marries a new man who is plotting to sell the family's magazine empire.

Anne Tyler published her first novel in 1964 and released four best-selling novels in the 1980s: *Morgan's Passing* (1980), *Dinner at the Homesick Restaurant* (1982), *The Accidental Tourist* (1985), and *Breathing Lessons* (1988). *Breathing Lessons*, which won a Pulitzer Prize, focuses on Ira and Maggie Moran, who are journeying from Baltimore to attend a funeral in a small town in Pennsylvania, where they conclude that their dreams of years past had gone away and their lives had become ordinary. Throughout the trip, it becomes clear that Maggie tries to meddle with all of her relationships to make them come out the way she wants, often alienating people with her overzealous opinions and by pouring her heart out to anyone who will listen. She has a strained relationship with her son Jesse and daughter-in-law Fiona, two high school dropouts who have become teen parents. Ira is her silent, but internally fuming, husband, whose logical viewpoint often leads him to be judgmental about his wife's antics. The book's success is owed to the depth given to both Ira and Maggie and their relationship in general, which reveals how complicated long-term marriages can be.

Salman Rushdie is an Indian writer from Britain who released his first novel in 1975. His fiction is mostly set in India and Pakistan. Rushdie started to experience mainstream success for the first time with the publication of *Midnight's Children* (1981), about a boy who grew up in the period when India earned its independence from Britain. Some critics have asserted that the story must be at least somewhat autobiographical, but Rushdie denies this. Rushdie also released *Shame* (1983), based on real-life political disorder in Pakistan, as well as a nonfiction title, *The Jaguar Smile* (1987), based on the Sandinistas in Nicaragua in the 1980s.

Rushie's most controversial work (which, for many in the general public, is the only mainstream title known outside his core fan base) is *The Satanic Verses* (1988), which was shocking to the worldwide Muslim community. In Muslim tradition, Muhammad added three verses to the Qur'an that accepted three goddesses who had been worshipped as divine. Muhammad later claims that the Devil made him say the verses, so he removes them. The controversy in *The Satanic Verses* is that its narrator says that the Archangel Gabriel, not the Devil, had made Muhammad say the verses, so ultimately they did not have to be removed. Rushdie explained on a radio program that Muhammad, being human according to doctrine, was not perfect, but that message was not well received by devout Muslims. The book was not only banned in every Muslim country, but bookstores were routinely firebombed for carrying the book. The most alarming development was that the Ayatollah Khomeini of Iran issued a fatwa calling for Rushdie's execution for committing blasphemy against Islam. A bounty was placed on his head, and Rushdie went into seclusion for a number of years.

Scott Turow has successfully combined his work as both an attorney and a fiction writer, releasing detective legal thrillers throughout the 1990s. His first book, *Presumed Innocent* (1987), follows Rusty Sabich, a legal prosecutor charged with the murder of Carolyn Polhemus, his female colleague that he had an affair with after his wife left him. Polhemus is discovered dead of blunt head trauma in her apartment, with evidence that initially suggested consensual sexual bondage that had gone awry. Sabich is assigned the case by the district attorney, who is facing a reelection campaign against Nico Guardia. Tommy Molto is in charge of the police force's homicide division and a Guardia supporter. After Guardia's election, Sabich becomes the focus of the investigation by Molto; evidence such as a beer glass with fingerprints, seems to have been tampered with in a way that only a prosecutor would know. The story twists as the former district attorney is found to also have a relationship with Polhemus, and that Polhemus had discovered a bribery case before her death that included Molto as the prosecutor. Sabich is put on trial for Polhemus's murder but ultimately is acquitted; in the end, it comes out that Sabich's wife actually killed Polhemus in a fit of mental imbalance.

Anne Rice is well known for her historically inspired novels, including a number that revolve around vampire stories. Her first, *Interview with the Vampire* (1976), was adapted into a motion picture and brought her significant recognition. Her books in the 1980s include two vampire tales (*The Vampire Lestat*, in 1985; and *The Queen of the Damned*, in 1988), and two others that are not about vampires. *Cry to Heaven* (1982) is a story about two castrati opera singers in Italy, and *The Mummy, or Ramses the Damned* (1989), concerns the mummy of Ramses II, which has been left in the care of an archeologist's daughter after her father's death. Ramses II has been made immortal because of an ancient elxir. *The Queen of the Damned* identifies that the lineage of vampires can be traced back to ancient Egypt, where the matriarch Queen Akasha is married to King Enkil.

Garrison Keillor has been a well-known radio personality on National Public Radio since the mid-1970s due to his popular variety show, *A Prairie Home Companion*. As a part of the show, there is a semicomic segment called "News from Lake Wobegon," in which Keillor discusses activities in this fictitious small town of Scandinavian and German decedents (where "all the women are strong, all the men are good-looking, and the children are above average"). Keillor developed two books based on the segment, *Lake Wobegon Days* (1985) and *Leaving Home: A Collection of Lake Wobegon Stories* (1986), both of which were top sellers. Both are in a short-story format that resembles the radio show and were in other forms before coming out in print: *Wobegon Days* was initially released as an audio book, while the stories in *Leaving Home* were used on the show first. Keillor also released *Happy to Be Here* in 1981, which maintained the same short-story format and upper Midwest subject matter, but it was less successful.

Like Keillor, Sidney Sheldon came from another type of media background. Sheldon wrote for television shows in the 1960s (*Patty Duke Show*, *I Dream of Jeannie*) before shifting to writing fiction in the 1970s. The 1980s was the most fruitful period of Sheldon's career, producing top books such as *Rage of Angels* (1980), *If Tomorrow Comes* (1985), *Windmills of the Gods* (1987), and *The Sands of Time* (1988). *Master of the Game* (1982) was adapted into a 1984 television miniseries. The storyline chronicles the MacGregor/Blackwell family over six generations. The matriarch of the family, Kate Blackwell, is celebrating her 90th birthday with her family and reminisces about her past. Her father, Scotland-born Jamie MacGregor, moves to South Africa to find his fortune in the diamond industry. He enters into a shady deal with Salomon Van Der Merwe, a Dutch investor, and is beaten when he confronts him. After being nursed to health by the investor's servant, Banda, Jamie and Banda work together to steal a fortune in diamonds. Jamie establishes a new company in Africa, and while on a tour of Scotland, seduces Salomon's daughter Margaret, who has his child. Although Jamie marries Margaret, he treats her poorly and keeps a mistress, before finally having a second child, Kate, with his wife.

Kate grows up working in Kruger-Brent, the family business, with her father Jamie's partner, David Blackwell. As Kate becomes an adult, her relationship with David turns romantic. David and Kate's relationship is strained because Kate wants to sell weapons during World War I against his wishes. David is killed in the war, but fathers a son with Kate, named Tony, before his death. Tony's mother becomes a successful businesswoman while raising her son. At the end of World War II, Tony seeks to live the life of an artist in France. Kate disapproves of his life choices, so she manipulates Tony, ruining Tony's career. Adding to Tony's tragic story is the death of his wife as she is giving birth to his twin girls, Eva and Alexandra. Tony is eventually committed to an asylum, while Eva and Alexandra are eventually poised to become heirs to the company.

Tom Wolfe was another author with a background in another medium (journalism, in Wolfe's case). A journalist since the 1960s, Wolfe became known as a leader of the New Journalism movement, particularly through the nonfictional account of Ken Kesey and his Merry Pranksters that followed the Grateful Dead, Hells Angels, and other countercultural figures. Wolfe continued to write nonfiction into the early 1980s, with *In Our Time* (1980), *From Bauhaus to Our House* (1981), and *The Purple Decades* (1982).

Wolfe's first novel was *The Bonfire of the Vanities* (1987), a contemporary tale set in the bond-trading market of New York City. The stories started as a long-form article in *Rolling Stone* magazine before Wolfe revised them into a book. The central character is Sherman McCoy, an egotistical bond trader who is having an affair with Maria Ruskin, a society wife. While they are driving in the Bronx, two African American boys block their car and approach them. Fearing they are about to be robbed, McCoy and Maria flee in their car, hitting one of the alleged assailants during their escape.

Peter Fallow, a journalist for a local tabloid, begins an investigative series into Henry Lamb, the boy who was struck. McCoy's involvement in the incident comes out, and the district attorney arrests him. McCoy's life completely unravels: not only is he branded a criminal in the press, he makes a significant mistake in a bond deal at work and is fired. Fallow discovers that Maria was with McCoy and wants to talk to her, but she has fled the country. In an attempt to find out where she is, Fallow interviews Ruskin's elderly husband at a restaurant, but the old man dies during the interview. Maria returns to New York to attend her husband's funeral, and the district attorney offers her a deal: immunity if she will trap McCoy and testify against him. McCoy is put on trial for the incident, and even though the case initially gets dismissed, the justice system continues to pursue him. His life is ruined, and his wife ends up leaving him (taking their young daughter).

This book is considered one of the most important books of the decade, as it graphically illustrates the greed and power of Wall Street, the materialistic lifestyle of the rich and famous, and the often-unscrupulous tactics of the media. The next section discusses some major best sellers intended to help the emerging entrepreneur.

FINANCE, BUSINESS, AND INVESTMENT

Donald Trump, elected the U.S. president in 2016, was one of the decade's most notorious figures, embodying the powerful, and often greedy, business entrepreneur. Trump collaborated with Tony Schwartz on *Trump: The Art of the Deal* (1987). Though the book has many elements of an autobiography (not much of a surprise considering Trump's drive and ego), his 11 points to success was inspirational to many budding businesspeople in the 1980s. In their review, *People* magazine stated that though the book "might not necessarily turn anyone into an instant competitor of Trump's, his book is full of clearly stated business tips. His 11 commandments of deal making, for instance, include: Think big; fight back; deliver the goods; and have fun." Trump is not big on personal insight, though, summarizing his philosophy in the book as "I don't do it for the money . . . I do it to do it." The book was a major best seller, released at a time when it seemed he could do no wrong, but a few years before his financial empire took significant losses in the 1990s.

Robert Allen's *Nothing Down* (1984) was the first in a series of books that Allen has released over 30 years. His message advocates that investors should invest in real estate sooner rather than later, as the cost of properties will continue to increase. This increase will prevent many Americans from owning a home, and thus create the need for more apartment buildings. To accomplish this, Allen recommends that the reader "find out where you are, focus on a specific intention, formulate a specific game plan, flood your imagination with vision, and force yourself to take at least one small step a day toward achieving your purpose." Allen also notes seven helpful techniques for buying property with no down payment. His *Creating Wealth* (1985) claims that financial self-reliance, using a model of 80 percent in real estate, 10 percent in liquid assets such as Treasury bills, and 10 percent in precious metals, can help propel the savvy investor into "automatic pilot." As a result, he advocates carrying debt to use as leverage to acquire more properties, as well as making profits in discounted mortgages. Allen's methods advocate buying one property a year for ten years and selling some of the properties to pay off the ones that are kept, all the while giving advice on restricting liability, avoiding lawyers, and finding ways of paying little or nothing in taxes. In a decade of financial ambition, both of Allen's books were big sellers.

Not all the financial books from the 1980s were about obtaining more wealth, however. Economists Milton and Rose Friedman's *Free to Choose: A Personal Statement* (1980) explains what they see as the problems with the U.S. economy, including scrutinizing the stock market, the Federal Reserve's failure to regulate inflation, failed pension policies, school systems, and protection for both consumers and workers. The Friedmans compare the United States to other countries and question whether American citizens are getting their "fair share" of the spoils of the global economy. In retrospect, this book acts as a warning about what could happen to the U.S. economy in the coming years, and many of the authors' predictions played out in the recession of the mid-2000s.

John Naisbitt's best seller, *Megatrends: Ten New Directions Transforming Our Lives* (1982), was key to foretelling the changes coming to American society in its movement to an information-based society, which took place in the 1990s. Alvin Toffler's *The Third Wave* (1980), described the movement from an agricultural society (the first wave), to an industrialized society (the second wave), to an informational one (the third wave). Echoing *Megatrends*, Toffler identifies that mass media are forced to share their influence, noting the decline in newspaper readership as an example. He notes that new media will emerge and that the economy will accelerate as information becomes "de-massified" and corporations will become less top heavy: rather, they will "consist of small components linked together in temporary configurations." Like *Free to Choose* and *Megatrends, The Third Wave* was curiously prescient about the way American society and business developed as the 20th century closed and the 21st century opened.

Thomas J. Peters and Robert H. Waterman Jr., the authors of *In Search of Excellence: Lessons from America's Best-Run Companies* (1982) were prominent researchers in business leadership and management in the 1980s. In this book, Peters and Waterman identify their McKinsey's 7-S Framework, which helps establish a firm management plan that will enable effective business leadership; they also identify companies that fit this criteria. Although some of the book focuses on business theory, much of the discussion provides insight into helping workers become more productive by being "hands-on and value driven."

Other business leadership books that were popular include *A Passion for Excellence: The Leadership Difference* (1985), by Thomas J. Peters and Nancy K. Austin; and *Talking Straight* (1988), coauthored by Lee Iacocca and Sonny Kleinfield. Iacocca (discussed in more detail later in this chapter) took Chrysler from the brink of bankruptcy back to profitability in the 1980s, which established him as a prominent businessman. Herb Cohen's *You Can Negotiate Anything* (1980) was one of the first books to discuss the topic of negotiation. The premise of his book revolves around three crucial variables: power, time, and information. Power is particularly important, comprising eight principles: Competition, Options, Legitimacy, Risk Taking, Commitment, Expertise, Knowledge of Needs, and Investment. Cohen finds that by playing the negotiator position as a strength, the adversary will recognize the negotiator's advantage. The aspect of Cohen's book that makes it so important to the business literature is that its negotiating techniques can be applied to many different aspects of business and professional life, not strictly in real estate or investments.

Spencer Johnson and Larry Wilson's book on sales, *The One Minute Salesperson* (1984), also offers advice that can be applied in a variety of areas. Some of the topics are fairly straightforward, such as preparation, goals, and objectives, but the text also discusses some other important aspects, such as trust, honesty, integrity, the buyer's self-interest, and the 80-20 rule: 20 percent of what we do provides 80 percent of the results. Johnson had previously collaborated (this time with Kenneth Blancards) on *The One Minute Manager* (1982), which included 43 essays, each portraying a scenario at a successful company. Like its predecessor, there are sections on one-minute topics such as goals, praise, and reprimands. Harvey Mackay's business advice book, *Swim with the Sharks Without Being Eaten Alive* (1988) incorporates a "short course in salesmanship," written in a straightforward manner that helps an entrepreneur close any deal, no matter how difficult. The next section of the book, a "short course on negotiation," helps develop the principles to make the business adversary come to an agreement that is favorable to the reader's terms, including walking away from the negotiating table if necessary. The next section, a "short course in management," is a thorough treatment of how be an effective supervisor of personnel, and the importance of little details and the timing of the delivery of bad news. The book ends with short thoughts on the overall aspects of business and inspiration.

Mark H. McCormack added another competing title to the literature, *What They Don't Teach You at Harvard Business School: Notes from a Street-Smart Executive* (1984), which was a best seller in its own right. Like some of the other books described in this section, this title describes strategies in selling, negotiating, managing, organizing, and communicating that can help one become a successful entrepreneur. How his book differs is that he also provides information on how to spend money on hotels and lunches most effectively, and he gives what he describes as the "Ten Commandments of Street Smarts." With the larger influence by business writers in the 1980s, there is little surprise that biographies of those men became big sellers during that period.

BIOGRAPHIES

Actress Shirley MacLaine brought attention to her spiritual side—subject matter that many considered questionable—in her series of biographies, running from *Dancing in the Light* (1986) to *It's All in the Playing* (1988). She noted that in particular, members of the entertainment industry had achieved "higher consciousness" and had understood their own past lives. The book was released near the time of her Oscar-winning performance in the film *Terms of Endearment*, which brought attention to the book that it might not have received otherwise. Although a discussion of a spiritual journey would not usually be controversial, her thoughts on reincarnation and her spirit guides, and how they assisted her relationships with her family and partner, were received with some criticism and a good deal of skepticism.

William Novak collaborated to write biographies with two important figures in American society during the 1980s. Lee Iacocca was a well-regarded celebrity in the 1980s because of his leadership in revitalizing the Chrysler Corporation and his likeable demeanor with the press. His biography, *Iacocca: An Autobiography* (1986), discusses his early years briefly but spends more time discussing his employment with Ford Motor Company, his departure from Ford, his move to Chrysler when it was a "sinking ship," his tenure there, where he bailed out the company, and the final section: his thoughts on "how to save lives on the road," the high cost of labor, the Japanese challenge to the American auto industry, and how to meet those challenges. His story proved to be inspirational to Americans both in and out of the business environment.

Novak also collaborated with Thomas P. "Tip" O'Neill Jr. on *Man of the House: The Life and Political Memoirs of Speaker Tip O'Neill* (1987). O'Neill was a long-serving politician from Massachusetts, whose career included a 34-year term in Congress and a 10-year spate as the Speaker of the House of Representatives (the longest in U.S. history). In his memoirs, the speaker devotes thoughts on his relationship with the Kennedy family, including President John F. Kennedy and Senator Ted Kennedy, and discusses his relationships with the many presidents who served during his tenure, including Kennedy, Lyndon Johnson, Richard Nixon (including details about the Watergate scandal), Jimmy Carter, and Ronald Reagan.

Biographies and autobiographies written about and by comedians were staples in the 1980s; almost all of them were well received. Roseanne Barr's autobiography, *Roseanne: My Life as a Woman* (1989), was a hit upon its release, not long after her sitcom was beginning its lengthy stint on television. She details her life as someone "born in Salt Lake City and grew up there amongst Mormons as a Jewish girl." The first part of the book discusses her upbringing and family, the second part deals with her life in Colorado, and finally, the third part gives a series of tales from her comedic career.

Comedian George Burns's touching memoir of his wife, Grace Allen, *Gracie: A Love Story* (1988) was popular because of its straightforward, affectionate storytelling. Burns and Allen were not only married but also were partners in a comedy act; he claimed, "for forty years my act consisted of one joke. And then she died." Burns and Allen were considered members of Hollywood royalty, and stories of their relationships with Jack Benny, Rosemary Clooney, and José Ferrer made the book a hit with older readers. Comedian Gilda Radner noted that she had intended to write a book called *A Portrait of the Artist as a Housewife* before she was diagnosed with ovarian cancer. Instead, she wrote *It's Always Something* (1989), about her battle with the disease. (The title is a riff from one of her enduring SNL characters, Roseanne Roseannadanna.) She reminisces about her disappointments with miscarriages, the details of her surgery and chemotherapy, and the strength of her husband, comedian Gene Wilder, and her friends during her ordeal. Published after her death, the book became a best seller.

Newspaper humorist/columnist Erma Bombeck had been widely read since the late 1960s. Like Barr, her humorous biography, *Family: The Ties That Bind . . . and Gag!* (1987) discusses her early life, but she focuses almost exclusively on funny anecdotes about her domestic life, including her husband, children, and pets. In many instances, she refers to specific situations on specific days and times to put her candid stories into context. A few years earlier, Bombeck released *Motherhood: The Second Oldest Profession* (1983), explaining events in her own life that became inspirational for many mothers through its warmth and humor. Comedian Bill Cosby's take on *Fatherhood* (1987) had a similar effect on men. He describes his experiences raising his children in an accessible, humorous way that echoed his stand-up routines. Many readers could relate to having your son turn the music down in his room, inspiring your daughter to get good grades in school, and giving your children their allowance. Cosby quips at one point that his five children are "gifted beggars. Not one of them ever ran into the room, looked up at me, and said, 'I'm really happy that you're my father, and as a tangible token of my appreciation, here's a dollar.'"

Kitty Kelley has been one of the more controversial biographers since the 1980s, with books about the British royal family, Elizabeth Taylor, and Nancy Reagan, among other celebrities. Kelley's book *His Way: The Unauthorized Biography of Frank Sinatra* (1986) was one of the top sellers in the 1980s because she painted a salacious picture of Sinatra living a double life, associating with members of the mafia, which readers found compelling. Sinatra vigorously fought to keep the book from getting published, which ironically may have brought it more publicity and made it even more successful. Priscilla Beaulieu Presley's book *Elvis and Me*, published in 1985, discusses her life with her ex-husband, Elvis Presley. Presley's involvement with the legendary pop star, first as a teen friend/fan, later as girlfriend and wife, and then finally as the divorced single mother of their daughter, had been well covered by the tabloids before the book's release. However, it went further, giving intimate and honest details about the couple's complicated relationship, including Elvis's prescription drug abuse, his affairs with a plethora of "assistants," and the family's general lack of a private life.

Nancy Reagan's memoir *My Turn: The Memoirs of Nancy Reagan* (1989) was about her relationship with her famous husband, President Ronald Reagan. Details about the President's shooting opens the book, followed by thoughts on her adjustment to the role as First Lady, her experience in Hollywood before meeting "Ronnie," a fellow actor' as she thought she had married a career actor. Chapters of particular interest describe their daily lives, ranging from minutiae such as what they ate for breakfast and the president's daily routine to the relationship she had with "the Russians" (that is, Soviet president Mikhail Gorbachev and his wife) at a time when the Cold War was thawing.

David Heymann's biography of former First Lady Jacqueline Kennedy Onassis, *A Woman Named Jackie*, released the same year, was another top seller that revealed some of the behind-the-scenes activity in the White House. As expected, Onassis's life with President John F. Kennedy was featured prominently, but one of those details—her amphetamine injections while she was renovating the White House—generated some controversy among her many fans. Her life with second husband Aristotle Onassis was also featured in the book, although Heymann makes the point that even though she was a favorite subject of tabloid writers at the time, it was questionable whether anyone could truly know what the former First Lady was like.

Peter Wright's memoir of his more than two decades in the British Security Service (MI5) was a surprise best seller in 1987. *Spycatcher: The Candid Autobiography of a Senior Intelligence Officer* details many stories about situations that he experienced in a manner that was as intriguing as any fictional story. As expected, the book is interspersed with juicy tales about American spy work against the Russians, including maneuvers while the United States was conducting the Bay of Pigs operation. As Wright remarks, "espionage is a crime almost devoid of evidence, which is why intuition, for better or worse, always has a large part to play in its successful detection." The book, which had a particular slant toward and interest in the Cold War, received a warm reception largely due to the period when the book was released.

HEALTH, DIET, AND SELF-HELP

The 1980s was also a decade where consumers' attitudes toward health were changing for the better. Many people were embracing fitness like they never had before. *Jane Fonda's Workout Book* (1981), written by the Oscar-winning actress, helped sparked an interest in working out, particulary aerobics. This was the case despite Fonda's somewhat checkered reputation—though her fans considered her Hollywood royalty, others thought she was a traitor due to her activism against the Vietnam War in the early 1970s. Later in the decade, Fonda released a video of her doing the workout routines, which reinforced book sales and inspired a slew of imitators. Both men and women began dressing in workout clothes both in and out of the gym, including leg warmers and pastel-colored leotards, tights, and headbands. For example, Olivia Newton-John chose to feature a collection of handsome men working out in the music video for her steamy song "Physical."

Soap opera actress Victoria Principal, who was making a big splash at the time for her role in *Dallas*, wrote *The Body Principal: The Exercise Program for Life* (1983), a book about exercise and health intended for busy women. Internet fitness critic Yin Teing (2009) noted on his health blog that the book "introduced a series of isometric contraction exercises." Principal showed how these exercises could be performed anywhere—while waiting in line at the grocery store, sitting at the hairstylist, or driving. No one will even notice when you are tightening your butt or stretching/contracting your calf muscles. Those exercises worked for her because at the time she wrote the book, she led a very busy life herself—working full time as an actress, running her own home, doing her own cooking, leading an active social life, and regularly volunteering. It was something that many working women could relate to.

Elizabeth Taylor was one of the most popular celebrities of the 20th century, beginning with her work in film as a child star and continuing as a glamorous (and Oscar-winning) actress into old age. In the 1980s, in her fifties, she wrote *Elizabeth Takes Off*, which was divided into two parts: the first, published in 1987, discussed her own weight gain, and the second, published in 1998, contained advice on finding a long-term solution for healthy living through diet, sample recipes, and exercise suggestions. Callan Pinckney developed a new type of exercise method, which she described in her 1989 book, *Callanetics: Ten Years Younger in Ten Hours*, which showed how consumers could hold poses for periods of time to firm muscles to lose weight. She wrote several follow-up books on this topic, and her methods helped reawaken interest in studying yoga and Pilates in some who were using exercise to lose weight.

As a result of these books, the sales of cookbooks marketed to consumers in order to be healthier escalated in sales. Television workout personality Richard Simmons put out *Richard Simmons' Never-Say-Diet Cookbook* in 1980, marketed to his fan base, which had grown considerably among homemakers. The *Weight Watchers 365-Day Menu Cookbook* (1981) gave its readers a step-by-step plan for every meal that they would eat for a year. The plan revolved around a main dish of one's choice for one meal a day, and the other meals and snacks would be adjusted accordingly to achieve the right food combination for optimal weight loss. *Weight Watchers Quick Start Program Cookbook* (1986), by Weight Watchers cofounder Jean Nidetch, was another big hit to help overweight people get started on a new way of eating.

Other cookbook authors were looking for approaches that they deemed more "scientific" in order to encourage new ways of eating. Stuart M. Berger, the author of *Dr. Berger's Immune Power Diet* (1985), advocated eating to give your body more energy. *Eat to Win: The Sports Nutrition Bible* (1982), by Dr. Robert Haas, embraced the mentality of becoming competitive through good eating habits. Harvey and Marilyn Diamond took a different approach in *Fit for Life* (1987), in which a person would eat only fruit in the morning and eat specific combinations of foods for other meals, in particular not mixing starches and proteins. Martin Katahn's *The Rotation Diet: Lose Up to a Pound a Day and Never Get It Back* (1986) had elements similar to the *Fit for Life* approach, which regulated what was eaten and when.

Durk Pearson and Sandy Shaw wrote *Life Extension: Adding Years to Your Life And Life to Your Years—A Practical Scientific Approach* in 1983; it was the first book that advocated adding supplements in pill or powder form to a person's diet, which fueled the rise of stores such as the General Nutrition Corporation (GNC) and the sales of herbal supplements that became a major factor in producing digestible solutions. Judy Mazel's *The Beverly Hills Diet* (1982) was a best-selling diet book during the decade. Mazel's approach was to understand the role of the enzyme in food and the importance of added sugar as a contributor to weight gain. Although the title might sound like a fad diet, the book is actually divided between motivational encouragement and a six-week regimen of regulated eating. The book assured readers that, by taking this approach, they would enjoy "lifelong slimhood." However, in the majority of cases (applying to diet books in general), readers followed the principles for only brief periods before returning to their original way of eating (and, usually, gaining the weight back). Many in the medical community were critical of the Beverly Hills Diet, which required a complete fruit-only diet for the first 10 days of the plan.

The most traditional cookbooks, the *Betty Crocker Cookbook* and the *Better Homes and Gardens New Cook Book,* were still relevant in the 1980s after decades of use. However, there were some new faces as well. For instance, Craig Claiborne with Pierre Franey produced *Craig Claiborne's Gourmet Diet* in 1981, and the *Frugal Gourmet* series of cookbooks by Jeff Smith, including the top-selling titles *The Frugal Gourmet* (1984), *The Frugal Gourmet Cooks with Wine* (1986), *The Frugal Gourmet Cooks American* (1987), and *The Frugal Gourmet Cooks Three Ancient Cuisines: China, Greece, and Rome* (1989) found a yuppie audience..

Leo Buscaglia wrote two books on the power of love to heal human relationships in the 1980s, *Living, Loving, and Learning* (1982) and *Loving Each Other* (1984). The former identified love as a "behavior modifier" that helps people be the best that they can be by choosing and teaching life, love, and being fully human. Another important focus is his discussion of the "anti-you," the self-defeatist part of our nature that hinders our happiness. Buscaglia's follow-up defined the loving relationship and how it is enhanced through communication, honesty, forgiveness, joy, intimacy, and dealing with jealousy. Inspirational sections about knowing yourself, ridding your life of petty irritants, and embracing spontaneity and thoughtfulness were well received by readers. Dr. Robert Schuller took a more religious/spiritual approach, asking readers to reexamine what makes them happy through eight statements of Jesus that can be applied to anyone seeking happiness by "bouncing back" from adversity, being calm, doing the right thing, treating others the way they would like to be treated, choosing to be happy, and acting as a bridge builder regardless of circumstances.

In another type of contrast, Norman Cousins, in *Anatomy of an Illness as Perceived by the Patient—Reflections on Healing and Regeneration* (1981), implored readers to accept a degree of responsibility into the recovery of any disease or disability. Cousins was skeptical of hospitals and convinced that pain can be caused by attitudes; he was also an advocate for holistic medicine, while pointing out that pain is not the enemy; he said that he was basing his opinions on what he learned from "three thousand doctors."

Wayne W. Dyer's *The Sky's the Limit* (1980) is an influential inspirational book on fulfilling one's potential. He listed a number of "false masters" that foster a sense of authoritarianism that hinders a person's ability to progress toward their goals. Dyer advocated becoming more natural and childlike (through laughter and spontaneity) and focusing on the basics of existence ("being an animal") that respects the person's spiritual needs and sense of purpose and meaning. The book cumulated by taking an attitude of "winning one hundred percent of the time" to live a more fulfilling life.

SPECIAL INTEREST AND SCIENCE

Throughout the 1970s, Robert Fulghum wrote columns for *The New York Times*, and they were released in book form in 1988 as *All I Really Need to Know I Learned in Kindergarten: Uncommon Thoughts on Common Things*. In a decade when many Americans seemed overly driven to succeed at the expense of the simpler pleasures of life, Fulghum's book was a welcome refuge, focusing on the everyday items that made life special—and enough people agreed with him to make the book a best seller. His thoughts on simple items, such as a child's love of puddles, laundry and the chore of doing it, taxis, and the act of yelling have proven timeless for many readers in the years that followed.

Andy Rooney, one of television's most recognizable commentators, released two books in the 1980s that found a receptive audience: *A Few Minutes with Andy Rooney* (1981) and *And More by Andy Rooney* (1982). Both wide-ranging books discussed different aspects of life. The former took a lighthearted look at "belongings" such as chairs, soap, jeans, and the differences in the size of nearly any tangible item, since he proclaimed himself an "all-American consumer." He also commented on "surroundings" such as street names, football on television, polls, debates, and the presidential electoral process, and "ourselves," including hair, gender, and "dirty words." His discussion on the state slogans on license plates is explored in the "advertising" section, and he questioned nearly every one.

The follow-up, *And More* addressed a wide range of topics, including items that were made by hand, old friends, eating and living, prejudices, occasions, the rich and famous, what we do, and life in general. He would also create questions that he would like to ask the president, such as 'Is being President as good as you thought it would be? Who's the biggest jerk you've met in government? Democrat or Republican? Could we just have a look at what you carry in your pockets and in your wallet?" As expected, Rooney's observations struck a chord with people during the 1980s, and both books provided keen insight into American society in a lighthearted way.

More serious was Bob Woodward's view of the CIA in *Veil: The Secret Wars of the CIA, 1981–1987*, which boasted the veteran journalist's extensive knowledge of secret documents and insider information. Woodward is particularly focused on William J. Casey, the CIA director, including a detailed examination of the Nicaraguan contras, terrorism, Israel, Iran and Libya, and Casey's relationship with President Ronald Reagan. Although some readers saw the book as a critical account of important events of the decade, it is actually a better example of how powerful governments can be in furthering their agendas and showcases Casey in particular as a powerful man with great influence on U.S. foreign policy.

Although not considered traditional literature, *Dungeons and Dragons* is a book-based game with multisided dice based on fantasy scenarios. The game features several specific scenarios; but through the direction of a player called a dungeon master, who helps create a map for them to follow, the stories and dangers constantly evolve as the game is played. David Ewalt (2013, 5) remarked that the game is

> inspired by centuries of storytelling and literature. Books like J.R.R. Tolkien's *Lord of the Rings* helped set the tone: heroic knights and wise old magicians battling the forces of evil. A typical D&D session might find a party of adventures setting off to search an underground caves system for treasure and having to fight all the slobbering monsters lurking in the dark. But D&D isn't a board game with a preprinted map and randomized game play. Instead each setting is conceived in advance by one of the participants and then actively navigated by the players.

The game turned into a considerable trend, particularly for teenage boys, and generated considerable controversy (as discussed in Chapter 8, "Controversies").

The 1980s also had best sellers that featured animals in some fashion. For instance, James Herriot wrote a series of heartwarming books based on his experience as a country veterinarian in Yorkshire, England. Set after the end of World War II, the country veterinarian encounters both domestic and farm animals and takes a trip to the Soviet Union on a freighter with sheep. Herriot's compassionate tales read as fiction in the sense that they seem too good (and too well-rounded) to be true, but that is what made the readers of *The Lord God Made Them All* (1981) and its sequels so motivated to read them. Dog trainer Barbara Woodhouse's *No Bad Dogs: The Woodhouse Way* (1984) discussed dogs that were nervous, had phobias or schizophrenia, and were generally mentally unstable—but none of them were bad. More practical advice on eating, reproduction, food, and guarding their owners too aggressively followed, buoyed by Woodhouse's conviction that any animal could be trained. She identified common mistakes made by dog owners, the ideal way of indulging and understanding your pet, and how to praise and correct. As Woodhouse said, "the mind of a dog is forever open to taking in, by touch, by telepathy, and by talking, the feelings, ideas, emotions, and wishes of its owner."

Astronomer Carl Sagan released *Cosmos* (1980), one of the first books written by an academic for the general reader community to be a significant success. He provided details about space, the way that the planets revolve in the Milky Way, and what at the time was the recent exploration of Mars. Sagan also offered some historical context of scientists such as Galileo and Christiaan Huygens, while discussing the images sent to the United States by the *Voyageur* series of explorers. In addition, Sagan wrote about other solar systems and how they evolved over time, including star formations such as the Big Dipper. The enthusiastic public response to that book opened the door for Stephen W. Hawking, who published one of his most famous tomes, *A Brief History of Time,* in 1988. Like Sagan's *Cosmos,* its success was predicated largely on how it presented a complicated subject matter in an eminently approachable way, with readable text and the occasional diagram. Hawking's descriptions of the solar system, space and time, and how the universe has been expanding from its initial creation at the "big bang" and will eventually meet its demise in the "big crunch" helped the lay public understand black holes, elementary particles in nature, and other physics concepts. Its critical acclaim and commercial success established Hawking as one of the top physicists of the 20th century.

Henry Louis Gates, Jr.'s, groundbreaking work, *The Signifying Monkey* (1989), helped establish a relationship between African American literature and the traditions of how African Americans lived in the United States after the "middle passage" from Africa, from slavery to the present. These traditions were formed by influences from Africa, such as the trickster Esu-Elegbara, from Yoruba mythology. His method of "signification" of describing semantic and rhetorical methods of writing, as well as its comparison of the "black vernacular" to Standard English, explained the details of the black poetry tradition. He further included examples of items from the past written in a vernacular tone so that African Americans could identify with them more easily. Alice Walker's *The Color Purple* (discussed in more detail earlier in the section "Fiction" of this chapter, as well as in Chapter 4, "Film") is scrutinized in Gates's work to put it in context.

Another important academic book was Richard Rorty's *Contingency, Irony, and Solidarity* (1989), which was considered a powerful book of the decade, selling well while discussing philosophy in the history of language and self being. The book also features discussions of irony and hope, and a moral discourse on cruelty and solidarity to establish a liberal philosophical frame of mind—which makes its popularity all the more remarkable because throughout most of the 1980s, the political climate was much more conservative. Rorty's book communicated ideals that were transformed into the more liberal philosophy of the 1990s. Note, however, that those liberal ideas couldn't have taken hold without the progress that occurred in all areas during the 1980s, including technology. The next chapter provides details on those developments.

FURTHER READING

Allen, Robert G. *Creating Wealth.* New York: Simon and Schuster, 1983.
Allen, Robert G. *Nothing Down.* New York: Simon and Schuster, 1984.
Ewalt, David M. *Of Dice and Men.* New York: Scribner, 2013.
Friedman, Milton, and Rose Friedman. *Free to Choose.* New York: Harcourt Brace Jovanovich, 1980.
McCormack, Mark. *What They Still Don't Teach You at Harvard Business School.* New York: Bantam Books, 1989.
Tieng, Yin. *The Body Principal.* Viewed at http://healthblog.yinteing.com/2009/06/11/the-body-principal-exercise-program-for-life/, 2009.
Toffler, Alvin. *The Third Wave.* New York: William Morrow, 1980.

CHAPTER 6

Technology

For decades, developments in technology have been used to help entertain the American public. The 1980s were no exception, as the developments in microprocessors that occurred in the 1970s allowed computer-based items to be more financially accessible to consumers. Other developments from the 1970s, such as smaller portable cassette players, videocassette recorders, and camcorders, became more affordable for home purchase.

Developments in fax machines, answering machines, and cellular telephones had been occurring for decades before the 1980s. The first commercial version of a facsimile (more commonly referred to as "fax") machine was established by Xerox in 1964, though experiments in transmitting images were first conducted in the mid-19th century. In 1980, Japan's domestic telephone company, NTT, established uniform guidelines for faxes, known as the ITU G3 Facsimile standard. This standard was adopted by many manufacturers, which led to a significant increase in the popularity of the fax machine in the 1980s. Tape-based answering machines had been used for years, but in the 1980s, the price of those machines dropped, adding to their popularity. In 1983, Kazuo Hashimoto developed the first digital machine, which expanded the impact of the answering machine further.

Cellular telephones had undergone some development years in the past, but it was in the 1980s that the technology improved enough to foster cellular telephone companies (though it was not until the 1990s that the technology and service was inexpensive enough to be adopted by a wide audience). The Advanced Mobile Phone System (AMPS) emerged in the United States in 1983. Later in the decade, it was replaced by the Motorola DynaTAC system. The government developed the Internet as a way of communication during this decade, but the Web did not become commercially exploited until the 1990s. The 1980s was less about significant advances in communication technology. Rather, technology for the home-based user reflected a cultural shift in ideals.

TANGIBLE MEDIA

In the 1970s, the videocassette recorder (VCR) was introduced to consumers. Two types of systems were released in 1976: JVC developed VHS, and Sony featured Betamax. Betamax was released a few months before the VHS format, and as such, the Japanese Ministry of International Trade and Industry was encouraging JVC to drop their work with VHS in order to present a more unified offering to consumers. JVC and Sony had some mutual history, as they had worked together on a format called the U-Matic. Sony's adaptation of the U-Matic ran into technical problems, which led JVC to rethink their strategies with a new format. JVC decided on certain criteria that would need to be included with the new format, known as the Development Matrix. As Rick Maybury explains on his informative website (http://www.rickmaybury.com/Altarcs/homent/he97/vhstoryhtm.htm):

> It listed five key features the system must have: the equipment had to be compatible with any ordinary TV; picture quality must be similar to a normal off-air broadcast; it must have at least a 2-hour recording capacity; tapes must be interchangeable between machines, and it should be versatile, which appears to imply that it should be able to tape TV programs, and be used with a video

The videocassette recorder (VCR) changed how home viewers watched both television shows and movies. Shows could be recorded for future viewing, while movies could be rented from stores and viewed at home. Two formats, VHS (shown here) and Betamax, competed for the market share, with VHS ultimately becoming the standard. (Zoltan Pataki/Dreamstime.com)

camera. They identified six key consumer and manufacturing requirements: players should be affordable, easy to operate and have low maintenance costs. It must be capable of being produced in high volumes, parts must be interchangeable, and decks must be easy to service. Lastly, and unusually for 1971, JVC considered the social implications of a new technology, recognizing the role it would have to play in what they dubbed the "information society."

Companies that embraced the VHS format included Akai, Hitachi, JVC, Mitsubishi, Panasonic, and Sharp. The VHS format emerged as the leading format because consumers considered the VHS platform more reliable, its tapes could record longer programs, and the machines were less expensive to both purchase and repair.

To try to compete with the VHS format, Betamax made improvements to the technology that would enhance quality, but then VHS countered by enhancing their features in their own right. Betamax companies included Sony, Sanyo, Toshiba, and NEC. Both formats were used in portable camera formats (camcorders), and since the Betamax tapes were smaller, the VHS format was adapted into a newer, smaller VHS-C variant. The initial Betamax I version had higher-quality audio at its release. Betamax recorded at a speed of 1.5 inches per second and had a more detailed horizontal resolution (250 lines instead of 240 with VHS), but the trade-off was that since Betamax recorded faster, it could not record programs as long as the VHS format. The advantage that VHS tapes had over Betamax was that VHS tapes could initially record two hours of video, with less video noise. Betamax II reduced its speed to try to compete with the VHS recording length, but doing so sacrificed horizontal resolution to 240 lines, the same as VHS.

As VHS became more popular, Betamax tried to gain ground by releasing Beta-HD, but then Super VHS came out, quickly countering the Betamax improvements. Ultimately, Betamax was discontinued, and what led to its demise was that the VHS format was adopted exclusively by the videotape rental industry. Although some video stores had versions of each format for commercial release, VHS tapes were largely more popular, and consumers purchased more of the recorders/players.

The Video 2000 format was created by European manufacturers Philips and Grundig to compete with the VHS and Betamax formats. Released in February 1980, the Video 2000 was one of the most advanced home recorders, as eight hours could be recorded onto one cassette that was approximately the size of a paperback book, for a price of around $40. The reason for the extended recording time was the reversible, dual-track cassette that Philips had developed. Each of the two tracks on standard half-inch tape gave four hours of playing time in both directions. Although the format was incompatible with the Japanese formats, the Video 2000 was more efficient in tape economy and boasted superior technical features. The tracks themselves were very narrow, similar to the professional line that Philips had developed in the 1970s, the N1700. The Video 2000 also used a new feature among consumer products called *dynamic track following (DTF)* for precise control of the machine. The frequency range for the stereo audio went up to 12.5 kHz—not quite high fidelity but certainly a formidable competitor to the Japanese formats. Video 2000 had the ability to locate specific recordings anywhere on the tape, which were visually identified by a four-digit numeric counter on the machine and could be searched for.

The Video 2000 was equipped for the automatic recording of TV programs using a microprocessor circuit that could store instructions for 26 television channels, and five programs on different stations could be preselected up to 16 days in advance. Since the recorder could detect which of four tape lengths was being used, the microprocessor could alert the user if the available recording time was being exceeded.

Pye and Magnavox, affiliates of Philips, marketed the video machine in the United States with the intention of addressing the shortfalls of the other two formats. However, like Betamax, it was left behind in the wake of the videotape format war. Though current releases of movies were not widely distributed to video to ensure that consumers would still go to movie theaters, the development of the format did have an impact on the entertainment industry. The videotape industry allowed users to record home videos for their use at a higher quality than earlier formats, and it also made entertainment more convenient for consumers, who could now watch movies in the privacy of their homes. More information on the controversy between VHS and Betamax is presented in Chapter 8, "Controversies."

Convenience was an important part of the way consumers enjoyed music in the 1980s. In the mid-1970s, large "boom boxes" emerged, becoming an important part of the development of urban music. As rap music became popular, break dancers used the portable sound systems as they performed on city sidewalks. Initially, the systems featured an AM/FM radio receiver and a cassette player. Later, the systems were expanded to include two cassette players, equalizers, balance (panning) controls, and input and output connections so they could be further amplified or could incorporate the use of a microphone. The devices were powered by AC current or via batteries. Popular models included the JVC RC-M90 and the Sharp GF-777.

In 1980, the Sony Walkman was introduced in the United States. This allowed listeners to enjoy music without people around them having to hear it too, and the Walkman was a very portable, convenient device (however, early cassette-based Walkmans had two headphones, and a talking microphone that allowed each listener to communicate with the other). The Walkman's most influential period came with the ascendancy of the cassette-based format in the 1980s; the device became something of an icon. With the popularity of the Walkman, cassette tapes became the preferred medium outside the home, and the 8-track tape declined in popularity. Eventually, more cassette tapes were sold than vinyl records. Other Japanese manufacturers followed Sony's lead, developing their own version of the device. The Sony D-50 was a later development that allowed compact discs (CDs) to be played in a similarly portable way. Eventually, Minidisc and MPEG-1 and/or MPEG-2 Audio Layer III (more commonly known as MP3) versions were released, eroding the Walkman's influence and popularity.

The use of cassette-based formats began to decline in the late 1980s, and by the 1990s, it was virtually eliminated in the recorded music market. Philips, based in Amsterdam, presented the CD to approximately 300 journalists in 1979. By 1980, Philips and Sony entered into a partnership, agreeing on a standardized format. Peek, Bermans, van Haaren, Toolenaar, and Stan, researchers in the history of the CD, explained in a 2009 paper that the new system was "the conclusion of a successful merger of two major existing technologies: the optical readout, by using a laser, of information stored on a disc; and the digital coding/decoding and digital processing of signals (419)." The disc itself was much smaller than a vinyl recording—only 115 mm in diameter and 1.1 mm thick. The disc was a helical track of etched pits commencing at the center, and could initially record 60 minutes of material. Unlike the vinyl record, with which bass response was eroded as it became more filled, there was no change in quality if the material either filled the disc or fell short.

Since the CD contained binary numeric code, the recorder only had to read the numbers on the disc. It was established that the new medium would be able to extend to frequencies beyond human hearing (which is typically 20–20,000 Hz) by implementation of the Nyquist Theorem. The sample rate, or number of numeric pictures per second, must be twice as fast as the highest frequency, represented as 2HF=SR. A sample rate of 44,100 was selected since the medium could accommodate frequencies up to 22,000 Hz. Further, there was a quantization rate of 16 bits for each sample. Quantization rate is twice the exponent of how many bits were available, which allowed 65,536 different details per sample.

The new technology was impressive and made a big hit with consumers, helped along by Sony's release of the Discman, the CD counterpart of the Walkman, in 1984. The CD's popularity began to be reflected in recordings. The album *The Visitors*, by ABBA, was the first CD to be released in 1982 in Europe. Billy Joel's *52nd Street* (1978) was recorded in CD format, but it was initially released in Japan in 1982; the first CD to be released in the United States was Bruce Springsteen's megahit album *Born in the U.S.A.* (1984). David Bowe was the first major artist to have his complete catalog converted to CD in 1985, and the first CD to sell a million copies or more was *Brothers in Arms* by Dire Straits, released that same year. The medium, created to replace the vinyl record, was slowly becoming the industry standard. Fans of the CD format spanned across genres. Fans of popular music liked the fact that there was little noise with the CD, as opposed to the pops and crackles from a vinyl recording and the tape hiss of a cassette tape, while classical fans championed the expanded dynamic range that the new digital format embraced.

LaserDiscs were the digital equivalent of the CDs, in that they were both digital and could not record material (at least upon their initial development in the 1980s). Since they were much larger (12 inches in diameter) than either a CD or its successor, the digital versatile disc (DVD), and also because of the density of information required to play the video and audio of a full-length movie, they were not intended to be used outside the home. One difference between the LaserDisc and the DVD is that the former recorded analog video that was stored in a composite domain, with pulse code modulation digital audio. Similar to CDs and DVDs, the information is read using pits and lands, but the LaserDisc is an analog video source without binary coding. The players initially used a gas helium-neon laser, but that technology was replaced by wider infrared laser diodes in later models.

Consumers were initially interested in the LaserDisc medium because of its superior picture quality (425 horizontal lines for the LaserDisc, as opposed to 240 for VHS, as noted earlier). Since the audio was digital, alternative versions of the audio (such as a director's commentary) could be accessed alongside the analog video information. Ultimately, the LaserDisc lost its popularity because it could not record programs to the medium as the VHS format could. Not only were games enhanced for arcade use alongside the favorite genre of the 1970s (the pinball machine), but Americans were also playing video games in their own homes in the 1980s. These developments are discussed next.

ARCADE GAMES

The 1980s saw significant advancements in computer-based arcade games. These video games largely replaced the pinball machines that were popular in the 1970s. The first two important games of the 1980s were *Space Invaders* and *Asteroids*, both in the "space shooters" category. Taito in Japan initially released *Space Invaders*, a two-dimensional fixed shooter game, in 1978; the game was distributed in the United States by Midway. The game features a movable cannon shielded by barriers as it tries to shoot five rows of 11 aliens that descend toward the cannon. If the aliens either touch the cannon or destroy it by shooting, the player loses. As the player completes levels, the aliens descend faster, making the game more challenging. *Asteroids* features a spaceship surrounded by large asteroids (and the occasional flying saucer). The spaceship shoots the asteroids to break them up. When the asteroids and saucer are cleared, a new level appears, with the components moving faster (and when an asteroid breaks up, its parts move faster too). The latter game, released by Atari, was an immediate hit.

The most popular of the arcade games was *Pac-Man*, along with its popular companion, *Ms. Pac-Man* (as well as many subsequent imitation games). The game, which was unlike any that had been introduced, was an immediate hit among a variety of players; however, its primary appeal was to preteens and teenagers. The premise of the game was simple enough: The Pac-Man, a little yellow blob, maneuvers around a maze, eating pellets while being chased by four ghosts (named Blinky, Pinky, Inky, and Clyde in the original version). At various points in the maze are power pellets, and if the Pac-Man eats one of those, the ghosts turn blue, move more slowly, and can be eaten for additional points. After the Pac-Man eats all the pellets in a maze, a new level appears. As the player moves from level to level, the ghosts become vulnerable via the power pellets for shorter periods of time and the particulars of the maze also change at times. Although *Pac-Man* was designed for the user to play as many levels as they could before losing all three of their lives, it had a software glitch that limited the player to 255 levels; at that point, a "split-screen" display

Led by the popularity of *Pac-Man*, video games became an important feature of American culture in the 1980s. The video game arcade became a popular hangout among teenagers, where they played games such as *Asteroids, Galaga, Tempest*, and *Defender*. (ilbusca/iStockphoto.com)

would appear, rendering the game useless afterward. Few could achieve this level, though, so the game's popularity was largely unaffected.

Pac-Man is considered the best-selling video game of all time. In the opinion of DeMaria and Wilson (2002, 62), "Pac-Man was the first electronic game superstar and the first game character to join the ranks of pop icons like Mickey Mouse and Bugs Bunny." It is tough to disagree with this statement, as the game was licensed to companies interested in making money off the sales of toys, cereals, and cartoon shows, among others. Namco was the Japanese group who developed *Pac-Man*, but *Ms. Pac-Man* was an unauthorized sequel developed by American company General Computer Corporation and sold to Midway Video Game Company. However, Namco eventually wrested copyright control of both games for themselves.

The success of *Space Invaders* and *Pac-Man* set up a rivalry between Atari and Midway that dominated video game culture throughout most of the 1980s. Midway president David Marofske (Kent, 2001, 137) explained that "in the late 1970s and early 1980s, our main competitor was Atari. I always looked at it as we had a hit, they had a hit, etc. It was great because we were creating a constant interest out there. Regardless of who had it, there was always something new, and people put their quarters in the slot and enjoyed what they were playing." However, it would be incorrect to claim that these were the only two significant game manufacturers in the 1980s; the strides made by each of the companies led to innovations by other manufacturers.

Space Panic, developed by Universal, was among the first to use a new genre, a platform game, that requires the player to jump or climb between suspended platforms to advance to new levels. However, *Space Panic's* success pales in comparison to another platform game, *Donkey Kong*, developed by Nintendo. The main character is Mario, who is trying to save Lady, a princess, from Donkey Kong, a large monkey. Mario, originally named "Jumpman," became one of the most enduring characters in video game history. Donkey Kong rolls barrels down the platforms to deter Mario's efforts to save the princess. When Mario gets to the point where he can seemingly save the princess, Donkey Kong grabs her and moves to the next level. New sets of platforms, with additional pitfalls, are provided. Like *Pac-Man*, *Donkey Kong* also spawned knock-off games and became a significant part of popular culture in the 1980s.

Frogger, *Dig Dug*, and *Zaxxon* were games that started in the arcade that were also widely licensed for home use. *Frogger* was developed by Konami; its objective is to maneuver a frog from his home, first across a busy street while avoiding vehicles, and then across a river by jumping on logs or turtles to avoid falling in the water, and finally avoiding snakes and alligators to get to a new home in a specific amount of time. If the frog gets squashed or eaten, or falls in the water, the player loses. Sometimes an alligator or a snake will occupy the home that the frog is trying to reach; that also causes the player to lose a "frog" (life). The pace of play increases as the player completes each level. On occasion, the character is joined by Ms. Frogger to achieve a bonus score.

Dig Dug requires the player to destroy underground-based monsters in two ways: dropping rocks on them or pumping them with air until they explode. The main character burrows underground, making tunnels along the way, while avoiding two types of monsters: the round Pooka and the fire-breathing Fygar. The character also has to make sure that a rock doesn't drop on him, usually by way of the tunnels that he digs. Demaria and Wilson (202, 83) noted, "in contrast to the early arcade maze games, *Dig Dug* was like a make-your-own maze game." *Zaxxon*, another game that was distributed to home platforms, is a shooting game where the player controls an airplane-type craft, flying over targets in an enemy fortress. The player shoots missiles launched by the enemy all while avoiding being shot down. Fuel can be replenished by destroying the enemy's fuel drums. DeMaria and Wilson (2002, 87) called *Zaxxon's* point of view an "isometric perspective" that was unique to games of its time.

Tron (1982) was a successful movie for Disney that featured unique visual technology. Its storyline revolved around Jeff Flynn, a computer programmer who is transported into one of the game machines at an arcade. In an attempt to counter the actions of a coworker at his former employer who has plagiarized a number of his games, Flynn gets digitized and trapped within the company's security software. He tries to escape from the system, and in the process, is forced to play the games inside it. One of the games, and two of the scenes from the film, were then adapted for use in a video game (alongside a tank battle game) by Bally, which became more popular than the film itself. The two scenes are the input/output tower, where the player destroys "grid bugs," and the MCP cone in a game called "Master Control Program." The game has 12 levels, each using a keyword found in computer programming. The game features what DeMaria and Wilson (2002, 85) described as "that glow of neon that was just cool, and the joystick was completely satisfying in your hand. The game itself was plenty hard, which meant lots of quarters spent in order to experience all of its scenes, the best of which was based on the famous light cycle sequence in the movie."

Tempest was a "shoot-up" game that used Atari's color vector graphics. Its objective is to use a claw-looking shooter to destroy enemies who chase the shooter around the perimeter of three-dimensional shape divided into segments, or by using a "superzapper" that destroys all the enemies. Each level has a different shape; the first 16 levels feature unique shapes and after the 16th level, the shapes cycle through in order again (the first level the same as the 17th, etc.), with additional pulsating features that restrict the shooter from entering that particular segment. The colors of the shapes change, to the point where the shapes are not even visible (i.e., they are black) in levels 65–80. Making each level more complicated are spikes generated by enemies that need to be shot to open the segment as the shooter moves down to where the level is on the verge of completion. Despite the complex structure of this game, it was very well received by the general public. One reason for its popularity is that the player could choose which level to start on, with a point bonus given for completing each level. Initially, players could choose up to level 9, but once they lost the game, and if they chose to play again, they would start at a level near where they had finished. That feature, which meant that they did not have to start all over from the beginning, encouraged users to continue to play.

Galaga and *Defender* were popular space-based shooter games released in 1979; both remained big hits throughout the early and mid-1980s. *Galaga*'s fixed shooter/spaceship moves left and right to shoot insect-type enemies (such as bees and flies) that appear in formation and then fly down toward the ship to destroy it, either by crashing into it or shooting it with bullets. A specialized insect enemy in a type of "tractor beam" can also capture the ship. After completing a few levels, the player could compete in a bonus round called the Challenging Stage to earn more points. In higher levels, enemies chase the player's now-movable spaceship.

Defender was considered by Steven Kent (2001, 147) as "one of the toughest games in arcade history." The player controls a spaceship over a scrolling display of the surface of a planet. The screen moves back and forth as the ship flies either vertically or horizontally. The premise is that the main character will destroy flying, slow green or faster red aliens, and protect astronauts who are on the surface of the planet from abduction. The astronauts who are abducted from the surface of the planet turn into mutants and attack the player's ship. A two-way joystick controls the ship's elevation, and five buttons control its direction (Thrust, Reverse, or Hyperspace) and weapon of choice (Fire or Smart Bomb). If too many mutants populated the planet, it explodes. One feature of the game was that the player could see the immediate view of the aliens on the bottom portion of the screen, and there was also a smaller, radar-like topside scanner that enabled players to attack and defend themselves simultaneously.

Two games that were successful in both upright and cockpit/environmental formats were *Pole Position* and *Star Wars*. *Pole Position*, released in the United States by Namco and Atari in 1982, is a racing simulation that defined the genre of racing games. The controls include a steering wheel, gear shifter, and accelerator pedal (though the cockpit version also includes a brake control). The player races a Formula One car around a track, first to qualify, and then to race against seven other cars. The game emulated the Fuji Racetrack in Japan. *Pole Position* was mimicked for years by many other games in various formats. Atari developed *Star Wars* (1983), based on scenes from the first of the famous movie series. The game features three different phases: a space fight with TIE fighters, followed by a battle on the surface of the Death Star (where the player destroys towers), and finally, a trench battle to destroy the Death Star to complete the level.

Q*bert was one of the more unusual games of the decade. The player controls the character Q*bert, who starts the game at a 28-cube pyramid and jumps from cube to cube to change their colors. DeMaria and Wilson (2002, 84) noted, "this nonviolent critter just had a need to hop around, changing the colors of the platform tiles on a playfield that gave the illusion of being 3D—no doubt part of its appeal." One of the significant differences about the *Q*bert* game is that it relied on strategy, not shooting. Programmer Warren Davis initially had designed a typical goal of killing enemies but eventually changed the focus to just saving the main character. When Q*bert succeeds in changing all of the cubes to the same color, a new level starts. As the levels progress, the character must jump on a cube twice for the cube to change color instead of only once, and on even higher levels, a cube changes color when Q*bert lands on it a second time (so he then has to jump on it again to change it back). Both elements are then combined in still more advanced stages. Jumping off the pyramid results in the character's death. Unfortunately for Q*bert, he also has to deal with Slick and Sam, two green monsters that can change the cubes back to their original color, and he can be "killed" by getting caught by his purple enemies Colly, Ugg, and Wrongway, or by jumping off the pyramid. *Q*bert's* simplicity was appealing to novice video gamers, but it also presented quite a challenge as it progressed through the higher levels.

Centipede was another unusual-looking game that came out during the 1980s. The player moves horizontally along the base of the screen, shooting what begins as a multisegment, centipede enemy that moves through a series of mushrooms toward the shooter. If the shooter successfully hits a segment of the centipede, it is turned into a mushroom, but it also breaks the centipede into more parts, each with its own head. If any of the parts of the centipede reaches the bottom of the screen, the portion moves back and forth around the shooter with new heads until it reaches the shooter, ending its life. The level is completed when all the heads and segments are eliminated; with every new level, a new centipede appears. Demaria and Wilson (2002, 78) wrote,

"*Centipede* was a brilliant game in every respect. The smoothness of motion using the Trak-Ball and the rapid-fire attack, could whittle away a mushroom faster than you could say 'millipede.'" The mushrooms can be eliminated after they are shot four times, allowing the player a better opportunity to shoot a centipede. Since the mushrooms push the centipede closer to the bottom of the screen, eliminating them gives the shooter more time to complete the level. The shooter must also deal with other enemies: fleas drop toward him, leaving more mushrooms in the path of their descent. Spiders eat some of the mushrooms, which helps the shooter; but scorpions also poison some of the mushrooms. When the centipede touches a poisoned mushroom, the mushroom drops toward the shooter, and if it should touch the shooter, the player loses a "life." The player can also lose a life if the shooter makes contact with any of the fleas, spiders, or scorpions. The game was one of the biggest hits for the Atari game system, both in arcades and the home market.

Joust was another game that had an unusual design. Gravity played a major role in the game since the main character, a knight riding a flying ostrich, needs to stay airborne. The knight is fighting against opponents riding on flying buzzards; the opponent that is higher will win the "joust." If the enemy is defeated, the enemy becomes an egg that falls to the bottom of the screen. The player can then collect the egg for additional points, but if the egg is not collected, it turns into another enemy knight. The enemy knights (named Bounder, Hunter, or Shadow Lord) have different values. Complicating the jousts is a pterodactyl that flies across the screen to attack the player. Ultimately, *Joust* spilled over into the home video game market, which expanded significantly during the decade.

HOME AND PORTABLE VIDEO GAMES

In the early 1970s, Ralph Baer developed a system that became the Magnavox *Odyssey*, which featured removable cartridges housing printed circuit boards and a gun-type peripheral for the game *Shooting Gallery*. The console made a big hit, largely because of the popularity of the game *Tennis*. Atari released a similar game, *Pong*, as an arcade version in the mid-1970s. Although Atari ultimately paid Magnavox handsomely in a copyright settlement, it turned out to be worth it—the success of *Pong* helped propel the home video game market into the 1980s. After *Pong* was released to arcades, Atari discovered that the coin-op distribution system in the United States limited its ability to profit from the game. The success of *Pong* in the arcades helped fund the Atari Video Computer System (later known as the 2600 game console), the widest-selling video console in the early 1980s. The console included the game *Combat*, two joysticks, and two paddle controllers. Atari decided to license the technology to Sears and Roebuck, who came up with an identical game, known as *Tele-games*, which helped expand Atari's meager beginnings. The console was one of the most prominent gifts for children in 1979.

The console also supported other games via a cartridge format similar to the Magnavox system. Users would purchase additional games, ranging from traditional games such as *Tic-Tac-Toe* and *Video Checkers*, to sports games such as

Bowling, Indy 500, and *Football,* to rebranded arcade games such as *Space Invaders, Dig Dug,* and most successfully, *Pac-Man. Space Invaders* changed Atari's fortunes, as its release inspired children and teens to purchase the console simply so they could play that game away from the arcade. Activision was a company that profited from Atari's success, as their games were compatible with the Atari system. Activision cartridges *kaboom!, Barnstorming,* and *Pitfall* were all significant successes for the company.

Video game fans had been eagerly awaiting *Pac-Man* before its eventual Atari debut, and the game brought an even more expanded fan base to home gaming. The company even had licenses with movie companies. Atari featured games based on *Star Wars, Raiders of the Lost Ark,* and *Ghostbusters.* Ultimately, however, the ill-fated decision to license a game based on the wildly successful movie *E.T.* caused Atari a number of serious problems. The license fees were high, and fans rejected the game because it was not easily playable. Atari introduced the 2600's successor, the 5200, in 1982, but by the time it was released, there was plenty of competition in the home video market, and Atari never recovered.

The most formidable competitor to Atari was Mattel's Intellivision platform. Mattel had developed a series of handheld sports games that were a big hit with preteen boys (as discussed later in this chapter). The executives at Mattel believed that their earlier successes with handheld games would allow consumers to identify with a Mattel-made console. Since Intellivision was more powerful than the Atari 2600 system, the graphics had more detail. JCPenney's Al Nilsen, who purchased the games for the national department store chain, explained (Kent, 2001, 195):

> Two things made Intellivision good. The graphics were superior, less stick figure–oriented, with more bright and vibrant colors. The second thing was the lineup of the sports games. Baseball, football, hockey, soccer, backgammon, bowling. Mattel wanted to have every sport under the sun, all licensed from the right organizations. Sports really brought new players to video games.

Nilsen was correct, as in the years that followed, sports-based video games, including the *John Madden* series of football games, became among the biggest sellers for subsequent consoles. Intellivision controllers also featured a 12-button keypad and a disc that the user could control with the thumbs while also having the option of using the Atari joystick. Intellivision led an aggressive marketing campaign against other manufacturers, a first in the industry. They were also the first company to develop an add-on module, IntelliVoice, which would turn voice into a synthesized format that could be used in select games, most notably, *B-17 Bomber.*

Coleco had some success with handheld video games in the 1970s (detailed later in this chapter), and put out the Coleco Vision console in the early 1980s. The Coleco Vision format had more detailed graphics than Atari and Intellivision. Coleco made a deal with Nintendo to adopt *Donkey Kong* for the home format. Steven Kent (2001, 94) remarked that Coleco paid "one or two dollars per cartridge, a great deal back then, but they also wanted $200,000 wired to them within 24 hours." This development led to the initial popularity of the Coleco Vision format. Those who were interested in the Atari format started to consider the Coleco Vision console because it supported "Expansion Module #1," which enabled the user to play Atari games. A lawsuit by Atari followed, which Coleco won. Coleco also released Adam, another computer system, but it was rejected by the public. Interestingly, Coleco's fortunes turned for the better because of the success of the Cabbage Patch Kids, a toy that became a cultural force in the 1980s.

Then, on December 7, 1982, the video game world was shaken by the news that Atari had announced that it expected a 10 to 15 percent increase in sales in the fourth quarter—a positive number, but well below expectations of nearly 50 percent. Atari's shares on the New York Stock Exchange tumbled to half their value, and the bottom dropped out of the entire video game market as a result. This change came about for a number of reasons. First, the U.S. economy plunged into recession in late 1982, and gasoline had become more expensive, so consumers had less money to spend on luxuries like games. The videocassette recorder had become more popular, and children became more interested in recording and watching movies, music videos, and television shows. The salaries of young video game executives were high, and these executives operated by the belief that, according to Steven Kent (2001, 235), they "could sell anything packaged with a video game." But Atari over-manufactured *Pac-Man*—only 10 million consoles were in circulation, but they made 12 million copies of the game. The design of the game was also weak due to its rushed development, and some consumers even demanded refunds. A similar hurried approach was taken in the development of the *E.T.* game, but to make matters worse, the consumers did not like the game itself, in spite of the movie's worldwide popularity.

In the end, Atari had a tremendous inventory of worthless cartridges, which they ultimately buried in the New Mexico desert. With the demise of Coleco's Adam and Mattel's new Intellivision II, the market dried up nearly completely. The home console market had dwindled from $3.2 billion annual revenue in 1983 to a mere $100 million by 1986. Mattel lost tens of millions in 1983. Magnavox canceled the release of the Odyssey 3 console system that it had been developing, and the Texas Instruments IT-99/4a was discontinued as well. Coleco's Adam was not as popular as expected.

Accelerating the demise of the console systems even further was the emergence of the home computer, led by Apple and IBM. Before long, personal computers (PCs) became popular among all segments of the population. For a brief period, Commodore International thought they had the solution, putting out the Commodore 64, a console that could function as both a computer and a game system. The Commodore 64's graphics were more advanced than the Apple II, the IBM PC, and Atari's attempt at a computer, the 800. The model was sold in retail stores, not just computer and electronics stores, making it more mainstream. The Commodore 64 helped bring along the video game crash because of a promotion that was announced, in which Commodore would issue a voucher of $100 toward the purchase of the 64 to any customer who surrendered older consoles.

Eventually, Atari decided to compete with the Commodore 64 by releasing the 8-bit 400 computer, soon followed by the 800 and XL series, highlighted with the release of a game called *Star Raiders.* There were two main views in *Star Raiders:* a more global "galactic chart," which gave details on sectors of the galaxy that could be reached via "hyperspace," and a fighter screen for individual sectors. When players were in fighter mode, they would be confronted by Zylons. Ultimately, the damage had been done, and the home video game market crashed and burned like a Zylon fighter.

New video game developers, such as Electronic Arts, had to refocus their efforts toward producing games that could be played on personal computers, such as the Commodore 64 and the Apple II system. As part of that development, computer keyboards were replacing joysticks in console formats. Games could be saved on floppy disks, which had been impossible with previous consoles. Electronic Arts found its niche in sports games, sold under the imprint EA Sports. Among their first successes were the *One on One* games, first pitting Julius Erving (aka Dr. J) against Larry Bird, and then later, Bird against Michael Jordan. *Earl Weaver Baseball,* named for the legendary Orioles manager, inspired users to buy the Commodore Amiga console. EA Sports then aligned itself with the legendary football coach and commentator John Madden to release *John Madden Football.* In the 1980s, the game received limited attention, but years later, it became among the most popular titles in home gaming and spawned numerous imitators.

In the late 1980s, home game systems rebounded when the Japanese-based Nintendo began making inroads into the United States. *Super Mario Brothers* was a smash hit for the platform, as was the home version of the arcade game *Tetris* and *The Legend of Zelda,* a fantasy action-adventure game. Eventually, Nintendo became the top console of the 1990s, but it faced considerable competition from the Sega/Genesis system which, like Nintendo, featured games in all genres, ranging from fantasy, sports, and action to fighting games.

As discussed earlier, Mattel was a significant manufacturer of handheld games in the late 1970s. In 1977, *Football* was released, followed by *Football II, Baseball, Basketball, Hockey,* and *Soccer* in 1978. Coleco responded by releasing its own version of the games, *Head to Head,* which allowed two or three players to compete with each other. Nearly a decade later, handheld electronic games were introduced into the youth gamer market. Nintendo released the Game Boy in 1989, fueled by the success of the home console popularity of *Super Mario Brothers.* The Game Boy was a significant development, as it allowed the user to have interchangeable game cartridges with the handheld device. Tetris became an international craze partly because of its popularity on the Game Boy platform.

PERSONAL COMPUTERS

The semiconductor firm Intel developed the microprocessor in the early 1970s. The 4004 processor was used in the new scientific calculators that came on the market, and eventually, the firms Motorola, Z9log, and Mostek put out other processors. Eventually, these microprocessors were used by what Martin

Campbell-Kelly and William Aspry (1996) called "hobbyists"—those who were inspired by the information technology pioneer Ted Nelson, who was considered something of a maverick among them. Eventually the hobbyists, who often read the magazine *Popular Electronics*, stumbled upon the Altair 8800 computer kit. Two Seattle hobbyists, Bill Gates and Paul Allen, collaborated on designing software for the Altair using Beginner's All-purpose Symbolic Instruction Code, or BASIC, which had been developed at Dartmouth University in the 1960s. Eventually, the duo created a software company that became known as Microsoft.

Gates became interested in computers as a youth, and eventually learned BASIC. He became close friends with another student, Allen, at the Lakeside private school in Seattle, Washington. The two formed the Lakeside Programming Group, a group of hobbyists that Allen described to Walter Issacson (2014, 316) as "a boy's club, with lots of one-upmanship and testosterone in the air." After a few years, the two became interested in Intel's 8008 microprocessor and focused on writing software that could be used by new developments in hardware such as the 8008. Eventually, the pair started a processor for BASIC that would work with Intel's 8080 microprocessor. The translator became the first commercial, native high-level programming language for a microprocessor and was widely used on computers made by Altair. The software-based translator's success led to the development of Microsoft, one of the leaders in the computer software industry, both in the 1980s and continuing today.

Meanwhile, the Homebrew Computer Club, similar to the Lakeside Programming Group, was organized in Cupertino, California. Steve Wozniak was a key member of this group. In time, he met Steve Jobs, who was also interested in electronics. Wozniak focused on the development of the computer itself, where Jobs concentrated on finding ways that their computer could operate beyond the limited computer hobbyist market. This attitude continued throughout their history at Apple Computers, the company they founded together; Wozniak has always focused on the technical developments of any product that they were working on, while Steve Jobs drove the marketing and vision. An early device was known as the "Blue Box," which was used to fool the Bell telephone system so that the user could make free long-distance telephone calls by emitting a series of specific tones. Wozniak had worked at Atari (on video games such as *Breakout*) and Hewlett-Packard (on calculator design) at night. Their first product, the Apple I, enjoyed moderate success in the late 1970s. The Apple I had a number of specific features: a computer keyboard for entering data, a visual monitor to see what was entered and processed, and a means to store the information.

It was followed by the Apple II, which in the words of Walter Issacson (2014, 58), was "the first personal computer to be simple and fully integrated, from the hardware to the software." What helped the Apple II become accepted by the business community was that it had VisiCalc, the first financial spreadsheet program, created by Dan Bricklin. Two additional products followed shortly afterwards, AppleWriter and Easy Writer, two word-processing programs. The Apple II was intentionally designed to look more like a home appliance rather than an electronic device.

Steve Jobs (left), chairman of Apple Computers; John Sculley (center), president and CEO; and Steve Wozniak, co-founder of Apple, unveil the new Apple IIc computer in San Francisco in 1984. Jobs and Wozniak were two of the four computer mavericks (along with Microsoft's Bill Gates and Paul Allen) who helped revolutionize the home computer industry in the 1980s. (AP Photo/Sal Veder)

Two other systems emerged to compete with Apple II: the Commodore PET and the Tandy TRS-80, the latter company being the parent of the Radio Shack electronics chain. Software developers began to write programs for personal enjoyment, particularly video games, but they were very basic compared to others in the market. The framework that was laid during this period, bringing forward software that the user could interact with, understand easily, and use effectively, became an important part of the success of the PC. Soon, educational software followed that adopted the same approach.

IBM was initially only interested in licensing Microsoft BASIC, but thanks to Gates and his excellent salesmanship, he was able to convince IBM to license any product that Microsoft developed, including the languages Fortran and COBOL. The operating system IBM used, MS-DOS, became a critical element of the way that computing worked outside Apple in the 1980s. Business software such as VisiCalc was developed as a visual calculator and met the simple interface requirement. Reliable word processing was still in its infancy, and the typewriter, particularly electronic models by IBM, was still used by many in the workplace.

IBM recognized that in order to stay relevant and competitive with Apple and its other rivals, they also would need to embrace computer technology. IBM then became affiliated with Gates and Allen of Microsoft, who developed the MS-DOS programming platform for them. IBM also decided to affiliate with other companies to make related components: Epson for printing and Zenith for monitors are two examples of this approach. Because of these affiliations, as well as IBM's existing reputation in the business world, the IBM computer became the preferred machine for use by businesses globally. IBM was also eager to license its framework with other manufacturers, such as Compaq, since it knew that the real measure of success would not be in hardware developments, but in software. More details about this entire history can be found in Chapter 10.

Business software, such as a spreadsheet known as Multiplan and the spreadsheet Lotus 1-2-3, became essential tools in American business. In order for Apple to maintain their place in the business marketplace, the company began a new project: Lisa. With 1 MB of random access memory (RAM), two floppy disk drives, a hard drive, and seven application programs, the system sold for $9,995. Printer prices ranged from $700 for a dot-matrix printer to $2,100 for a laser printer. Buying either type was prohibitively expensive, even for businesses (never mind the individual user). Soon after, Jobs announced the launch of a new project called the Macintosh, which would be significantly less costly than Lisa. Ultimately, the Lisa software and files were not compatible with either IBM or the Macintosh, so they quickly disappeared from the marketplace. Nevertheless, the Lisa was innovative, in that it demonstrated the graphical user interface (GUI) that Apple had developed and would use later to great fanfare.

Inspired by the developments made at the Xerox Palo Alto Research Center (PARC), the Macintosh GUI was significantly more user-friendly than BASIC. The idea of the GUI dated to 1950, when electric engineer Douglas Englebart (Donovan, 2011, 143) "concluded that computers would be easier to use if people interacted with them via television screens rather than keyboards, punch cards, or switches," made possible by bitmapping, another innovation pioneered at Xerox PARC. Until then, most computers, including the Apple II, would merely generate numerals or letters on the screen, which usually were green against a black background. Bitmapping allowed each pixel on the screen to be controlled by the computer—turned off or on in any color. The Macintosh's ability to produce graphics was far superior to anything that had come before.

The simple text commands used by BASIC were now replaced by new terms: *windows, icons, pull-down menus,* and the *mouse,* and the interface was laid out on what was now described as a *desktop.* Files and programs could be easily found and restored on the computer. The size of the machine also became much more manageable: physically, it was not much larger than a phone book, and it had a detached keyboard (where the Apple II had a connected keyboard), an internal monitor and floppy drives (both whom were disconnected in the Apple II). Although there was no possible way to expand the computer's hardware in terms of a hard drive or memory, Apple licensed its source code to other companies to create software for the new system. Apple changed their marketing approach so that the Macintosh didn't compete directly with IBM, who had a firm foothold in the business market. Led by John Scully, the company started to market its products to home users, but the price of the machines ($2,500, a sizeable sum for the mid-1980s) still did not match the demographic.

As a result, Apple started to collaborate with Microsoft so that they could develop business software so their system could compete with IBM. After an impressive presentation of the new Macintosh computer, Jobs began to discuss partnering with Microsoft to develop new software that would be shipped with the Macintosh line, including a spreadsheet (Multiplan), a chart program (MacGraph), and a BASIC interpreter. Meanwhile, Apple developers Bruce Horn and Steve Capps created the Finder program for file and program control in the desktop environment. An interface program (Toolbox), a drawing program (MacPaint), and a word-processing program (MacWrite) were also developed for the new system. By 1986, next-generation models of the Macintosh were emerging: Macintosh Plus, Macintosh SE, and most significantly, the Macintosh II, each bringing a higher functionality. The Macintosh II used a Motorola MC68020 microprocessor with a floating-point coprocessor. It also featured 1 MB of RAM, which could be increased to 8 MB, making this the first computer with the capacity for expansion. The Macintosh II was significantly faster than the Macintosh SE, and it incorporated the NuBus architecture, which had recently been developed at the Massachusetts Institute of Technology to allow users to interface with the computer using cards by other manufacturers to support specific software. In 1991, a significant development in the system software, System 7, was released that allowed object-based technology and preemptive multitasking.

Throughout much of the 1980s, Microsoft was relying on MS-DOS coding for the software it was providing to IBM. As noted earlier, Microsoft had worked with Apple in the beginning of the 1980s on software for the Apple II. Jobs met with Gates regularly because of the agreement between Microsoft and Apple. It was in August 1981 that Microsoft learned about the Macintosh GUI platform, and they eventually developed their own operating system, known as Windows. Although Apple sued Microsoft for copyright infringement, the case was dismissed, and Windows gained significant popularity throughout the 1990s, to the point that, as Issacson (2014, 369) remarked, "Windows eventually clawed its way to dominance, not because its design was better but because its business model was better." By the end of the decade, Windows had taken over 80 percent of the computer market. The key reason for this was that the operating system was made available to outside hardware developers. Users had more choices, and companies such as Dell and Compaq could create foreign-made, Windows-capable machines, for a mere fraction of the price of the IBM or Apple computers. A Windows machine could be "hot-rodded" by removing and replacing motherboards freely (though both platforms allowed hard drives and memory to be upgraded).

Apple, on the other hand, wanted all their components to be proprietary, and that made the costs higher. However, the Macintosh inspired great loyalty in their fans, who were willing to pay for a unique computing experience (embodied in Apple's slogan "Think different") that focused on users' comfort rather than just productivity.

While Apple and Microsoft dominated the computer landscape during the 1980s, Tandy made two significant contributions. The first was the TRS-80 Pocket Computer, which measured 7 inches by 2.75 inches by 0.5 inches and used four mercury batteries. It resembled a calculator, but it was much more powerful and laid the groundwork for the future development of the portable computer. The second was the TRS-80 model 100, which became the first laptop computer, and its design powerfully influenced the design of future models by both Apple and IBM-related manufacturers.

Eventually, each of these computer technologies would become integrated via the World Wide Web and Ethernet networking technology. The 1990s was the decade where home users became completely comfortable using the Internet, e-mail, electronic bulletin boards, and modems. However, none of these new developments would have happened without the technological progress that took place in the 1980s.

FURTHER READING

Abramson, Albert, and Christopher H. Sterling. *The History of Television, 1942–2000.* Jefferson, NC: McFarland and Company, Inc., 2003.

DeMaria, Rusel, and Johnny L. Wilson. *High Score!* New York: McGraw-Hill/Osborne, 2002.

Donovan, Tristan. *Replay: The History of Video Games.* East Sussex, UK: Yellow Ant, 2010.

Issacson, Walter. *The Innovators.* New York: Simon and Schuster, 2014.

Kent, Steven. *The Ultimate History of Video Games.* New York: Three Rivers Press, 2001.

Peek, J. B. H., Jan Bermans, J. A. M. M. van Haaren, Frank Toolenaar, and S. G. Stan. *Origins and Successors of the Compact Disc: Contributions of Philips to Optical Storage.* Springer: New York, 2009.

CHAPTER 7

Visual Arts

Before the 1980s, abstract and modernist artists were considered the new and emerging artists of the 20th century. However, as those ideas fell out of fashion, there was a reemergence of figuration painting. Significant exhibitions in London and Berlin in the early 1980s helped realize this change of taste. As John Russell (1981, 13) wrote at the beginning of the 1980s, "when art is made new, we are made new with it. We have a sense of solidarity with our own time, and of psychic energies shared and redoubled, which is just about the most satisfying thing that life has to offer." An example of the change came when a new style of Italian painting, described as "Trans-avant-garde" by Achille Bonito Olivia in 1980 (Chilvers, 620), such as in the art of Francesco Clemente, began to gain traction. In response, photography-related art began to emerge as a true representation of real-life subjects. Often, the most popular were also controversial. Newer technology in the manner of video art was also beginning to gain traction in the art community in the 1980s, which is not surprising since art will often have modern influences as they emerge in any decade. In addition, there were advances in architectural design, fashion, toy design, and theme parks, and there were changes in selling products through new advertisements. All these items helped establish what was specifically trendsetting and idiomatic of the 1980s and made the decade among the most nostalgic of the 20th century.

PHOTOGRAPHY

Photography became one of the most recognizable art forms of the 1980s. Redden and Stadler (1987, 80) remarked that "the difference between photography and high art seems to turn on the question of whether or not the photographer's exploitation of advances in technology (and chemistry) should make one hesitate to classify photography alongside painting, etching, woodblock carving, and the like." Photography as art is an active experience, whereas photos that are taken simply to use in advertising become more of a passive one. Lines of what was taboo were blurring. Anthony Julius (2002, 149, italic in original) considered that in art, "taboos compromise precisely those practices and belief that cannot be defended. If they *were* defensible, they would be something else: laws, or principles or morality, or good manners. To describe a modern belief as a taboo is thus to condemn it." Among the most condemned, recognized, and controversial photographers was Robert Mapplethorpe.

Robert Mapplethorpe's photography can be best classified into three categories: flowers, faces, and figures. The "figures" category is where Mapplethorpe has generated the greatest controversy. Photography of figures, particularly if they are nude, is a two-way process for Mapplethorpe: The viewers are looking at the image in the same manner that the person is looking at the camera. This connection between looking at something and being looked at works both ways, and that in itself becomes something that can be interpreted as sexual, electric, and inasmuch a promise of pleasure. Mapplethorpe had plenty of supporters, one of the strongest of which was Richard Howard, who acknowledged that

> no feature of a body of work, then, can be so important as it seems in our discussion of it—there will be in Mapplethorpe's copious oeuvre, almost invariably, a contradiction to the perceived drift, or even to the tyrannous current; he is venturesome enough, as I say, to inspect the nostalgias of the life we all live, of the sights we all see, as well as his own visions and vilifications. Yet for the rapt artist, the life we all live is not enough of a subject, and for the photographer, not enough of an object. It must be life with an inclination, a leaning, *a certain slant of light* a tendency to shape itself only in certain forms, to afford its most valued and valuable revelations only in certain . . . darkness. (Karndon, 158)

It is in the context described by Howard that Mapplethorpe's work should be something to be embraced, not feared. The photographs are simply a way of telling a story about us. Arthur C. Danto remarked (1986, 214–215) that the phallus is the focus of Mapplethorpe's exhibitions, agreeing with critic Howard in that Mapplethorpe has "aestheticized the genitals, drawing attention to the correspondence in form and function between these and flowers, which are 'the sexual organs of plants.'" Danto further states that in his own self-portraits, Mapplethorpe is "dressed in a sort of jerkin, and in those backless tights, looking over his shoulder at us, his Pan-like head with its small soft bearing glowering in a sort of defiance. He is holding the handle of a cruel bullwhip up his anus. The visual equalization between the phallus and the agency of pain contributes another component to genital aesthetics."

Mapplethorpe starts that story in his book *Certain People: A Book of Portraits* (1985) but focusing on himself first, as the book features self-portraits on the front and back covers before moving on to a plethora of images of others. In contrast, in the book *Lady, Lisa Lyon* (1983, 43), Mapplethorpe focuses on the bodybuilder, within "interplay between phallic drive and passiveness—or guild—is enacted not on the boy of the male photographer but on the body of

Robert Mapplethorpe was a controversial photographer active in the 1980s. His subjects included celebrities, nudes, and BDSM, and before his death in 1989, his work was celebrated with a national tour. Critics in the 1980s questioned if government funding should be used to display what some considered to be offensive displays of art. (Rose Hartman/ Archive Photos/Getty Images)

a woman." Throughout the book, there is a cohesive narrative that brings the art into two levels of the reader's conscience: as individual images and the book as a body of work of its own. In Mapplethorpe's next project, *Black Book* (1988), the focus becomes isolated on black men in conventional images that represent the stereotypes that society holds for them, including classical nudes, jungle inhabitants, athletes, allegorical figures, soldiers, and tough guys. These images help shape both active and passive portraits of a wide-ranging spectrum within one group of people.

Lorna Simpson's projects focusing on African American women have a similar tone. Unlike the Caucasian Mapplethorpe, Simpson brings a uniquely African American viewpoint to the images that she captures. Okwui Enwezor (2006, 51) opined that what Simpson was "most concerned with was not 'self-evident' truth." Rather, she was invested in "historical" truth, that is to say, those images calcified like plaque in the social unconscious. In this way, Simpson captures images that are aligned with some of the struggles of African American women, from surface issues such as their hair, to more important things, such as their ability to be seen as an equal to the other gender and races. Simpson's images are not simply photographs; some of them are in mixed media, including video and Plexiglas. Her works betray a nakedness about her own view of the struggles of the women she is portraying.

David Salle's works with nude models have raised questions among art critics. Kuspit (1988, 312) remarks that "the secret of representation is that it is a problem of object relations, psychoanalytically understood. Salle's art is a brilliant demonstration of the general character of object relations, as well as a deconstructive odyssey—as full of unpredictable adventures as that of Ulysses and Leopold Bloom—of his own relations to that personally most dramatic, socially most vivid object, woman. No mater how naked, his woman is still veiled with his own ambivalent attitude toward her." Levin (1988, 228) adds, "It isn't easy to offend viewers anymore, but Salle's art raises theory questions. Is it ironic, sarcastic, or neutral? Are his images of women misogynist, pornographic, or simply confrontational, bringing into the open a visual tradition of objectified female nudes? Is he an archmoralist or is his work really, as he has insisted (there's no narrative, there really is none, there isn't one) devoid of content, stripped of meaning?" Arthur C. Donta (1986, 77) considers that Salle had five different components to his work. Two of which are important to note, first, "an appropriated image, usually from a work or a fragment of a work that has a locus in the history of art but sometimes a locus just in the stock of banal images of everyday life. Then there is a component that looks, though painted, like a photograph in hideous monochrome, often of a nude or seminude woman displayed in a sexually humiliating posture." Salle's importance in the 1980s was further reinforced by the fact that critics—whether positive or negative—at least were talking about him.

When discussing his critics, Salle (Avedon, 1987, 58) responded, "perhaps more acute but no less wrongheaded, because they have also posited a certain set of ideas about the audience which I think are offensive, especially in the ballet world. Ideas about what's 'avant-garde' or 'unconventional', that kind of nonsense. They are not even very observant, as the writing gives a tone of almost scientific data-gathering-like detachment from which deductions are made, while their ability to actually visually discriminate between thing A and B is very dim." In 1985, Robert Rosenblum (1999, 322) posited that Salle's work could be considered among the new reality of artists. He writes that Salle's work is "conjured up as if by free association, a mirage of seemingly disconnected fragments from art and life is suspended in an elusive twilight zone that never stops seesawing between tangible matter and filmy phantoms, between the codified languages of abstraction and those of figurative art." Salle, who continues to live and work in New York City, remains a leader of the postmodern art world.

PAINTING

Judy Chicago generated considerable attention in the 1980s through her series of works that collectively became known as the *Birth Project* (1980–1985). Chicago had emerged as a leader in feminist art in the 1970s, and she was interested in the female sexual anatomy in the sense of power of birth giving, rather than of sexual pleasure or freedom. As she states (Lippert, 2002, 68), "to my dismay, I discovered that there were too few images of birth in Western art, an omission I set out to counter through an extended series of painted and needle worked images of birth. To behold the vulva in labor as a woman is giving birth is to be confronted with sheer female power. I wanted to celebrate that power and to explore and express the range of birth experiences—the painful and the joyous—and the act of creation itself." Chicago has also reinterpreted the story of creation in the book of Genesis, where she claims that man, without a woman's involvement, created life; this idea became one inspiration for the beginning of her series (Fedler and Rosen, 281).

Some critics saw the female subjects in Cindy Sherman's work to be less empowering. Sherman became popular through her series *Untitled Film Stills* (1977–1981), which, in the opinion of Donald Kuspit (2002, 166), shows that "immaturity exists in the form of a young woman, on the verge of adulthood but still adolescent in her attitude, trying out various roles in search of an identity she doesn't not believe in, that is, a womanhood she is skeptical of even as she playacts it. Sherman seems to be exploring a labyrinth of exciting female identities, but all are stale, predetermined, and somewhat tarnished cliché's, as indicated by the fact that they are the products of Hollywood convention and artifice." Sherman's thoughts on her work differ, as quoted by Julius (2002, 201): "I wanted to make it very clear what my concerns were about, and try to be different and challenging. I've always been so well received publicly that it started to bother me. I wanted to make something that would be hard to be well received publicly. It's still been pretty well received." What Kuspit failed to recognize, though, is that the images are for "pop's sake" (pop culture, that is), and can be enjoyed without making a statement that some might consider rebellious or antiestablishment.

Roy Lichtenstein is often associated with the Pop Art movement of the late 1960s through his cartoon-influenced art. His earlier works focused on what Irving Sandler (1997, 149) considered "big themes—love and war—but for fear of sentimentality, he counteracted their human drama by appropriating images from comic strips. He also culled images from the history of art, particularly those that had been widely circulated as postcards or posters." By the 1980s, Lichtenstein's style had moved toward expressionism, as opined by Levin (1988, 234), "Lichtenstein's Pop style has congealed into a stunning caricature of itself. It's partly the desperation of a successful artist who has painted himself into a corner, and partly as if he's boldly turning the whole outmoded idea of modern stylization into his own brilliantly decorative semi-postmodern décor." Lawrence Alloway (1985, 96) added, "Lichtenstein no longer systematizes the turbulent, but confers a contradictory humbleness and elegance upon it." Among those, Lichtenstein's top works in the 1980s was *Mural with Blue Brushstroke* (1986), which Rondeau and Wagstaff (2012, 24) called "a veritable catalogue of Lichtenstein's formal preoccupations in terms of motifs, specific paintings, series, and favored artists."

Keith Haring's pop art could be seen in a wide variety of forums, from painting clothing for 1980s' pop icons Madonna and Grace Jones, to designing sets for dance pieces, to a curtain for a Roland Petit ballet that was presented in 1985. He was initially influenced by graffiti art and was arrested for criminal mischief while "decorating" a subway in 1982. In the 1980s, his approach was an attempt to bring together high art and low art, but critics did not always see eye to eye with him; "there is neither age nor wisdom nor survival, only colorful, cavorting infantile figures, stripped of all distinguishing signs, including those of gender. They are ageless figurines full of energy, existing for its own utopian sake" (Kuspit, 2000, 168). Haring drew his quasi-human graphic characters across any surface that he could find, vividly projecting themes about the power of media such as television, the futility of the pursuit of money, the joys of homosexuality, and the threat of AIDS. Haring's most famous graphic character, "Radiant Baby," was inspired by his involvement in the Christian group *The Jesus Movement* in the 1970s. On a blog dedicated to Haring (http:// keith-haring-100a.blogspot.com), the anonymous fan quoted Haring's thoughts on the character, calling it "purest and most positive experience of human existence." Haring was openly gay, and he was diagnosed with the AIDS virus in the mid-1980s; at that point, his street-influenced art took on a decidedly social tone, drawing the public's attention to the plight of those affected by the disease. Haring died at the age of just 31 in 1990.

Julian Schnabel became one of the best-known artists in the 1980s, working in a style known as *neoexpressionism*. By the age of 31, Schnabel was the only young American artist to be included in the *A New Spirit in Painting* show at the Royal Academy in London in 1981. As Suzi Gablik remarked in Irving Sander's article on popular culture, "it became impossible in certain circles to attend a dinner party where Schnabel was not the center of conversation. Everybody, it seemed, was asking everybody, in an effort to get at the heart of the matter, 'what do *you* think about Julian Schnabel?'" (1996, 149). Donald Kuspit (1998, 289–291) added,

> Schnabel's most notorious additions are velvet and crockery. Like the newspaper many of the original Cubist collages incorporated, velvet and crockery are mass-produced domestic materials. Velvet is a romantic material epitomizing the everyday idea of luxury. Crockery is a primitive substance given civilized shape and put to personal use. Crockery is as necessary for everyday life as velvet is unnecessary, yet both are peculiarly intimate in import even if it is a vulgar idea of intimacy—intimacy turned inside out into conspicuous material, that is, intimate sensation, these materials convey a philistine coziness.

However, Levin (1998, 224) was less than impressed, decrying that the "surfaces Schnabel usually paints on are meant for other uses or else they're tarps that have been dragged through the dirt. But these Kabuki backgrounds aren't just material: they're readymade images, opening up a stylized theatrical landscape. They set the stage. And onto the surface of these preexisting vistas Schnabel's images wander like malfunctioning props." With the attention, both positive and negative, Schnabel came to reflect the 1980s, or as Irving Sandler (1996, 430) says, he is an "ego monster—a kind of Donald Trump of art or the artist laureate of the Reagan era." It is that capacity that made Schnabel something of a maverick—an attitude that was well embraced by an emerging type of art: video art.

VIDEO ART

Video art was one of the more radical art movements in the 1980s. The use of surveillance tapes became a form of expression by a number of artists in the 1980s. The use of the cameras highlights the ever-intrusive eye of the government in both repressive regimes and supposedly democratic societies. Vito Acconci was one of the leaders in this field in the 1980s; his career started in the 1960s, and by the 1980s, he was using video, furniture, landscape art, and installations for his expressions. Acconci (2005, 132) remarked, "Video installation is the conjunction of opposites (or, to put it another way: video installation is like having your cake and eating it, too). On the one hand, 'installation' places an artwork at a specific site, for a specific time (a specific duration and also, possibly, a specific historic time). On the other hand, 'video' (with its consequences followed through) but a video broadcast on television is placeless; at least, its place can't be determined—there's no way of knowing the particular look of all those millions of homes that receive the TV broadcast. Video installation, then, places placelessness; video installation is an attempt to stop time." Acconci used "mass-media tools to promote a more complex understanding and experience of the individual human being in the social world. In Acconci's *sub-Urb* at Artpark, 1983, the viewer-participant's intense isolation in underground 'rooms,' coupled with the experience of collective address as evoked by the printed, poster like words on the walls, serves to acknowledge both the tension and the relationship between the realms of public and private" (Kuspit, 1988, 426). Dieter Froese had a well-received exhibition called *Not a Model for Big Brother's Sp-Cycle* in 1987, in which he used closed-circuit television to present a two-channel, pretaped video. Julia Scher, a member of New York's Burglar and Firearm Association who is considered a "certified alarm installer," used the commercial surveillance motif in a more extreme setting than Dieter in her installation *Security by Julia.* The exhibit featured performers in specific scenes while the video cameras captured the footage and broadcast it to the audience. A pink-uniformed woman wearing a "Security by Julia" badge met visitors to the exhibit, which toured nationally.

One of the most important artists in the video art medium is Bill Viola, an artist and instructor at the California Institute of the Arts in Los Angeles. He was very active in the 1980s, with installations in France, New York, Houston, Sweden, and Japan. Viola's 1983 work *Reasons for Knocking at an Empty House* featured a video of a dark room that contains a man in a wooden chair, implying that he is about to be executed, staring at a camera. The exhibit also shows a monitor showing footage of the man in the chair being battered in the head by another man, who is standing behind the seated man. The complementary images of the two cameras, juxtaposed into the same piece, changed the approach to video art in the years following the 1980s.

Andy Warhol was one of the most controversial yet celebrated artists of the 20th century. His career began in the 1950s, and throughout the 1960s and 1970s, his pop art pieces like painting of objects (most famously Campbell's soup cans) made him a household name. He produced and appeared in three cable television series during the 1980s. All of the programs were produced for cable television: *Andy Warhol's Fashion* for Manhattan Cable, *Andy Warhol's TV* for the Madison Square Garden Network, and *Andy Warhol's Fifteen Minutes*, which was named for his flippant quote that "everyone will be world-famous for 15 minutes," for MTV. Warhol's death of a heart attack in 1987 took place before the last episode of *Fifteen Minutes* aired. Donald Kuspit (1988, 397) remarked that "his career makes it clear—perhaps for the first time in the history of capitalist art—that it didn't much matter whether one was seen for one's art or one's money. Preferably one was seen for both."

ARCHITECTURE

Both traditional and abstract approaches in architecture flourished in the 1980s. Works from Michael Graves during the decade included the Portland Building in Oregon in 1980, replete with quotations from the classical language that included a tiered stylobate at the street level. He was also a force in reintroducing color into 20th-century architecture, as with the green terracotta columns and tan flanking walls punctured by square windows. Graves also designed the Swan and the Dolphin hotels at the Walt Disney World resort in Florida, which were two of the most popular hotels in central Florida in the 1980s.

The Italian master Renzo Piano was a top architect in the 1980s who designed a variety of structures both in the United States and internationally. Piano lived in Houston for a portion of the 1980s and served in academic capacities at Columbia University and the University of Pennsylvania. His creations included a multifunctional food center in Genoa, a structural system with steel beams similar to the World Trade Center in Milan, an exhibition area featuring a great platform in Milan, a spatial grid of reinforced concrete pyramidal elements, and a variety of rehabilitation projects, such as the renewal of a street block in the Turin city center and the conversion of a 15th-century Benedictine abbey into a cultural and exhibition center in Perugia. Piano also was commissioned by IBM to create a temporary, travelling exhibition building of polycarbonate pyramidal elements, laminated wood, and aluminum to be placed in urban parks internationally, including in Rome, Milan, Lyon, and London. In the United States, Piano designed a building consisting of an articulated platform filtering light from above and transmitting it into the interior of the exhibition area for the Menil Collection in Houston.

Richard Meier gained exposure for his work on the High Museum of Art in Atlanta, with a stark white exterior made of plain paneling that in the words of Moffett, Fazio, and Wodehouse (2004, 551) featured a "dominant circulation path around the circumference of a quarter-cylinder glass-enclosed atrium, off which he arranged more conventional orthogonal galleries with artificial illumination." Meier's work was rooted in the early traditions of modernism, including his design for the Museum of Decorative Arts in Frankfurt, Germany, and the billion-dollar Getty Museum, started in 1984 and completed in 1997, which featured porcelain-emblem panels with modular but textured stone. Meier's work was seen as a response to newer technologies.

This contrast would be seen in the deconstructionist work of Peter Eisenman. Charles Jencks (Moffett, Fazio and Wodehouse, 2004, 557) considered deconstruction as the art that "always deepens for its meaning on that which is previously constructed. It always posits an orthodoxy which it 'subverts,' a norm which I break, an assumption and ideology which it undermines." Deconstructive architects do not merely have the ability to destroy what already exists; rather, they unlock what a building could be while removing barriers that were part of the original design process. Eisenman was a leader in this area; though he has reinvented himself over the years, his works in the 1980s are neat examples of the deconstructivist approach. A collusion of geometries remains, overlaid with biological metaphor, which is certainly more apparent to the designer than the casual onlooker of his Biocentrum in Frankfurt am Main. Eisenman's buildings are typically distorted and unbalanced.

Frank Gehry's deconstructive approach in an important building in the 1980s, the Winton Guest House in Wayzata, Minnesota, incorporated basic forms (shed-roofed box, a vaulted-box, other boxes with flat roofs) that hover around a central pyramid. When it came to commenting on deconstructionist style, Eisenman was quick to remark that "if there is a Deconstructionist style, I would certainly be the first one to turn against it. That is when I become anti. . . . Something to be against. I have always been against something that becomes fashionable" (Papadakis, Cooke, and Benjamin, 1989, 146).

Maya Lin won a competition to design the Vietnam Veterans Memorial in Washington, D.C., at 21, selected from a pool of over 1,400 applicants. The guidelines for the competition (as chronicled on the official website, http:// thewall-usa.com) stated that the memorial was to be "reflective and contemplative in character, harmonious with its surroundings, contain the names of those who had died in the conflict or who were still missing, and make no political statement about the war." The memorial generated some discussion due to its color. Harriet F. Senie (1992, 33) noted, "Black was interpreted by many as a state of shame and dishonor, especially in contrast to the many white memorials in Washington. But Lin found black 'a lot more peaceful and gentle than white,' and more important, able to reflect its surroundings when polished. Black is also the traditional color of mourning, but this association implied a negative interpretation of the war. In the minds of many, the color black made it difficult to separate honoring the veterans from damning the war." The Vietnam Veterans Memorial has a time line on a structure that is completely closed, making a statement about the war's length and closure, and Lin made a similar statement with her Memorial for Civil Rights (1989) in Montgomery, Alabama, a closed circle with a larger interval between the first date, 1954, and the last, 1968. Visitors can project themselves as a link to and an extension of the struggle. Lin herself (2000, 103 and 401) noted that a "still photograph of any of my works does not afford an understanding of the piece, unless one has already seen it. I always wanted the names to be chronological, to make it so that those who served and returned from the war could find their place in the memorial."

OTHER TRENDS IN VISUAL ART

Richard Prince was active in appropriation art in the 1980s, where he rephotographed advertisements to present them as new works. He used Marlboro cigarette advertisements, making a new piece out of an easily identifiable macho, masculine, and loner image that had become romanticized as a part of the American vernacular. Some critics found this practice terribly unoriginal, but Hal Foster (1996, 101) defended it, stating, "the critique of appropriation art was often dubious in its own right, but at least it retained critique as a value. Moreover, it attempted to elaborate rather than to reverse the deconstructive techniques of related practices: conceptual art, institutional critique, feminist art, and so on." Transgressive art's intent is too profound in other ways; much that is valued as art remains shocking, disturbing, and problematic. Such art has been endorsed with the generic description *transgressive*—suggesting that this art shocks only by virtue of its uncompromising mission to interrogate conservative views and subvert conventional moral beliefs. However, many consider that this mission has become excessive in that transgression "goes too far"; and violates the responsibility of enlightened culture to embrace it as art.

Magdalena Abakanowicz has utilized both soft and hard surfaces in pursuit of presenting analogies to the animal, plant, and mineral forms of nature. Her 1987 work, *War Games*, represents "one extreme of Abakanowicz's thematic repertoire: the consequences, seen in the double-edge image of weapon and victim, of the instinct for destruction" (Rose, 1994, 138). They evoke a response of mural outrage that we can compare only with that aroused by the mangled corpses and hideous scenes of bloody carnage depicted by Fancicso Goya in his *Disasters of War,* and like Goya, Abakanowicz witnessed murder and mutilation during the terror of the Warsaw uprising and its aftermath.

Graffiti was popularized in 1970 by Taki, but as art, it is without a past and with a questionable future. However, it has a history of its own, which according to Kim Levin (1988, 204) accidentally collides with recent art's own history. Nicholas Ganz (2004, 18) goes on to point out that the "USA was the birthplace of graffiti, which spread like wildfire from cities such as New York or Philadelphia throughout the whole country—and later throughout the whole world. The quality of both lettering and figurative work has risen to amazing heights, and artists such as Dalek and Craola have created completely new worlds around their characters. Many of the early writers are now freelance artist or work for key companies in the clothing industry as designers. Murals have become popular as they often help American artists secure paid work."

Jean-Michel Basquiat, a native of Brooklyn, started graffiti with a friend, Al Diaz, using the text motif "SAMO" in each of their works. SAMO became recognized throughout New York, was featured in the *Village Voice,* and eventually became a copyrighted symbol. Their work would feature different sayings and became a downtown fixture similar to Keith Haring's "Radiant Baby" slogan, discussed earlier in this chapter. Diaz and Basquiat parted ways, and the latter moved on to create gallery-based art, including what Terry Smith (2011, 56) called "confrontational paintings that combined a sophisticated response

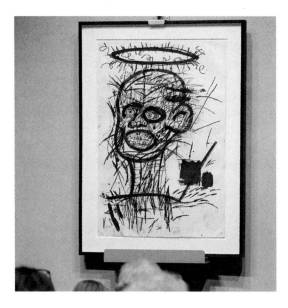

Jean-Michel Basquiat initially found fame as part of the graffiti art duo SAMO, with fellow artist Al Diaz. As the duo parted ways, Basquiat began to focus on creating gallery-based art, much of which contained underlying criticisms of political and social situations. The image above is a 1982 gallery work, *Untitled*. (AP Photo/Kathy Willens)

to sources ranging from Dubuffet, Rauschenberg, and Twombly, to Leonardo's sketchbooks and *Gray's Anatomy*." Basquiat developed a heroin addiction and passed away in 1988, at only 27; yet he brought the culture of the street into the sensibility of the refined art community, and this influence affected fashion in the 1980s in a similar manner.

FASHION

Fashion has always reflected the entirety of popular culture. The 1980s were no exception, and with the rise of yuppies, the idea that fashion would reflect power and wealth is not surprising. Changes in fashion often seem to run counter to what was popular in previous years—some liken this to a cyclical model, in which fashion always repeats itself. Although those involved in the industry would be among the first to argue that changes in fashion do not occur fast enough, fashion trends often return to the forefront of popular culture. The 1970s was largely considered the "Me Decade," and for good reason, as strides were made in personal liberties (such as women's liberation and sexual freedom, which followed the development of the birth control pill in 1960) that were resulting in self-reflection that by the 1980s became self-indulgence. The social revolution of the late 1960s spawned a generation of teenagers, many of whom questioned authority, but by the time they reached adulthood in the early 1980s, many of these former rebels had become self-confident (even arrogant sometimes) and desired success and money above all. In short, the 1980s nickname of the "Greed Decade" made a lot of sense. Anne Slowey (Demacy and Baudot, 2003, 5) reinforces this thought, saying that "even though the 1980s were known as the Greed Decade, fashion experts would probably refer to it as the decade of individualism and extremes." The new heroes were male professionals, such as stockbrokers, who wanted "top designers, including Thierry Mugler and Kenzo began to add menswear to their collections, a development that was paralleled by the expansion of the specialized male fashion press. For women, who entered the workforce in greater numbers than ever during the eighties, the big-shouldered power suit became a potent symbol and acted both as a protective shield and a statement of authority" (Mendes and de la Haye, 1999, 213).

Similarly, John Peacock (1998, 7–8) observed:

> In the 1980s, youth culture no longer dominated fashion. In male dress, the peacock look of the seventies gave way to a more sophisticated, formal elegance. Men wanted clothes that were both business-like and comfortable, as well as being of a recognizably high quality in a decade that was greatly concerned with status. A typical outfit for men consistent of a double-breasted jacket worn with straight-cut trousers with pleats from the waist. For smart occasions, a designer-label jacket was often combined with blue denim jeans and an open-necked silk shirt.

Peacock is on solid ground here, but what is essential to note is that the most influential consumers in fashion were women. Women, now competing with men for similar jobs, wanted to show their power through their dress (even if they did not make the same amount of money as their male colleagues). Designers such as Ralph Lauren and Calvin Klein became household names, and each year they would make insignificant changes to their lines to fuel further sales.

High fashion is the most financially lucrative portion of the industry. Often, it is through this area that the most experimental and avant-garde designs are revealed, to be embraced or rejected. What many in the mainstream do not realize is that there is a trickle-down effect, as the most exclusive designers influence their more mainstream compatriots. In the 1980s, two important events helped change high fashion: the wedding of Lady Diana Spencer and Charles, Prince of Wales, and Ronald and Nancy Reagan's move to the White House. Both of these events inspired designers to pursue luxury and romance. As a result, *Vogue* (Mulvagh, 1998, 275) noted that in 1981, the "spring silhouette was either emphatically short, body-skimming, and sexy, or blousy and romantic. London's New Romanticism and its new Princess sported velvet bloomers, breeches and cavalier clothes. This fancy-dress look could be both escapist and cheap, as the young and brave raided charity shops and second-hand stores." Designers continued their designs throughout 1982, but in that year saw an important development as Japanese designers dominated the Paris collections. In 1983, the androgynous look emerged, breaking down any preconceived notion of proper gender roles. In 1984, fashion focused on the London subculture (discussed later in this chapter), while in 1985, the classic silhouette took a soft turn, emphasizing a voluptuous profile in both the breasts and bottom. In 1986, the collections sent the message that you should flaunt your assets—whether they be your figure or your money. Curves were favored, while high heels brought a focus on women's legs.

The changes in fashion for both women and men were reflected in popular culture outside the high fashion world. For example, in the evening soap operas popular on television during the 1980s, Linda Gray and Victoria Principal (*Dallas)*, and Joan Collins and Linda Evans (*Dynasty*) wore suits by designers such as Ungaro and Valentino. The men followed their lead, as can be seen in the Armani-influenced pastel suits worn by Don Johnson and Phillip Michael-Thomas on *Miami Vice*.

Trends such as power dressing, cross-dressing, and status dressing, the invention of high-tech fabrics, the use of vibrant colors and abstract-expressionist graphic prints, the Japanese invasion, the birth of the graffiti, logs, streetwear and hip hop the popularity of preppy-punk, and hyperaccented silhouettes with large shoulder pads made the 1980s one of the most creative and outrageous periods of fashion in the entire 20th century. This decade was about power, and the bold statements of fashion included accessories. Paula Reed (2013, 8) commented, "The *Dynasty* women were never knowingly under-accessorized. Liberal helpings of statement costume jewelry were worn day and night by the show's female stars and drifted into mainstream fashion."

The best symbol of the female power dressing through fashion was the abovementioned shoulder pads. Dressing like an executive, for both men and women, became known as *power dressing*. When the yuppies left work, they adopted a preppy look, with ironed jeans and khaki pants with loafers or deck shoes and traditional plaid or striped shirts, polo shirts featuring an alligator or other emblem, or turtlenecks. Yuppies draped crew- or V-neck sweaters around their shoulders. These low-priced coordinates were copied worldwide. *Vogue* criticized the recent extremes and exaggerations: the retrospective and overdone shoulders were too square, shirts too brief, jackets too tight. Cotton knits in soft, smudged pastels added color and contrast to the tweed jackets or skirts, full easy linen trousers, and leather garments.

Some changes in fashion arrived via an unlikely source: a new culture of physical fitness. Olivia Newton-John's music video for "Physical" in 1981 incorporated the look—leggings, leotards, and sweat bands—early on, and actress Jane Fonda, who kicked off the trend of workout videos in the 1980s, sported similar attire. Paula Reed (2013, 68) considered "the fashionable preoccupations of the decade became health, beauty, youthfulness and sex appeal. Accordingly, the diet, health-club, and fitness equipment industries boomed. Biker shorts, headbands, sweatshirts, and legwarmers became streetwear and Lycra was transformed from a fiber known mostly to lingerie and hosiery manufacturers into a global mega-brand from its developer and manufacturer, DuPont." Jane Mulvugh (1988, 371) identified the new trend as well: "[S]portswear was seen on every city street this year—leotards, running shorts, track suits, exercise shoes, dance pumps and trainers. There was a transport strike in New York and many walked to work in neat gabardine suits with, literally, training shoes, Adidas, Nike, Etonic, Saucony and New Balance being the most popular. The fitness craze had become a fashion craze. Norma Kamali launched her 'sweats' collection: rah-rah skirts, leggings and jogging suits cut in gray and brightly colored cotton sweaters." As the fitness craze expanded, clothing made of Lycra, a new synthetic that was tight fitting and easy to work out in, became widespread (sometimes even worn outside the gym). In another similar look, Jennifer Beals, the star of the movie *Flashdance* (1983), wore slashed sweatshirts and leggings, and many young girls copied her look. Many of them wore white Reebok high-tops with their leggings (though the more affluent, fashion-conscious of them sported designs by the Paris-based Azzedine Alaia instead).

Business was good in the 1980s: the economy was booming, and the tech industry flourished. Overall, American society was full of a hubris and extravagance that it had not seen at any point in the century since the 1920s. As society was enjoying high levels of excess, fashion in mainstream society was following a similar path, reinforced by "street cred." Thanks to the emergence of punk rock, fashion was now a protest statement. The roots of street cred started in the punk era in London in the late 1970s, and that bled over into the 1980s. Valarie Mendes and Amy de la Haye (1999, 221) noted that

> Punk first manifested itself among groups of unemployed young people and students, many from the capital's art schools, who congregated around Vivienne Westwood and Malcolm McLaren's famous boutique in the King's Road, Chelsea. Punk was anarchic, nihilistic style that deliberately set out to shock. In stark contrast to the naturalism colorful garments worn by the generally utopian Hippies, Punk clothing was almost entirely black and consciously menacing.

In time, designers Vivienne Westwood and Malcolm McLaren morphed punk fashion into a new style, known as the New Romantic. The rebellion of the punk movement also shifted the mentality of the new street-cred traits of being obsessed by money and success, including wearing recognizable designer clothing and accessories. Louis Vuitton and Chanel released handbags; Moschino's large belt buckles and buttons were popular fashion icons; and Mont Blanc pens, Rolex watches, and Filofax organizers emerged as coveted status symbols. Westwood's Buffalo Girl collection of 1982 was featured in the style of the pop group Bow Wow Wow. Big words placed on printed shirts became a major trend, originally pioneered by British designer Katherine Hamnett; and two British designers, Stevie Stewart and David Holah, under the name Body-Map, were the first to design dancewear as fashion, with cutout details.

By the end of the decade, overaccentuated hourglass shapes, epitomized by those black-clad femme fatale backup musicians in Robert Palmer's "Addicted to Love" video, were among the dominant images in popular music. Before the AIDS crisis and the stock market crash devastated New York City and the world beginning in 1987, American artists tuned into fashion's kinetic wavelength and commented on gestalt of commercial fashion. For instance, Keith Haring (discussed earlier in this chapter) was mass-producing his urban graffiti characters on T-shirts and paraphernalia on the streets of lower Manhattan. Stephen Sprouse went one step further, bringing the bravado of the streets to the forefront of fashion circles when he launched a line of neon suits and glow-in-the-dark graffiti print dresses that were featured in the 1985 movie *Desperately Seeking Susan*.

Hip hop sparked a fashion trend of its own that brought street cred to a more mainstream sensibility, though it never became as widely influential as the New Romantic movement. Run-D.M.C. was one of the biggest crossover rap groups of the 1980s, and they were trendsetters for both their fans and their fellow artists for a number of years. The group routinely wore Adidas sporting track suits and unlaced Adidas shoes, large faux gold chains, Kangol hats, leather jackets, and fashionable sunglasses. Their approach to fashion was in stark contrast to earlier rappers, whose clothing choices were reminiscent of the disco era of the 1970s. Run-D.M.C.'s attire would be appropriated by nearly every hip hop group for the rest of the decade, and fans, both inner city and rural, African American and Caucasian, brought the look to the mainstream.

Though their effects were less dramatic, rock bands in the late 1980s, particularly Bon Jovi, also began to influence the style of dress of both men and women, including denim, stonewashed jackets and pants, and leather jackets with fringe on the sleeves. The fashion styles were absorbed into the success of the genre (as discussed in Chapter 3, "Music") and have been criticized in the years since its demise. Fashion is part art and part product, and any analysis of the decade of the 1980s must recognize the role that advertising plays in selling fashion (not to mention other products).

ADVERTISING AND MEDIA

Before the 1980s, there were essentially only two American newspapers that were widely read nationally: the *Wall Street Journal* and *The New York Times.* Both were popular in terms of daily subscriptions in this period, before the Internet took hold of the mainstream in the 1990s and the beginning of the 21st century. The *Wall Street Journal* has long had its finger on the financial pulse of American society, and its business focus is influential for businessmen and women throughout the country. For its part, *The New York Times* has arguably been the most influential newspaper in the nation since its founding in the mid-19th century, publishing as their logo states, "All the News That's Fit to Print." What makes it stand out from other newspapers is that its columns are among the best and most intelligently written pieces of journalism in the United States, and writers across the nation and the world often consider it an honor to work for the esteemed "Gray Lady."

However, neither of these newspapers was marketed to mainstream Americans. To fill that niche, *USA Today* began publication in 1982. The publishing giant Gannett has distributed *USA Today* since its release, which initially was limited to Washington, D.C., and the Baltimore metropolitan area. However, it gradually expanded, and the paper was among the top sellers nationally just three years later. An international edition began in 1986, which focused on American news geared to the audience of a specific country. At the same time, print advertisements were on the rise in newspapers throughout the decade.

The number of magazine titles expanded in the 1980s, mostly focused on one topic (which in turn gave their readerships very particular demographics that could be targeted by advertising). Computers became more and more heavily employed in the 1980s, and a number of computer magazines came out to fulfill the needs and interests of computer users, including *PC World, PC Week,* and *Family Computing.* The new interest in science, encouraged by the writings of Carl Sagan and Stephen Hawking, led to the popularity of *Discover* magazine.

In addition, several new magazines on parenting appeared, including *Families, Parenting,* and *Baby Times*. Health and fitness magazines included *Cooking Light* and *American Health*. Other magazines targeting specific subjects, such as *New England Monthly* and travel magazines such as *Condé Nast Traveler* and *Southern Travel,* emerged as well. Fashion magazines such as *Mirabella,* edited by veteran *Vogue* editor Grace Mirabella, was aimed at women between the ages of 30 and 50; and it continued a tradition of age-focused magazines such as *Seventeen* (early teens), *Cosmopolitan* (late teens), and *Vogue* (between 20 and perhaps 40). Sports magazines were prevalent as well, including the flagship of the genre, *Sports Illustrated,* which has dominated that market since the 1950s; journals that previewed the upcoming season for each sport, such as *Basketball Digest;* and even traditional titles such as *Newsweek,* which released an imprint tailored to the college market, *Newsweek on Campus*.

As discussed in Chapter 6, "Technology," the emergence of cable television and its specialty channels helped streamline advertisement dollars since the demographics of the viewership could be isolated better. As a result, more television commercials were aired in the 1980s than in the past, simply because there were more channels to air ads on.

Any television advertising campaign needs to be memorable, and one of the common ways for that to happen is to have a jingle—a short tune, easy to memorize and recognize, featuring catchy lyrics that will make the listener remember the product. The ideal is that the consumer will see the product at a store, recall the jingle (and thus the message from the commercial), and buy the product. For instance, Band-Aid featured the jingle, "I am stuck on Band Aids cause Band Aids stuck on me!" GLAD storage bags became indelibly associated with "Hefty Hefty Hefty wimpy wimpy wimpy"; and Meow Mix was called by name by cats, especially the ones singing "Meow meow meow meow." Personal hygiene products were promoted in the same way, such as Nair hair removal ("Nair for short shorts"), Sure deodorant ("Raise your hand! Raise your hand if you're sure!"), and Arrid Extra Dry ("Get a little closer. Now don't be shy!"). Even repackaged versions of classic hit songs were sometimes used; the California Raisin Commission featuring raisins that sang Marvin Gaye's "I Heard It Through the Grapevine"; Sunkist used the Beach Boy's "Good Vibrations"; and the Genesis hit "In the Air Tonight" was featured in Michelob beer ads. (At times, the use of a song in an ad reawakened listeners' interest in the song itself, and it would make its way onto the charts again.)

The 1980s were full of catchphrases that became part of the period's vernacular. Wendy's had "Where's the beef?" cried by an old woman (played by Clara Peller) to mock how little meat the competitors' hamburgers had. McDonald's featured people trying to say the ingredients of their Big Mac as quickly as possible; ads for Eggo waffles proclaimed "Leggo of my Eggo," and Bartles & Jaymes commercials presented two older men who would "thank you for your support."

Though the campaign started in the 1970s, Bounty paper towel ads featuring Rosie and the "quicker picker upper" remained in circulation through the 1980s. One of the most unusual ad campaigns of the period included a character known as Ernest P. Worrell, who began each commercial with "Hey Vern!" before explaining what great news he was sharing; the commercials were for different products, but Ernest and the actor who played him (Jim Varney) became a national celebrity. He even went on to star in a couple of movies in the 1980s: *Ernest Goes to Camp* (1987) and *Ernest Saves Christmas* (1988).

The decade included a number of advertising-related contests, such as McDonald's $1,000,000 promo in which customers were given a song on a small record, and by listening to it (as well as sales information on the actual food), they would find out if they had won prizes of up to $1 million. The Pepsi Challenge was a taste test to see if Pepsi truly tasted better than its competitors, and Captain Crunch cereal launched the "Where's the Captain?" contest.

Commercials sometimes became well known and popular for their imagery or impact, such as Apple's un-Orwellian prediction for 1984 for the Macintosh line, arguing "why 1984 won't be like *1984*." A bull terrier named Spuds Mackenzie became the cool figure associated with Bud Light; Bonkers candy, marketing toward children, ran ads where the elderly person in the commercial got crushed by giant fruit falling from the sky. The ads would sometimes backfire— people would remember the commercial but not buy the product (or even remember what product was being advertised).

The concept of the celebrity pitchman (or pitchwoman) was popular in advertising in the 1980s. For instance, Calvin Klein ads featured actress Brooke Shields, who looked at the camera and cooed, "Do you wanna know what comes between me and my Calvin's. . . . NOTHING." Another 1980s icon, Michael J. Fox, ran through rain, over car hoods, and through traffic to get a Diet Pepsi for his girlfriend. And, as discussed in other chapters of this book, the use of popular figures such as Michael Jordan, Michael Jackson, and Madonna in ads encouraged fans to buy products because of the impression that the celebrities were endorsing them.

Sometimes an ad could succeed even if it was annoying. For instance, Dominos Pizza's Noid, though decidedly unpopular, was identifiable with the company. The Noid campaign was similar to others in that its focus became repurposed to different areas, such as the sales of a video game (the Noid), T-shirts with slogans on them (Wendy's "Where's the Beef?"), and even toys (the California Raisins).

Print and billboard ads left lasting impressions on the public as well. Joe Camel was a cool cartoon figure, smoking Camel cigarettes in the most desirable settings, such as surrounded by attractive women at a swimming pool or watching football with his buddies at a bar. The cigarette industry was forced by the Tobacco Master Settlement Agreement of 1998 to drop its use of cartoons in advertising, and all cigarette advertising, including the iconic masculine Marlboro Man, was eliminated shortly afterward.

Few segments of products become as trendy as children's toys, thanks to the power of ads. Children who grew up in the 1980s fondly recognize the toys of their past and are filled with a sense of nostalgia (including celebrities who speak about their favorites on television). In 1980 and 1981, teenage boys and girls purchased the Rubik's Cube in droves, and the question of who could solve the puzzle the quickest was a topic of discussion in nearly every household that had a teen in it. *Pac-Man* led the new video game craze, and companies developed new gaming platforms for the home market as well, as discussed in Chapter 6. Fantasy toys featuring characters from hit movies and shows like *Clash of the Titans, Masters of the Universe,* and *Buck Rogers in the 25th Century* became favorites with boys, and girls were fans of puffy stickers, Strawberry Shortcake dolls, and the Smurfs.

In 1982 and 1983, the board game *Trivial Pursuit* was released and became a favorite with a wide range of players, from kids to older adults. Products based on popular movies, such as *E.T., The Extra Terrestrial, Indiana Jones* and the third installment of the *Star Wars* series, *Return of the Jedi,* became big hits as well. Two trendy items, Chia Pets and Cabbage Patch Kids, were among the top American icons of the decade. Chia Pets were small containers shaped like dogs, cats, and other animals that sprouted greenery (the animals' "fur") when watered. Cabbage Patch Kids had "birth certificates" for each individual doll, and parents frequently argued over the purchase of a specific doll.

Though toys related to television shows, such as *Knight Rider, M*A*S*H*, Alvin and the Chipmunks, the A-Team,* and *Fraggle Rock,* were successful, the reverse occurred as well. For instance, the Transformers line of robots became a big hit in themselves—so much so, in fact, that a television show about the characters followed, and its success fueled even more sales of the toys. Transformers continue to be popular to the present day with a new generation of fans, mostly (though not exclusively) boys.

The year 1985 saw the emergence of a series of toys that were embraced by younger children. The Muppet Babies, inspired by the eponymous television show, were young versions of the original characters featured on *Sesame Street.* Teddy Ruxpin, a mechanical stuffed animal that would tell stories to infants, was a big seller, as were Pound Puppies and Ewoks (the furry characters introduced in *The Return of the Jedi*).

Older children preferred the ThunderCats (action figures based on the 1980s' animated series), or they collected the Garbage Pail Kids, trading cards inspired by the Cabbage Patch Kids that were intended to gross out parents. In 1986, a stuffed toy based on the main character from the hit television show *Alf* was also popular, as was the fantasy-based Bionic Six (part human, part metal) and Inhumanoids.

The biggest news from 1986, though, was the reemergence of video gaming as Nintendo and Sega Master System changed the industry with innovative graphics. By the end of the decade, the fantasy toys Silverhawks, Dino-Riders, Captain Power and Soldiers of the Future, Robocop (based on the eponymous hit movie), SuperNaturals, and Visionaries were popular, as were Game Boy, a pocket-sized Nintendo game console, and the Teenage Mutant Ninja Turtles, heroic crime fighters featured on a cartoon show that became a cultural icon in the 1990s. Games and toys were marketed aggressively on each type of media, not specialized into market demographics as had been done before. This development made the 1980s among the favorite decades for adults in the years since their youth.

EPCOT Center (Experimental Protype Community of Tomorrow) was the second theme park to open at Disney World in Florida. Opening in 1982, the park was inspired by an original concept conceived by Walt Disney himself and was divided into two sections: Future World and World Showcase. (Wangkun Jia/Dreamstime.com)

An examination of popular culture must include the amusement park. The 1980s was an important decade in terms of both the rise and the prominence of theme parks. The most significant of these were (and are) located at Walt Disney World, outside Orlando, Florida. Disney World started in the early 1970s, and like its sister park in California that emerged in the 1950s, it became a major vacation destination for families. It experienced such a degree of success (along with the unrelated SeaWorld resort, discussed later in this chapter) that it completely revitalized an entire region that had been severely underutilized in the past. The entire Orlando area was transformed from a military and aerospace town to the top tourist destination worldwide.

In 1982, EPCOT opened at Disney World. The park was initially conceived by Walt Disney in 1964, but it did not fully begin to be explored until after Disney's death in 1966, and it took almost 20 years to come to fruition. EPCOT was conceived as a breathtaking voyage into the world of the future and a contemporary journey through the nations of the world. It is the world of the possible. In Future World, the challenges of life are vividly explored. EPCOT Center is also the world of today and yesterday. In World Showcase, the cultures and achievements of different nations are presented in all their colorful diversity. The World Showcase includes many countries, and the staff in each country are actually from there. The park became a significant success, evolving to feature more thrilling rides, such as "Soarin'" and "Test Track," in the years that followed.

A third Disney theme park, Disney–MGM Studios, opened in 1989, following a licensing agreement between Disney and the historic movie studio. Though there were many legal challenges concerning what would be allowed at the park and what would be at MGM's Las Vegas Hotel, the naming partnership would continue for nearly 20 years. The park includes rides set in the mythical Hollywood of the 1930s and 1940s, such as the attraction "The Great Movie Ride." Even though both parks are constantly evolving, their emergence in the 1980s helped expand the impact of all theme parks from then on.

One of the beneficiaries of Disney's success was the Six Flags group of theme parks. Six Flags had seen successful at parks in Texas and Georgia in the 1970s, but the company decided to purchase an existing park, Marriott's Great America, in 1984 to expand its reach. The purchase also gave Six Flags rights to the Warner Brothers *Loony Tunes* characters for use at their theme parks. Great America added a number of attractions in the 1980s, such as "The Edge," a free-fall ride, in 1983, and "Splash Water Falls," a water ride, in 1986. Both of these inspired the free-fall "Tower of Terror" and Typhoon Lagoon and Blizzard Beach water parks at Disney. The Bally Corporation, the owner of the Six Flags franchise, decided to sell it to Wesray Capital in 1987. By this time, the parks focused more on thrill-based attractions and less on themed entertainment.

SeaWorld has been a competitor to Disney World since the Florida version of the park opened in the 1970s. Part of a franchise of amusement parks, the first park was based in San Diego, and SeaWorld expanded into the San Antonio area in 1988. The park was a smash, featuring a new show with the killer whale Shamu called "One Ocean" and a synchronized swimming and diving show called "Azul," which included beluga whales. Three roller coasters, as well as the water animal shows and exhibits, helped make the park so popular. "The Great White" is an inverted steel roller coaster; "Journey to Atlantis," based on the mythical Greek city, features a roller coaster and drop combination; and "Steel Eel" is a roller coaster that reaches heights up to 150 feet.

Ohio-based Cedar Point expanded their theme park rides significantly in the 1980s, with the goal of being the "roller coaster capital of the world." The new rides were much more varied than mere roller coasters, however; they included water attractions as well, and new 3D and IMAX movies were shown virtually every year in the Cedar Point Cinema, as the theater was one of the first in the country to embrace that new movie format. "Oceana" was a dolphin stadium and aqua zoo, while "White Water Landing," "Thunder Canyon," and "Soak City" featured raft and traditional water park rides. Cedar Point also featured a number of extreme rides, including "Demon Drop," "Avalanche Run," and "Iron Dragon." "Magnum XL-200," the world's first coaster to top the elusive 200-foot-tall threshold, also opened in the 1980s.

Other parks that gained more regional than national attention flourished in the 1980s as well. Knott's Berry Farm, located in Buena Park, California, is an underrated theme park that unfortunately is often overshadowed by Disneyland, which is close by in Anaheim. Though family patriarch Walter Knott died in 1981, his family continued to operate the park through the rest of the decade. Knott's Berry Farm capitalized on the "Urban Cowboy" craze (covered in Chapter 4, "Film") via its "Barn Dance" attraction. The park also created two other attractions to compete with Disneyland: "Kingdom of the Dinosaurs" in 1987, and a popular water park ride, "Bigfoot Rapids," in 1988.

Dollywood was founded in the late 1980s when singer and entertainer Dolly Parton bought Silver Dollar City Tennessee, a small theme park in Pigeon Forge, Tennessee. As Parton was a native of the area, she was emotionally attached to the park and worked very hard to ensure its success. She hired many of the local population (including family members) to work at the park, and it quickly became a favorite tourist attraction for those visiting the Great Smoky Mountains. In contrast with other, larger theme parks such as Disneyland and Knott's Berry Farm, the more intimate Dollywood featured rides that were more typical of amusement parks; as to be expected, Parton's park also featured extensive live entertainment. In the decades that followed, increasingly thrilling rides (including roller coasters) were implemented, and Dollywood continues to be popular today.

FURTHER READING

Demacy, Jean, and Francois Baudot. *Elle Style: The 1980s.* Paris: Filipacci Publishing, 2003.

Enwezo, Okwui. *Lorna Simpson.* New York: American Federation of the Arts, 2006.

Felder, Deborah G., and Diana Rosen. *Fifty Jewish Women Who Changed the World.* New York: Kensington/Citadel Press, 2005.

Karndon, Janet. *Robert Mapplethorpe: The Perfect Moment.* Philadelphia: Institute of Contemporary Art at the University of Pennsylvania, 1988.

Kuspit, Donald. *The New Subjective: Art in the 1980s.* Ann Arbor, MI: UMI Research Press, 1988.

Mapplethorpe, Robert. *Lady, Lisa.* Lyon and London: St. Martin's Press, 1983.

Massimo, Dini. *Renzo Piano, Projects and Buildings, 1964–1983.* New York: Electa/Rizzoli, 1984.

Mendes, Valarie, and Amy de la Haye. *20th-Century Fashion.* London: Thames and Hudson, Ltd., 1999.

Mulvagh, Jane. *Vogue History of 20th-Century Fashion.* London: Viking, 1988.

Peacock, John. *The 1980s.* New York: Thames and Hudson, 1998.

Reed, Paula. *Fifty Fashion Looks that Changed the 1980s.* New York: Conran Octopus, 2013.

CHAPTER 8

Controversies

CONTROVERSIES IN HEALTH AND THE ENVIRONMENT

Few topics were as controversial in the 1980s than the outbreak of the human immunodeficiency virus (HIV). Initially diagnosed in 1981 by Michael Gottleib, a Los Angeles doctor who noticed that five young men in the gay community had similar types of pneumonia, the condition was brought to the Centers for Disease Control and Prevention (CDC) after discovering that a rare organism, *Pneumocystis carinii* (PCP), was present in each case. In the months that followed, the disease was given the name *acquired immune deficiency syndrome (AIDS).* The U.S. government, then led by the conservative Republican Ronald Reagan, was slow to react to the disease, which some ascribed to the fact that the initial victims were gay men and intravenous drug users (i.e., marginal members of society). The government became more proactive after the public realized that the disease could be spread through the exchange of body fluid passively to anyone, even through blood transfusions. Members of the gay community were shunned by many heterosexuals out of fear that they would acquire the disease by casual contact, such as swimming in a pool or even through contact with body sweat. Both claims were eventually proven false, and it was established that the disease was most commonly transmitted via sexual contact or intravenous drug use.

For many in the conservative community, gay sex and intravenous drug use are among the most immoral acts in American society, and therefore, the religious right lost little time condemning both the disease and the lifestyles of those afflicted. What began to sway public opinion the other way, though, was when the legendary Hollywood movie star Rock Hudson was diagnosed in 1985. It also became clear that AIDS could be transmitted by blood transfusions, so concerns arose about the safety of that procedure. All donated blood underwent testing to ensure that it was clear of the HIV virus, and additional precautions were taken to make sure hospital patients were not exposed. Another alarming discovery was that many people who were infected did not have symptoms of the disease and could pass the disease on to others unknowingly. In some cases, HIV would take nearly 10 years to develop into full-blown AIDS, while many others did not progress to the disease at all. By 1992, the CDC estimated that over 1 million people had been infected nationally, with 40,000 new cases every year.

As with any health crisis, it is imperative that citizens become educated about it in order to quell panic and counter misconceptions and prejudices. The controversy of AIDS and HIV was not that the disease was deadly but rather that it was a result of supposedly questionable lifestyle choices that were endangering the whole of American society. Those quick to judge, or who preferred to avoid the facts about the disease to strengthen their own agendas dictated by their value judgments, were just as much a part of the controversy as the AIDS victims who were being scrutinized. Fortunately, with the rise of talk shows and more news channels on television, information was disseminated quicker than ever before, and eventually, people began to focus more on the actual causes of AIDS than on judging the people suffering from it.

A controversial political issue in the 1980s was the practice of apartheid by the government of South Africa, which had been going on since the late 1940s. Many in the international community decried apartheid, as the policy was racist toward native Africans by the largely white-controlled South African government. This condemnation had been going on for some time, but the protests increased and grew louder and more vociferous in the 1980s. Countries had placed an embargo against trade of any type with South Africa to pressure the government to abandon apartheid. This affected a resort area called Sun City, one of the top vacation destinations in the country, which was largely divided on racial lines. A few entertainment and sports figures were associated with the resort in the early 1980s and were the target of much approbation for doing so; for instance, Ivan Lendl and Jimmy Connors participated in a tennis tournament there in 1983, and both tennis fans and the general public disapproved of this. Musicians such as Elton John, Frank Sinatra, Queen, Julio Iglesias, and Ray Charles performed in the 6,000-person-capacity Sun Bowl, seemingly without regard to the country's apartheid policies. In time, many noted members of the entertainment and sports world began to criticize the country openly and refused to visit or perform anywhere in the country, including Sun City.

Guitarist Steven Van Zandt banded together with many other leading artists (including Bob Dylan, Pat Benatar, Herbie Hancock, Ringo Starr, and Peter Gabriel) in 1985 to form Artists United Against Apartheid. Inspired by the success of "We Are the World," which helped raise money for famine relief in Africa, the group cut a single called "Sun City" to bring awareness to apartheid. The project's definitive statement was that no one in Artists United Against Apartheid would perform at Sun City until apartheid was lifted. An album was released with the single, "Sun City," and one led by U2, "Silver and Gold," which helped bring awareness to the situation. What separated

Apartheid was the system of institutionalized racism in South Africa. Some American art-ists refused to perform in South Africa and recorded the *Sun City* record in protest of apartheid. In this photo from 1985, "Little Steven" Van Zandt presents two $25,000 checks, royalties from the record sales, to Coretta Scott King (widow of Dr. Martin Luther King, Jr.) and the mayor of Atlanta, Andrew Young. (AP Photo/Charles Kelly)

this particular project was that artists who sought a militant voice against oppression were shaming some of the artists who had already played Sun City.

One of the biggest controversies of the 1980s was the War on Drugs. Presi-dent Reagan was just one year into his first term when he announced the war on drugs, and he appointed Vice President George H. W. Bush to spearhead the new policy, partly because Bush was a former head of the Central Intelli-gence Agency (CIA). In the eyes of the administration, American society was becoming more vulnerable to a consistent influx of marijuana and cocaine spilling over the borders into the United States, particularly from Mexico, but also from both Central and South America.

Bush's plan was to utilize all the government resources—the Internal Reve-nue Service (IRS), the Border Patrol, the Drug Enforcement Administration (DEA), and even the armed forces—to quash the drug trade. The policy was a long time coming, as drug use in the United States had increased steadily since the late 1960s and throughout the 1970s. Cocaine, in its most pure form, had become the drug of choice for young urban professionals. Crack cocaine, a concentrated cooked version, was favored by many of the poorer populations because it was cheaper. In short, cocaine was was affecting all areas of Ameri-can life in one way or the other. The idea of reducing drug use was not really much of a problem in itself; it was the way that the resources were used to curb the war on drugs that became controversial. At the time, the Reagan administration was eager to overthrow the Sandinista rebels in Nicaragua, so General Manuel Noriega, Panama's president, was being funded by the CIA to funnel arms to the Sandinistas' enemy, the Contras, even though he was allied with the Medellin and Cali cartels that were bringing drugs into the United States. The government was willing to ignore this fact to further a goal that they were more commited to. These facts came out in the course of the Iran-Contra hearings toward the end of the decade, which tainted the Reagan administration with scandal.

In another effect to combat the drug epidemic, First Lady Nancy Reagan spearheaded a campaign called "Just Say No." The (admittedly simplistic and naïve idea) idea was that if Americans just refused to use drugs, the demand would go away, and so there would be no market for drugs to be sold in the United States. Unfortunately, most drug-using members of society simply ignored her appeals, and little has been accomplished in the many years since Reagan's charge was initially given. Drugs continue to be a scourge on the health and well-being of American citizens. The 1980s featured three controversial, high-profile cases that involved newborn babies: one that questioned the rights of parents to decide medical treatment for their children; one about the rights of surrogate parents versus birth parents; and one concerning the transplantation of a baboon heart into a human being. In 1982, a baby was born suffering from Down's syndrome, as well as problems with its throat and esophagus that made it unable to eat or drink by mouth. In addition, babies with Down's syndrome often have a birth defect in the heart, and this child did as well; but the parents of this baby elected not to have surgeons operate to correct it. The hospital, on the other hand, believed that the child should be saved at any cost, so it filed appeals to mandate the surgery. However, the baby, known as Baby Doe, died after six days, before the operation could be performed. President Reagan and the U.S. Department of Health and Human Services (HHS) established a protocol to prevent parents from making a similar decision in the future. Immediately, controversy emerged about who ought to have this right: the parents, as the guardians; the hospital, which supposedly has the duty to save every life; or the government itself. By 1984, the Child Above Amendment to the Child Abuse Prevention and Treatment Act stated that health care providers must treat ill newborns unless death seems inevitable. Again, debates about the right to life were reintroduced by both sides of the abortion question; however, the HHS ultimately withdrew its protocol, leaving this decision at least somewhat open ended, in the realm of both the parents and health care providers.

In 1978, Louise Brown, the world's first "test tube baby," was born in England. In this procedure, now known as *in-vitro fertilization*, an egg from a mother is mixed with sperm from a father in a laboratory. When the egg gets fertilized, the result, known as a *zygote*, is placed in the mother's uterus, where it can develop in the same manner as a traditional pregnancy. Zygotes could also be frozen for later implementation, in the event that the parents were not ready to have children at that moment.

Surrogacy also came to be in the 1980s. If a woman was not capable of carrying (or willing to carry) a zygote to full term, a surrogate mother would be asked to do so instead. Often, the surrogate mother would be paid for her services, and the birth mother would be the legal mother at birth. That was the planned arrangement, at any rate, but that required that everyone involved agree to it. But that did not always happen. In 1985, a New Jersey couple, William and Elizabeth Stern, paid Mary Beth Whitehead $10,000 to be a surrogate mother for them. After the baby was born, however, Whitehead decided that she had made a mistake; she asked for a visit with the child and kidnapped her. The child, who became known as Baby M, was returned to the Sterns, and after a legal battle, the Sterns were granted custody of the baby. However, the New Jersey Supreme Court reversed the ruling, outlawing surrogate contracts for pay and granting Whitehead visitation rights. With New Jersey's decision, other states began to consider new laws requiring certain actions of the surrogate, such as avoiding alcohol, tobacco, and drugs, in the best interests of both the baby and the birth parents. Other concerns revolved around the ethics of payment, particularly in cases like Baby M, in which the Sterns were financially stable and well educated while Whitehead was in a lower income bracket and poorly educated. Controversies also occurred regarding the custody of unborn zygotes in the event that the relationship between the two birth parents ended.

In 1984, a baby named Fae was born with a defective heart. The fatal deformity was known as *hypoplastic left heart sydrome,* which meant that the heart simply did not function. After it was determined that the heart could not keep the baby alive, she was given a baboon heart transplant. As with any transplant, there was a risk that the new organ would be rejected. Initially the operation seemed to be a success; but on the 14th day, Fae's body started to reject the heart. Antirejection drugs were administered to try to help the body accept the organ, and Fae was placed on a respirator. Her kidneys then began to fail, leading to failure of the rest of her organs, including the heart.

There were a few reasons that could have led to the failure: the heart was a different blood type than the child's, and the child's frail immune system was ill equipped to handle such a foreign organ like a baboon heart at such a young age. But she lived longer than any other recipient of a nonhuman organ had, which was something of a breakthrough.

In retrospect, medical experts decided that transplants such as the one for baby Fae could be used as a temporary bridge. But the move came under fire from the animal rights community, sensing that the success of a transplant of this nature could have an impact on baboons, and eventually many other species. In addition, some religious and medical professionals questioned if there was an ethical argument against this type of transplant, including how a person would feel later in life when she found out that she had the heart of a baboon or some other animal.

For older patients, there were alternatives to the baboon heart. Human heart transplants had been performed since the late 1960s. The first artificial heart approved for implementation into humans, the Jarvik-7, was first used in 1982; however, its recipient, Barney Clark, died in March 1983 because of other complications with his lungs and kidneys. Nevertheless, the artificial heart was considered a success, and other recipients came forward. Unfortunately, the majority of these patients suffered a stroke soon after their operations, and many observers questioned if the new device could be used on a temporary basis before a donor heart was found or if it should be used at all. Eventually, the Jarvik-7 was discontinued.

Further controversy surrounded the use of the pacemaker but not because it was not effective. Rather, there was concern over how much was being charged for the device and whether the device was being implemented in patients unnecessarily. Eventually, HHS began to investigate if doctors were receiving financial benefits for choosing a specific model (i.e., pay for play). More controversy surrounded the use of lasers to help battle coronary artery disease, as there were concerns about the accuracy of using the laser in an artery to displace plaque in such a delicate organ. As heart disease had become the top killer among American citizens because of years of poor diet, smoking, lack of exercise, and other bad habits, much work took place during the 1980s to try to reduce it.

In the 1980s, there were also significant strides made in genetic engineering of deoxyribonucleic acid (DNA), specifically in the genes of bacteria. This way, insulin could be created for diabetics, and human growth hormone could be programmed to help those who did not gain a normal height. The DNA of one person could be "spliced" in the laboratory to help enhance his or her quality of life. In 1989, white blood cells were transferred into skin cancer patients who were considered terminal in less than 90 days, with the intention to destroy the cancerous cells, and the experiment proved a success. In spite of the undoubted benefits of these technological advances, there were concerns that prolonging life in such a manner would be unethical and unnatural. Employers could profile potential employees on the basis of their genetics and base their hiring decisions on their findings—a troubling notion. There was even the charge that scientists could perform unnatural experiments, such as creating harmful viruses in the laboratory and releasing them on an unsuspecting population, with no known antibodies to counteract them.

Product tampering became a concern in 1982, as seven Chicago residents died after taking Extra-Strength Tylenol, which had been laced with cyanide. After an investigation, it was concluded that the gelatin-based capsules were the ones that were tainted, and they had been tampered with after they had left the manufacturing plant. The culprit was never found, though a man trying to convince authorities that the poisonings would cease if he were paid $1 million was later convicted of extortion. The concern with the poisonings caused a national panic, as sale of over-the-counter medication dropped precipitously for a few months. However, Johnson & Johnsons, the makers of Tylenol, recognized that the gelatin pills, which were popular as they were easier to swallow, were also the easiest to tamper with, so the company began selling only solid capsules. More importantly, each pill manufacturer in the United States implemented new packaging practices. A sealed top made of thick paper and foil was placed under the cap of each bottle, making it evident to purchasers if there was any irregularity in the packaging. Similar panics occurred in the years that followed, but none had the effect that the 1982 killings did.

Toxic shock syndrome is a rare but sometimes fatal disease. It was thought that the disease was caused by the use of tampons. Initially promoted by Proctor & Gamble under the brand name Tampax in the 1930s, a "digital" version of a tampon (i.e., it could be inserted by hand, without an applicator) was developed in the 1940s. Toxic shock syndrome occurred in 344 women who became infected with *Staphylococcus aureus*, which then needed to be treated with strong antibiotics. The syndrome's symptoms were sudden and included high fever, vomiting, and diarrhea, with more severe cases including dizziness and fatal shock.

In 1982, Proctor & Gamble, the distributor of the Rely brand of tampons, and four other manufacturers were sued by hundreds. A federal jury found that the companies were negligent but did not award the plaintiff financial damages. Later, Proctor & Gamble paid $300,000 in damages to another plaintiff, while Johnson & Johnson was ordered to pay yet another plaintiff $10.5 million. It was discovered that brands that were marketed as "superabsorbent" contained cellulose chips that absorbed magnesium, and bacteria fed off these chips. Ultimately, superabsorbent tampons were removed from the market, and an extensive campaign in the safe usage of tampons was promoted.

The 1980s was also the decade where concerns about the ozone layer arose. The ozone layer at higher altitudes and at the poles of the planet had been decreasing slowly over a number of years because of global warming exacerbated by activities of the industrial sector. At high altitudes, the ozone helps shield the Earth from harmful ultraviolet rays from the sun, which can cause skin cancer in humans. On the other hand, too much ozone (as is prevalent in urban areas) can be as bad as too little, causing pollution harmful to human health.

It was determined that chlorofluorocarbons (CFCs), used since the 1920s as refrigerant, Styrofoam (used in disposable cups and packaging for fast food), propellants in aerosol sprays, and cleaning chemicals played a large part in eroding the ozone layer. Although industries around the world began to implement new measures to help eliminate these harmful substances, it was clear by 1985 that the ozone layer near the poles was depleting, causing the poles themselves to begin to melt. As a result, global warming has increased water levels worldwide, causing destruction to coastlines in all locations that continues into the present day.

The initial developments in nuclear power for consumer use began after World War II. Nuclear power plants were used throughout the decades that followed and became popular among a segment of the population because of their relatively low cost after the initial investment. In the United States, concerns were raised about the safety of nuclear power plants and their effect on the environment. There was an accident on March 28, 1979, at Three Mile Island in Pennsylvania, where one of the core's reactors was close to a meltdown, causing nearby residents to evacuate. Soon after the accident, residents in Seabrook, New Hampshire, and Shoreham, New York, protested vigorously over safety concerns against a company that owned nuclear reactors in both locations.

The biggest controversy over nuclear power plants came about not because of an accident in the United States, but rather the Chernobyl reactor meltdown in the Ukraine. Unlike American nuclear plants, including Three Mile Island, the Chernobyl reactor was not in a containment building, exposing the plant to the environment. The accident caused contamination over hundreds of miles of the forest, and Americans were made aware yet again of the safety concerns of nuclear power. Accidents were not the only worry, however; the used nuclear fuel rods, necessary isotopes crucial to nuclear fission, needed to be discarded, and this was a hazardous process. Ultimately, the uranium would be buried in locations with stable rock formations nowhere near water supplies (but this solution did not please everybody).

Similar toxic waste had been recklessly released into the environment for years since the Industrial Revolution in the 19th century. By the 1980s, citizens were beginning to see the results of these practices, with chemicals appearing in rivers and often killing great numbers of fish. To help combat the damage, Congress established the Superfund, which not only provided funding for the cleanup of toxic areas, but also fined corporations who had contributed to the original problems.

The Environmental Protection Agency (EPA), established in 1970, had already established regulations for corporations to follow, but the 1980s brought attention to this issue into the mainstream. In the late 1970s, Love Canal, near Niagara Falls in New York, was one of the highest-profile areas affected. Inadequately sealed large metal drum containers held chemicals from a plastics company, and the contents were seeping into the water. Residents were unaware of the danger as houses were being built close to the site, and this caused physical calamities among the children growing up close to the new housing development. Eventually, the Superfund's National Priorities List identified 50 top areas of pollution, and the EPA was vigorous in the cleanup during the decade.

CONTROVERSIES INVOLVING AFRICAN AMERICANS

As discussed in Chapter 1, "Television," the emergence of MTV was one of the most important cultural developments of the decade. As music videos were considered a promotion for the recording artists, the artists and songwriters were not paid, as opposed to radio, where these artists received royalties each time a song was played. The first promotional video shown on the new network, on August 1, 1981, was the Buggles' "Video Killed the Radio Star." The video was shot with a limited budget, as was typical of the period. Soon, videos such as Devo's "Whip It" would incorporate a strong visual element that would be just as appealing as the song itself. As a result, some videos were successful even though their songs were weaker than those of other less visually appealing performers.

The main controversy was in how teenagers would react to the new channel. Teenagers watched the channel hour after hour, in a way that they had never done with any other channel. Critics of MTV saw it as a harmful influence on teens and children in that they were glued to the television set, soaking in whatever content was being delivered by video producers and record companies (not to mention advertising), like unthinking sponges. Roles of gender, race, and sex become more prevalent, and more distorted, than ever in all aspects of American society, and parents were becoming increasingly aware of those topics. Programmers at MTV recognized that their main audience was white teenagers in the Midwest, and they thought that African American musicians would not only be unpopular but even offensive enough for viewers to change the channel. But Michael Jackson broke through that barrier. After "Billie Jean," Jackson's second video, was added to regular rotation on MTV, he became the most popular artist in pop music. With his success, MTV was more apt to program pop and rock artists of various racial backgrounds.

Jackson was a true crossover artist, becoming known for more than just his singing. He entertained audiences of his videos through both his dancing and his singing, making him the right artist at the right time for the rise of such a visual medium. He was stylistically rooted in Motown, as he was an artist for that record company, whose roster had been accepted by a white, middle-class audience for years. Berry Gordy created Jackson's first record company, Motown, to cross over into what Reebee Garofalo (2008, 170) has described as "assimilation into the mainstream of American life." This goal was met to such a degree that in 1984, the company celebrated its 25th anniversary with a television special. Of course, since Jackson had started his career with Motown, it was only fitting that he be involved. Jackson's performance was a resounding success. This television special brought his moonwalk to a national audience, and it became a key component of 1980s' culture. An estimated 47 million viewers saw the special, which featured other Motown artists such as Smokey Robinson and the Supremes, but Jackson's breakthrough performance was even compared to appearances by Elvis Presley and the Beatles on the *Ed Sullivan Show* two decades earlier.

Acceptance on MTV was the mark of success for any group, singer, or even entire genre in the 1980s. Although MTV programmers ignored African American artists earlier in the decade, rap music arrived as a force to be reckoned with when *Yo! MTV Raps* debuted in August 1988. The show, which played on MTV until 1995, quickly became one of the network's most popular shows; its success signaled that the network was beginning to focus on conceptual programs (including *Top 5 at 5,* featuring the hits of the day; a hard rock and heavy metal show called *Headbanger's Ball;* and an indie and college music show called *120 Minutes*) rather than just a nonstop barrage of music videos. The result was that for select periods of the day, a specific demographic (male Caucasian teenagers, for example) was likely to watch the network, which resulted in more exclusive/expensive advertising at that time of the day.

Rap—both the music and the accompanying culture—started in the urban center of New York City, an area that has had poor sections for decades. Usually, in the poor regions of a city, crime and violence are prevalent. To reduce this, Jamaican immigrant, disc jockey, and social activist Afrika Bambaataa established the Zulu Nation in 1974, with the goal of making connections between different neighborhoods and avoiding crime.

New York was a perfect incubator for rap for two reasons: First, the subways displayed graffiti, which helped publicize emerging rap artists for free; and, second, the Zulu Nation promoted parties in the streets and city parks as occurred in their native land, with entertainment by a DJ, which often featured rap music. Break dancing was a major phenomenon in New York in the early 1980s. It could be done cheaply, as the only requirements for it were music and a piece of plastic or cardboard to allow the dancers to dance and roll around on the floor more easily with less injury. The young performers were creating their own culture, independent of the rest of society. Ivor Miller (2002, 71) claims the culture has

> produced some of the languages that contemporary youth has created to define themselves. When young B-boys carry boom boxes down the street, they take over the environment, both visually and acoustically. The spray-painted pieces on the subways and walls of New York City dominate the transit system, claiming it as the territory of the writers. No matter how short lived the effects of their presence, urban youth create another landscape, one that reflects them and one in which they rule.

Eventually, the culture was showcased in *Beat Street,* a 1984 movie about the New York rap scene that featured break dancing, DJs, and graffiti. Graffiti had been a part of urban lifestyle for decades, and many associated it indelibly with minorities. Those opposed to it considered all forms of graffiti to be vandalism, as its signatures, or "tags," would often be painted on privately owned businesses and means of transportation, including trains, subways, and buses. On the other hand, its proponents saw graffiti as artistic expression worthy of First Amendment protection.

Graffiti became embraced by the art community, particularly at Fashion/Moda, a gallery in the South Bronx of New York City in the early 1980s—a controversial turn in the eyes of those who didn't consider graffiti to be artistic expression. Keith Haring was the most prominent graffiti artists of the time, and he invited artists of all ethnicities to join him to tag the areas around Fashion/Moda. Jean-Michel Basquiat was featured at the Times Square Show, with nearly unreadable messages that were elaborately displayed. The head of the New York City Transit Authority's vandal squad, Alfred Oliveri, was openly critical of graffiti, yet his way of decrying the practice—"If this is art, then to hell with art" (https://medium.com/@timmaughan/graffiti-40-years-of-hacking-new-york-city-6c72b99c6039#.ux1bl2e3i)—became a rallying cry among artists eager to bring in a new era of expression.

Rap songs differed from others in their extensive use of new advances in digital music technology, called *sampling.* The basic premise, originated by the Beastie Boys in the early 1980s, was that a group or individual artist would record short snippets on digital recorders that could be accessed via keyboard (and, eventually via computer using the new Musical Instrument Digital

Interface [MIDI] communication protocol). They could create short samples on their own, in addition to using the recordings of others.

This use of sampling became the standard in most rap music and remained so through the first decade of the 20th century. Those who use samples are required to pay a fee to both the songwriter and the recording company to use the copyright holder's material, but if they are successful, there is more than enough money for everyone. Nevertheless, many groups during the 1980s attempted to use material without securing copyrights. What made the Beastie Boys such an enduring group was that not only did they do sampling, they performed on live instruments. As a result, groups who simply relied on the samples of others had less staying power than those who could create their own beats as the Beastie Boys had.

Doug E. Fresh gained attention in the 1980s for his technique that became known as "beatbox." The beatbox performer vocally emulated the sounds that would be made by a drum machine. He became nationally recognized for his performance in *Beat Street*. Fresh, alongside the early rap performers Treacherous Three, helped bring rap culture (recognized later as hip hop) to rural America. With that focus, rap became popularized. Matt Diehl (Light, 1999, 122) has noted that "for many rap fans, such an approach inherently means gentrification of hip-hop—yet hip-hop's original intent was always about sucking the biggest possible audience in its groove." In this context, Diehl referred to the popularization of rap to a younger audience. The turning point in rap came with the success Vanilla Ice's "Ice Ice Baby" in 1990, by a 23-year-old white break dancer. Vanilla Ice used a bass line from the hit "Under Pressure" by Queen and David Bowie as the backdrop to his rapping.

The fact that rap did not make inroads into a white audience until it was performed by a white rapper was characterized by some African American rappers as "cultural imperialism." But by the late 1980s, rap had become ripe for assimilation into popular culture. DJ Jazzy Jeff and the Fresh Prince scored a commercial mainstream hit with "Girls Ain't Nothing but Trouble" (1987), largely because of its universal message and appeal to all fans regardless of background. Likewise, the follow-up, "Parents Just Don't Understand" (from *He's the D.J., I'm the Rapper*, 1988), was relatable to young fans, as it was a simple yet effective demonstration of a new wave of music. Rap was becoming innocuous and started to lose its underground, "street" identity.

Throughout its history, rap has been controversial in a variety of ways. Critics, especially those in the rock industry, argued that early rap was not really music because the rapping was not melodic and was essentially rhythmic talking over drum machines programmed to repeat specific, short beats. This brought additional criticism that the music was not even performed and, later, that rap artists "stole" recordings from rock records via sampling. Other criticism revolved around the language of rap, which was considered vulgar, especially by the end of the decade. However, Tricia Rose (1994, 85), in defense of the genre, presents a different definition: that "rap music is a technological form that relies on the reformulation of recorded sound in conjunction with rhymed lyrics to create its distinctive sound." She goes on to argue that the music fit into the oral traditions of African Americans and that many of the genre's detractors were Caucasians who did not understand this history. Most important, veiled racism was believed to be behind the criticism, simply because most rappers were African American. In addition, rap was presented as a way for young people in the inner city, often growing up in an environment full of violence, drug abuse and crime, absent parents, and few opportunities, to succeed.

The division between race and class differences is not new, however. Rock and roll went through similar pains in the mid-1950s, when white musicians were influenced by R&B artists and black musicians were influenced by country artists. And any critics of the use of preexisting music should keep in mind that composers have been quoting elements of the work of others for centuries; in jazz, for instance, some chord progressions have been used so often that they have become part of the standard repertoire.

As early rock and roll was combining two questionable types of music considered unrefined by the social establishment (i.e., R&B and country), it is not surprising that by the end of the 1980s, two similar types of unrefined music, heavy metal and rap, started to cross-pollinate, helping to define music into the 1990s. At that point, hip hop had firmly established itself as one of the dominant genres in American society.

By the mid-1990s, the by-product of the rap scene that became hip hop had become the biggest cultural development among teenagers. By looking back at the genre's meager beginnings, some find it surprising that rap has become such a mainstream staple. To the genre's defenders, however, this is no surprise at all, as the genre has always been about bringing the reality of urban life to the masses regardless of geographic location, social class, or economic standing.

The Compton area of Los Angeles County, California, had become a hotbed of crime, violence, and drug abuse, and the rap group N.W.A., led by Dr. Dre, Ice Cube, Eazy-E, and Arabian Prince, told of the angry horrors of their everyday lives through their music. The group's lyrics, revolving around violence, drug use, and the inner city, got a grip on the rap community, and gangsta rap was the stylistic result. N.W.A.'s first album, *Straight Outta Compton* (1988), was initially released on the independent record label Ruthless Records. By the time their second album, *EFIL4ZAGGIN* (1991), was released, the group had become the most important, and arguably the most dangerous, group in rap in two ways. First, the group's lyrics were seen as offensive by politicians (mainly because they presented a belligerent attitude toward authorities such as the police), and, second, the group came from a real gang lifestyle that was perceived as physically threatening.

The imagery that the group painted in their songs told what they felt was the truth about the harsh realities of the streets of Compton, California. They were bringing their own lawless and dangerous lives to every person interested in the genre—most of whom had never even been to Compton. Many of their fans, regardless of geographic location or ethnicity, loved the gangsta lifestyle as a symbol of rebellious power. The details allowed listeners to imagine themselves on the streets with the group; the songs were gangster-influenced rants on drinking, women, and violence.

Television shows that focused on African American casts became a significant part of media in the 1970s, including the hits *Good Times, The Jeffersons, Sanford and Son,* and *WKRP in Cincinnati,* and some of these shows continued into the 1980s. In the 1990s, there were newly created hits such as *In Living Color, Martin,* and *Living Single.* In between both of those decades, however, was the 1980s, a time where relatively few new shows featured an African American cast. Rather, the 1980s included some African American actors, but their roles (usually playing sidekicks or other supporting characters) were not particularly groundbreaking. For instance, in *Gimme a Break!* (1981–1987), Nell Carter played the housekeeper in a home of a white father and two motherless daughters. Former NFL defensive end Bubba Smith played a grocery store manager in the short-lived sitcom *Open All Night* (1981–1987). On *Fame,* about a New York performing arts school, Debbie Allen played a dance instructor (as well as choreographing the dance numbers for the show), and Erica Gimpel and Gene Anthony Ray had supporting roles as well. *Diff'rent Strokes,* which ran from 1978 to 1985, made some strides in the way African Americans were portrayed; although the Drummond family was headed by a white man, the two adopted brothers in the family were African American, and Gary Coleman, who played the youngest son Arnold, became one of the favorite characters of all on network television for the decade.

The show that proved that a series focusing primarily on African American characters could be a hit with mainstream television audiences was *The Cosby Show.* Bill Cosby was already a popular comic, as well as being a writer and voice actor in the important cartoon series, *Fat Albert and the Cosby Kids,* which ran from 1972–1985. The success of *The Cosby Show* lay not simply in who was playing the main characters, but also in the high-quality content. Television humor in a family setting was coming back to mainstream television. *The Cosby Show* was truly revolutionary, as American audiences now could see an example of a stable, upper-middle-class, educated African American family on television every week, and the humor did not rely on the slapstick that had often been part of earlier portrayals of African American characters.

The Cosby Show was the 1980s' version of the classic family sitcoms from the 1950s, such as *Father Knows Best* and *Leave it to Beaver.* As such, both Caucasian and African American audiences easily accepted the show, propelling it to the top spot in the ratings for most of the decade. *The Cosby Show* helped the NBC network as a whole return to prominence in the 1980s, opening the door to more family-oriented comedies in the years that followed. Its success paved the way for other comedies featuring African Americans, such as *The Robert Guillaume Show, Charlie & Co., 227, Frank's Place, Family Matters,* and *Fresh Prince of Bel Air.*

The controversy behind *The Cosby Show* and shows like it was that television executives were reluctant to present an African American family on network television in a prime spot, for fear of alienating Caucasian audiences. Once *Cosby* took hold as a nationwide hit, though, it became obvious that if a show had good writing and acting, it would find a wide audience. The fact that the nation was exposed to positive images of African Americans may have countered the prejudices of some members of the audience and also may have inspired other minorities who identified with characters that looked like them.

How, and by whom, television news is delivered will always have an impact on the way that viewers interpret its message. There were few African American newscasters in the mainstream media. J. Fred MacDonald (1992, 234) states that "by the early 1980s, there was a growing concern among blacks that they had hit their peak in nonfiction TV, and that progress toward integrating video news would remain incomplete." One of the reasons for the lack of such programming is that there were few African Americans in higher positions on networks who could decide what was to be included. MacDonald (1992, 235) continues, noting that if the networks "desired to integrate their operations, blacks would have been hired specifically for executive operations." This was in contrast to comments by the president of ABC News, Roone Arledge, who stated on *Viewpoint* that he wanted more African Americans to be included in the news world. Regardless, the only African American to become widely successful was Oprah Winfrey, initially on the show *A.M. Chicago* before moving to her own successful television show in the years that followed.

CONTROVERSIES IN CENSORSHIP AND SEXUALITY

Sex was a prevailing source of controversy in the 1980s. In both his music and his music videos, Prince included blatant references to sexual images, questioning gender roles. At the end of the 1970s and early 1980s, he defined a sound that became a cross between R&B, rock, and new wave. *Dirty Mind* (1980) and *Controversy* (1981) enjoyed some success among R&B fans in spite of (or perhaps because of) their raunchiness. Prince's lyrics, such as in "Soft and Wet" (from *For You*, 1978), "Head" and "Do It All Night" (from *Prince*, 1979), and "Do Me, Baby" and "Jack U Off" (from *Dirty Mind*) leave little to the imagination about his intentions and messages. Prince's animal sexuality has appealed strongly to his fans since the beginning of his career. In addition, he used visual symbols and wore clothes that could be considered sexually charged and even androgynous.

Madonna's fashion approach had sexual overtones, beginning with her videos "Borderline" and "Lucky Star," and her style was widely copied by teenage girls across the country. She wore a cross on a necklace, but she also wore lacy, low-cut blouses, tight skirts, and fishnet stockings, contrasting religion and sex. She was also known for wearing a belt inscribed with the words "boy toy," and she wore a dog chain on the cover of *Madonna*, which created even more controversy among the parents of her teenage fans. Madonna's videos and fashion impact would widely influence important elements of the new, visually based medium of music television, though in some ways, her music did not receive as much attention as the videos themselves. Madonna was the new breed of pop star, changing forever the way that pop artists were marketed. Her fourth album, *Like a Prayer* (1989), continued her tradition of pushing the boundaries by addressing uncomfortable song topics. The "Like a Prayer" video questioned racial and religious issues, with an underlying questioning of her own power as a woman. The video debuted in a Pepsi commercial as per the terms of an endorsement contract with the soft drink company, one of the first of its time—however, its racy content made Pepsi pull it from its advertising campaign.

Throughout Madonna's stylistic development in the 1980s, the use of synthesizers and current trends in dance music were always at the forefront of her writing and production style. By constantly keeping abreast of the next trend in the underground dance scene, Madonna always managed to stay relevant throughout the 1980s and beyond. In a similar manner, she was aware of fashion, keeping in touch with the times and setting the latest trends.

Not everyone has been kind to her, however. Many see Madonna as a person who thrives on publicity to such a degree that she was always looking for ways to shock people and draw attention to herself. Others have considered that her role as a musician and producer was secondary to her role as a dancer. Regardless, Madonna was an artist who pushed the boundaries of what a visually charged MTV artist could achieve and broke ground for the performers who followed, especially women. In 1985, nude photos that she had taken prior to her recording contract appeared in the men's magazine *Playboy*, but it was her *Like a Virgin* album that bothered many of her critics the most because of the songs' lyrical content. Another female artist, Cyndi Lauper, actually preceded Madonna in including sexual content in her songs (for example, she hinted at female masturbation in "She-Bop" in 1984), but she generated less controversy than Madonna, probably because Lauper was more coy and fun in her approach to the subject matter. In the case of Lauper, she was a singer and songwriter first and pop culture icon second; with Madonna, it was largely the opposite.

2 Live Crew's "Me So Horny" was a deliberate attempt to gain media attention by trying to push the establishment's view of appropriate lyrics, a response to new parental guidance labeling championed by the Parents Music Resource Center (PMRC). Rap music had become fun, easy to understand by the mainstream pop audience, removed from the genre's style as originally intended. It is only natural to expect that groups would begin to want to bring the genre back to its original, street-cred roots. Gangsta rap achieved that goal.

The Dead Kennedys' lyrical content established itself as vulgar, yet full of politically charged commentary, critical of President Ronald Reagan, the religious right, and the upper class. The group was clearly a hardcore punk band on their first two releases, *Fresh Fruit for Rotting Vegetables* (1980) and *In God We Trust, Inc.* (1981). In 1985, their *Frakenchrist* album generated controversy in that the state of California charged the members (and anyone else involved with the album's manufacture) with "distribution of harmful material to minors," after the mother of a fan complained to the Los Angeles district attorney. Not only were the group's lyrics under attack, but the cover featured a painting by H. R. Giger, *Work 219: Landscape XX* (1973), which depicted penises entering vaginas (the case ended with a hung jury and was not retried). By 1986, the Dead Kennedys released *Bedtime for Democracy*, but it never moved into the mainstream.

The Parents Music Resource Center (PMRC), founded by the spouses of some American politicians, were concerned about the lyrical content of popular music recordings released in the 1980s. Tipper Gore (wife of Senator and future Vice President Al Gore) and Susan Baker (wife of Secretary of State James Baker) were leading members of the organization and appeared at the Senate hearings that resulted in the adoption of warning labels for records that may contain objectionable content. (AP Photo/Lana Harris)

In the mid-1980s, several wives of U.S. politicians (led by Tipper Gore, the wife of Tennessee senator Al Gore) gathered to organize a group called the PMRC. They had concerns about the types of lyrical content in commercial hit songs. The group received a good deal of media attention, and ultimately congressional hearings, to help further their cause.

The organization's influence ended up changing the music industry. Musical artists certainly did not appreciate the results of the women's cause. Twisted Sister vocalist Dee Snider considered that he and his fellow musicians were the targets of what he referred to as "character assassination." Artists ranging from Snider, to composer/bandleader Frank Zappa, to even the wholesome John Denver all called to testified before Congress about what they saw as censorship, each espousing their defense of lyrics as protected by the freedom of speech provision in the First Amendment.

Ultimately, the PMRC was working to define what was immoral, and their members advocated putting labels on musical recordings to help "inform" parents about what music their child was purchasing. Musicologist Robert Walser (1990, 138) noted that

Although the MPRC has been accused of not really being a "resource center" because its publications display little familiarity with the scholarly literature on popular music, it is unmistakably "parental." The fullest articulation of the MPRC brief is Tipper Gore's *Raising PG Kids in an X-Rated Society*, published in 1987. In it, Gore takes care to establish her authority as a social and cultural critic by emphasizing that she is a parent; she dwells on the numbers and genders of the children of PMRC leaders, while neglecting to mention that her main opponents at the Senate hearings, musicians Frank Zappa and Dee Snider, are also concerned parents. Her references to twenty-year-old "boys" mark her concern to represented heavy metal as a threat to youth, enabling her to mobilize parental hysteria while avoiding the adult word *censorship*. Objecting to eroticism and "lesbian undertones" in popular music, along with sadism and brutality, she conflates sex and violence, which have in common their threat to parental control.

Walser was speaking from his position as an expert on one frequently attacked genre, heavy metal. However, it was certainly not the only genre to receive criticism from the organization—indeed, the PMRC released the "Filthy Fifteen," a list of the most objectionable songs:

Artist	Song	Hot Topics
Prince	"Darling Nikki"	Sex, masturbation
Sheena Easton	"Sugar Walls"	Sex
Judas Priest	"Eat Me Alive"	Sex
Vanity	"Strap on Robbie Baby"	Sex
Mötley Crüe	"Bastard"	Violence
AC/DC	"Let Me Put My Love Into You"	Sex
Twisted Sister	"We're Not Gonna Take It"	Violence
Madonna	"Dress You Up"	Sex
W.A.S.P.	"Animal (Fuck Like A Beast)"	Sex
Def Leppard	"High 'n' Dry"	Drug and alcohol use
Mercyful Fate	"Into the Coven"	Occult
Black Sabbath	"Trashed"	Drug and alcohol use
Mary Jane Girls	"In My House"	Sex
Venom	"Possessed"	Occult
Cyndi Lauper	"She-Bop"	Sex, masturbation

The central question to the controversy was: What right does the U.S. government have to decide what is protected by freedom of speech and what ought to be censored? With any type of artistic expression, the integration of the work comes from the audience, and responsible parents should keep an eye on what their children are doing, so it is a good thing if they are involved enough in their children's lives to pay attention to what they are listening to.

Years after the PMRC's influence has waned, the industry still has labels on recordings that are sold commercially, but now fans use this as a badge of interest (or even honor), knowing that the recording could contain some forbidden or controversial content. Recording topics, particularly in hip hop, have become even more sexual and violent in nature, and perhaps they would have regardless of the PMRC's involvement. Before lyrics can be challenged, a view of socioeconomic problems in the United States would be a more prudent approach.

The PMRC's concerns about sex and violence were intermingled with another element that they considered dangerous—the occult. In the 1980s, many religious Americans became concerned about the effect on children of what they deemed to be Satanism. Most of these concerns were voiced by fundamentalist Protestant communities. There was the idea, known as the Satanic Panic, that Satan was actively trying to target children, both physically and psychologically, so that they would become his followers and reject God, their parents, and society as a whole. Followers of Satanic Panic began to behave in a manner that bordered on illogical, and over time, the members of the religious community would become more obsessed with finding the truth about allegations. The panic could even be compared to what occurred during the 16th-century witch trials of Salem, where children were asked leading questions that might be used to condemn an adult.

Heavy metal recording artists were particular targets of these concerns in the 1980s. For instance, Ozzy Osborne was accused of placing subliminal messages in his recordings, encouraging young teenagers to commit suicide, that could be heard when played backward. Judas Priest was the target of similar accusations; both artists had fans that led troubled lives as teenagers, and once in a while one of them would indeed commit suicide, but that had nothing to do with the recordings or the artists.

Teachers and day care workers were beginning to come under examination to make sure that groups of children were not molested en masse, which became known as Satanic Ritual Abuse (SRA). Michelle Smith published a book in the 1980s called *Michelle Remembers*, where she gives details of how she had been subjected to Satanic rituals as a child. Smith was a patient of psychiatrist Lawrence Pazer, who claimed that she had "repressed memories" of Satanic rituals. It was only after Smith received therapy from Pazer that these older memories of Satanic rituals were discovered. (Smith later became Pazer's wife.) However, the Federal Bureau of Investigation (FBI) concluded that the rituals that she detailed were myths. Groups began to question many childcare organizations. An investigation of the St. Cross Episcopal Church in Hermosa Beach, California, by the Children's Institute International looked into the question of teachers at the church's schools. About 100 teachers were accused of child molestation and/or Satanic rituals in the course of the investigation. Children were pressured by parents to claim that they had been molested and/or were made to participate in Satanic rituals, and interviewers used suggestive and repeated questions—techniques that would almost guarantee the implantation of false memories in the children's minds. But the sense of hysteria expanded beyond clear Satanism, as in the case of the McMartin preschool in Manhattan Beach, California, which was investigated for a number of months because of allegations of animal sacrifice and inappropriate sexual contact with some of the students. However, the children's testimony was deemed unreliable. One final aspect of Satanic Panic was the idea that children were being bred for sacrifice, as claimed by Lauren Stratford in her 1988 book *Satan's Underground* (though the book was later exposed as a fabrication by the Christian magazine *Cornerstone*). Satanic Panic was made even more widespread was because of the expansion of televangelists on mainstream television.

Sexuality was an important part of movies in the 1980s, which marked the beginning of a shift in values toward what was proper to show on screen, including attitudes toward gay men and violence. *Cruising* (1980) is a movie about a detective who is trying to find a serial killer targeting gay men. The title of the movie had a double meaning: police officers going cruising on patrol, and people cruising bars and nightclubs to find sexual partners. In the movie, Al Pacino plays a policeman who goes undercover in the underground S&M subculture to try to solve the case. A serial killer had been frequenting bars in the West Village area of New York City; he would pick up a man and, after taking him back to a motel, the killer would tie the victim before stabbing him to death. Steve Burns (Pacino) physically resembled the victims, so he decides to move into an apartment to become assimilated into the gay scene. He befriends a gay man, Ted, who is in a complicated relationship with a dancer. Burns tips his police colleagues that a waiter could be responsible, and the waiter is taken into custody and beaten during interrogation. Convinced that the police are prejudiced against gays, Burns considers leaving his position. Eventually a university music student is found to be the killer and taken into custody, and Burns returns to his straight life with his girlfriend. Though Pacino was a well-established star by the time the film was released, *Cruising* came under a good deal of critical scrutiny by gay activists shortly after it was released. The main critique was that the movie painted an unfairly negative picture of what gay people were like, making it look like they were all perverts and miscreants. Pacino went on record to defend the movie, though, drawing a comparison to the portrayal of Italian Americans in his most successful films in *The Godfather* series.

Although it received a lot of critical acclaim, *Blue Velvet* (1986) was also considered controversial upon its release because of its sexually charged and violent content. Director David Lynch, who already had a reputation for creativity due to his avant-garde films *Eraserhead* (1977) and *The Elephant Man* (1980), cemented his status as an auteur with this film. Set in Lumberton, a small town in the South, Jeffrey Beaumont, an all-American teen (Kyle MacLaughlin), finds a cut-off ear in a field after leaving the hospital where his father was recovering from a heart attack. He brings the ear to the police and befriends Sandy (Laura Dern), the daughter of a detective; they decide to try to find out where the ear came from. They eventually are led to a nightclub and meet sultry singer Dorothy Vallens (Isabella Rossellini), who is singing "Blue Velvet," the 1960s' Bobby Vinton hit.

The story takes a dramatic turn when Jeffrey, while hiding in a closet, watches Dorothy undress. When caught, she forces him to disrobe so she can molest him at knifepoint. The subject becomes the object, and vice versa. Dorothy is later raped by a drug-addicted psychopath (Dennis Hopper), in which the man acts as both father and baby, while Jeffrey is powerless to help. Adding fuel to the fire is the fact that after Frank leaves, Dorothy pleads to be further abused by Jeffrey. Through its sadomasochism and violent images, the movie produced a disturbing effect that stoked controversy, and it made an impact that changed the industry, similar to that of previously violent films, such as *Psycho* (1960).

In the mid-1980s, President Ronald Reagan identified that some of his strongest supporters came from the religious right. Reagan had hosted televangelists to the White House, and with good reason: they were essential to his initial election in 1980 and his reelection in 1984. As such, Reagan charged his Attorney General's office, headed by Edwin Meese, to do a study on the effects of pornography on American society. The call for a study of this nature was not new; President Lyndon Johnson founded a Commission on Obscenity and Pornography before his term ended, and the commission hired Berl Kutchinsky, a criminology professor, to do a study similar to the one in his native Denmark. When it came out in 1970, Kutchinsky's report noted that pornography posed no threat to society, but President Richard Nixon promptly dismissed its conclusions.

The Meese commission, staffed by ultraconservative members, found otherwise, detailing the harmful effects of pornography and its connection to organized crime. It recognized that the pornography industry had become more violent since the 1970 study. The constitutional expert, University of Michigan professor Frederick Schauer, opined that the First Amendment did not protect pornography since it was just sexual activity, not a form of speech. There were extensive public hearings, at an overall budget exceeding $1.5 million. The commission even sought out so-called victims of pornography to testify how their lives had been harmed. Many claimed that the pornography industry had contributed to their partner's infidelity and drug use. Cartoons in *Playboy, Penthouse,* and *Hustler,* the most prominent examples of racy magazines, were analyzed and found to be part of the problem. In the end, the commission's report condemned the industry, but a large number of critics found the report flawed in nearly every way. This is unsurprising, as the commission members held a bias about what they expected to find.

CONTROVERSIES IN RELIGION

The Catholic Church has the most members of any religious organization in the United States, and their members' voting and political activity in the United States reflect their faith. With the influx of additional immigrants from Central and South America, the percentage of Catholics in the United States was growing to heights not seen before, yet the numbers of clergy leading the congregations were dwindling because of a lack of new priests. In addition, women were becoming more concerned about their role in the church—some of them were interested in becoming priests instead of only nuns, but the Catholic Church strictly forbade this. There were also few opportunities for nuns to advance to high positions in the church. In 1971, Father Robert Drinan became a Democratic representative from Massachusetts, where he became initially known for his stance against the Vietnam War. He also began to voice views regarding abortion rights that conflicted with the Church. To counteract Drinan's views, the Vatican established a new policy that restricted the ability for a priest or nun to serve in public office, which was created in response to the desire of Drinan to continue to serve in Congress in the 1980s.

The official position of the Church was to be against abortion, which considering the controversies that arose in the wake of the 1972 *Roe v. Wade* decision that expanded upon a woman's right to have an abortion, polarized segments of the population. Though Pope John Paul II was among the most popular pontiffs in the church's recent history, he was staunchly against abortion, and church leaders were strongly encouraged to denounce the practice. Similar battles occurred over homosexuality, as the number of Americans supporting gay rights was starting to increase. Local churches were advised to withdraw their support of any organization that supported gay rights, and eventually this idea spilled over into the debate on AIDS, as discussed earlier in this chapter. Many churches began to provide condoms for homosexual men, but many still adhered to the stringent instructions from the Vatican against gay sex. Further, Catholics were beginning to voice concerns about the growing economic divide between the wealthy and the poor in the United States.

The Protestants were among the most active religious groups in the 1980s, but they also were led by the decade's most controversial figures. The leaders of their movement were Jerry Falwell, Richard Zone, James Robison, and Pat Robertson. Falwell was instrumental in founding the Moral Majority, an organization focused on bringing Christian values into politics with a conservative agenda. Zone founded Christian Voice, a similar lobbying group that openly admitted an interest in funding political candidates. Edward MacAteer headed the Roundtable, another group that lobbied for political candidates with a fundamentalist slant.

These groups, as well as many smaller ones, became known collectively as the New Christian Right, or the New Right. The New Right was very critical of the *Roe vs. Wade* abortion decision and have actively sought to overturn it ever since. They were also intent on having silent prayer in public schools, which was considered to violate the separation between church and state. In 1988, Jesse Jackson, a liberal African American activist with ties to the Rev. Martin Luther King, Jr., and the Reverend Pat Robertson both ran for president, but neither candidate generated much support for their political parties (Democratic and Republican, respectively).

A resurgence in religions outside the Judeo-Christian realm increased in the 1980s, if only slightly. These religions had an Eastern influence, such as Hinduism, Buddhism, and metaphysical crystals. These were lumped together into a movement called "New Age" and became more noticeable when celebrities, particularly Shirley MacClaine, began to publicly discuss them. Marilyn Ferguson was a vocal advocate in her book, *The Aquarian Conspiracy* (1980), that reintroduced religions that had long been ignored in the West, but people aligned with Christianity found them to be controversial. These religions promoted self-help and a stronger relationship with the Earth, its elements, and the heavens. As expected, the reintroduction of these religions came under scrutiny by Christian churches and was most commonly embraced by former members of the 1960s counterculture and those aligned with its values.

The 1970s was the decade where American society began to see the so-called electronic church, a term to describe religious television programming. By the 1980s, televangelism shows hosted ministers were gaining more viewers, and with that, more financial donations to their church. In turn, this made the church-oriented networks more powerful than ever. The Christian Broadcast Network (CBN) offered one of the most popular of these shows, *The 700 Club;* in the words of Jeffery K. Haden and Charles E. Swann (1981, 12), the show "matched *The Tonight Show* of Johnny Carson in almost every detail—band, desk and sofa set, sidekick, and appreciative audience. One might even find Hollywood stars as guests, but only those who are born again or Spirit-filled need have their agents book an appearance. Instead of sharing show-biz gossip, guests swap miracles and personal testimonies." CBN was powerful enough that they encouraged the founding of Regent University in Virginia Beach by Pat Robertson. Robertson also arranged broadcasting contracts for CBN to be shown on local stations throughout the country. The contracts became the model for other religious networks.

CBN's main competitor was the PTL network, based in South Carolina and started by two of CBN's hosts, Jim and Tammy Faye Bakker. The Bakkers were featured on the television show *The PTL Club* (the initials stand for either "Praise the Lord" or "People That Love"). Jim and Tammy Faye became significant celebrities in the 1980s, in part because of Tammy Faye's outrageous persona and appearance, including wearing very heavy makeup.

The network began to receive scrutiny in 1987 when it came out that PTL was accepting $1,000 as payment for a lifetime membership to the church, and donors' fees entitled them to a three-night stay at PTL's resort, Heritage USA. The membership fees were to be used to build the resort and hotel, but Bakker took much of the money for himself. Eventually, Jessica Hahn, a church employee, claimed that she had been drugged and raped by Jim Bakker and an associate. She went public with the allegations, causing Bakker to resign his position, though she later dropped the charges (which she was later found to have done in exchange for a payoff). Bakker eventually admitted that he had consensual sex with Hahn and was wrong in doing so, but more damning was a financial audit that proved that there were two versions of the company's accounting. Jerry Falwell took over the network, but the scandal damaged PTL's popularity. Bakker was convicted in 1988 but only for mail fraud.

Televangelist Jimmy Swaggart was even more rigorously scrutinized in the 1980s for his relationship with a prostitute. Swaggart had initially exposed a fellow minister and colleague at the Assemblies of God church organization, Marvin Gorman, for extramarital affairs in 1986. Perhaps wanting to settle the score, Gorman enlisted his son to watch Swaggart to catch him in his own indiscretions. Although Swaggart and Gorman had made an agreement to reinstate Gorman to Assemblies of God, this did not happen in a timely enough manner, and Gorman approached church executives about Swaggart's activities. Their efforts paid off, and Swaggart was caught with Debra Murphree, a prostitute, at a New Orleans motel; photos of the pair were taken, both in and out of the room. After Murphree failed a polygraph test, Swaggart publicly appeared on television with what is now known as his "I have sinned" confession. Murphree then revealed to the media that while Swaggart was a regular client, they did not have sex and Swaggart only took pictures of her. Though Swaggart was involved in another prostitution accusation in 1991, he continued to serve as a minister for several years. Though controversial in the mainstream, the religious right community did not seem to care very much about these allegations. Televangelism has continued to be a lucrative business model to the present day and has avoided the scandals that were prominent in the 1980s.

Another controversial aspect of popular culture in the 1980s revolved around Dungeons and Dragons, a fantasy game set in an era of magic, swords, sorcery, elves, and castles. Developed by Gary Gygax, the game, and its successor, Advanced Dungeons and Dragons, relied on the development of stories by a dungeon master, where players would be put in situations where they could battle each other and acquire treasure. One set of critics was less than fond of the fighting aspect of the game, since the swords, spells, and other medieval weapons involved were violent. More often, parents simply didn't understand why their teenage sons (and, rarely, daughters) were so enamored with the game. Those teenagers included a young David Ewalt, who remarked that even playing as an adult, he "needed to play [Dungeons and Dragons], too—I was dependent on it, like a junkie needs a fix. If my Tuesday-night game was canceled because someone had to work late, I was agitated and restless for the rest of the week" (Ewalt, 2014, 46). It became another avenue for the usual conflict between parents and teenagers over an activity that the teenagers are passionate about but that the parents find concerning.

For some parents, there was the additional concern that this story-game, most often played by so-called nerds or geeks, was in violation of the parents' religious principles. Witchcraft had long been scrutinized by the religious community, and some parents thought that playing Dungeons and Dragons would make their children more vulnerable to the influence of alternative religious or even satanic beliefs. This was most noticeable in Heber City, Utah, a farming town with an overwhelming Mormon population, in May 1980. Parents there complained to the local school board that the organizers of an after-school Dungeons and Dragons club were "working with the Antichrist and fermenting Communist subversion," while local Christian minister Norman Springer told *The New York Times* that the game was "very definitively" anti-religious: "These books are filled with things that are not fantasy, but are actual in the real daemon world and can be very dangerous for anyone involved in the game because it leaves them so open to Satanic spirits." In response, TSR, the company that owned Dungeons and Dragons, ran an ad in a magazine dedicated to the game's enthusiasts, *The Dragon,* calling for "real-life clerics: TSR Hobbies needs you," in an appeal to any member of the clergy, regardless of religion, to share how Dungeons and Dragons was a positive influence on the lives of their parishioner who played the game.

The movie *The Last Temptation of Christ* (1988) generated enormous controversy among devout Christians because of how Jesus Christ was portrayed in the film, inspired by a 1953 book of the same name. In the film, Jesus collaborates with the Romans to persecute Jewish rebels by helping to build crosses. As he is crucified, he begins to imagine how his life could have been different, including marrying prostitute Mary Magdalene, fathering children, and living into old age. He later learns that he had ultimately been tempted by Satan to have this alternative reality, which he chose to reject to achieve his destiny as the son of God.

Despite the fact that all of this was depicted as being from the influence of Satan, Christian fundamentalists were critical of this narrative because they considered it outside of traditional biblical accounts. In response, they launched a series of widespread, public protests, including outside the offices of the film production studio and any movie theater that showed the film. Some cinemas were afraid to show the movie at all. And once *The Last Temptation of Christ* was made available on video, many video stores, including the Blockbuster chain, refused to carry it. In some countries, the movie was simply banned. The film was critically well received, however, and Martin Scorsese was nominated for an Oscar for his direction.

CONTROVERSIES IN FILM AND TELEVISION

Other controversies in movies and television focused on how the films were made or the way they turned out. The film *Heaven's Gate* (1980) was controversial in two ways: animal cruelty allegations and how much funding and control was given to directors for specific projects in the years that followed. The American Humane Association (AHA) became critical of the production, claiming that horses were killed and injured during the filming, including the death of a horse by dynamite in the final scene. Further allegations included that the producers removed cow intestines to represent human intestines in battle scenes and that there was cockfighting on the set. Due to all this controversy, future films began to have AHA supervision over the use of animals in films.

Meanwhile, the process of making the film required a huge budget, which made *Heaven's Gate* the most expensive film made to date. Expectations were high in terms of quality as well, since Michael Cimino, the director, had made the highly acclaimed, Oscar-winning movie *The Deer Hunter* in 1978. But the critics' opinion of the film was almost universally very poor—in the end, it was considered one of the worst movies of all time. The audience stayed away in droves, and so *Heaven's Gate* was a historic box-office bomb. This brought down the reputation of the film company, United Artists, and harmed Transamerica, its parent corporation.

The film's epic failure sparked the end of what was considered America's New Wave of Filmmaking that had flourished with young directors since the mid-1960s. Furthermore, companies now started to be more careful with their budgets to try to minimize the financial consequence of a flop at the box office.

The Evil Dead (1981) was a low-budget film that marked the debut of a 23-year-old director, Sam Raimi. Its storyline was familiar enough: teenagers go to an isolated cabin/vacation home in the Tennessee woods and encounter a supernatural danger. They find the *Book of the Dead* bound with human skin, accompanied by a cassette tape recorder. By playing the tape, they release demons that terrorize them. The five become zombies one by one, until only Ash (Bruce Campbell) is left. Ash must dismember each of the zombies to survive. What set this film apart from the standard-issue thriller was the level of violence, imaginative imagery, and drawn-out sequences of terror—the action simply did not let up, and the audience was swept along with it, leaving them with a lingering uneasiness. But these defining features of the film stirred up a great amount of controversy. The film has been described by Jürgen Muller (1994, 194) as a "roller coaster ride: the audience is dragged into the action when the invisible demon—represented exclusively by the 'excursions' of a charmingly documentary-like, subjective hand-held camera and special sound effects—races through the undergrowth, splitting and shattering trees in its wake." Another aspect of its impact is that the film opened the door to the "slasher" genre—a plethora of gory films released later in the decade, such as the *Friday the 13th* and *Nightmare on Elm Street* franchises. There was also an even bloodier sequel, *Evil Dead II* (1987).

Twilight Zone: The Movie (1983) differs from the other movies described so far because the controversy surrounding it came from an accident on the movie set, rather than its storyline, budget, or special effects. Four episodes from the classic television series were adapted for the film, and each segment was helmed by a different director (John Landis, Steven Spielberg, Joe Dante, and George Miller). The segment that Landis directed, "Time Out," required a stunt that incorporated a helicopter for a scene set in the Vietnam era. The helicopter careened out of control, and three actors, Vic Morrow, seven-year-old Myca Dinh Le, and six-year-old Renee Shin-Yi Chen, were killed. Apart from the sheer tragedy of the event, it was in violation of several laws: The scene was shot at 2:30 a.m., and California law prohibited children from working at night, working without being accompanied by a teacher or social worker, and working around explosions and other dangerous situations. To further complicate matters, the child actors' parents were told not to reveal to the firefighters that the children were part of the scene; in addition, the children were being paid "under the table" to avoid child labor laws. The controversy cumulated in lengthy criminal and civil lawsuits, which took years to resolve. The tragedy and negative publicity also tainted the movie as a whole, which may have suppressed its performance at the box office.

One of the most important political topics in the 1980s was the Cold War between the United States and the Soviet Union. At the time, the United States had begun a significant buildup in nuclear arms in order to deter the Soviets from attacking. The buildup was in concern for the safety of the country, and the threat of the Soviet Union was very real for many Americans. However, the level of anxiety about it was not as high as it had been during the late 1950s and early 1960s, which brought the two countries to the brink of war. Nevertheless, in the 1980s, the fear of thermonuclear war was the subject of several films that illustrated the uneasy fear between the two superpowers, which led to them develop more weapons, including a missile defense system (nicknamed "Star Wars") that was championed by President Ronald Reagan.

One example was *The Atomic Café*, a documentary released in 1982, early in the Reagan presidency. It highlighted the history of nuclear warfare, including historical television footage. *WarGames* (1983) certainly fit in with those panicked thoughts as well. A teenager hacks into a computer that does war simulations, and the U.S. military reacts by preparing for war, believing that the computer is the Soviet military. *The Hunt for Red October* (1990) was a movie about a Soviet submarine that has been taken over by a rogue Soviet submarine commander who intends to defect to the United States. The United States, who was unaware of Ramius's true intention to defect, is unclear about whether the captain (played by Sean Connery) is insane enough to attack the United States alone. Another movie where the United States was under attack was *Red Dawn* (1984), where the country is being invaded by Soviet, Cuban, and Nicaraguan troops. A band of Colorado teenagers, who call themselves Wolverines after their school mascot, fight valiantly against the invaders.

Another invasion occurs during *Invasion USA* (1985), a Chuck Norris action film that pits Norris's character Matt Hunter against Cuban guerillas who have invaded Florida. One of the largest hits of the decade was *Top Gun* (1986), which pits ambitious and competitive pilots against Soviet flyers in a dogfight after undergoing training at a flight school. Not all of these movies were based on conflicts between the Soviet and U.S. militaries, though. In *Red Heat* (1988), Arnold Schwarzenegger portrays a Moscow detective working on a case about a drug lord from Soviet Georgia who makes his way to the United States. After the drug lord's capture in Chicago, an American detective escorts him back to Russia, where he escapes. Regardless of their cultural and political differences, the two detectives team up to find the criminal.

The impact of the Cold War in the 1980s was even incorporated into *Rocky IV* (1985), where a Soviet boxer who seems to be physically engineered by the government comes to the United States to fight Apollo Creed, killing him in the ring. Rocky then goes to train in the Soviet Union to avenge Creed's death, but after doing so, he comments that both countries should set aside their differences and work together.

In 1987, the Alliance of Motion Picture and Television Producers (AMPTP) started to demand that television writers accept a sliding scale on residual royalties, as the revenues generated by syndicating older television programs had dropped. In response, the Writers Guild of America (WGA) protested, insisting that they actually deserved a higher percentage over revenue coming in from outside the United States, as well as more creative control over their scripts. The negotiations persisted for weeks, and eventually the writers resorted to going on strike. The television industry came to a grinding halt for 22 weeks (from March 7 until August 7, 1988).

Network television had already been feeling the effects of a strengthening cable television landscape, so it was in a weaker position than it had been in the past. Viewer outrage at the lack of original programming from the "Big Three" networks pushed viewers toward cable television; as a result, the major networks lost approximately 9 percent of their total audience, and the effect has continued to be felt to the present day. Because of the strike, the networks had to postpone their fall season until the Christmas holidays. Writers not only lost money, but affiliated workers such as actors, production members, caterers, and shipping services—a sizable portion of the economy in Los Angeles—failed to work.

However, there were some beneficiaries from the strike. Carsey-Werner Co., producer of *The Cosby Show*, was able to continue production on that show, as well as a new sitcom, *Roseanne*, which shot to No. 2 in the ratings that season, because they hired independent writers. The lack of scripted shows also sparked the rise of early versions of reality television, such as *Unsolved Mysteries* and *COPS*. The strike ended because of the efforts by attorney Ken Ziffren and negotiator Nick Counter, as the sliding scale and an increase in international royalties for writers were agreed upon.

Another controversial aspect of the 1980s was the impact that young urban professional workers (yuppies) were having on society. What seemed to be a worthwhile approach—what could be wrong with being successful in life?—has come under scrutiny since the 1980s, but films of the 1980s mostly highlighted the positive aspects of the yuppie work ethic and the negative aspects of yuppies' consumption habits.

Business-oriented films were very big at the box office. *Wall Street* (1987) was one of the most important such movies, becoming known for its catchphrase, "Greed is good." Bud Fox (Charlie Sheen) is a young stockbroker who begins to work for Gordon Gekko (Michael Douglas), a corporate raider. The persistent Fox finally wangles a meeting with Gekko, providing him with some insider information about an airline. Gekko is impressed, so he hires Fox. Fox begins to make significant money, and when Gekko takes over the airline, Fox becomes its president. However, Fox is eventually arrested for insider trading, so in exchange for a lighter sentence, he wears a wire and helps trap Gekko for the government.

Working Girl (1988) was another movie with a Wall Street backdrop. Tess McGill (Melanie Griffith) is a secretary at an investment company in the mergers and acquisitions department, but she really wants to become a trader. She comes to work for Katherine Parker, a female executive (Sigourney Weaver), and initially she hopes that Parker will be her mentor. But then she makes a suggestion about a merger idea to Parker, and Parker steals it. In the meantime, Parker travels on vacation to Switzerland and breaks her leg. While her boss is away, Tess decides to take her career into her own hands. She meets Jack Trainer (Harrison Ford), an executive with another company, to propose the merger, and the two embark on the deal together. They also become romantically involved, and in the end, the deal goes through, Parker is revealed as a thief, and Tess winds up as a junior executive (with her own office!).

In *The Secret of My Success* (1987), Brantley Foster (Michael J. Fox) moves to New York from Kansas to work in the finance industry. After working in the mailroom at the Primrose Corporation (a job that his Uncle Howard, the company's chief executive officer, helped him get), he eventually sees a way for the company to make more money. Inventing a new persona as an executive, Carlton Whitfield, he starts working in both positions. Though he discovers that his uncle is having an affair with the object of his affection, Christy, Brantley ends up being seduced by Howard's wife, Vera. In the end, Vera and Brantley team up for a newer merger without Howard or Christy. The young yuppie gets not only the company, but also the elder woman.

Fox appeared in another movie about yuppies during the decade, *Bright Lights, Big City* (1988), as Jamie Conway, a fact checker at a New York magazine. Conway leads a frantic, cocaine- and alcohol-driven lifestyle, full of equal amounts of ambition and entertainment, often with his best friend, Tad Allagash (Kiefer Sutherland), at a nightclub called Heartbreak. A year before, Conway had married a model, but she left him to work in Paris and for another man. Conway meets Tad's cousin, Vicky (Tracy Pollan). He has dinner with her, and then in the bathroom, Conway decides not to use more cocaine and to try to get through the night without chemicals. After another lost weekend of partying, he reaches out to Vicky for help to clean up his life. Cocaine was the drug of choice for many yuppies, and it was controversial because some cocaine users saw the drug as necessary for success.

CONTROVERSIES IN BUSINESS

In the 1980s, the United States was still recovering from the 1973–1975 recession and faced a stagnant economy highlighted by oil prices that rose at a faster rate than the rest of the economy. President Ronald Reagan understood that the U.S. economy needed to change, and he proposed a controversial way of doing so. During his presidential campaign, he advocated "supply-side" economic policies, which would provide incentives to businesses with less government intervention. Supply-side economic policy advocated for lower tax rates that would flood the economy with more money (since consumers would have more to spend), hence improving business; the government would not have to spend as much itself, so taxes weren't as crucial. As a result, the government would have less influence on any restrictions or how businesses could pursue the American market. Businesses, ideally, would thrive with a lower tax responsibility to the government. The plan became problematic, though, when Reagan's defense budget grew even as taxes went down, increasing the national debt significantly. Reaganomics, the name given to what some describe as "trickle–down" economics, strengthened big business; the idea was that as companies' profits increased, lower-level employees would see benefits trickle down to them. Reagan also continued the deregulation trends began by his predecessor, Jimmy Carter. The airline industry was one of the most affected, as prices for flights went down considerably. Meanwhile, air traffic controllers went on strike in 1981, but Reagan just directed the Department of Transportation to fire them and replace them with nonunion workers. However, housing sales dropped, which affected profits for lenders and banks. In what became known as the "Savings and Loan crisis," savings and loan companies lent money at rates that motivated sellers to purchase homes at prices that were less than what they had borrowed. However, when the rates provided to savings and loan companies increased to a higher rate than what they had previously lent to consumers, the companies became insolvent. Rather than asking for assistance, the companies began to look for investments to make up for their lost profits. They were now allowed to invest as they chose, and when the investments didn't materialize, the accounts, guaranteed by the government, required funds to stabilize. Some investors used the system to speculate on future earnings. The middle and lower classes were beginning to suffer, while the upper class was controlling more of the economy than ever before.

Since the Industrial Revolution, the manufacturing of what is called "heavy industry" was the backbone of the U.S. economy. Though the decline of heavy industry started after the end of World War II, it became more precipitous in the 1980s. The automobile industry was among those hardest hit, as foreign cars, especially from Japan, began to saturate the market. Many consumers, whether correct or not, considered Japanese cars more reliable (not to mention better on gas in many cases). German cars were seen as status symbols by the segment of the population who could afford them. Cars from both countries were more technologically advanced than their American counterparts.

Steel used in cars and other pieces of heavy equipment was also declining. Textile manufacturing was particularly hard hit, as companies began to explore opportunities for cheaper labor abroad, rather than investing in new technology that would keep Americans employed and generate more products for the same (or even less) cost. The economy was embroiled in controversy because the government was not committed to helping industries that were failing, preferring to invest in defense, increasing the national debt. One could argue that the main political issue facing the United States was the Soviet Union; but by the end of the decade, the Americans had essentially outspent the Soviets to the point that the Soviet Union was near collapse (it dissolved fully in 1990).

With developments in technology, the computer sector grew significantly while the country moved from an industrial age to an information age in the 1980s. Unfortunately, the American farmer was not a participant in this development, and the farming industry was among the most affected by the decade's economic policies. As smaller countries were having trouble paying their debts to the United States, they imported fewer goods from it, particularly wheat. Land prices were dropping, and farms started closing. Farmers were given subsidies, a measure taken by the government that evoked some controversy but also slowed the decline. In the meantime, Wall Street investment speculators profited from the drop in grain prices. As young professionals graduated into the business world, greed became a trait to be proud of (remember "greed is good"). As the government did not seem to mind going into debt, consumers followed suit, purchasing more items on credit than ever.

Ivan Boesky was a controversial figure in the 1980s because of the success of his activities on Wall Street (and his less-than-scrupulous methods). He was hailed by some as the top deal maker on Wall Street, but it turned out that he was doing so well because he had confidential information that allowed him to engage in corporate takeovers, in violation of the law. On November 14, 1986 (which became known as "Boesky Day"), he was convicted of insider trading, which included a $100 million fine and a prison sentence (however, he did help the government catch other miscreant traders like Carl Icahn, Michael Milken, and Victor Posner, so he got a lighter punishment than he would have). Wall Street investors were shaken at the conviction of a person who had been considered a hero in the business community and the inspiration for films such as *Wall Street*.

Michael Milken was another example of 1980s' greed in the business community. His company, Drexel Burnham Lambert, was the firm where Boesky had hidden his funds while making his insider deals, and Drexel executives had signed documents that alleged that Boesky's money was held in payment for consulting services. Milken was a driven investor, intelligent but egotistical; part of his appeal to up-and-coming investors was that Milken did not indulge in expensive personal items such as cars or clothes, and his toupee was often seen with some type of reverence (along with some ridicule). Milken sought employees committed to their families and paid them well, but he also demanded vigorous work schedules that prevented them from spending time at home with their families.

As with Boesky, many in the Wall Street community saw Milken as a hero, but his success came from high-yield (also known as "junk") bonds of companies with poor credit ratings rather than from corporate takeovers. The companies would often owe their creditors significant amounts of money and had trouble finding investors, so the companies were forced to take out short-term loans. Drexel served as the underwriter for these loans so that investors would be motivated to funnel money into these companies; as a result, Milken's company received funds with few restrictions. Drexel was also involved in more stable investments, and both its low-risk and high-risk accounts brought the company nearly $100 billion by the 1980s. Ultimately, Boesky's allegations against Drexel led to Milken being dismissed by the company; Drexel pleaded guilty to some trading violations, but Milken himself did not go to jail.

Of the controversial figures in business during the 1980s, Donald Trump was certainly the most polarizing. Trump came from a wealthy family with holdings in houses and apartments, but it was Donald who convinced his father to enter the commercial real estate business. Trump's specialty was to purchase derelict properties, renovate them, and then sell them at an immense profit. In order to accomplish this feat, Trump had to battle New York City officials and politicians to rezone properties. Where he excelled was in self-promotion, and though many found his manner of doing business controversial and unscrupulous, nearly every American in the 1980s was at least familiar with "the Donald."

In addition to renovating hotels in both New York and Atlantic City, he wrote two books in the 1980s and sponsored a board game, all of which cemented his ego and persona as an executive who wins at all costs. Trump was cunning, and at times even sneaky, but in the 1980s, the yuppie mentality saw him as a hero who could enjoy immense wealth. He also had a stunning wife for most of the 1980s, Ivana. Nevertheless, as greed would expect, Trump began an affair with a beautiful mistress, Marla Maples; as a result, Ivana enjoyed taking a considerable amount of his fortune in the divorce. After the 1980s, Trump fell on tough financial times, and in 2015, he launched a presidential campaign that was instantly controversial due to his brash, often insulting public statements. In spite of (or perhaps because of) his branding as an outspoken, unpolitically correct figure, he won the Republican nomination and was elected U.S. president in the 2016 election, defeating Hillary Clinton.

Ross Perot was another billionaire businessman who played a major part in politics, running for president in 1992. Perot, like Trump, was a prominent example of capitalism, but where the two men differ is that Perot was a self–made billionaire. Perot led Electronic Data Systems (EDS) after a period of service in the U.S. Navy. He was a tough leader for EDS and later worked with General Motors, though he clashed with the chairman on finding ways to invigorate the company. By the end of the 1980s, he was the founder of Perot Systems Corporation and one of the richest men in the United States. What made him controversial was that he had a blunt, outspoken style, and this almost certainly made him enemies on his way to significant wealth.

CONTROVERSY IN TECHNOLOGY, ART, AND LITERATURE

Somewhat more controversial in consumer selection was in the preference of personal computer platform. The Apple II platform was widely successful among home users, while business users seemed to prefer IBM and its PC-DOS operating system. Eventually, Apple's Macintosh, with its innovative graphical user interface (GUI), changed the computer landscape in the mid-1980s, and Microsoft's development of Windows changed the ways that users could operate personal computers, making them more accessible to a mainstream audience. Apple was unsuccessful in a lawsuit with Microsoft claiming that Windows was a derivative of the Macintosh operating system, but that controversy was somewhat short-lived, as Apple and Microsoft have licensed software (particularly the Microsoft Office suite of products) for years. Many Americans embraced Microsoft founder Bill Gates as a smart businessman and generous philanthropist since Microsoft created the industry-standard Windows software package. Windows replaced the earlier operating system, known as DOS, and became the most popular operating system in the world. The Macintosh line has proved itself to stand the test of time. However, more companies wrote software for Windows than any other operating system.

The 1980s had three controversial episodes about technology, all of which revolved around the selection of a format that would hope to become the industry standard. The first of these was between the format choice for the tapes used in videocassette recorders, VHS or Betamax. As noted in Chapter 6, "Technology," JVC released VHS and Sony released Betamax in 1976. The Betamax format was widely recognized for its quality in both picture and audio, whereas the VHS format could record more on a single tape, allowing longer programs to be recorded without interruption. Another factor that made Betamax less desirable was the fact that it was more expensive than VHS. Further, the Betamax machine itself was prone to more mechanical problems, and the repair of those problems cost much more than the repair of the VHS machine. Movie distributors leaned toward the VHS format in commercial releases, and as a result, some retailers and tape rental stores began to shun the Betamax to appeal to more customers. Betamax tried in vain later in the decade to counter VHS's strength in longer recording times by reducing the recording speed (which affected the quality), but the VHS format had a firm grip on the market at that time. One other alleged aspect of the format war (ultimately debunked) was the impact of the pornography industry. The rumor was that Sony, based on ethical principles, would not allow pornographic films to be distributed on Betamax tapes for commercial release, whereas JVC made no restriction on whether VHS could be used for pornographic distribution. In reality, all commercial movie distributors, regardless of genre, favored the VHS format.

Less controversial was the competition between the home gaming console formats. Atari had the clear hold on the home video game market in the early 1980s. Like the controversy surrounding the videotape format war, consumer preference was not related to quality. The other competitors, particularly Mattel's Intellivision and Coleco's Coleco-Vision, had more detailed graphics than Atari, but the latter maintained its ascendancy thanks to the popularity of specific games, particularly *Space Invaders* and *Asteroids*.

Robert Mapplethorpe was one of the most controversial figures in the art world in the 1980s, largely because of his focus on nude images. There are homosexual clues in Mapplethorpe's work, as well as nude images of women; as Jane Kardon (1988, 10) remarks, "depicting blatant sexuality in a pristine photographic language infuses the words with enormous impact and energy; the contrast between the subject and its manner of presentation allows the viewer the option of being voyeur or connoisseur." Nevertheless, for the more conservative members of American society, his art delivered a different message, and criticism began to mount. The controversy became national news when North Carolina senator Jesse Helms considered some art, in particular Robert Mapplethorpe's photography, to be so "obscene or indecent" that it ought to be banned. David Joselit (Kardon, 1988, 18) comes to Mapplethorpe's defense:

> The enormous popularity of Mapplethorpe's photographs is often explained as a form of sophisticated naughtiness. His frequent characterization as, in the words of one critic, "the imp of the perverse" is an easy kind of dismissal: it labels him a campy gay man. It is undeniable that his photographs form a position of sexual marginality, but he occupies a margin that has much to say to the center. As Craig Owens has argued, the social conventions of homosexuality are meant to regulate the behavior of all men, gay and heterosexual alike. It is his broader relevance that is typically denied to him, by ignoring the hauntingly unstable vision of masculinity and femininity of his art proposes. Mapplethorpe's complex,

compound dramatization of the interplay between sexual aggression and submission—in men and women, heterosexual and homosexual—is clearly evident in the relationship he establishes between his own self-portraits and the photographs of his models.

In 1989, 100 days after Mapplethorpe died of AIDS, Helms and his supporters pressured the Corcoran Gallery of Art in Washington, D.C., to cancel a major traveling exhibit of his work. The exhibition had been supported by the National Endowment for the Arts (NEA), but with it losing its funding, a private corporation stepped in and provided the funding so that the exhibition could be put on.

Another art target by critics was the photograph, *Piss Christ*, a work by Andres Serrano that showed a cross in a jar of the artist's urine. The photo won in the "Awards in the Visual Arts" division from the Southeastern Center for Contemporary Art in Winston-Salem, North Carolina. The religious right objected to the catalogue of visual arts competition winners, largely because *Piss Christ* was placed on its cover. Critics, such as Grant Kester (1998, 126), acknowledged that the work was a "disturbing and challenging artistic statement, (which) explores how spiritual belief has been exploited and spiritual values debased." Lucy Lippard (1990, 232) added that the piece is "part of the 'polyphonies discourse' many Third World scholars have been calling for; he challenges the boundaries formed by class and race, between abstraction and representation, photography and painting, belief and disbelief." For religious Americans, any display of Jesus Christ in less than the most reverent of settings was unacceptable.

In 1988, Salman Rushdie, a British-Indian author, published *The Satanic Verses*. The book caused immediate uproar in the Islamic community, including a *fatwa* (decree) by Ayatollah Ruhollah Khomeini

Salman Rushdie's book *The Satanic Verses* generated significant controversy in the 1980s. The Iranian Muslim leader Ayatollah Khomeini issued a *fatwa* sentencing him to death, but Rushdie was able to successfully elude those who intended him harm. However, some of the bookstores that carried the novel were bombed by extremists. (Terry Smith/ The LIFE Images Collection/Getty Images) of Iran that stated, "the author of the *Satanic Verses* book, which is against Islam, the Prophet, and the Koran, and all those involved in its publication that were aware of its content, are sentenced to death" (http://www.nytimes.com/books /99/04/18/specials/rushdie-khomeini.html). As a further incentive to Rushdie's murder (besides striking a blow for religious purity), Khomeini offered a bounty of over $1 million. Khomeini's threat immediately forced Rushdie into hiding, in fear for his life. He later apologized, but that did nothing to ease the tensions, which caused riots in India and Pakistan. Rushdie's book was among, if not the most, controversial releases of the decade.

The situation had the potential to escalate into an international crisis, as Western countries contemplated imposing sanctions on Iran. European diplomats were expelled from Iran to their home countries, and President George H. W. Bush remarked that "inciting murder and offering rewards for its perpetration are deeply offensive to the norms of civilized behavior" (http://www .nytimes.com/books/99/04/18/specials/rushdie-bush.html). This seemed to not be an issue even with some American writers who protested against the book, including Susan Sontag, Norman Mailer, Larry McMurtry, and Joan Didion. Rushdie's American publisher, Viking/Penguin, had to close its offices temporarily because of bomb threats, and many booksellers were refusing to stock *The Satanic Verses* at all, citing safety concerns, while still acknowledging that the whole situation was truly about censorship. Some American writers were courageous enough to march on some booksellers, such as the B. Dalton chain, to encourage them to stand up to the pressure and restock the book. Ultimately, Khomeini used this whole issue as a political cudgel to wield against the debauchery of Western society. On the other hand, the book sales probably increased due to all the publicity.

CONTROVERSIES IN SPORTS

The Major League Baseball (MLB) players' strike, which lasted seven weeks and one day in 1981, was the first labor stoppage in the 1980s by a sports league. It was the culmination of an ugly, public spat over issues with the baseball owners' plan for free agency. When the strike was called on June 12, the blame was immediately placed upon the owners. They were trying to regain concessions that they had made at the last collective bargaining agreement meetings, and they expected to be able to replace players that were lost in a free-agent draft with additional roster spots. The plan was that if a player left to join another team, then a player from the middle of the ranks of the new team would have to join the old team; this player became known as the "Sixteenth Man." From the owners' perspective, this move would keep talent on their team, but from the players' perspective, it hurt the bargaining position of the free agent.

To protect themselves, the owners took out an insurance policy before the onset of the strike with Lloyds of London. The owners were immovable for weeks—at least until the money from the insurance payments started to dwindle. Behind the owners was Ray Grebey, a ruthless negotiator who had an almost hostile relationship with Marvin Miller, the head of the players' union. In the end, though, the owners caved in, and the free agency plan would not be implemented.

But the strike angered fans, threatening to alienate them from the game altogether. Players were angry too, at the loss of games that would affect their statistics (a factor often ignored in the discussion of any strike), and the owners lamented their loss of revenue. The strike made the 1981 season one of the most chaotic in history (as discussed in detail in Chapter 2, "Sports"). The players went on another brief, two-day strike in 1985, but things were smoothed over and games resumed.

The 1982 National Football League (NFL) players' strike was a 57-day ordeal that resulted in seven weeks of the regular season being canceled. After the league signed a five-year, $2.1 billion contract with the three major television networks, the NFL Players' Association wanted a larger portion (55%) of the gross revenues. The owners' response was to simply close the teams down; they believed that using replacement players would be bad for the long-term image of the league.

In the end, both sides agreed to the following terms to end the strike: the owners would spend $1.6 billion over four years on players' salaries, including $60 million in immediately payable bonuses. By 1987, the players were beginning to believe that they should have held out for more at that time, so they went on strike themselves. This time, the issue was not only the sharing of revenue but also because of the restrictions imposed by the league on free agency. Players were interested in unlimited free agency, and yet some owners were concerned that competition would be hindered to the point that only the richest clubs could afford the best players. In contrast to the 1982 strike, owners decided to use replacement players, so the players gave in. It would not be until the 1990s that the issue of free agency was resolved.

In the 1980s, the NFL had 28 teams, expanding from 26 in the mid-1970s. It didn't seem as if the league was planning on expanding, and for some businessmen, the ownership of a professional football team was an important accolade. Because of the limited number of NFL squads, there were few opportunities to "join the club." The United States Football League (USFL) was an attempt by some businessmen, including Donald Trump, to own a football team. The new league was designed not to compete with the established league, as its 18-game season would be held during the spring and summer.

The USFL began to gain credibility when it signed one of the most celebrated college football athletes in history, University of Georgia standout Herschel Walker, to a contract. At the time, NFL rules wouldn't allow a student player to declare for its draft until he completed his senior year, but the USFL had different rules, and the then-junior Walker was allowed to sign with a team. This brought immediate concern from the NFL, since it viewed the new league as tapping into its talent pool. In short time, USFL owners became obsessed with signing stars away from the NFL or keeping them from going to the NFL in the first place, including Steve Young, Mike Rozier, Marcus Duprec, Jim Kelly, and Doug Flutie.

However, for some owners, signing some of college football's biggest stars to spite the NFL wasn't enough. Led by Trump, the USFL began to explore moving its schedule to compete directly with the NFL. Unfortunately, none of the major television networks, concerned about their existing relationship with the NFL, were willing to sign a contract with the USFL. USFL owners were furious, thinking that the NFL had a monopoly over the television stations. So the USFL sued the NFL for violating U.S. antitrust laws, seeking $1.69 billion. The court found in favor of the USFL on the antitrust matter, but awarded the USFL only a single dollar. As the league needed at least $300 million to continue with the 1986 season, it folded after only two years.

Denver Broncos quarterback John Elway had one of the most celebrated careers in NFL history by the time he retired in 1998, resulting in two Super Bowl wins, three additional Super Bowl appearances, and an induction to the Pro Football Hall of Fame. At the beginning of his professional career, though, Elway was at the center of a controversy. In 1983, he was considering what NFL team to play for. He was not only the top football recruit to emerge from the high school ranks when he graduated from Granada Hills High School in California; the New York Yankees also selected him in their baseball draft. While a star quarterback at Stanford, he was overwhelmingly viewed as the best player available in the 1983 NFL draft. But the top pick belonged to the Baltimore Colts. The Colts head coach, Frank Kush, had a reputation of being abrasive with his players. Elway's father, Jack, had been a longtime collegiate coach and was understandably protective of his son. The idea of playing for Kush concerned both Elways tremendously. Elway felt that he had two options rather than play for Kush: force the Colts' decision to trade the first pick so that he could play for another team, or play professional baseball full time.

Elway began by quietly negotiating with the Colts, explaining that the perfect excuse for the Colts trading their pick would be that Elway preferred to play football on the West Coast. At the same time, he stated publicly that he was considering playing for the Yankees and would play baseball and not football if the Colts selected him. Although the San Diego Chargers and the San Francisco 49ers showed interest (as well as the New England Patriots, a division rival of the Colts), the Colts' general manager was concerned that while the 1983 draft had a large number of talented quarterbacks (the 1983 "class" is considered one of the best in history, featuring such future stars as Jim Kelly and Dan Marino), there were few in the 1984 draft that intrigued him.

Elway ended up being selected by the Colts, and so he continued his threat to play baseball for the Yankees instead. The Colts traded Elway to the Denver Broncos for a rookie that the Colts coveted before the draft, the Broncos' top pick in the next draft, and an additional quarterback. Many were critical of Elway's stance, which they considered selfish. Though Elway struggled in his first year (typical of many rookie quarterbacks in the NFL), by his fourth year he had led the Broncos to the Super Bowl.

For his part, Kush was fired from the Colts, which now was based in Indianapolis, after just two more seasons, which prompted many longtime Colts fans to question the team's decision. The Colts would not have a winning season until the 1987 arrival of running back Eric Dickerson. The Colts did not have a "franchise" quarterback until they drafted Peyton Manning in 1998.

In the early 1980s, Al Davis, the Oakland Raiders managing general partner (though most fans saw him as the team's owner), approached the city of Oakland about upgrades to the Oakland Coliseum. Davis's main argument was that in order to compete financially with other teams around the league, the city should install luxury (or corporate) boxes to which groups (mostly businesses) would purchase annual rights. The boxes would offer some of the best seating in the stadium and come with full catering and a bar. Mainstream fans would typically pay ticket prices ranging from $20 to $100 in the 1980s, but these corporate boxes were lucrative to owners, as the overhead was not particularly expensive. When the city showed no interest in providing the boxes, Davis began negotiations with a commission at the Los Angeles Memorial Coliseum, which had previously hosted the Los Angeles Rams and was seeking a new team.

But when Davis announced his plans, both the league and the fellow owners voted it down unanimously. Though he continued with his plans, the league filed an injunction to prevent it. A lawsuit was filed by the Los Angeles Coliseum, and in 1982, a jury found in favor of Davis and the Los Angeles group, which allowed the team to move. The controversy shook the league, but teams began to notice that there was an antitrust violation when a privately operated league prevented moves of businesses owned by a private enterprise, including football teams.

In 1983, Robert Irsay, the owner of the Baltimore Colts, began to have discussions with his own city in a similar manner as Davis had with Oakland. Irsay's position was that Baltimore's Memorial Stadium, the team's home since their inception in 1953, was also in need of significant upgrades, if not replaced entirely. Though Irsay's public stance was to stay in Baltimore, he was secretly negotiating with officials in both Phoenix and Indianapolis. The Maryland legislature began the process of passing a bill that would allow the state to seize the team under eminent domain. Knowing this, Irsay moved quickly, negotiating a deal to relocate the team to Indianapolis.

The controversy became more complicated when Irsay made arrangements with a moving company to move the team in the middle of the night, so that the team could leave with neither fan protests nor government intervention. The Colts fans in Baltimore were understandably shocked, as were most fans of the league, but the team's arrival in Indianapolis instantly made the city recognizable at a higher level. The team's new domed stadium (RCA Dome) was used from 1984 until 2007, before a new stadium, Lucas Oil Stadium, was constructed.

In the years that followed, more teams relocated: The St. Louis Cardinals went to Phoenix (eventually playing as the Arizona Cardinals), the Houston Oilers played in Nashville (eventually coined the Tennessee Titans), the Cleveland Browns left for Baltimore (as the Baltimore Ravens), the Los Angeles Rams went to St. Louis, and ironically, the Raiders eventually returned to Oakland. Cities were now forced to upgrade their facilities, often with taxpayer funds, or run the risk of losing their team.

There were few events in baseball that caused as much controversy as the "Pine Tar Incident" that marred the July 24, 1983 game between the Kansas

City Royals and the New York Yankees. Both were top teams in the American League, with a fierce rivalry that dated back to the mid-1970s. The Royals star third baseman, George Brett, was a significant reason for the success of his team. Meanwhile, the Yankees manager, Billy Martin, was well known for his volatile personality.

In the ninth inning of that game, the Royals were trailing the Yankees 4-3, with two outs and one player on base. Brett was the next player up to bat for the Royals. He hit a home run, but as he was crossing the plate, Martin ran out onto the baseball diamond to protest that Brett had violated a rule mandating that there could be no sticky substance, such as pine tar, more than 18 inches from the bottom of the bat. Brett's bat had pine tar on it in an illegal area, so the home run was deemed an out by the umpire, ending the game.

Brett was understandably angry about this, and the Royals argued to the American League office that the excess pine tar did not influence his ability to hit the home run. Though the Yankees did not dispute this issue, Brett's bat did violate the rule. After four days, American League president Lee McPhail (Wallace, 261) "cited that the sprit, if not the letter, of the law, decreed that the home run counted, the Royals once again led 5–4 in the ninth inning, and the remainder of the game would be played at a future time." He went on to comment that "the original meaning of the rule was to keep the ball in play from being discolored by pine tar on the bat, and that a discolored ball actually helped the *pitcher*, making it harder to see." The Yankees were furious, but eventually the two teams played out the rest of the game from the point where it had ended, and the Royals ended up winning.

Another controversial issue in the 1980s came with Pete Rose's banishment from professional baseball. Rose was one of the most popular and accomplished baseball players in the 1970s, playing for the Cincinnati Reds and briefly the Philadelphia Phillies. Nicknamed "Charlie Hustle," he set records for more hits and runs than anyone in league history, as well as many other records. After he retired from playing in 1986, he went to managing the Reds, and he shoved an umpire in 1988. National League president Bart Giamatti gave Rose a significant punishment for the offense, fining him $10,000 and barring him from the team for 30 days.

By 1989, Giamatti had Rose under investigation for gambling on baseball games, which potentially affected the integrity of the game to its core, especially since he gambled on his own team's games. Rose's position was that he never bet on games in which he was involved, but that did not change much. Giamatti and Rose came to a deal where Rose received a lifetime ban under the condition that he would be able to apply for reinstatement after one year. Since then, Rose has unsuccessfully lobbied for reinstatement so he could be considered for baseball's highest honor, the Hall of Fame. To this writing, Rose has not been reinstated and has been kept out of the Hall, which is controversial because otherwise, he almost certainly would have been voted in on the merits of his career accomplishments by now.

The 1980s also saw sports collide with international politics. In the late 1970s, the Soviet Union invaded Afghanistan, attempting to quell the Mujahideen rebels that were fighting the pro-Soviet government. Since it was typical of U.S. foreign policy to support any enemy of the Soviet Union, the U.S. government gave the Mujahideen weapons. The Soviets invaded Afghanistan in 1979 to support the existing Afghan government. After the Winter Olympics in Lake Placid, New York, ended, the United States decided that they would forgo the 1980 Summer Olympics, which were to be held in Moscow, in protest of the Soviet invasion. The United States was joined by a large number of their allies.

The controversy that surfaced was based on a matter of principle: Should amateur athletes who have been training their entire lives have to forgo the opportunity to compete in what may be a once-in-a-lifetime event, just to make a political statement? The American athletes decided to follow their government's lead and did not participate in the games. In an expected response, the Soviet Union ordered their athletes not to appear at the 1984 Summer Games, to be held in Los Angeles. The Soviets did not pull out of the games until a few weeks in advance, and they ultimately blamed the situation on a lack of security in Los Angeles for their team.

FURTHER READING

Abramson, Albert, and Christopher H. Sterling. *The History of Television, 1942–2000.* Jefferson, NC: McFarland and Company, Inc., 2003.

Crepeau, Richard C. *NFL Football: A History of America's New National Pastime.* Champaign, IL: University of Illinois Press, 2014.

Ewalt, David. *Of Dice and Men.* New York: Scribner, 2014.

George-Warren, H., P. Romanowski, and J. Pareles. *The Rolling Stone Encyclopedia of Rock & Roll (Revised and Updated for the 21st Century).* New York: Fireside, 2001.

Larkin, Colin, ed. *The Encyclopedia of Popular Music.* 4th ed. New York: Oxford, 2006.

Vecsey, George. *Baseball: A History of America's Favorite Game.* New York: Modern Library/Random House, 2008.

Wexman, Virginia Wright. *A History of Film.* 7th ed. New York: Pearson, 2009.

Wood, Robin. *Hollywood from Vietnam to Reagan.* New York: Columbia University Press, 1986.

CHAPTER 9

Game Changers

In the 1980s, there were several well-recognized members of American society who helped define the qualities of the decade and established new standards, ideals, and accomplishments that truly made them "Game Changers." The reach of these individuals was wide; some come from the financial world, the sporting world, and all areas of entertainment.

DONALD TRUMP

Donald Trump became one of the most polarizing figures of the 1980s. To many, Trump was the defining businessman of the decade—one who accumulated wealth via real estate with seemingly little effort. Based in New York City and New Jersey, Trump began to gain notice in the 1970s, as he became affiliated with building projects. One of his signature projects in the 1980s was Trump Tower, located on Fifth Avenue at East 56th Street in Manhattan. The 68-story opulent building is a retail and office (the first 26 floors) and residential (the final 42 floors) complex, complete with a marble and brass interior and a five-story waterfall. He renovated a 1920s building into Trump Parc, flanking Central Park, which became a well-known residential building. In Jersey City, he developed Trump Plaza, a 55-story residential building right on the waterfront, with a clear view of New York City.

Trump developed the Plaza Hotel in New York and sold it in the mid-1990s. He purchased an older hotel in New York, the Commodore, and redeveloped it into the Grand Central Hyatt. Trump Castle was a development in Atlantic City, New Jersey, formerly known as the Golden Nugget, which opened in 1985 (it was renamed Trump Marina in 1997). Trump beat out television magnate and investor Merv Griffin in a very competitive bidding process to get the project. In short, Trump was in the business of winning, and it seemed that during the 1980s, he could not be stopped. What made him a Game Changer was that he was the inspiration for a 1980s' generation of yuppies and ambitious businessmen. He fit the moniker "greed is good" better than anyone.

In addition to his real estate holdings, he purchased a yacht (the *Trump Princess*), owned a professional football team (the USFL's New Jersey Generals), promoted a heavyweight championship fight (Michael Spinks vs. Mike Tyson), and created the Tour de Trump, a bicycle race, in the late 1980s. He was married to a beautiful Russian woman, Ivana, and even after he was caught having an affair with Marla Maples in 1991, his legions of followers forgave his antics as being typical of "The Donald." He chronicled his own success with a best-selling book, *Trump: The Art of the Deal* (1987), which he cowrote with Tony Schwartz. Though Trump's fortunes took a significant tumble in the 1990s, and he had a controversial (but ultimately successful) run for president in 2015 and 2016 that brought him plenty of negative attention, he epitomizes the general feeling of the 1980s better than most.

TED TURNER

Though not involved in self-promotion à la Trump, Ted Turner was another powerful 1980s' icon, as he helped change television from a three-network broadcast format into a cable-based format that has been the backbone of the American news and entertainment industries since the mid-1980s. His Cable News Network (CNN) and WTBS Superstation ventures opened the door to multiple cable television channels, which established him firmly as a Game Changer. Though he failed in his bid to purchase CBS, he did buy the Metro-Goldwyn-Mayer/United Artists (MGM/UA) movie production conglomerates and promptly began showing their catalog of movies on his television station, Turner Network Television (TNT), bringing an even wider viewership to his Turner Broadcasting Company umbrella. As discussed in Chapter 8, "Controversies," Turner also began to add color to the black-and-white movies in the MGM/UA catalogue, a move that sparked intense criticism.

Turner also got involved in professional wrestling, which expanded the national impact of a previously regional sport. In addition, he helped launch the Goodwill Games in the Soviet Union to create an alternative event to the Olympics—another controversial action during the decade. As with Trump, Turner was involved with professional sports, owning both the Atlanta Braves baseball and the Atlanta Hawks basketball teams. Throughout most of the 1980s, he was married to Jane Shirley Smith, and the couple were important philanthropists. Turner's public persona was as a shrewd entrepreneur, even though he developed a reputation for making outrageous statements that were sometimes offensive.

DAVID LETTERMAN

The late-night talk show format did not start in the 1980s—it has been around nearly as long as television itself. *The Tonight Show* has been broadcast since 1954; since that time, the show has gone through a number of hosts, including Steve Allen, Jack Paar, and Johnny Carson. But by the start of the

1980s, the format had gotten a little tired, even stale. In 1982, *Late Night with David Letterman* followed *The Tonight Show* on weekday evenings, and David Letterman, the groundbreaking comic who hosted it, began to make his mark. Letterman widely gave Johnny Carson credit for being a close friend and mentor to him. Jeff Jarvis at *People* magazine (August 13, 1984, 97) had this to say about Letterman:

> He is America's No. 1 smartass. He is also, by far, the most inventive man on TV today. Letterman is a talk show host without fear. He flirts with the boundaries of politeness and humor; he'll try anything once. Like Carson (but unlike [Alan] Thicke), he knows what to do when a joke bombs—and bomb they do, for that is the price of experimentation. Once, to apologize for a groaner, Letterman paid everyone in the audience $1. He gleefully lets people make fools of themselves, and it's wonderful to watch. For as cynical and near nasty as he can be, Letterman is still one of the more likable and most entertaining people on TV.

Letterman was worth staying up late to watch because he was funny. He would laugh at himself as well as others, a skill he had honed doing stand-up comedy. His innovative skits, "Stupid Human Tricks," and "Top 10 List" set him apart from Carson. On occasion, children would demonstrate their science projects. In segments that echoed Carson's on *The Tonight Show,* zoo trainers would bring exotic animals onto the set, sometimes to his amusement, sometimes to his horror or surprise. His celebrity guests, ranging from comedians (like Bill Murray at the top of his career), to musicians (like Madonna, complete with an extensively vulgar vocabulary), to politicians, wanted to be on his show simply because of his presence. But when those celebrities arrived, Letterman knew the right questions to ask, not only for his audience, but to further enhance the appearance by the guest, who was likely promoting a movie, television show, musical recording, and the like. Letterman, who had expected (or perhaps, just hoped) to replace Johnny Carson when he retired from *The Tonight Show* in 1992, moved to CBS when the job was given to Jay Leno instead. He started a late-night competitor to Leno called *The Late Show* in 1993.

Letterman qualifies as a Game Changer because he brought fresh excitement to late-night television, which had grown stagnant before his arrival. His tenure as a prominent public figure lasted 30 years until he finally retired from *The Late Show* in 2015.

PHIL DONAHUE

The daytime talk-show format underwent a number of changes in the 1980s as well. Through his show *The Phil Donahue Show* (more commonly known as *Donahue*), Phil Donahue was instrumental in developing the "tabloid" talk-show format that addressed controversial issues in the news. The show had both straight talk and entertainment woven together into a unique place in the mind of its viewers. Donahue was comfortable discussing political and social issues, including the acquired immune deficiency syndrome (AIDS) and savings and loan crises of the 1980s. In the process, he developed a passionate core audience while maintaining critical acclaim. Donahue featured inner-city rap culture and break dancing on his show when those things were considered not relatable to a national audience.

Donahue was also part of the "Space Bridge," where viewers from the Soviet Union and the United States could participate in a live teleconference; viewership in the United States was somewhat fleeting, though the show was popular in the Soviet Union. Donahue's show, which started in Chicago and eventually moved to New York City, helped establish him as a Game Changer by pioneering the audience-interaction talk shows that became prevalent in the decades to follow.

OPRAH WINFREY

Oprah Winfrey took the Donahue talk-show format to a new level. As a starting point, she had a compelling personal history: an African American woman growing up poor in Tennessee, working in broadcast media in her late teens, and recovering from a background of sexual abuse and difficult teenage years (including a miscarriage). Her audience related to her and embraced the feel-good story of a woman who overcame adversity and succeeded.

Winfrey's easy-to-approach manner made her a natural for what has been termed the confessional talk show. Her topics were less controversial than the talk shows that emerged later (such as *Ricki Lake, Jerry Springer,* and *Jenny Jones*), but Winfrey turned her show into a positive experience for viewers, with self-help discussions, book recommendations (which were amazingly effective—a word from Oprah was enough to make a book a best seller, even if it had been published long ago, like Elie Wiesel's *Night* and Gabriel García Márquez's *Love in the Time of Cholera*), and even prizes for members of the studio audience. Winfrey's approach of empowering viewers through positive programming, and the tremendous success and influence that she wielded in the process, is what establishes her as a Game Changer.

Winfrey has become, and continues to be, a trend-setter since her program became nationally televised. Winfrey helped popularize specific products through featuring them not only on her program, but in *O* magazine and the OWN network she eventually founded after the 1980s. It is through those endeavors that she transcends multiple types of media. She has been an outspoken supporter of the gay community; in the 1980s, when AIDS and HIV paranoia was at its height, she took her show to Williamson, West Virginia, in support of an HIV-positive gay man who lived there. The man had caused paranoia among the town's residents, and Winfrey asked these people simple questions about their Christian beliefs and how they aligned with the way the man was treated. In the end, at least some people may have been inspired to look at the issue differently. Winfrey also put on an episode where each member of the studio audience "came out" as gay on her show; and in another episode, she hosted an experiment in which all blue-eyed people in the audience were discriminated against in the way that African Americans often were. African Americans have certainly seen her as a role model, but Winfrey has extended her influence throughout the United States to people of all ages and backgrounds.

MICHAEL JACKSON

Michael Jackson had a long and storied history in the music industry. He got his start as a key member of the Jackson 5, a group from Gary, Indiana, comprised of his brothers that recorded for Motown Records. Jackson became a child star in the late 1960s and early 1970s. By the end of the 1970s, he had been featured regularly on network television and had starred in a movie musical, an adaptation of *The Wizard of Oz* called *The Wiz*. Both of those credits featured not only Jackson the singer and musician but also the dancer and overall entertainer. Via his role on *The Wiz*, he started to work with producer Quincy Jones, a jazz musician who had played trumpet for jazz legend Dizzy Gillespie and had a successful career in arranging and producing both jazz and pop music. Their first collaboration resulted in a disco record, *Off the Wall* (1979). Musically, the record was a good transition for Jackson into the pop music of the 1980s, where he set the standard.

Jackson's music featured the strong rhythmic drive of 1970s' disco and funk, with modern synthesizer technology added. Various musicians on the *Thriller* album from differing ethnic and musical backgrounds (including rock icon Eddie Van Halen, discussed later in this chapter) helped mold this music into forms that appealed to just about everyone. Jackson's music in the 1980s sounded modern upon its release, and in the years after his unexpected death in 2009, his music still sounds current because it has superb core elements: easy-to-identify and listenable melodies, harmonies that have good tension and release, production items that are still used, and the catchy rhythms noted here.

It is only fitting that Jackson's overall talent as a dancer would come into its prime with the emergence of MTV. With videos from his blockbuster album *Thriller*, Jackson used directors who could frame a song in the context of a compelling story. His first video, "Beat It," featured not only choreographed dancers in a fight scene, but also rock guitarist Eddie Van Halen of Van Halen, the most popular hard rock band of the era. Two points are important in situating Jackson as a Game Changer: First, dancing became seen as the norm in pop videos, particularly ones with an R&B background. Second, Van Halen's performance on the song and in the video gave some sort of legitimacy to an artist who usually might not appeal to a white audience.

As Jackson's impact became greater, videos that were more elaborate could be created, and the release of the video became a specialized event. The video for "Thriller," helmed by veteran Hollywood director John Landis, had an extended introduction featuring a horror movie–type setting, further enhanced with a voice-over by horror movie actor Vincent Price. Jackson was also a key participant in a number of philanthropic endeavors. He collaborated with Lionel Richie (discussed later in this chapter) and a number of other American pop and rock stars on the song "We Are the World." The profits from sales of that single, as well as the album it was on, went to feed children in Africa.

MADONNA

Madonna (born Madonna Louise Ciccone) became a cultural phenomenon in the 1980s by releasing well-crafted pop/dance music, provocative music videos, progressive attitudes of sex and racial crossover, and an innovative fashion sense. Originally from Michigan, Madonna worked in the art and pop scenes in New York before releasing her self-titled debut in 1982. The initial reaction from her fan base, largely teens and children as young as six years old, was to her fashion sense. Her use of lacey gloves, religious jewelry, and headbands created trends that were emulated almost immediately. Madonna became a Game Changer by pushing the boundaries in her music as well, including an infamous performance at the MTV 1984 Video Music Awards, where she sang "Like A Virgin" in a white bridal gown and danced suggestively in a sexual manner.

Madonna's video for "Like a Prayer," featuring religious iconography and an interracial relationship between a white girl and a black man that is set in the South, sparked a great deal of controversy as well. Romona Curry (1990, 26) commented, "[I]n a narrative parallel to that of the murder and false accusation, Madonna worships a statue of a black male saint in the church, who is thus moved to life, and first blesses and later erotically kisses Madonna as she is sprawled on her back on a pew." This type of imagery was certainly not considered safe in the 1980s. The sexually charged images in "Like a Virgin" and other Madonna videos helped other women performers embrace their sexuality in music videos.

Madonna was also trained as a dancer, and since she could dance so well, she had a profound impact on what pop artists needed to do to be successful in the 1980s and the decades after. Similar to the impact of Michael Jackson, Madonna put on stage shows featuring synchronized dancing and extravagant productions. Many of the dancers were African American, and nearly all of them were gay, which made Madonna something of an icon to the gay community. As groundbreaking as dance was in her delivery of music, the music itself was always just a step ahead of the next trend in pop/dance music. She teamed up with producers such as Jellybean Benitez, Niles Rodgers, Stephen Bray, and Patrick Leonard to put out numerous top singles throughout the decade.

EDDIE VAN HALEN

To many outside the rock world, considering a rock band's guitarist, rather than the lead singer, as a Game Changer might seem unusual or even questionable. However, among rock fans, and certainly among guitarists, Eddie Van Halen's significance cannot be understated. As acknowledged earlier in this chapter in the discussion of Michael Jackson, he was the most respected guitarist in rock in the early 1980s. His group, Van Halen, was one of the most popular rock groups at the same time that Jackson was the most popular pop artist.

The group had many important elements, ranging from vocalist David Lee Roth's showmanship, to bassist Michael Anthony's solid playing and unique backing vocals, to drummer Alex Van Halen's style (ranging from flashy to powerful). But Van Halen the group was important because of Van Halen the guitarist. His solos incorporated techniques not widely used by other guitarists—the hammer-on (slur) technique and the innovative use of the "whammy" (tremolo) bar—while his rhythm guitar playing was an extension of his innovative lead guitar. The way that he customized his guitar, with a Gibson humbucker pickup into a Fender Stratocaster copy body, became the most emulated design for guitars in the decades that followed. His use of a "variac" voltage controller gave his guitar amp a timbre not seen before—one that was the envy of every guitarist of the period.

Van Halen's writing style became the norm among guitarists from the Los Angeles/Hollywood area in the early 1980s, and that helped establish hard rock and heavy metal as the most popular genres in popular music during the decade. Even as Eddie began to focus on a songwriting-first approach by the middle of the decade, his respect among musicians stayed at a consistent level. It was just at this time that the group Van Halen was becoming more popular in the mainstream, coupled with its new vocalist, Sammy Hagar, who replaced Roth in 1985. Thanks to Eddie Van Halen, the term *guitar hero* became widely used, and a decade of guitar heroes are indebted to him for popularizing the instrument and bringing it into the mainstream through the increased sales of guitar magazines and instruments. Playing the guitar turned into a cool hobby for a generation of musicians in an age before digital recording on a computer became widespread.

BON JOVI

Bon Jovi was one of the decade's most successful rock artists, largely through the popularity of two albums: *Slippery When Wet* (1986) and *New Jersey* (1988). The game-changing aspect of Bon Jovi was that *Slippery When Wet* helped split heavy metal and hard rock into two distinct forms. Prior to the album's release, groups such as Mötley Crüe, Van Halen, Ratt, Quiet Riot, Iron Maiden, and Judas Priest were classified as both hard rock and heavy metal, terms that were fairly synonymous in the early 1980s; but after 1986, few would describe these groups using both terms interchangeably. Bon Jovi's third album was released in August 1986, the same year as Poison (who released their debut in May, but did not pick up momentum until later in 1986). Both albums were stylistically apart from Metallica's third album *Master of Puppets* (which was released in March but still in the underground). It was at this point that hard rock groups such as Bon Jovi and Poison became distinguished from heavy metal groups such as Metallica. By the time Bon Jovi's album became a mainstream sensation, it opened the door for Poison's success. Bon Jovi helped separate two genres, verifying their place as a Game Changer in the 1980s.

Bon Jovi, led by vocalist Jon Bon Jovi, did something else that had not been seen in the 1980s: it tapped into a mainstream audience outside of rock, consisting of all demographics. Young children were now singing along to "You

Give Love a Bad Name," while women in their 50s were singing "Livin' on a Prayer." The reason for this was that the group has always been accessible, in an almost everyman capacity. Jon Bon Jovi became a poster boy not just for teenage hard rock fans (admittedly, most of whom were female) but also for younger ones; and these fans were eager to buy merchandise at levels not seen by a hard rock group before.

Guitarist Richie Sambora brought back the use of the guitar Talk-Box effect, not heard since Peter Frampton in the 1970s, giving older fans a sense of nostalgia. The feeling of authenticity communicated to the audience made Bon Jovi (the band from New Jersey, not from the big city of New York) the one fans wanted to root for. Their music videos showed them at their most vulnerable ("Dead or Alive"), and their lyrics had imagery that was relatable by many who attended high school or who had done so in the past ("Never Say Goodbye"). In order to help fans participate in the band's performances, the group made a video called "Bad Medicine," which integrated footage of the band recorded by fans using cheap camcorders. It seemed that the only ones who didn't like Bon Jovi were fans of the other genere: fans of heavy metal, like Metallica, who saw the group as weak or effeminate.

RUN-D.M.C.

As discussed in Chapter 8, there was a deep divide between rock and rap in the 1980s. Before Run-D.M.C., rap music was the music of the streets, talking about the struggles of inner-city youths who were trying to find their identity in pop music in a post-disco era. The rock community, who felt that the only way to create music was to also perform it, immediately criticized the single act of rapping over prerecorded material. The closest thing to dancing in the rock community would be some type of mosh pit action, though those were reserved for the more aggressive types of metal with a punk thread in their history. Mainstream hard rock fans simply didn't dance to Van Halen.

Nevertheless, for early rap, and the rest of 1980s' pop, break dancing was paramount. Easily performed on a piece of cardboard on a sidewalk, this type of dancing would be performed over music from an easily transportable cassette/stereo system (known as a "ghetto-blaster" by members of the audience). The DJ would perform spinning and scratching on two turntables, an impressive display of technique, while an MC would rap over the transition. Eventually, the stereo would diminish to make room for beatboxing or sampling prerecorded audio clips via hardware samplers (such as the Akai S-900).

Many rock fans didn't see rap music as real music—to them, it was just uncreative noise. That was the case for Run-D.M.C. too, at the start of their career; the group was a formidable force in rap music in the early 1980s, but their audience was restricted to just rap fans. But the group's collaboration with Aerosmith helped break down those barriers. Producer Rick Rubin had a brilliant idea: Run-D.M.C. should record its take on "Walk This Way," a 1970s' song by Aerosmith, a group whose popularity was fading. The result ended up having far-reaching consequences for both groups. Run-D.M.C. scored a top five hit (a better performance on the charts than the original version, in fact), gained fans from the rock community, and went mainstream. Meanwhile, Aerosmith was seen as being in touch with the youth of the 1980s, revitalizing their career.

Run-D.M.C. made an important impact on fashion as well. Each member wore a three-striped Adidas tracksuit emblazoned with a three-leafed motif. The members also wore gold "dookie rope" chains around their necks and black fedoras. They also wore unlaced white Adidas shell toe "Superstars," sneakers with the tongues pushed up, allegedly in impersonation of the "prison style" worn by prison inmates. The style was street credible in New York, and fashionable, especially among hip hop fans of all cultures, in all rural areas and suburbs across the country. For detractors, this was something that only African American kids should wear, but that opinion did not discourage white teens from wearing this style of clothing.

NWA

The music of the inner city had been brought to the mainstream via Run-D.M.C., but few in the early 1980s, even those among their fans, would have predicted the impact of N.W.A. Already controversial with such a coarse name (as noted in Chapter 3, "Music," the acronym stands for "Niggaz Wit Attitude"), N.W.A. was the first successful gangsta rap group to emerge from the Los Angeles area. As different as LA's inner city is from New York, the lyrical content of each urban center's music reflected the same amount of contrast. At this time, the Compton area was a hotbed of crime, violence, and drug abuse, and N.W.A. told of the angry horrors of everyday life through their music, an innovation that made the group a Game Changer. The group's lyrics, revolving around violence, drug use, and the inner city, got a grip on the rap community, and gangsta rap was the stylistic result.

Born Eric Wright, Eazy-E was a drug dealer who changed his life by forging a partnership with club DJ Andre Young (Dr. Dre) to focus on records that reflected the lifestyle in their neighborhood. Cheo Horari Coker (in Light, 1999, 253) stated that Dre wanted "to combine the profane and sexually provocative humor of Richard Pryor and Dolemite with the lurid, nihilistic violence of Al Pacino's *Scarface*." Thanks to the help of a white businessman named Jerry Heller, the group eventually signed with Priority Records. The label released the group's first album, *N.W.A. and the Posse*, in 1987, with little impact, but their 1988 release *Straight Outta Compton* became the defining moment of their career (which ended in 1991). The details of life in Compton, communicated in gangster-influenced rants on drinking, women, and violence, afforded listeners the opportunity to imagine themselves on the streets with the group.

By the time N.W.A.'s second album, *EFIL4ZAGGIN* (1991), was released, politicians saw the group's lyrical content as a threat, and the group came from a real gang lifestyle that could pose a physical threat to their enemies. The imagery that the group painted in their songs told the truth about the harsh realities of the streets of Compton, California. They were telling stories of their own lawless and dangerous lives to every person who wanted to hear them—and in most cases, their new fans were people who had never even been to Compton or experienced the street life anywhere. Many of their fans, regardless of geographic location or ethnicity, appreciated the gangsta lifestyle simply as a symbol of rebellion and power; this sense became the most significant attribute credited to the group, and it encouraged groups in the years ahead to write lyrics that embraced the reality of street life.

MICHAEL JORDAN

Michael Jordan was a tremendously skilled basketball player, a true legend of the sporting world in the 1980s. He was part of a championship team at the University of North Carolina (UNC), as a freshman sensation from Wilmington. After Jordan's junior season at UNC, he was the second player drafted in the 1984 NBA draft. In only three seasons, Jordan's new team, the Chicago Bulls, was a contender for the NBA championship—an achievement that Jordan was to repeat with the Bulls for the rest of the 1980s and into the 1990s (when they actually started winning championships, one after another). As great a player as he was, though, it was Jordan's marketability and impact as a product endorser that really made him a Game Changer.

In 1984, Jordan was selected by Nike to be part of a global campaign to market a line of basketball shoes. Nike was seeking a new image, as the company had lost a significant size of the world athletic shoe market to Reebok. Jordan was an easy selection for this task, largely because of the dynamic way he played basketball. It was common for Jordan to score what seemed to be impossible shots from long distances, or under tremendous pressure, with routine ease. The basketball dunk had been around for many years, but Jordan took it to new heights. He would steal the ball and leap 15 feet across the court, floating in midair, and then execute a slam-dunk, with his arm stretched outward for maximum impact. Even when the Bulls themselves were struggling, Jordan was always a sight worth seeing.

The contract that Jordan signed with Nike was for $18 million—certainly a sizable amount in itself—but he also earned royalties on each pair of shoes that was sold, which actually brought him the majority of his earnings. Jordan appealed to a global audience because of his athletic prowess; in fairness, he also received high royalties for other products he endorsed, such as McDonald's and Coca-Cola, but the latter didn't have the same impact as the Nike contract. The Chinese in particular were attracted to Jordan the person as well as the player (not being terribly familiar with or interested in the game of basketball itself). Between 1987 and 1989, sales doubled for Nike to $1.7 billion, attributable primarily to Jordan's appeal.

The shoe design itself was a genius in marketing. Taking advantage of Jordan's ability to leap through the air during his dunks, Nike dubbed the new shoe the "Air Jordan," complete with a tiny air pump that would allow the wearer to pump air into the shoe to make it more comfortable. To the target audience—many of whom were teenage boys with an interest in basketball—it seemed to promise to somehow give its wearers the ability to jump higher and run faster—maybe not as high or fast as Jordan, but better than they could have done otherwise. The NBA banned the shoes from game play by all of its players (Jordan included) because they did not match most teams' uniforms, and because a player's teammates might not want to wear that design. Nike began a new marketing campaign with Jordan as the centerpiece: the slogan "Just Do It" would appear on numerous T-shirts and television commercials throughout the 1980s. Eventually, fans wanted to "Be Like Mike" (another Nike campaign) because Jordan was so likeable and talented. In addition, as Jordan's reputation as a player grew, in a time when cable television was expanding its reach through an increased number of channels, pro basketball became more popular than ever.

SAN FRANCISCO 49ERS AND ITS "WEST COAST OFFENSE"

The impact of the West Coast Offense of the San Francisco 49ers NFL team was reflected in their on-field reputation, as opposed to in the world at large. Though it might seem unusual for a team and its coaching staff to be considered a Game Changer, it is less so if you remember that football is a team sport, and that each of the parts contribute something important to the whole. The impact starts with Bill Walsh, the designer of the legendary offense, which is predicated on a short passing game that opens up the run game. Walsh initially designed the game plan while he was an assistant coach with the Cincinnati Bengals in the 1970s, and then he used it again in his tenure as the head coach for Stanford at the collegiate level. The offense utilizes a number of adjustments before the ball is snapped into play, and the quarterback often rolls out of the pocket before throwing to a receiver for a short gain.

In the years prior to the offense's emergence, the running game would require the linebackers and defensive backs to come closer to the line of scrimmage to open up the long, vertical passing game; short passes were essentially an extension of the running game, with passes out of the backfield to the running backs as part of the basic plan. Short passes were also more accurate than a consistent long-pass approach. The development of the offense led to teams shifting from a run-oriented offense to a pass-oriented offense. With the threat of the short passing game, faster defensive backs would be required who would be physically less capable of defending against the run.

In the years since, teams have relied more on the passing game than in any of the previous decades. The 49ers won four Super Bowls by using the offensive approach. Other coaches, such as George Seifert, Mike Holmgren, and Mike Shanahan won their own championships in the years ahead using Walsh's principles.

Joe Montana, the 49ers quarterback, was the ideal person to direct this offense, as he had the ability to run out of the pocket to throw to receivers in short passing routes, keeping the linebackers and defensive backs in place before using an effective running game. Later in the decade, Steve Young replaced Montana, though Young had struggled in Tampa Bay after a prolific college football career. As Montana became a victim of injuries, Young came in and gave an additional dimension to the offense with his excellent running ability. Early in the decade, Wendell Tyler was the team's running back, but the offense hit its true stride with Roger Craiz, who was equally adept at running the football and catching it, playing that position. Possession receivers who ran reliable, crisp routes were essential to the offense's success—initially Dwight Clark took this role, but beginning in the mid-1980s, Jerry Rice joined the team, becoming one of the most respected wide receivers of all time. Rice, from the small Mississippi Valley State University, didn't have the incredible speed that other receivers had, but his consistency to get open to receive the ball was unparalleled. Rice was hard on himself physically, training all year to be the best that he could be, and his results inspired others on the offense. Other important parts to the offense included wide receivers such as Freddie Solomon, John Taylor, and tight end Brent Jones.

BO JACKSON

Bo Jackson's professional sports career was somewhat brief, but it packed a powerful punch. Almost from the moment he entered college at Auburn University, it became clear that the running back was going to be a special player; but no one would have predicted that Jackson would be a tremendous player in two sports. Jackson was named an All-American in two popular sports, football and baseball. The New York Yankees drafted Jackson immediately after he graduated high school in Bessemer, Alabama—where he not only played football and baseball, but also competed in the decathlon. He chose to go to college instead, playing both football and baseball at Auburn University.

On the football field, Jackson had a superb yards-per-carry average, and one highlight early in his career was when he led Auburn to a win over Alabama in their yearly "Iron Bowl," which had been dominated by Alabama for a number of years. Auburn upset Alabama with Jackson diving over the Alabama defensive line, further attesting to his physical skills. Jackson was expected by many to be drafted with the first pick in the 1986 NFL draft.

Jackson was also a formidable force playing baseball. He was an outfielder for three seasons (he was injured for his sophomore season), but his senior season was cut short, as the National Collegiate Athletic Association (NCAA) had deemed him ineligible. Before the NFL draft, the team with the first pick, the Tampa Bay Buccaneers, had insisted that it would not hurt his baseball eligibility if he were to accept a plane ticket to Tampa for a physical. When Jackson found out otherwise, he refused to play for the Buccaneers, promptly deciding to play major league baseball for the Kansas City Royals instead.

Where Jackson emerges as a Game Changer is that he excelled in two major professional sports in the same year. While he was still playing for the Royals, Jackson was drafted by the Los Angeles Raiders the following year. Raiders owner Al Davis came to an agreement with Jackson that he could play with the Raiders around the baseball schedule. When he played with the Raiders as a running back, Jackson was nearly impossible to stop because of the combination of his size and speed, making him look superhuman to his fans. It was only after a severe hip injury in 1989 that Jackson became more mortal. He could only return to the baseball field; he was less of the player than he once was, and his football career was over. For the years he did play, though, it seemed that there was little that Jackson could not do, as exploited by Nike via a series of television commercials for his signature shoe, which stated "Bo Knows . . ."

MIKE TYSON

Mike Tyson had many of the same qualities as Bo Jackson, in that it seemed that both were nearly unstoppable physically while playing their sport. His fighting style was ferocious, not the finesse approach that was seen with the most famous heavyweight boxer before him, Muhammad Ali. Tyson helped bring boxing into the mainstream (for good and ill at times), which was the main reason that he can be considered a Game Changer in the 1980s. As testimony to his popularity, Tyson was the first boxer to be featured in a video game.

The speed at which Tyson retired his opponents was spectacular. He established a new record in the Junior Olympics for the quickest knockout (eight seconds). His first fight as a professional was another knockout, defeating his opponent in the first round. This became common for Tyson, and fans tuned in not to see who would win the fight, but rather, how fast Tyson could do it. Of his 28 victories, 26 of them were by knockout or technical knockout; these fights lasted just 74 rounds in total, whereas championship fights can last a maximum of 15 rounds (also known as "going the distance"). His reign of holding the three title belts (WBA, WBC, IBF) lasted from 1987 until 1990.

He also established a new record as the youngest heavyweight titleholder, at just 20 years and 4 months of age. Ultimately, he became too comfortable and was upset by Buster Douglas in 1990; his career and life went downhill from there. He was convicted of rape and served time in prison in the 1990s; his fights afterward seemed to have some type of controversy attached to them (including his 1997 fight with Evander Holyfield, during which Tyson bit off part of his ear). But Tyson changed how mainstream fans would embrace boxing forever.

SYLVESTER STALLONE

Of course, as much as a giant to the boxing world that Tyson was in the 1980s, it is only fitting that he is followed in this chapter by an actor who was initially known for portraying a boxer—Sylvester Stallone. Stallone, who went to high school in Philadelphia, portrayed a boxer who was an unknown, largely disrespected, local talent, but he got the opportunity to rise to the top of his profession (in this case, fighting for the heavyweight championship). The rags-to-riches story of Stallone's breakthrough film, *Rocky*, echoed Stallone's real life: he went from being a struggling actor and screenwriter, to getting his break from United Artists, which agreed to a contract with him to make *Rocky*, to ultimately convincing the studio executives that he was the one who should play the lead role. The gamble paid off, for all concerned: *Rocky* was a smash at the box office and was nominated for Best Picture, and Stallone became an iconic movie star. This all took place in the 1970s, but it set the stage for Stallone's emergence in the 1980s.

At the beginning of the decade, he was continuing his series of films based on Rocky. *Rocky III* (1982) showed Rocky as the mainstream success that was so important to American citizens in the 1980s, and *Rocky IV* (1985) featured him fighting a fearsome Soviet boxer, who seems to have been manufactured to ensure that he would not fail against the Americans, highlighting the struggles of the Cold War.

Stallone the hero took a different turn for the rest of the decade, ironically through another movie series, featuring Stallone as the Vietnam vet John Rambo. *First Blood* (1982) established Rambo as an important action hero in the 1980s, and several sequels followed. It was common for stories about Vietnam veterans to be included in the storylines of movies. For many Vietnam veterans, the code that they followed on the battlefield differed from the code in American society. As Jürgen Muller (1994, 376) explains,

> for the Vietnam Vets, the way back into civilian life is blocked as they've learned to live according to other laws. "In the field, we had a code of honor: you watch my back, I watch yours. Back here there's nothing." Honor and morality weren't just necessary to the soldier's survival; they were also the values he was supposed to be defending. And now a so-called law keeper is persecuting him, just because he's moving around freely in his own country—a country that embodies the idea of freedom like no other. It could be argued that *Rambo* is formulating a certain measure of ideological criticism: how can a government send people to war in defense of values that have long since lost all validity in their home country? Precisely because the solider is the last man left with a code of honor, society regards him as a troublemaker in peacetime, for his presence alone is enough to remind everyone else of their lack of morality.

Though *First Blood* chronicles the story of a Vietnam veteran fighting for individual freedom in a land that seemed to have developed a different set of rules, some movie viewers saw *Rambo: First Blood Part II* (1985) as the vehicle that showed Rambo as a true hero; in this film, he is fighting for the release of American POW/MIAs that were left behind during Vietnam. After losing most of the equipment that he brought with him during the parachute drop into the jungle, Rambo becomes a guerilla, using anything that he can to survive and keep fighting.

In *Rambo III*, Stallone returns to fighting the Soviets, this time in the Afghanistan war, another fight that would be seen as heroic by American audiences. The Rambo character takes a new slant—this time, he is rescuing his commanding officer, and for the first time, he is well equipped with gear. Though violent, the sense of action and heroism was equated with Stallone himself. Stallone's role as a Game Changer lies in his strength and heroic persona, which he expressed through different characters embraced by a large number of fans.

HARRISON FORD

Harrison Ford represents a different kind of masculinity than Stallone. His work with characters in the 1980s was of a wider variety than Stallone's but equally as masculine. Ford is most commonly known for two roles during his career: Han Solo, from the *Star Wars* series, and Indiana Jones, from the *Raiders of the Lost Ark* series. As Solo, Ford embodies the maverick smuggler, who doesn't seem to have much of a heart initially, but he ends up falling for a princess and joining a rebel cause. He is skilled with a laser gun and has the courage to fight—for the right price. As Jones, Ford is the adventurer and the academic. This time, he is armed with a whip, and he too is courageous—not in the fighting sense, but rather the discovery sense in exotic and dangerous situations.

Audiences see these roles in a heroic light, but additional roles from the 1980s showcased Ford's masculinity as well. As Rick Deckard in *Blade Runner* (1982), he is the retired police officer who becomes a hero in a science-fiction setting. In *Witness*, he plays Detective John Book, looking for a killer with ties to his own police department. He is forced to go into hiding in the Amish community where his witness (an eight-year-old boy) lives with his mother. The Amish love him, as he knows carpentry, and he winds up falling in love with the Amish woman he is staying with; however, he can't resist fighting to defend those who are wrong, so he must leave the Amish community. Ford becomes the head of a family in *The Mosquito Coast* (1986), as they go to live a simpler life in the Central American jungle. And in *Frantic* (1988), he is a concerned husband whose wife has been kidnapped. He must labor valiantly to rescue her. In all his films of the 1980s, Ford is the masculine hero but one that every man can relate to. Similar to Stallone, Ford's ability to adapt to different roles effectively while maintaining varying types of masculinity makes him a Game Changer in the 1980s.

SIGOURNEY WEAVER

Sigourney Weaver leads the charge for the heroic women of the decade for her role in *Alien* (1979) and its 1980s sequel, *Aliens* (1986). Before she played Ellen Ripley, few heroines had ever been included in feature roles in action movies, making her a Game Changer in the 1980s. Ripley is passionate and mentally strong, thoughtful, and courageous, without having the sheer strength of a Stallone or a Ford. How Ripley differs from Han Solo and Indiana Jones is that she has no room in her story for any type of sexualized portrayal, because she simply has to survive. Her appearances in *Ghostbusters* (1983) and its follow-up *Ghostbusters II* (1989) are sexier, but allowed her to show her comedic talents as well. In contrast, she appears as primatologist Dian Fossey in *Gorillas in the Midst: The Dian Fossey Story* (1988). Here, Weaver played a different type of person, a compassionate and courageous advocate for gorillas. It is through the *Alien* series that she is most transformative, however.

STEVEN SPIELBERG AND GEORGE LUCAS

The biggest Game Changers in film in the 1980s were two close friends, Steven Spielberg and George Lucas. Movies that Spielberg was involved with, as either producer or director, were among the top ones of the decade: *The Blues Brothers* (1980), *Raiders of the Lost Ark* (1981), *E.T. the Extra-Terrestrial* (1982), *Poltergeist* (1982), *Twilight Zone: The Movie* (1983), *Gremlins* (1984), *Indiana Jones and the Temple of Doom* (1984), *Back to the Future* (1985), *The Color Purple* (1985), *The Goonies* (1985), *Young Sherlock Holmes* (1985), and *Who Framed Roger Rabbit* (1985). Lucas's films in the 1980s include *Star Wars: The Empire Strikes Back* (1980), *Raiders of the Lost Ark* (1981), *Body Heat* (1981), *Return of the Jedi* (1983), *Indiana Jones and the Temple of Doom* (1984), and *Indiana Jones and the Last Crusade* (1989)—as well as one of the biggest turkeys of all time, *Howard the Duck* (1986).

A number of researchers have scrutinized Lucas's and Spielberg's works. Elizabeth Traube (1992) noted that researchers could see that the political climate of the 1980s had affected the way that the pair made movies, noting the explicit cultural program of the Lucas and Spielberg movies was to infantilize movie audiences, just as the heroes are compelled in the narratives to repudiate adulthood and return to childlike "innocence." Peter Biskind (Traube, 1992, 174) argues further that an unintended effect of the infantilization was the "rise of a new patriarchy intratexturally and a heightened receptiveness of

Steven Spielberg (left) and George Lucas became giants in the film industry in the 1980s. Between the two of them, they created six films that became mainstays in popular culture throughout the decade and some of the most popular films in history. (AP Photo/Wally Fong)

patriarchal figures, from Obi Wan and Yoda, to Henry Jones, authorize in the movies the reversion of the heroes to childhood." In other words, the characters who took on leadership, mentoring roles were now heroes. From a political perspective, which Biskind stresses were not conscious to the moviemakers, were realized in Ronald Reagan, the "ideal president for the Age of Star Wars." Like the acceptable authorities in the movies, Reagan's public style was a "blend of adult and child."

Subconscious codes in art forms have been noted in a variety of areas, especially music. In the context of movies, filmmakers are influenced by what is happening around them. President Ronald Reagan was the adult figure/leader of the free world against communism, as well as a youthful idealist in the technological sense. Reagan's influence made films by Lucas and Spielberg accessible to the audience of the 1980s. After the political turmoil in the 1960s and 1970s, it is not surprising that filmmakers were looking for a sense of nostalgia, the "good old days" unconsciously, and that feeling also permeated films by these two top director/producers. Elizabeth Traube (1992) adds,

> Critics have shown how the two trilogies affirm regressive, backward-looking values at multiple levels, while packaging their nostalgic message for consumption by a high-tech, middle-class audience, and they have suggested, as did we, that in celebrating a represented return to innocence, the movies anticipated and reinforced the rightward turn in American political culture. What we foregrounded in our interpretation of Indiana Jones was the movie's own inadvertent resistance to its regressive trajectory. By "reading against the grain," as I have since learned to call the interpretative practice, we deducted the traces of an alternative narrative that, we argued, could have subverted the dominant narrative of return to an idealized earlier state.

The movies that both of these men worked on led audiences to simply feel better about their lives. Americans could now have a new, though repackaged, hero inspired by a film genre from the past, the western. The traditional western had declined by the 1980s, but Indiana Jones fits the description of this new type of hero, with his rugged clothing (leather jacket and hat, canvas trousers), a whip that he uses instead of a gun, and the way that he rides a horse while eluding his pursuers in desert scenes in *Raiders of the Lost Ark*. Nigel Morris (2007, 74) continues that Jones's "rugged individualism recalls the pioneering spirit enshrined in the principle of Manifest Destiny to conquer the wilderness." Indiana Jones represents the maverick cowboy and the intellectual professor at the same time.

Both Spielberg and Lucas were comfortable creating science fiction movies. What makes Spielberg effective in the science fiction realm was that he "explores how encounters between humans and nonhuman life forms—whether from outer space or futuristic laboratories—drastically alter daily life" Friedman (2006, 29). Friedman goes on to comment that in *E.T.*, "humans and aliens equally share the narrative in scenes that run the gamut from comic, compassionate, to exploitative and to potentially tragic."

Lucas, on the other hand, had the imagination (and facility with technology) to create worlds that had never existed before. Dale Pollock (1983, 55) opined,

"Lucas' sophisticated visual sense further enhances his editing skills. Lucas and the Industrial Light and Magic (ILM) staff often run special effects footage in a screening room. The ILM staff are trained professionals who can spot minute flaws in a segment of film ten seconds long." Lucas can "see something wrong in a shot, and he'll know whether or not we can get away with it."

Lucas and Spielberg were pushing the boundaries of what creativity could do through technology, while maintaining the values of older Hollywood in the roots of their films, making them the most important filmmakers and Game Changers of the decade.

JAMES CAMERON

Spielberg and Lucas were not the only filmmakers that were Game Changers in the 1980s. James Cameron helped define action films in the decade and create the model for future action blockbusters. *The Terminator* (1984) was Cameron's first success. He had written the screenplay and was trying to find a movie studio that would purchase it. Cameron was willing to sell it but only on the condition that he would also direct the movie, regardless of his lack of experience; eventually, the small studio Hemdale Pictures agreed. *The Terminator* featured Arnold Schwarzenegger as a strong muscleman, and the film raised his profile and put the actor in great demand.

In addition, Cameron's work with Sigourney Weaver in *Aliens* (as discussed earlier in this chapter) highlighted her groundbreaking status as an action heroine. Cameron approaches the movie from the backdrop of the U.S. involvement in the Vietnam War (to the point where he uses the term "Colonial Marines" to refer to the military group in the film), making a parallel to armed forces with a technological advantage struggling against guerilla tactics in an antagonistic environment. Cameron was also involved in guiding visual effects in conjunction with the staff at George Lucas's ILM company. Cameron's work on *The Abyss* (1989), also in collaboration with ILM, was considered one of the most innovative use of special effects. Computer-based visual effects were key to the development of the final product. What was also important to the film's production was the largely underwater filming process, since computer technology had not quite advanced to that level at the time. Costly giant tanks for water had to be built for the production, the largest being 55 feet deep. The film was a commercial success, and Cameron's work on films in the decades after the 1980s have cemented his reputation as a major filmmaker.

JOHN HUGHES

John Hughes (1959–2009) was one of the most successful comedy writers working on films in the 1980s. He is best known for movies that were about and written for teenagers. His success in the early part of the decade had some impact, as he was a writer on the hit comedies *National Lampoon's Class Reunion* (1982), *Mr. Mom* (1983), *National Lampoon's Vacation* (1983), and *European Vacation* (1985). Where Hughes made his game-changing impact, though, was with

Sixteen Candles and *The Breakfast Club* in 1984 and *Weird Science* in 1985; on all three, he served as director as well as writer. *The Breakfast Club* has particular significance, as it highlights the wide range of personalities that nearly any teenager could identify with.

In addition to writing the very successful *Pretty in Pink* (1986), he directed *Ferris Bueller's Day Off*, released the same year. The latter is viewed as making considerable commentary on 1980s' society. For example, "Whereas teen comedies may be generically constrained to subvert or in some way question whatever versions of adult values they present, in *Ferris Bueller* the antiauthoritarian impulse is carried to an extreme, leaving no space for any form of reconciliation between generations. *Ferris Bueller* also contrasts with other Hughes films in its intentionally open, fragmented story line, repeatedly interrupted by Ferris's asides to the audience." This comment illustrates how effective Hughes's approach to making films was. He could make teenagers see how the movie relates to them, either by identifying directly with characters, or in the case of Ferris Bueller, to live vicariously through someone doing things that you might not have the nerve to do yourself. Hughes's ability to relate to a teen audience makes him a Game Changer for the 1980s.

Though Hughes is most often noted for his teen movies, the latter half of the decade included a period of prolific success for Hughes in other genres. He directed, wrote, and produced three hits: *Planes, Trains and Automobiles* (1987), *She's Having a Baby* (1988), and *Uncle Buck* (1989) that furthered showcased his comedic flair. He became more active as a film producer as well, working on *Some Kind of Wonderful* (1987), *The Great Outdoors* (1988), and *National Lampoon's Christmas Vacation* (1989).

Directors who cite Hughes's influence include Judd Apatow (Saperstein, 2009), who remarked after Hughes's recent death, "basically, my stuff is just John Hughes films with four-letter words. I feel like a part of my childhood has died. Nobody made me laugh harder or more often than John Hughes." Where Apatow is most on target is how important Hughes's films were to the teenagers who grew up watching them.

STEPHEN KING

Stephen King had already established a reputation as a horror author by the beginning of the 1980s. His first book, *Carrie* (1973), was written in the epistolary style, and later became a hit movie. *Salem's Lot* (1975) was adapted as a television movie to great fanfare, and his further books in the 1970s, *The Shining* (1977) and *The Stand* (1978) solidified his reputation. King became a Game Changer in the 1980s because of the number of his books that became significant films during this period, expanding his reputation among people who did not read novels. For instance, *Firestarter* (1980) features Andy McGee and his daughter, Charlie, who are being pursued by a government agency. Andy and his wife, Vicky, had performed experiments with a psychotic drug called Lot 6, and as a result, both developed psychic abilities. Andy, in particular, could use his mind to control others, which he called "the push." Charlie, in turn, was born with the ability to start fires telekinetically, and so the government wanted to capture the McGees and further study their abilities (and perhaps develop Charlie to use as a weapon). The movie was made into a film in 1984.

Cujo (1981) is named for a family dog that is bitten by a bat, giving him a violent form of rabies. Set in Maine, Joe Cambers is a mechanic who is visited by new residents Donna Trenton and her son, Tad. While Donna's husband, Vic, is out of town on business, she takes her car to the Cambers' shop for repair, and she and Tad are trapped in her increasingly hot car by the rabid animal. Though this novel did not have a supernatural basis, it was still a thrilling story.

King's *Christine* (1983) is about a car that seems to be possessed. A teenager, Arnie Cunningham, buys Christine, an antique Plymouth Fury, from Roland LeBay. Arnie begins to restore the car, and his behavior changes while doing so; it comes out later that he is developing the personality traits of LeBay, an abusive, angry man whose daughter and wife died tragically in the car in separate incidents. Arnie finds a new girlfriend, Leigh, who chokes on a hamburger in the car (similar to the way LeBay's daughter died) and blames it on the car. After Arnie's parents disallow him to keep the car at home, Arnie parks it in a parking garage, where the car is vandalized. The car begins to hunt and kill the ones who vandalized the car. The vandals are also LeBay's enemies as well. Arnie's Leigh and friend Dennis start their own relationship, begin to feel as if the car will attack them, and decides to get to the car first to save Arnie and themselves. The car is destroyed, but unfortunately Arnie dies as well. *Christine* was made into a film in 1983.

Pet Sematary (1983) is a story about a cemetery where children in rural Maine bury their pets; the cemetary seems to have magical restorative powers. Dr. Louis Creed had recently become the doctor for the University of Maine and recently moved into the area. As Creed's family goes out of town, he discovers that their family cat has been killed. In order to replay Louis for saving his wife's life, their neighbor, Jud, leads him to the pet cemetery, part of which is on an ancient Indian burial ground that has the ability to reanimate the dead, so that the cat can be resurrected. The cat returns, but its character has undergone a sinister transformation. Nevertheless, when Louis's infant son is killed, he is compelled to bury him in the same cemetery, with tragic results. *Pet Sematary* was made into a film in 1988.

Cycle of the Werewolf (1983), like most of King's works, is set in rural Maine, and focuses on Marty, an 11-year-old in a wheelchair, and a rash of killings that occur in the area on each full moon. The victims are both people and animals, and the town of Tarker's Mill lives in fear of these events. The town cancels Independence Day fireworks, but Marty's uncle, sensing Marty's disappointment, buys Marty his own fireworks. While Marty sets them off, a werewolf, who has been responsible for the killing, attacks him. Marty maims the werewolf by forcing fireworks into the animal's eye. At Halloween, Marty sees the Reverend Lowe wearing an eye patch, determines that Lowe is the werewolf, and begins to send the Reverend letters asking him to commit suicide to save the town. Meanwhile, Marty asks his uncle to prepare silver bullets so he can defend himself from the werewolf. The silver bullets are finally used when the werewolf comes to kill Marty. *Cycle of the Werewolf* was made into the movie *Silver Bullet* in 1985.

Misery (1987) tells the tale of Paul Sheldon, a writer who has an auto accident while driving from Boulder to Los Angeles in a snowstorm. A nurse, Annie Wilkes, rescues him and takes him to her home, and as fate would have it, she is a huge fan of Paul's romance novels featuring Misery Chastain. Sheldon has broken his legs in the accident, and Wilkes starts to nurse him back to health (with the help of copious amounts of painkillers). Unfortunately for Paul, Annie is a bit of a psycho. When she finds out that Paul killed Misery off in the latest entry in the *Misery* series, she tortures him to force him to write a new novel bringing her back to life. *Misery* ends with a violent confrontation between Paul and Annie, in which Annie is finally killed.

Misery became one of King's most popular books in the 1980s, establishing him as the king of horror for the decade. It was also made into one of King's most successful movies in 1990, and Kathy Bates won an Oscar for her compelling portrayal of Annie.

THE FOUR COMPUTER MAVERICKS

The popularity of the personal computer expanded significantly in the 1980s. Four men (or, more accurately, two pairs of men), contributed to its significant development, and hence qualify as Game Changers. The Seattle-based duo, Paul Allen and Bill Gates, founded Microsoft, the software company that developed a suite of office tools, as well as the Windows operating system, which became the most widely used in the decade. Starting as hobbyists in high school, the young men joined a computer-programming group at their private high school (Lakeside). After high school, Gates attended Harvard for two years, and then, after he dropped out of college, he eventually reconnected with Allen to develop their company.

Hobbyists using the Altair 8000 computer could purchase Microsoft's software to program their computers at home, and eventually, the company developed software for larger companies. Microsoft's impact, in the words of Walter Issacson (2014, 340), was that the company could "meet software deadlines that seemed insane, beat other competitors to the market for each new product, and charge such a low price that computer manufactures rarely thought of writing or controlling their own software." Microsoft aligned itself with two prominent manufacturers, IBM and Apple. When they entered into those software-programming agreements, Allen and Gates became Game Changers.

The PC-DOS operating system used for the IBM was the first of these agreements to make a name for Microsoft. Gates could also license the same operating system to other personal computer makers under the name MS-DOS. Microsoft kept control of the source code, which meant that IBM couldn't modify or evolve the software into something that became proprietary to its machines. Only Microsoft could make changes, and then it could license each new version to any company that wanted it.

Microsoft had also established a relationship with Apple, whose Apple II models were competing with IBM. Headed by Steve Wozniak and Steve Jobs, the other game-changing pair, the Apple Computer company had evolved out of the same culture as Gates and Allen: the hobbyist computer market. Wozniak and Jobs hailed from Cupertino, California (near San Francisco), and like Gates and Allen, they joined a computer club at their high school so they could pursue their interests. Wozniak focused on programming computers, and Jobs thought of ideas to help market the computers to a wider audience. In the view of Issacson, (2014, 353), the Apple II was the "first personal computer to be simple and fully integrated, from the hardware to the software," which helped bring upon the decline of the computer hobbyist culture.

The development of the Apple and Microsoft software allowed users into the world of word processing. The software would change how documents could be typed, edited, and saved digitally, in contrast to a process of typing with a typewriter, editing with correction fluid, not being able to cut, copy, and paste sections of the document into other areas, or saving offices the trouble to store boxes of documents that might need to be accessed at a later time. Furthermore, spreadsheet and database use changed the way that both businesses and consumers could organize and present information—quite a departure from ledger books. The hardware on both Apple- and IBM-affiliated systems now supported the software, as well as provided a mechanism to support entertainment, including gaming.

The widespread use of both the hardware and software made these four computer experts Game Changers because of their impact on how computers could be used in both the workplace and home environments. With the development of Apple's Macintosh series, the landscape was changed even further, making computer use even more accessible to a larger number of consumers.

FURTHER READING

Biskind, Peter. *Easy Riders, Raging Bulls: How the Sex-Drugs-and Rock 'n' Roll Generation Changed Hollywood.* New York: Bloomsbury, 1999.

Curry, Romona. "Madonna from Marilyn to Marlene—Pastiche and/or Parody." *Journal of Film and Video*, vol. 42, no. 2, p. 26, 1990.

Friedman, Lester D. *Citizen Spielberg.* Urbana, IL: University of Illinois Press, 2006.

Issacson, Walter. *The Innovators.* New York: Simon and Schuster, 2014.

LaFaber, Walter. *Michael Jordan and the New Global Capitalism.* New York: Norton, 2002.

Light, Alan, ed. *The Vibe History of Hip-Hop*, New York: Three Rivers Press, 1999.

McClary, Susan. *Feminine Endings.* Minneapolis: University of Minnesota Press, 1991.

Morris, Nigel. *The Cinema of Steven Spielberg: Empire of Light.* London: Wallflower Press, 2007.

Muller, Jürgen, ed. *Movies of the 80s.* Koln, Germany: Taschen, 1994.

Pollock, Dale. *Skywalking.* New York: Harmony Press, 1983.

Traube, Elizabeth. *Dreaming Identities: Class, Gender, and Generation in 1980s Hollywood Movies.* Boulder, CO: Westview Press, 1992.

CHAPTER 10

Legacy

As a decade, the 1980s greatly influenced a number of areas in popular culture, including in the delivery and content of television, music, sports, and movies. This final chapter of the book explores some elements from the 1980s that helped build the legacy of popular culture in the years that followed.

THE LEGACY OF 1980s' SITUATION COMEDIES

Situation comedies (or sitcoms) have been an integral part of the entertainment industry since the mid-1940s, initially via radio programming. With the emergence of television in the 1950s, audiences could appreciate how visual, nonverbal cues could enhance the writing. The 1980s continued that tradition, and the legacy of sitcom writing can be divided into three categories: family-based, friendship-based, and occupation-based. Family-based writing during the 1980s had the biggest impact: *The Cosby Show* was particularly groundbreaking, as it featured an upper-middle-class African American family as the main characters (the 1970s' sitcom *The Jeffersons* also centered around well-off African Americans, but George and Louise Jefferson did not have young children, while the Huxtables of *The Cosby Show* did). If not for *Cosby*, there might never have been shows like *The Fresh Prince of Bell-Air*, which was one of the top sitcoms of the 1990s.

Married . . . with Children had a cynical view of the middle-class American family; without that show's success, it would have been more difficult for a show like *Roseanne* to be accepted in the late 1980s and early 1990s. *Roseanne* helped serve as a neat transition between the 1980s and 1990s, featuring a working-class family with the mother as the clear head of the household. The boundaries of traditional families were challenged in 1980s' shows such as *Who's the Boss?* and *Full House*, which helped expand the role and prominence of parents and grandparents in the 1990s' homes of *Everyone Loves Raymond* and *Frasier*.

Any discussion of a group of elderly relatives and friends in the 1980s must include *The Golden Girls*, featuring (mostly) likable, sincere, and believable characters dealing with real-life situations. *The Golden Girls* pioneered the type of comedy that centered around groups of friends, which was echoed in other popular shows of the decade. *Cheers*, the 1980s' show that focused on the interactions of the denizens of a local bar, was reflected in two iconic, friend-centered comedies of the 1990s: *Friends*, following the exploits of six friends in New York City; and *Seinfeld*, the most popular show of the 1990s. Though the storylines differ, similar connections can be made to the four women in *Sex and the City*, as well as to the groundbreaking friendship between a gay man and a straight woman in *Will and Grace*.

Occupation-based sitcoms of the 1980s had less of an impact than family- and friend-based shows. However, shows like *Taxi* and *Night Court* proved to 1980s audiences that work situations could be funny, and that motif was explored further in 1990s' shows such as *Spin City* and *Frasier*.

THE LEGACY OF 1980s' TEEN CULTURE

Entertainment and media are essential aspects of any teen's life and have been since the 1950s. The 1980s was the decade that expanded the number of options and accessibility of different types of entertainment—aspects of pop culture that are taken for granted today. Movies focusing on teens, such as *Ferris Bueller's Day Off*, *Pretty in Pink*, and *Fast Times at Ridgemont High*, continued even after the 1980s, including *American Pie*, *Clueless*, *Easy A*, *Mean Girls*, and *Ten Things I Hate About You*. In each of these movies, high school is an essential setting for the plot. The school had not been a prevalent place in teen movies prior to the 1980s (with notable exceptions including 1955's *Blackboard Jungle* and 1967's *To Sir with Love* and *Up the Down Staircase*)—rather, there was more of a focus on the extracurricular activities of teenagers at a restaurant, drive-in, or even on the street.

Other trends included controversial musical artists, such as Madonna in the 1980s, who has gone on to influence artists such as Britney Spears and Lady Gaga in subsequent decades. Rap music in the 1980s, that was seen by some as a passing fad, has turned into a hip hop culture that encompasses not only music, but fashion. In the 21st century, hip hop fashion has become a badge of honor and a symbol of authenticity and pride for those interested in that culture—though some have unfairly characterized it as African American culture, not realizing that the message of rap can be embraced by the plurality of American society.

Technology also had an impact on teen culture. The development of the Sony Walkman made prerecorded music portable for the first time. Unlike portable radios, though, users could listen to whatever they wanted on cassette, either a full-length recording purchased at a store, or a "mix tape" of songs that they put together themselves to personalize their listening experience. The legacy of the Walkman was certainly prevalent after the 1980s. Portable CD players were very popular throughout the 1990s, and with the development of the iPod and iPhone, music became portable via digital files. Video game technology of the 1980s, such as Atari, Mattel's Intellivision, and

Coleco Vision, has had a long legacy, ranging from Sega Genesis, to as of this writing, four types of Sony PlayStation and its competitor, the XBox series.

THE LEGACY OF 1980s' POPULAR MUSIC

Delivery of popular music changed in the 1980s with the development of the music video. Madonna and Michael Jackson both incorporated dancing as an essential element to the delivery of pop music as an overall entertainment package. In the 1990s, Janet Jackson, Paula Abdul, and Ricky Martin displayed their considerable talents as dancers while lip-syncing the vocals in their music videos. Mariah Carey and Whitney Houston, two of the biggest artists of both the 1980s and 1990s, not known for their dancing, used backup dancers in their music videos. The 1980s also had teen pop sensations Debbie Gibson and Tiffany, whose successes were used as models for future teen pop artists in the 1980s and beyond. It was common for later vocal groups such as Boyz II Men, All-4-One, En Vogue, TLC, and the Spice Girls to incorporate synchronized dancing into their performances. By the end of the 1990s, the next wave of pop stars such as Britney Spears and Christina Aguilera were accomplished dancers and well as singers.

An important aspect from the 1980s that carried over to the 1990s and the decades that followed was the concept of the boy band. New Edition, Bell Biv Devoe, and New Kids on the Block were among the best-selling musical artists of the 1980s, largely because of the demographic they appealed to. Preteens and teenagers (mostly girls) have a significant amount of disposable income that has made stars of male performers for decades, including Frank Sinatra, Elvis Presley, and the Beatles; and these 1980s' groups continued in that fine tradition. The Backstreet Boys were among the first groups in the 1990s to emerge under the boy band umbrella. Assembled by music impresario Lou Pearlman, the Orlando-based group held auditions that included one former Walt Disney World entertainer, Kevin Richardson. After approximately two years performing in venues ranging from theme parks to high schools, the Backstreet Boys received a major recording contract. The Backstreet Boys left Pearlman's fold, and he responded by developing a second group, NSYNC. This group included another Disney performer, Justin Timberlake, who had performed on the *Mickey Mouse Club* reboot alongside Spears and Aguilera. By the turn of the millennium, NSYNC became one of the top pop groups of the 1990s. Other performers who got their start on Disney programs and then became widely successful include Miley Cyrus, the Jonas Brothers, Jessica Simpson, Selena Gomez, Lindsay Lohan, and Aly and AJ.

Ultimately, the simple idea that musical performers should make videos to go along with their hits cemented the legacy of 1980s' music. In pop and country, the music video has proved itself to be essential, as the storyline of the video gives the audience another avenue of connection to and interest in the music. As far as the industry is concerned, some labels value the video as a necessary element of promotion. Others are finding that selling their individual recordings (whether in hard copy or via downloading) is not the best way to make money off of their art anymore, and that the audio sale is a part of a global sales reach that includes merchandise, live performances, and personalized meetings with artists. One of the reasons why the video hasn't had the same impact for subgenres in rock is that cable television has changed its priorities, moving from a video format to a reality-based pop culture format, which began in the 1990s.

THE LEGACY OF 1980s' PRO FOOTBALL

Before the mid-1970s, the Super Bowl pitted the winners of the two divisions of the NFL against each other to determine the national champion, but it wasn't much more than that. By the end of the 1980s, though, the Super Bowl had become the most watched individual sporting event in the United States. In the years that followed, the Super Bowl became a cultural event, complete with elaborate halftime shows featuring pop and rock stars performing live. For many Americans, the Super Bowl was something of a national holiday. Tickets to the game itself were highly prized, selling for much more than face value.

Football had evolved from the run-heavy game of previous decades into a dynamic passing game. Quarterbacks of the 1980s, such as Dan Fouts, Joe Montana, Dan Marino, and John Elway, were passing for more yards than quarterbacks had ever done before. The passing game, particularly with the West Coast Offense made famous by the San Francisco 49ers, made short passing plays as effective as the running game. Moreover, as the passing game advanced, running backs were now expected to be versatile enough to run and catch.

The top defenders were not the big, hulking middle linebackers of years before, who could stop a running back in his tracks. The new heroes were the outside linebackers and defensive ends, who could provide the pass rush against the passing game. One outstanding example of this type of player was Lawrence Taylor. Top cornerbacks were expected to run as fast as the wide receivers. Rules were developed that helped protect the quarterback, putting all defenders, including cornerbacks, at a disadvantage. The cornerbacks were also hindered when the league outlawed the use of a sticky substance known as *stick-um* and restricted defensive backs so they could attack the receiver only beyond the first five yards from scrimmage.

Cornerbacks such as Michael Haynes and Lester Hayes were joined by fleet-footed safeties such as Ronnie Lott and Kenny Easley to help defend receivers such as Jerry Rice and James Lofton. The physiques of pro football players had changed in the 1980s. With the advance of the passing game, the players were expected to be faster than any in previous decades. William "The Refrigerator" Perry was the first star player to eclipse 300 pounds, but as the NFL is a league where all teams follow trends, in the decades that followed, nearly every lineman on both the offensive and defensive sides of play is now expected to be over 300 pounds. The use of steroids and other performance-enhancing drugs expanded in the 1980s, which changed the way the game was regulated in the coming years.

Another legacy of pro football in the 1980s was the increase in power by NFL owners. At the end of the decade, the Dallas Cowboys were purchased by Texas billionaire Jerry Jones. Jones became much more of a hands-on owner than most owners had historically been. By the 1990s, Jones became the club's general manager, making decisions on personnel for the team. His biggest impact was that future owners were expected to be billionaires, making team ownership an exclusive club, and that legacy has continued to the present day.

In another long-lasting aspect, municipalities were expected to support the billionaire team owners, and if they did not submit to demands for updated or new stadiums with lucrative seat licenses and luxury boxes, the owners threatened to leave for a new city. The two Los Angeles teams in the 1980s, the Rams and the Raiders, would leave for St. Louis and Oakland in 1994, respectively, because their owners were offended at apparently being slighted by the stadium executives. Newer teams, such as the Carolina Panthers in Charlotte and the Jacksonville Jaguars, both received stadiums that were either new or updated to include significant financial benefits. Stadiums now include the best technology, with a wide variety of beer and food options to help justify the higher ticket prices. With the increase in financial benefits, the owners have become even more powerful. In addition, the players make more money than ever, largely because they gained a larger percentage of the television funds thanks to negotiations during the two players' strikes that took place in the 1980s.

THE LEGACY OF 1980s' TELEVISION

The 1980s featured a number of programs that encouraged a new level of honesty about personal relationships and sex than those of previous decades. Dr. Ruth Westheimer, popularly known as "Dr. Ruth," became an important authority in the 1980s because she discussed sex with a frankness that helped Americans open up about their sex lives like never before. She was controversial because of her openness about a previously taboo topic, but many people found her information on sex useful. She started her media career on radio in New York, where she hosted the show *Sexually Speaking*. Westheimer's purpose was to help educate her audience and encourage them to have sex (so long as it was safe) so that the partners could live more fulfilling lives. Her advocacy of safe sex and masturbation was new to 1980s' society. For example, she (1992, 107) explains, "masturbation often doesn't come as naturally or easily for girls as it does boys. There are many reasons for this—from societal strictures to anatomy—but now is not the time to go into them. The important point is that women can give pleasure to themselves."

Television court programs in the 1980s helped develop the reality television programming that has become a staple of American society. Shows such as *The People's Court* (featuring Judge Joseph Wapner in the 1980s and early 1990s) enabled American viewers to see disputes between ordinary Americans that would often border on the ridiculous. Naturally, viewers would pick a side in the dispute, and if they watched the program with a friend, their friends might debate the pros and cons of the case on television. Guests on the show were more than willing to share the details of their disputes, regardless of how they would be portrayed to the viewing audience. Into the 1990s, the *People's Court* concept was expanded into increasingly ludicrous situations in *Judge Judy*, which featured a retired judge, Judy Sheindlin. A plethora of courtroom reality shows followed, including *Judge Mathis, Divorce Court,* and *Judge Joe Brown* (as well as *The People's Court,* which has continued to this day, but with Judge Marilyn Milian instead of Judge Wapner).

The most influential aspect of television in the 1980s (at least in terms of reality television) was the development of the "confessional" talk show format. Talk shows from the 1980s, *Donahue, Sally Jesse Raphael Show, The Ricki Lake Show,* and *Oprah,* brought the struggles of real people in a format that could be discussed and debated, not just by the episode's participants and audience, but by viewers at home as well. Experts on nearly every topic were interviewed on the stage, but what would make the show so intriguing is how eager ordinary audience members were to share their own perspectives on the topic on national television. The hosts would empathize with their guests and the audience members, encouraging them to discuss their own personal experiences even more.

The impact of these shows could be felt in similar shows in the 1990s, but with a more aggressive slant. The *Jerry Springer Show* quickly became the archetype of the "trash" talk show that featured some of the most controversial topics in American society, with largely low-class guests with some type of personal dispute, often including relationship infidelities and frequently involving paternity testing. Often, the guests would actually engage in physical combat with each other (to the extent that the shows would have to hire security staff to break up the fights).

Thanks to the openness on television pioneered in the 1980s, any type of reality television became viewed as partially shocking and partially acceptable. As such, post-1980s' audiences flocked to see shows such as MTV's *The Real World, Survivor, Big Brother, The Amazing Race,* and *The Bachelor.* The reality format ranged from competition shows (*Survivor, Big Brother,* and *The Amazing Race*), to supposed relationship-oriented programs (*The Bachelor* and *The Bachelorette*), to series that purported to show the adventures of real people (the *Real Housewives* franchise).

THE LEGACY OF 1980s' FILM TECHNOLOGY

Films in the 1980s made significant strides in the use of technology to create special effects, largely through the efforts of George Lucas's company, Industrial Light and Magic (ILM). In his movies, spaceships had to find a magical way to fly in space and look believable. When George Lucas was working on the idea of creating the first film in the *Star Wars* series, he had to devise new approaches to create special effects by using the technology of the mid-1970s in new ways, or simply creating something new from scratch. He started ILM in 1975 as a forum where creative artists and craftsman could think "outside the box" to find innovative solutions.

One of the ways ILM expanded the way that they made movies in the 1980s was by aligning themselves with Jim Henson. Henson took his Muppet creation, a puppet that had become popular on the 1960s children's show *Sesame Street*, and used the concept to create the character of Yoda for *The Empire Strikes Back*. In an age before computer animation, this was no easy feat. Stop-motion photography, a time-intensive process, was also used on films such as *The Empire Strikes Back, E.T., Raiders of the Lost Ark*, and *Dragonslayer*.

The implementation of computers in creating film-based special effects by ILM is a significant part of their legacy. The staff brought in to help build the special effects began using a new type of computer that exclusively focused on creating graphics: the Pixar. Movies such as *Star Trek II, Young Sherlock Holmes*, and *The Abyss* made significant strides in the basic design, which is still used even today, in the first two decades of the 21st century. Pixar was eventually sold to Steve Jobs (and they would make their own mark on the film industry, particularly through advances in computer animation as demonstrated in the blockbuster *Toy Story* series of films). However, until then, ILM used the technology for films other than ones that Lucas was making, such as *The Goonies, Cocoon*, and *Back to the Future*.

Of course, ILM's impact in the 1980s was significant for Lucas's own *Star Wars* films, *The Empire Strikes Back* and *Return of the Jedi*. For the former, creating a city in the clouds and having white snow speeders against a white background still show up convincingly on camera were certainly not easy illusions to pull off. Neither was creating the background of an interstellar fighting sequence between the rebels and the Empire, while the evil Emperor coaxed Luke Skywalker and Darth Vader to fight for the right to become the Emperor's apprentice moving forward.

Lucasfilm, an affiliated company owned by Lucas, also developed the THX standard for movie theaters. THX is not a specific process, but rather standards of theater design to support high-quality sound using multiple amplifiers and speakers, alongside a device called a *crossover*. The first use of the THX standard was in *Return of the Jedi*, one of the *Star Wars* series. In the years since, THX has become the standard sound system in nearly every movie theater in the United States.

THE LEGACY OF 1980s' HORROR MOVIES

The 1980s was the decade where horror films became a larger part of the mainstream. There were two reasons for this: Stephen King became a top-selling author of stories of horror and the supernatural, and second, horror movies started to incorporate a higher degree of violence (to the point that a new genre was invented: slasher films). He had creative settings and detailed, evocative characters, and his works explored themes of childhood, death, imagination, and family. Sharon Russell (1996, 23) adds, "the suspense genre shares much of its structure with horror. Both encourage identification with the central character or characters. In addition, both use the plot and the reader's expectations to create tension. If we know more than the characters, we can anticipate what might happen. If we share the viewpoint of the character, we identify with that character." King's influence has been extensive, inspiring such writers as Dan Simmons, Bentley Little, and particularly Clive Barker; the work by these authors and many others has been among King's biggest contributions to the legacy of horror writing in the 1980s. In addition, his strength in creating compelling characters made movies a natural transition for him, and those movies (like *Misery, Firestarter, Salem's Lot,* and *The Shining*) further expanded his audience.

The *Halloween, Friday the 13th,* and *A Nightmare on Elm Street* series focused on one central, psychopathic character who had one simple goal: kill everyone, for no apparent reason. Movies such as *Candyman* (1992), *Scream* (1996), and *I Know What You Did Last Summer* (1997) were influenced by these slasher movies of the 1980s, though it must be acknowledged that the number of the movies has decreased; it could be argued that the 1980s were something of a "golden age" for slasher films. The years that followed also included remakes of older classics, such as *Psycho* (originally 1960, remade in 1998), *Texas Chainsaw Massacre* (originally 1974, remade in 2003) and *A Nightmare on Elm Street* (originally 1984, remade in 2010), demonstrating that the genre was not extinct. In fact, it was so popular that a comedic parody, *Scary Movie,* came out in 2000.

The influence of the movie onto the literary scene has come full circle; writers such as Dean Koontz write in such a vivid style that the descriptions of the horror in his pages are just as shocking and compelling as visual images. Though horror has been a part of movies since the very beginning, the gore and violence of the 1980s was much more pronounced, and that will prove to be a lasting (if not entirely positive) legacy.

THE LEGACY OF 1980s' HOME USER TECHNOLOGY

The 1980s featured advances in technology that changed how information is captured and shared. The videocassette recorder (VCR) allowed viewers to have their videotaped programs available for many years if they recorded them personally, to keep them indefinitely if they had purchased the recording from a store, or to rent videos from a store and simply watch them at their leisure. The VCR could be considered the precursor for today's "on-demand" viewing.

The legacy of having videos available on request has shown itself in many ways in the decades following the 1980s. One of the most prominent of these is YouTube, the online video sharing website, which allows ordinary people to simply record a video and share it with whomever wants to view the recording at any time, as many times as they want. A new slant with such sites as YouTube concerns how many "hits" (views) the video receives. Advertisers have realized that hits mean people who can see their products, so they are motivated to invest in showing ads on the sites, supporting them further. Some musical recording artists, such as Justin Bieber, Carly Rae Jepsen, and PSY, have become stars in mainstream media because of their initial success on YouTube.

The home video recorder (camcorder) operated hand in hand with the VCR in the 1980s. Home movie recording had certainly been around for years before the 1980s, but playing back these movies was not easy to do. A screen (similar to a screen found in many classrooms) had to be set up, and a projector to play the movie would have to be set up several feet away from the screen. With the video recorder, a tape could simply be placed in the VCR and watched on the television. Users could now record home movies easier than before, and they could share them almost immediately.

The legacy that the camcorder helped to establish is that consumers now expected to be able to capture events in their personal lives and share them easily. Into the 21st century, that attitude has been facilitated by technology, particularly with the rise of the mobile smartphone. It is now possible to record the video of a special event and post it onto a social media website in mere minutes for all to enjoy (or mock, or criticize, as the case may be).

Of course, advances in personal computing constitute one of the most enduring legacies of the 1980s. A majority of households in the United States today owns a personal computer or a tablet that can function similarly to one. The computer might be a desktop, but currently, the laptop and the tablet (such as the iPad) are the items of choice. It is nearly impossible for many Americans under the age of 30 to consider how to function in society without immediate access to a computer. Typewriters have long since fallen out of favor, and it is common for Americans to watch a videotaped movie or television show right on their computer—particularly when traveling. Projects for both work and school are expected to be prepared on a computer, which is equipped with some type of word processing, spreadsheet, or presentation program, often in a suite of programs such as Microsoft Office.

As a result, the personal computer can allow people to interact with each other as never before. However, computer technology has evolved such that it is also easy to express insulting or otherwise offensive ideas while hiding your identity behind an avatar or other social media presence, or to overshare every detail of your personal life on the Internet, so that so that everyone can see exactly what you are doing, where you are going, or what you are eating.

FURTHER READING

Abramson, Albert, and Christopher H. Sterling. *The History of Television, 1942–2000.* Jefferson, NC: McFarland and Company, 2003.

Crepeau, Richard C. *NFL Football: A History of America's New National Pastime.* Champaign, IL: University of Illinois Press, 2014.

George-Warren, H., P. Romanowski, and J. Pareles. *The Rolling Stone Encyclopedia of Rock & Roll (Revised and Updated for the 21st Century).* New York: Fireside, 2001.

Kingsbury, Paul. *The Encyclopedia of Country Music.* New York: Oxford University Press, 1998.

Larkin, Colin, ed. *The Encyclopedia of Popular Music.* 4th ed. New York: Oxford University Press, 2006.

Shoals, Bethleham, and Jacob Weinstein. *FreeDarko Presents: The Undisputed Guide to Pro Basketball History.* New York: Bloomsbury, 2010.

Vecsey, George. *Baseball: A History of America's Favorite Game.* New York: Modern Library/Random House, 2008.

Westheimer, Ruth. *Dr. Ruth's Guide to Safer Sex.* New York: Warner Books, 1992.

Wexman, Virginia Wright. *A History of Film.* 7th ed. New York: Pearson, 2009.

Wood, Robin. *Hollywood from Vietnam to Reagan.* New York: Columbia, 1986.

Bibliography

Abramson, Albert. *The History of Television, 1942–2000.* Jefferson, NC: McFarland and Company, 2003.

Allen, Robert G. *Creating Wealth.* New York: Simon and Schuster, 1983.

Alloway, Lawrence. *Lichtenstein.* New York: Abbeville Press, 1985.

Avedon, Elizabeth. *Salle.* New York: Vintage Books, 1987.

Azerrad, Michael. *Our Band Could Be Your Life.* Boston: Back Bay Books, 2001.

Barr, Roseanne. *Roseanne: My Life as a Woman.* New York: Harper and Row, 1989.

Bellomo, Mark. *Totally Tubular '80s Toys.* Iola, WI: Krause Publications, 2010.

Biskind, Peter. *Easy Riders, Raging Bulls: How the Sex-Drugs-and-Rock 'n' Roll Generation Changed Hollywood.* New York: Bloomsbury, 1999.

Bombeck, Erma. *Family: The Ties That Bind . . . and Gag!* New York: McGraw-Hill, 1987.

Burns, George. *Gracie: A Love Story.* New York: G. P. Putnam's Sons, 1988.

Buscaglia, Leo. *Loving Each Other.* Thorofare, NJ: Slack Incorporated, 1984.

Campbell-Kelly, Martin, and William Asprey. *Computer: A History of the Information Machine.* New York: Basic Books, 1996.

Cashell, Kieran. *Aftershock: The Ethics of Contemporary Transgressive Art.* London: I. B. Taurus, 2009.

Cosby, Bill. *Fatherhood.* New York: Berkley Books, 1986.

Cousins, Norman. *Anatomy of an Illness as Perceived by the Patient.* New York: Norton, 1979.

Danto, Arthur C. *Encounters and Reflections: Art in the Historical Present.* New York: Farrar Straus Giroux, 1986.

DeMaria, Rusel, and Johnny L. Wilson. *High Score!* New York: McGraw-Hill/Osborne, 2002.

Dini, Massimo, and Renzo Piano. *Projects and Buildings, 1964–1983.* New York: Electa/Rizzoli, 1984.

Donovan, Tristan. *Replay.* Lewes, UK: Yellow Ant, 2010.

Dyer, Wayne W. *The Sky's the Limit.* New York: Simon and Schuster, 1980.

Engle, Lehman. *Words with Music: Creating the Broadway Musical Libretto.* New York: Applause Books, 2006.

Enwezo, Okwui. *Lorna Simpson.* New York: American Federation of the Arts, 2006.

Ewalt, David M. *Of Dice and Men.* New York: Scribner, 2013.

Felder, Deborah G., and Diana Rosen. *Fifty Jewish Women Who Changed the World.* New York: Kensington/Citadel Press, 2005.

Foster, Hal. *The Return of the Real.* Cambridge, MA: MIT Press, 1996.

Fox, Pamela. *Natural Acts.* Ann Arbor, MI: University of Michigan Press, 2009.

Friedman, Lester D. *Citizen Spielberg.* Urbana: University of Illinois Press, 2006.

Friedman, Milton, and Rose Friedman. *Free to Choose.* New York: Harcourt Brace Jovanovich, 1980.

Fulghum, Robert. *All I Really Need to Know I Learned in Kindergarten.* New York: Ballantine Books, 2003.

Ganz, Nicholas. *Graffiti World: Street Art from Five Continents.* New York: Harry N. Abrams. 2004.

Garafalo, Reebee. *Rockin' Out,* 5th ed. Upper Saddle River, NJ: Prentice-Hall, 2011.

Hadeen, Jeffery K., and Charles E. Swann. *Prime Time Preachers: The Rising Power of Televangelism.* New York: Addison-Wesley, 1981.

Hall, Doug, and Sally Jo Fifer. *Illuminating Video.* San Francisco: Aperture/Bay Area Video Coalition, 2005.

Harris, Blake J. *Console Wars.* New York: HarperCollins, 2014.

Hawking, Stephen W. *A Brief History of Time.* New York: Bantam, 1988.

Herriot, James. *The Lord God Made Them All.* New York: St. Martin's Press, 1981.

Hoban, Phoebe. *Basquiat.* New York: Viking, 1998.

Hopkins, David. *After Modern Art: 1945–2000.* Oxford, U.K.: Oxford University Press, 2000.

Iacocca, Lee, with William Novak. *Iacocca: An Autobiography.* New York: Bantam Books, 1984.

Issacson, Walter. *The Innovators.* New York: Simon and Schuster, 2014.

Jordan, Chris. *Movies and the Reagan Presidency.* Westport, CT: Praeger, 2003.

Julius, Anthony. *Transgressions: The Offences of Art.* Chicago: University of Chicago Press, 2002.

Karndon, Janet. *Robert Mapplethorpe: The Perfect Moment.* Philadelphia: Institute of Contemporary Art at the University of Pennsylvania, 1988.

Kent, Steven L. *The Ultimate History of Video Games.* New York: Three Rivers Press, 2001.

Kester, Grant H., ed. *Art, Activism, and Oppositionality: Essays from Afterimage.* Durham, NC: Duke University Press, 1998.

Keyes, Cheryl. *Rap Music and Street Consciousness.* Urbana, IL: University of Illinois Press, 2004.

Kulkarni, Neil. *Hip Hop: Bring the Noise.* New York: Thunder's Mouth Press, 2004.

Kuspit, Donald. *The Rebirth of Painting in the Late Twentieth Century.* New York: Cambridge University Press, 2000.

LaFaber, Walter. *Michael Jordan and the New Global Capitalism.* New York: Norton, 2002.

Larkin. Colin, ed. *The Encyclopedia of Popular Music,* 4th ed. New York: Oxford, 2006.

Light, Alan, ed. *The Vibe History of Hip-Hop.* New York: Three Rivers Press, 1999.

Lin, Maya. *Boundaries.* New York: Simon and Schuster, 2000.

Lippard, Lucy R. "Andres Serrano: The Spirit and the Letter." *Art in America,* p. 239, April 1990.

Lippard, Lucy R. *Judy Chicago.* New York: Watson-Guptill Publications, 2002.

MacDonald, J. Fred. *Blacks and White TV: African Americans in Television Since 1948*. Chicago: Nelson-Hall Publishers, 1992.

Marks, Craig, and Rob Tannenbaum. *I Want My MTV*. New York: Dutton, 2001.

Mazel, Judy. *The Beverly Hills Diet*. London: Sidgwick & Jackson, Ltd., 1981.

McClary, Susan. *Feminine Endings*. Minneapolis: University of Minnesota Press, 1991.

McCormack, Mark. *What They Still Don't Teach You at Harvard Business School*. New York: Bantam Books, 1989.

Mendes, Valerie, and Amy de la Haye. *20th Century Fashion*. London: Thames and Hudson, Ltd., 1999.

Miller, Ivor L. *Aerosol Kingdom: Subway Painters of New York City*. Jackson, MS: University of Mississippi Press, 2002.

Moffett, Marian, Michael Fazio, and Lawrence Wodehouse. *A World History of Architecture*. Boston: McGraw Hill, 2004.

Morddan, Ethan. *The Happiest Corpse I've Ever Seen*. Hampshire, UK: Palgrave Macmillan, 2004.

Morris, Nigel. *The Cinema of Steven Spielberg: Empire of Light*. London: Wallflower Press, 2007.

Muller, Jürgen, ed. *Movies of the 80s*. Koln, Germany: Taschen, 1994.

Mulvagh, Jane. *Vogue History of 20th Century Fashion*. London: Viking, 1988.

Nidetch, Jean. *The Weight Watchers Food Plan Diet Cookbook*. New York: Heathside Press, 1973.

Papadakis, Andreas, Catherine Cooke, and Andrew Benjamin, eds. *Deconstruction, Omnibus Volume*. New York: Rizzoli, 1989.

Peacock, John. *20th Century Fashion*. New York: Thames and Hudson, 1993.

Peek, Hans, Jan Bermans, Jos van Haaren, Frank Toolenaar, and Sorin Stan. *Origins and Successors of the Compact Disc*. New York: Springer, 2009.

Pollock, Dale. *Skywalking*. New York: Harmony Press, 1983.

Presley, Priscilla Beaulieu, with Sandra Harmon. *Elvis and Me*. New York: Berkley, 1986.

Radner, Gilda. *It's Always Something*. New York: Harper Entertainment, 1989.

Reed, Paula. *Fifty Fashion Looks that Changed the 1980s*. New York: Conran Octopus, 2013.

Reppen, Kyra, and Ingrid Stadler. "The Camera Observed," in Ingrid Stadler, *Contemporary Art and Its Philosophical Problems*. Buffalo: Prometheus Books, 1987.

Reynolds, Simon. *Rip It Up and Start Again: Postpunk 1978–1984*. New York: Penguin Books, 2005.

Rooney, Andrew A. *A Few Minutes with Andy Rooney*. New York: Athenaeum, 1981.

Rorty, Richard. *Contingency, Irony, and Solidarity*. New York: Cambridge University Press, 1989.

Rose, Barbara. *Magdalena Abakanowicz*. New York: Harry N. Abrams, Inc., 1994.

Rose, Tricia. *Black Noise*. Middletown, CT: Wesleyan University Press, 1994.

Rosenberg, Neil. *Bluegrass*. Urbana, IL: University of Illinois Press, 1985.

Rosenblum, Robert. *On Modern American Art: Selected Essays*. New York: Harry N. Abrams, 1999.

Russell, John. *The Meanings of Modern Art*. New York: Harper and Row, 1981.

Russell, Sharon. *Stephen King: A Critical Companion*. Westport, CT: Greenwood Press, 1996.

Sagan, Carl. *Cosmos*. New York: Random House, 1980.

Sander, Irving. "The Deluge of Popular Culture," in Betsy Fahlman, *American Images: The SBC Collection of Twentieth-Century American Art* (New York: Harry N. Abrams, 1996), 146–151.

Schnabel, Julian. *Julian Schnabel.* New York: Rizzoli International Publications, 2008.

Schwichtenberg, Cathy. *The Madonna Connection.* Boulder, CO: Westview Press, 1992.

Senie, Harriet F. *Contemporary Public Sculpture: Tradition, Transformation, and Controversy.* New York: Oxford University Press, 1992.

Smith, Sam. *The Jordan Rules.* New York: Simon & Schuster, 1992.

Smith, Terry. *Contemporary Art.* New York: Prentice-Hall, 2011.

Sternfield, Jessica. *The Megamusical.* Bloomington, IN: Indiana University Press, 2006.

Thomkins, Calvin. *Post to Neo: The Art World of the 1980s.* New York: Henry Holt and Company, 1988.

Tichi, Cecilia., ed. *Reading Country Music.* Durham, NC: Duke University Press, 1998.

Toffler, Alvin. *The Third Wave.* New York: William Morrow, 1980.

Traube, Elizabeth G. *Dreaming Identities.* Boulder, CO: Westview Press, 1992.

Wallace, Joseph, Neil Hamilton, and Marty Appel. *Baseball: 100 Classic Moments in the History of the Game.* London: Dorling Kindersley, 2000.

Westheimer, Ruth. *Dr. Ruth's Guide to Safer Sex.* New York: Warner Books, 1992.

Woodhouse, Barbara. *No Bad Dogs.* New York: Fireside, 1982.

Wright, Peter, with Paul Greengrass. *Spycatcher: The Candid Autobiography of a Senior Intelligence Officer.* New York: Viking, 1987.

Index

About the Author

Thomas Harrison, PhD, a native of Kailua, Hawaii, has been a musician since childhood. He has credits on recordings as a guitarist and bassist, and also as a recording producer and engineer. Dr. Harrison signed with 405 Hollywood/Atlantic Records in 2016, recording with artists Raven Cain, Tommy Harrison Group, and Glutton. Dr. Harrison also composes music for the classical concert hall. A noted musicologist, Dr. Harrison's contribution to the *Pop Goes the Decade* series is his sixth book. He holds a PhD from the University of Salford (UK) and is currently the Professor of Commercial Music, Music Business, and Recording at University of Central Florida.